Practicing Prayer for the Dead

Practicing Prayer for the Dead

Its Theological Meaning and Spiritual Value

JAMES B. GOULD

CASCADE *Books* • Eugene, Oregon

PRACTICING PRAYER FOR THE DEAD
Its Theological Meaning and Spiritual Value

Copyright © 2016 James B. Gould. All rights reserved. Except for brief quotations in critical publications or reviews, no part of this book may be reproduced in any manner without prior written permission from the publisher. Write: Permissions, Wipf and Stock Publishers, 199 W. 8th Ave., Suite 3, Eugene, OR 97401.

Cascade Books
An Imprint of Wipf and Stock Publishers
199 W. 8th Ave., Suite 3
Eugene, OR 97401

www.wipfandstock.com

PAPERBACK ISBN: 978-1-4982-8456-1
HARDCOVER ISBN: 978-1-4982-8458-5
EBOOK ISBN: 978-1-4982-8457-8

Cataloguing-in-Publication data:

Names: Gould, James B.

Title: Practicing prayer for the dead : its theological meaning and spiritual value / James B. Gould.

Description: Eugene, OR: Cascade Books, 2016 | Includes bibliographical references and index.

Identifiers: ISBN 978-1-4982-8456-1 (paperback) | ISBN 978-1-4982-8458-5 (hardcover) | ISBN 978-1-4982-8457-8 (ebook)

Subjects: LCSH: Prayers for the dead. | Prayer—Philosophy. | Prayer—Christianity. | Philosophical theology. | Universalism. | Title.

Classification: BV210.3 G69 2016 (print) | BV210.3 (ebook)

Manufactured in the U.S.A.

CONTENTS

Introduction | 1

Part I: The Theological Meaning of Prayer for the Dead

1 Looking Back: A Review of Volume One | 5
2 Consummation Prayer for All the Dead | 20
3 Growth Prayer for the Blessed Dead | 48
4 Purification Prayer for the Imperfect Dead | 73
5 Salvation Prayer for the Unsaved Dead | 104

Part II: The Spiritual Value of Prayer for the Dead

6 The General Spiritual Value of Praying for the Dead | 158
7 Particular Spiritual Benefits of Praying for the Dead | 184
8 Some Sample Prayers | 230

Appendix: Additional Notes | 247
Abbreviations | 278
Bibliography | 281
Names Index | 297
Scripture Index | 305

INTRODUCTION

It was raining hard, and traffic was barely moving—the Chicago interstate was more like a parking lot than an expressway. But not to worry, since my wife Jenna and I were engaged in a lively theological debate. She was raised and remains (with serious reservations) a member of the Christian Reformed Church—a conservative Protestant denomination in which praying for the dead is as foreign as speaking in tongues. Jenna was trying to understand my Anglican tradition, which cautiously accepts the practice. "So why exactly does your church pray for the dead?" she wanted to know. "And why do you think it matters?" This project is an answer to her questions. In it I argue that prayer for the dead integrates fundamental elements of theology. John Polkinghorne notes that "eschatology is . . . the keystone of the edifice of theological thinking, holding the whole building together." Prayers for the dead raise the most basic of theological questions, matters which go to the center of God's purpose in creating spiritual beings and redeeming sinful persons.[1]

My project on praying for the departed consists of two volumes. The first—*Understanding Prayer for the Dead*—considers the history and logic of prayer for the dead. It makes a case for prayer for the dead in general. This volume—*Practicing Prayer for the Dead*—concerns the theological meaning and spiritual value of praying for the dead. It examines four specific types of such prayer: prayer for final consummation of all things, growth of the blessed in heaven, purification of the imperfect in purgatory, and salvation of the unsaved in hell—and it identifies the necessary conception of the afterlife required by each particular prayer. This book also reflects on the formational benefits of praying for the dead—how it enhances faith, builds hope, and sharpens discipleship—and it provides

---

1. Polkinghorne, *God of Hope*, 140.

sample prayers that may be used both liturgically and devotionally. The Appendix includes additional theoretical considerations.

In these pages I develop few new positions on heaven, purgatory, or hell; there is an enormous literature on each of these questions, and interested readers will find resources in the footnotes. My unique contribution is to summarize and synthesize what others have written, assembling from established positions an explanation of prayer for the dead—hence, like the first volume, this book is packed with quotes. My account of prayer for the dead is *prescriptive* (it defines what we *ought* to mean when we make such prayers), not descriptive (it does not aim to express what people actually do think they are doing). My argument is *orthodox*. Its conclusions are revisionary in some ways, but its theological premises are conservative, drawing on basic doctrines—Trinity, creation, and salvation—which the historic churches and great theologians have held as fundamental to Christianity and which are common to all orthodox believers.[2] My position is *systematic*. It makes a variety of logical connections between biblical themes and doctrinal teachings. Eschatology "plays such an essential role that, without [it], Christianity loses its meaning," says Hilarion Alfeyev. The last things, as implied by praying for the dead, are not isolated doctrines; instead, "all dogmas of faith are directly related to it."[3] My position is *ecumenical*. The views developed here are not the exclusive possession of one branch of Christianity, but belong to its common heritage. I cite theologians of all persuasions to make a case for petitionary prayer for all of the departed which should be acceptable to all branches of the church. I do, however, reference the traditions of my own denomination—the Episcopal Church, part of the worldwide Anglican Communion. Finally, my analysis is *integrative*—it endeavors to discern the truth, as an Episcopal Church statement says, "through engaging the Bible, . . . the historic teachings and liturgy of the Church, and human reason."[4] Prayer for the dead involves complex and controversial issues—exegetical, theological, and philosophical. In addressing them I engage a range of academic disciplines in an attempt to be biblically accurate, historically informed, and philosophically reasoned.

Theology is, as Anselm of Canterbury put it, faith seeking understanding—*fides quaerens intellectum*. Given the finitude of human

---

2. I draw this language from Kronen and Reitan, *God's Final Victory*, 2.
3. Alfeyev, "Eschatology," 107.
4. Episcopal Church, "Episcopal Faith."

categories and the infinity of the living God, who remains shrouded in mystery, theological modesty is always required. As Eugene Petersen paraphrases 1 Corinthians 13:12 (*The Message*), "we don't yet see things clearly. We're squinting in a fog, peering through a mist." And yet—while we cannot have exhaustive knowledge of God, we can have true knowledge of God. In studying it is important to see beyond the sometimes narrow limits of our particular experience of Christianity, to listen to and learn from other expressions of the faith. In particular, Stephen Webb says, we "must be open to new readings of the Bible that challenge our customary habits and ingrained prejudices."[5] This can be hard work, against which we often push back. In the seventh century, Maximus the Confessor urged his readers—especially his opponents—to use the principle of charity:

> if anything in these chapters should prove useful to the soul, it will be revealed to the reader by the grace of God, provided that he reads, not out of curiosity, but in the fear and love of God. If a person reads this or any other work not to gain spiritual benefit, but to track down matter with which to abuse the author . . . , nothing profitable will ever be revealed to him in anything.[6]

We must practice a "hermeneutic of love" rather than an attitude of suspicion. In this book I analyze theological concepts and link them together in systematic ways. Whether my arguments are accepted or rejected, the reader will be forced to think about important questions—and will in the process gain new insights into Christian beliefs and how they are related to each other.

As the old saying goes, "if you are the smartest person in your group, find a new group." I have been blessed to be surrounded by wise colleagues and generous friends—Beth, Timothy and Larry—who have helped me think out ideas, have disagreed with certain conclusions, have pressed me on key points. Herb and Brian, you were there for me in moments of crisis—*gracia*. Thanks to the good people and priest of my home parish—St. James Episcopal Church, West Dundee, Illinois—where my faith is nurtured weekly. Thanks also to my editor, Robin Parry, for making a number of helpful suggestions and corrections that improved the manuscript. My deepest gratitude to God is for my parents, Fred and

---

5. Webb, *Good Eating*, 259.

6. Maximus, cited in Clendenin, *Eastern Orthodox Christianity*, 167. The phrase "hermeneutic of love" comes from page 139.

Helen Gould, my children—Becky, Sarah, and David—and for Jenna: you light up my world with your smile, you warm my heart with your kindness, you bring great joy to my life, and you surround me always with God's grace made visible.

Some of the material in this volume first appeared (in modified form) in previous publications of mine. Specifically, I have drawn material from the following articles:

> "Becoming Good: The Role of Spiritual Practice." *Philosophical Practice* 1 (2005) 135–47.

> "Broad Inclusive Salvation: The Logic of 'Anonymous Christianity.'" *Philosophy and Theology* 20 (2008) 175–98.

> "God's Saving Purpose and Prayer for All the Departed." *Journal of Anglican Studies* 10 (2012) 1–29. All materials are used with permission.

Unless otherwise indicated, Scripture is taken from the *New Revised Standard Version* of the Bible. Division of Christian Education of the National Council of Churches of Christ in the United States of America, 1989. Scripture marked NIV is taken from the *Holy Bible, New International Version*. International Bible Society, 1984. Passages from the Apocrypha are taken from the *New Revised Standard Version with the Apocrypha*. Oxford: Oxford University Press, 2009. Scripture marked KJV is taken from the *King James Version* of the Bible. Scripture marked as *The Message* is taken from Eugene Peterson, *The Message. The Bible in Contemporary Language*. Colorado Springs: NavPress, 2009.

In this book I use the term "Hebrew Scripture" to refer to what is usually called the Old Testament and "Christian Scripture" to refer to what is usually called the New Testament. My concern with language about "Old" and "New" Testaments is that it can imply a historically supersessionist view that I am not comfortable with. I appreciate that talking of the so-called New Testament as "Christian Scripture" is somewhat inaccurate because Christian Scripture also includes the so-called Old Testament, but I hope readers will understand my intention.

When I quote authors who refer to God using masculine terms, I change these to the gender-neutral word "God." I leave masculine biblical quotations unchanged.

chapter 1

LOOKING BACK:
A REPRISE OF VOLUME ONE
AFTERLIFE POSSIBILITIES
AND PRAYER FOR THE DEAD

It is December 6, 2015, the Sunday morning following the San Bernardino shootings at a facility for the disabled in which fourteen people were massacred. The offenders were chased and killed in a shoot-out with police. The Prayers of the People include, as usual, a petition for the faithful departed: "Lord of glory, you destroy the darkness of the shadow of death and open the Kingdom of heaven to your loved ones. We pray for the departed, especially remembering Sid [a member of the congregation who had just died after a lingering illness], that in your love they may rejoice in peace." I am pleased by Father Don's concluding collect, which asks for those who had been killed in San Bernardino—but I am astonished when he includes those who carried out the shootings. Not just the victims, but the perpetrators, are mentioned in our prayers. This raises questions, of course—uncomfortable questions perhaps. First, what is the *theological meaning* of praying for the dead? Whom do pray for—should we pray for the wicked?—and what do we pray for them? Second, what is the *spiritual value* of praying for all the departed? How does it form our lives as followers of Jesus?

My Position Stated

The position I defend in this volume and its predecessor is that Christians should offer

1. petitionary prayers (not simply thanksgivings)
2. for (not simply about, but on behalf of)
3. all the dead (not simply the saved dead).

There are four types of prayers for the departed. The first is *consummation prayer*, which asks for completion of God's plan—Christ's return, joyous resurrection, and new creation; it concerns all people, the living and the dead. There are three places where the dead reside: heaven is a place of comfort and happiness; purgatory is a place of cleansing, the entranceway to heaven; hell is a place of suffering and unhappiness. The three additional types of prayer, then, are:

1. *growth prayer*, which concerns the blessed in present heaven; they ask for rest and increasing participation in God's life;
2. *purification prayer*, which concerns the imperfect in purgatory; they ask for moral transformation into characters of holy love;
3. *salvation prayer*, which concerns the unsaved in hell; they ask for repentance and restored relationship with God.

I challenge all branches of Christianity to reformulate their traditions concerning prayer for the dead—to carefully examine what they believe and to modify established positions. I call Protestants to *begin* praying for the dead, to adopt this ancient and long-standing practice—and I call Roman Catholics and Eastern Orthodox to *broaden* their praying for the dead to include the unsaved.

In thinking about faith and practice the church must balance two needs that can be hard to reconcile—the need for continuity and the need for change. Julian Baggini makes a distinction between *traditions* (which are dynamic) and *heritages* (which are static). When a tradition stops evolving and adapting, when it denies the possibility of growth, it ossifies and becomes frozen in time like a museum piece. A living tradition, by contrast, while maintaining continuity with the past, does not simply preserve the old ways but is able to change, to be fresh and new. A living tradition, Baggini adds, looks both backward and forward—taking the good from the past into the future while allowing it to develop and grow.[1] Pope Benedict XVI agrees that *tradition* is different from *traditionalism*: the former allows renewal and change, new interpretations and understandings that rejuvenate faith, while the latter does not. There is a balance here: innovation is necessary to keep tradition alive—but without the anchor of tradition, innovation can be destructive. This book challenges the church to innovate in continuity with tradition. Revisions around the edges of a theological system—the kind of revisions in praying for the dead that I am calling for—are perfectly compatible with stability in general commitments to major Christian doctrines.[2]

Reading Scripture and developing theology, Benedict observes, involves two dimensions. There is a *personal* dimension, since God's truth is meant for each of us individually. This does not mean individualism, however; when we think alone—by ourselves, relying solely on our own wisdom—"we can easily slip into error." A too individualistic search for truth can lead away from correct belief, not toward it; personal interpretation and reflection that does not respect the common teaching of the church can create confusion. Acquiring knowledge is a social, collaborative enterprise, not an individual, entirely private endeavor. And so reading Scripture and developing theology always require a *communal* dimension: we think in communion with the church, the people of God. Only in harmony with tradition and the *regula fide*—the "rule of faith" based on apostolic tradition, which protects common catholic truth—are we "correctly attuned" to properly understand the Bible.[3] We must balance autonomy (freely using our own reason to think about matters for ourselves) and heteronomy (relying on the authority of others and deferring to tradition to tell us what to believe). Pride is dangerous when we are interpreting Scripture and developing theology; we must have humility to rely on argument and evidence given by others, to integrate our understandings with those of the broader church. In reaching our own conclusions, we must hear what tradition has to say—and yet we should not simply accept in an uncritical way what we are told.

The point I am making is, I hope, clear. In its ongoing attempt to understand its faith, the church should be both firm (holding to core

---

1. Baggini, *Virtues of Table*, 111 and 116.
2. Pope Benedict XVI, *Fathers of Church*, 15–17 and 32–35.
3. Ibid., 111 and 113–14. Protestants emphasize that the individual, inspired by the Holy Spirit, is sufficient for interpreting Scripture and developing doctrine. Roman Catholics, by contrast, claim that the teaching magisterium of the Catholic Church is necessary for correct biblical and theological understanding.

commitments and listening respectfully to the teachings of the past) and open (adjusting beliefs and practices in light of new understandings). Tradition should be respected where appropriate and revised when necessary. The principle of conservatism indicates that long-held positions should not be modified without good reason. There are, however, good reasons for Christians to reform their views of prayer for the departed—for Protestants to change their Reformation tradition by recovering ancient church practice, and for Catholics and Orthodox to change their traditions by revising existing practice, expanding prayer in new directions. Neither adopting prayer for the dead for the first time nor broadening it to include the unsaved are a reversal of biblical truth; instead, they constitute an enlargement of theological understanding.

The first book of this project—*Understanding Prayer for the Dead*—explores the foundations of praying for the dead in history and logic. This chapter briefly reviews what was argued there.

Scripture, Church Tradition, and Prayer for the Dead

There is no clear command, example or prohibition of prayer for the dead in the Bible. None of the possible references speak to the practice. The silence of Scripture on prayer for the dead is irrelevant, however, since the practice can be defended theologically, from things that are said in the Bible.

In the ancient church remembrance of the dead at the Eucharist began early and was widespread. It thanked God that the departed were at rest in Christ and asked that they be brought safely to resurrection in God's eternal kingdom. Following the conversion of Constantine and peace of the church, prayer for the dead gradually came to be associated with belief in a process of sanctification after death—culminating in the medieval doctrine of purgatory as a place of temporary punishment and purification for those who die in grace but unready for heaven. The idea that individuals in purgatory can be helped by the prayers and works of the church on earth gave rise to abuses—most notably, the promiscuous selling of indulgences, the proximate cause of the Reformation. Protestants affirmed justification by faith alone and rejected the idea that individuals must pay for their own sins after death. They claimed that prayer cannot help the dead because eternal destiny is settled at death, when—following immediate judgment—the saved are made perfect and united with Christ in heaven and the unsaved are separated from God in hell. While the Anglican tradition condemned intercession for the delivery of souls from purgatory, some accepted commemoration of the righteous dead as practiced by the early church. They rejected a punishing purgatory, but accepted a sanctifying process after death and prayer for the increased bliss of the Christian dead. Prayer for the dead is not unscriptural, incompatible with salvation by grace, and inseparable from belief in a punishing purgatory. Praying for the dead is currently practiced in both Roman Catholic and Eastern Orthodox churches as well as the Anglican Communion; it is entirely absent in conservative Protestantism and only occurs partially in progressive ecumenical Protestantism.

Logical Assumptions of Prayer for the Dead

Prayer for the dead requires three logical assumptions:

1. that prayer is effective;
2. that the dead exist as conscious, personal beings; and
3. that the life to come is temporal in nature.

Given continuing disagreement among scholars about these matters, it pays to be cautious and non-dogmatic. While these assumptions are not conclusively established, however, prayer for the dead does fit very nicely with—and seems to require—them.

The Effectiveness of Petitionary Prayer

Prayers for the dead, as intercessions which ask God to do something, must exert real influence on God. They must be effective in changing God's mind about what God will do and must therefore be able to shape how things go in the world. Petitionary prayers make best sense with a God who is personal and responsive and in a universe that is non-deterministic. The Bible depicts petitionary prayer as able to influence God's actions—changing the future and making it different that it would have been without prayer. Prayer is effective since God's actions are sometimes contingent on our requests; some things can only be achieved if God does not act unless we pray.[4]

---

4. Willard (*Divine Conspiracy*, 253) calls God, who can be changed by prayer, the

The Conscious and Personal Nature of the Intermediate State

I take it for granted that if Christianity is true then life after death is also true, since there is a tight connection between them. Life after death is a function and consequence of belief in God. As one of the characters in a dialogue by John Perry puts it: "God, who is just and merciful, would not permit such a travesty as that our short life on this earth should be the end of things. . . . I don't know how God could be excused, if this small sample of life is all that we are allotted; I don't know why God should have created us, if these few years of toil and torment are the end of it."[5]

In order for prayer for the dead to make sense the dead must be aware—they must think and feel—and they must exist as the very same people they were in life. Continuity of consciousness and personality are necessary for individual identity and afterlife survival. There are three philosophically possible accounts of conscious experience between death and resurrection; all are compatible, with varying degrees of plausibility, with Scripture.

Dualism claims that human beings consist of two parts—a body which is a material substance, and a soul which is an immaterial substance and to which the conscious life of thought and feeling belongs. Dualism implies a disembodied intermediate state. During this life consciousness and personality depend on the brain, but after death the soul separates from the body and continues in conscious existence, being re-embodied at resurrection.

Materialism asserts that we are identical with our bodies. Consciousness—every thought and emotion—is the product of brain activity. Brain function is necessary for the mental states which depend on it. What is conscious is not an immaterial soul but a physical body—a brain. In order to affirm an afterlife materialists must accept either immediate bodily resurrection or an embodied intermediate state. But immediate resurrection contradicts Scripture, and so the only viable materialist option consistent with prayer for the dead is an embodied intermediate state. This means that between death and resurrection we have temporary bodies of some kind. Perhaps God preserves the same body through body-snatching. At the moment of death God removes the earthly body and replaces it with a perfect physical duplicate. The body that is buried is a lookalike—while the original body is immediately reanimated by God

---

"Moved Mover."

5. Perry, *Dialogue on Personal Identity and Immortality*, 2 and 4.

as an intermediate state body. Or perhaps God preserves the same body through body-splitting. At the moment of death God divides the earthly body into two identical streams—a living intermediate state body and a dead corpse. This ensures that the afterlife body is causally connected to and materially continuous with the earthly body.

Constitutionism says that human beings are persons who are constituted by, but not identical to, physical bodies—just as a bronze statue is constituted by a particular piece of bronze but is not identical to it. Like materialism, constitutionism claims that human beings are purely physical organisms; there is no non-physical soul and consciousness requires a body. But just as computers of different types can run the same software program, so consciousness can take place in different physical systems—in different bodies. Constitutionism is consistent with post-mortem survival since at death God can relocate consciousness—the essence of a person—to a different afterlife body. The intermediate state must be embodied, and we survive death by body-switching. After death the mind is transferred into a different material medium; it is reduced to a software package and reinstalled in another physical system in the intermediate state.

The biblical view of the person is not that our bodies are, in Stephen Webb words, "transitional soul homes" which are destroyed once we depart this life. The soul (Hebrew, *nephesh*—Greek, *psyche*) is not a separate, immaterial substance, but is simply the breath of life (Gen 1:20-30) given to all living creatures—in the case of humans, individual consciousness that emerges from the organization of physical matter in the brain.[6] Prayer for the dead requires that its subjects consciously exist as the same persons between death and resurrection. Dualism says that we exist in the intermediate state as souls without any body at all. Materialism says that in the intermediate state we must have the same body we have now. Constitutionism says that the intermediate state allows a different body; we can exist without *this* body but not without *a* body. Prayer for the dead is consistent with all three theories of human nature: dualists can pray for the dead, materialists can pray for the dead, constitutionists can pray for the dead. All affirm personal conscious existence between death and resurrection. My own view is—in Amos Yong's words—that since "human beings are constituted by (even if not reducible to) their bodies,

---

6. Webb, *Good Eating*, 172. "God does not create souls and then plant them into bodies, using the flesh as a container that can be discarded when it has served its function."

then there can be no proper human 'existence' after death" without embodiment.[7] This means that the intermediate state is a spatial reality, a physical place.

Praying for the dead requires that they exist as the very same people they were in life, having the unique characteristics and social identities that make them who they are. There are three theories of identity which correspond to the three theories of human nature.

1. *If we are souls*, then an earthly individual is identical with an afterlife individual if they have the same soul.

2. *If we are bodies*, then an earthly individual is identical with an afterlife individual if they have the same body.

3. *If we are persons constituted by bodies*, then an earthly individual is identical with an afterlife individual if they have the same memories and personality.

What is essential to identity across time is psychological essence (since soul or body without personality is not the same person, while personality without soul or body is).

The Temporal Nature of the Intermediate State

In order for prayer for the dead to make sense history must remain unfinished (final consummation must be future for them) and their condition must be progressive, not static. Change is an inherently dynamic concept, and so time, both before and after death, flows in a sequential way. To be in time means to change, to experience reality successively (as a sequence of moments), rather than remain constant.

Consummation prayer for the completion of God's purpose in history requires an incomplete future; there must be actual future events that have not happened yet. If eschatological events (such as resurrection) happen at the moment of death, then consummation prayer makes no

---

7. Yong, *Theology and Down Syndrome*, 337. He adds that a materialist anthropology takes embodiment "as constitutive of human personhood and identity in the afterlife much more seriously than any dualist view can." The doctrine of creation means that God is responsible for the existence of the world; it does not identify the mechanism by which God created. In the same way, the doctrine of afterlife survival (resurrection, for example) means that God makes us continue to exist after we die; it does not identify the mechanism for how God ensures the connection of personality to a new afterlife body.

sense—but if they occur some time after death then it does. All the dead have futures which are consummation-incomplete. *Growth, purification,* and *salvation* prayers require that the post-mortem condition of the dead be dynamic, not static. If spiritual development and destiny become complete and final at death then prayer for the departed is pointless—but if futures after death are open to change then it is not. The blessed in heaven have futures that are growth-incomplete; the imperfect in purgatory have futures that are purification-incomplete; the unsaved in hell have futures that are salvation-open.

The dynamic theory of time claims that the fundamental feature of time is ordering of events in terms of tensed properties: past, present, and future. Time flows in an active process as things come into and go out of existence. The static theory claims that the fundamental feature of time is ordering of events in terms of tenseless properties: earlier than, simultaneous with, and later than. The experience of future events becoming present and then past is a subjective perception of the mind seeing reality from a particular position in time. The Bible depicts and theological reflection suggests that God's relationship to time, including eschatological and post-mortem events, is temporal rather than timeless. Both the incomplete future and the dynamic afterlife fit best with the theory of temporal becoming.[8]

These three requirements—that prayer is causally effective, that the dead are conscious, most likely embodied, retain the essential traits of personality, and are in a temporal condition—are individually necessary and jointly sufficient for prayer for the dead to be logically coherent.

A Theological Framework of Prayer for the Dead

My theology is guided by one overriding principle—the good news of God's unlimited and steadfast love. The love of God is the basic theme, Webb says, "that serves as a kind of logic or grammar to the Bible as a

---

8. The life to come, Habermas and Moreland (*Beyond Death*, 226) say, is endless time since "the very notion of timeless existence for finite conscious beings is unintelligible." In the afterlife we will be in a different time frame, not no time frame. "There will . . . be a flow to [afterlife] time, including both past and future. Moments will be realized and will recede into the past, while others await us in the future" (281). For an overview of the debate concerning time see Taliaferro, *Contemporary Philosophy of Religion*, 144–63.

whole."[9] We are made for the divine life of love, in this world and the next—and when relationship is broken God does everything possible to bring us back into communion. All of theology—including prayer for the dead—is framed by this relational understanding. All four types of petitions for the departed center on love: consummation prayer asks for the final triumph of love in God's kingdom (which is not yet complete); growth prayer asks for increase of love (because in heaven love always expands); purification prayer asks for development of love (because at death the love necessary for heaven can be underdeveloped); salvation prayer asks for acceptance of love (because in this life some persons refuse God's love).

Theology proper begins from the fact that God is relational. God's nature—seen in both Trinity and incarnation—is relational. God's purpose in *creation* is relational. God made us to take part in the current of love that is the Trinity. *Anthropology*—human nature—is relational. We are spiritual beings who are naturally inclined toward God, relational beings (the *imago dei* means that when we are in relationship with others God's very being is reflected in us) and free beings who must voluntarily decide for God. *Hamartiology*—sin, the betrayal of God's purpose—is relational. The essence of sin is breaking relationship, not rules (sin is disordered love, a curving in on oneself and away from others). The effect of sin is alienation—the disruption of relationships with God and neighbor. *Soteriology*—salvation, the restoration of God's purpose—is relational. Sin has two consequences both of which need mending. 1. Sin alienates us from God *objectively*; justification forgives the guilt of sin and puts us right with God. 2. Sin makes us self-centered *subjectively*; sanctification frees us from the power of sin, transforming us so we can love God and neighbor. The essence of salvation is becoming holy, not being forgiven. *Ethics and ecclesiology* are relational. Individually and corporately we are to live out God's love and pursue God's reign of justice and peace. *Eschatology*—the completion of God's purpose—is relational. Heaven is relational; its reality is friendship with both God and others. Purgatory is relational; its purpose is to prepare us for the relationships of heaven. Hell is relational; it is meant to correct sinners so they choose relationship with God in heaven. *Prayer*—including prayer for the dead—expresses relational concern. Petitionary prayer in general is an act of love for other people. Prayer for the *saved dead* assumes the doctrine of

---

9. Webb, *Good Eating*, 259; cf. 233.

the communion of saints—that the bond and interaction between God's people on earth and God's people in heaven is not broken by death. The saved dead can be helped by the actions and prayers of the living. Prayer for the *unsaved dead* assumes a principle that we might call the solidarity of humanity —that all individuals are loved by God. Just as we pray for unbelievers in this life, we pray for the unsaved in the next.

Hope, Expectation, and Prayer for the Dead

Prayers for the dead are prayers of hope. Ordinary hope differs from religious hope. While ordinary hope has an uncertainty requirement (hoping that an event happens entails that it might or might not), Christian eschatological hope has a certainty requirement (we await resurrection with sure and certain hope). This makes it a form of expectation. Hope involves incorporating beliefs and desires into one's way of life, making them part of our thoughts, feelings, and actions. A hopeful person sees the future as open (leading to action) while a despairing one sees it as closed (leading to capitulation). Action-hope enables us to live faithfully now as we await the future, and attitude-hope creates a sense of optimism and joy.

In the Bible hope is based on God's promises and God's faithfulness; it includes expectation of the future, trust, and the patience of waiting. Hope involves three elements:

1. *trust*—"hoping that" involves "trusting in," in particular trusting in God's faithfulness;

2. *promises*—speech-acts that define the future and commit God to act in particular ways;

3. *faithfulness*—the power and goodness of God ground our expectation that God will complete what God has promised.

The biblical metanarrative is comedic, not tragic—and so the hopeful Christian

a. *desires* particular eschatological outcomes: final consummation of all things, continual growth toward God, perfectly holy character and salvation of every person;

b. *believes* confidently that these outcomes will occur, given God's promises and faithfulness, power and love; and

c. *incorporates* these desires and beliefs into their way of being and doing.

Many people have run out of energy and hope, feeling that life is too much for them, that the world is beyond restoration. Praying for the dead is one way of incorporating hope (consummation hope, growth hope, purification hope, and salvation hope) into our characters and conduct.

Concluding Remarks: Afterlife Possibilities Summarized

Before proceeding to detailed analysis of each type of prayer for the dead, let me summarize the afterlife possibilities. The prayers we can logically make—consummation, growth, purification, and salvation—depend on what happens to someone when they die.

The logic of prayer for the dead involves two variables. Consummation prayer concerns the *timing* of final redemption—which occurs either immediately at death or sometime after death. If complete fulfillment has already happened for the dead then we cannot ask for it to come—but if it remains future, we can. Growth, purification, and salvation prayer concern the *nature* of post-mortem existence—which is either fixed or fluid. If the life to come is static immutability then we cannot ask for an increase of joy, moral transformation, or reconciliation with God—but if it is progressive development, we can.

The dead either enter the final state (experiencing consummation in death) or an intermediate state (in which they await the last things).

1. If they are in the *final state*, this condition is necessarily conscious; if consummation is unconscious existence, it is not personal survival. This conscious condition is either static (complete and unchanging) or dynamic (allowing growth and transformation for the saved and repentance for the unsaved).

2. If the dead are in an *intermediate state*, this condition is either conscious or unconscious—and if conscious, either static or dynamic. An intermediate state requires judgment directly at death so the person goes to the right place—heaven, purgatory, or hell.

Here, then, are the afterlife options correlated with the four types of prayer for the dead.

Afterlife Possibility 1: No Intermediate State

There is no intermediate state; the dead are in a conscious final state. The dead "right away die into the end"—as Dorothy and Gabriel Fackre put it—into the resurrection of the body, the return of Christ, final judgment, and everlasting life.[10]

Possibility 1 rules out consummation prayer, but may allow growth, purification, and salvation prayers. The conscious final state is either static or dynamic for the saved (the blessed and imperfect) and either closed or open for the unsaved. This creates four possibilities.

a. The conscious final state is dynamic for the saved (the blessed and the imperfect), but closed for the unsaved. This scenario allows growth and purification prayer, but not salvation prayer.

b. The conscious final state is dynamic for the imperfect, but static for the blessed and closed for the unsaved. This scenario allows purification prayer, but not growth and salvation prayer.

c. The conscious final state is dynamic for the imperfect and open for the unsaved, but static for the blessed. This scenario allows purification and salvation prayer, but not growth prayer.

d. The conscious final state is dynamic for the saved (the blessed and the imperfect) and open for the unsaved. This scenario allows growth, purification, and salvation prayer.

While consistent with some prayers for the dead, immediate resurrection at death contradicts the Bible's future consummation texts.[11] Option 1, while a possible afterlife scenario, is not actual.

Afterlife Possibility 2: Unconscious Intermediate State

The dead are in an unconscious intermediate state. They do not exist now at all—or if they do, are unconscious—but will exist and be conscious again in the future resurrection. "There is a period of 'soul sleep'"—in the Fackres' words—"a time we exist only in the mind of God, until a future resurrection."[12]

---

10. Fackre, *Christian Basics*, 137.
11. See Volume 1, chapter 6.
12. Fackre, *Christian Basics*, 137–38.

Possibility 2 allows consummation prayer, but not growth, purification, and salvation prayers.[13] Extinction or unconsciousness between death and resurrection, however, contradict the Bible's continuing existence texts.[14] Option 2, while a possible afterlife scenario, is not actual.

Afterlife Possibility 3: Conscious Intermediate State

The dead are in a conscious intermediate state. The dead are "awake" and in communion with or separate from God in the world beyond—their existence, the Fackres say, " is never interrupted" as they await the last things.[15]

Possibility 3 allows consummation prayer. The conscious intermediate state is either static or dynamic for the saved (the blessed and imperfect) and either closed or open for the unsaved—thus creating the same scenarios as in afterlife possibility 1:

a. the traditional Protestant—and to some extent Eastern Orthodox—view,

b. the traditional Roman Catholic view,

c. never a popular option, and

d. my—and to some extent Eastern Orthodox—view.[16]

A conscious intermediate state is a logical implication of combining the Bible's future consummation and continuing existence texts. The biblical data imply what Tom Wright calls a two-stage hope: "life after death" (the intermediate state) followed by "life after life after death" (the final state).[17] Possibility 3 is the actually true afterlife scenario.

The logical relationships are set out in the chart below.

---

13. In the most technical sense this is not true. Scenarios 1 and 2 both say that—experientially—we go directly to the final state, either immediately at death (1) or after a period of non-existence (2). Scenario 2 allows consummation prayer but scenario 1 does not—and as long as change is still possible in the final state, then growth, purification, and salvation prayers are possible on both scenarios 1 and 2. See Appendix Note 1.

14. See Volume 1, chapter 6.

15. Fackre, *Christian Basics*, 138.

16. I realize I am making sweeping generalizations by identifying these positions with particular churches. Still, broadly speaking and subject to qualifications, I think this is accurate.

17. Wright, *Resurrection of Son of God*, 129–30.

	Consummation prayers	Growth prayers	Purification prayers	Salvation prayers
Possibility 1: final state	not possible	1. possible if state of blessed is dynamic 2. not possible if static	1. possible if state of imperfect is dynamic 2. not possible if static	1. possible if state of unsaved is open 2. not possible if closed
Possibility 2: unconscious intermediate state	possible	not possible	not possible	not possible
Possibility 3: conscious intermediate state	possible	1. possible if state of blessed is dynamic 2. not possible if static	1. possible if state of imperfect is dynamic 2. not possible if static	1. possible if state of unsaved is open 2. not possible if closed

I now turn to examine the substance of consummation, growth, purification, and salvation prayers.

chapter 2

CONSUMMATION PRAYER FOR ALL THE DEPARTED

*Faithful God,
we commend to your mercy all who have died,
that your will for them—the consummation
of all things—may be fulfilled.*

AMEN.

Two stories from my childhood.

Waiting. And waiting. And still more waiting. That is what Advent was like for me as a child. As a missionary kid raised in Africa, I attended boarding school several hundred miles from home.[1] Our mission agency operated a fleet of light aircraft, and twice a year we travelled by Piper Comanche back home to our parents' place of work, often a remote mission station. Christmas break began in mid-December, and on December 1 the flight schedule—the listing of who was being shuttled home when—was posted. We waited expectantly for that event. We knew it

---

1. Many missionary kids struggle with homesickness while away at boarding school. The notion of being "homesick"—the distress reaction created by leaving home and being separated from relationships with loved ones—is a profound metaphor of our displacement from our highest good, eternal union with God in the life to come. See, for example, Bonhoeffer's references to a feeling of homelessness and homesickness during his year in Barcelona and while in prison (*Letters and Papers*, 168 and 184). He (*Christmas Sermons*, 21–22 and 25–26) says, "a kind of homesickness comes over us . . . , a blessed longing for a world without violence or hardness of heart, . . . a longing for the safe lodging of the everlasting Father."

would happen, we were confident it would happen—but the waiting was hard. And then finally the day came. We crowded around the bulletin board, edging our way in, to see when we were going home. And then, of course, we had to wait some more—between the "already" and the "not yet"—for that special day when school would be finished at last and we would fly home. We were ready—more than ready—for the fulfillment of the promise that the flight schedule represented. We knew we would go home, we were confident we would soon be on that plane—but the waiting had to come first. Sometimes it seemed like it would never happen. But it always did—finally—come.

The English word "advent" derives from two Latin words which mean "to come" or "arrival." Advent is the time in the church year when we prepare and wait. We read from the prophets: "the days are surely coming, says the Lord, when I will fulfill the promise I made to the house of Israel and the house of Judah" (Jer 33:14). A child will be born and "there shall be endless peace for the throne of David and his kingdom. He will establish and uphold it with justice and righteousness . . . forevermore" (Isa 9:7). We sing the songs: "Come Thou Long-expected Jesus"—and we say the prayers: "bring your reign of love and light among us who sit in darkness and in the shadow of death, that your glory be spread abroad over the earth." The promise is given and the people of God have waited, first for the advent of servant Messiah and now for the advent of King Messiah. We are ready—more than ready—for the fulfillment of these promises. We try to be patient, but our hearts cry out "Come, Lord Jesus, come. Change this world to be how you intend it to be—peaceful and perfect. Set what is wrong right. And bring us home to your final kingdom." We know that God will fulfill these promises. We are confident because we have seen in Jesus the dawning of what is to come. We live between the times, between the "already" and the "not yet," between promise and fulfillment. But the waiting is hard.

A second anecdote. As a boy I loved to put on my pajamas and listen, with my siblings, to bed-time stories. One summer my parents read us the entire *Chronicles of Narnia* by C. S. Lewis. I especially liked *The Voyage of the Dawn Treader* in which King Caspian and other passengers leave Narnia in search of lost friends. As an adult I came to appreciate one voyager, Reepicheep, as more than a brave little mouse—as someone with a deep yearning for heaven. Reepicheep wants to sail to Aslan's Country at the End of the World. He has heard that he will one day find all he seeks in the East; "the spell of it has been on me all my life," he tells his shipmates. Reepicheep is dedicated to reaching his heart's desire: "while I can, I sail east in the *Dawn Treader*. When she fails me, I paddle east in my coracle. When she sinks, I shall swim east with my four paws. And when I can swim no longer, if I have not reached Aslan's Country . . . , I shall sink with my nose to the sunrise." Near the end of the journey, Reepicheep does fall into the sea, disappear over the horizon, and come safely to the End of the World.[2] At times in my life I have been especially aware of the overwhelming brokenness of this world—when my student's car slides on black ice into the path of an oncoming train or when standing in the rail yard of Auschwitz death camp, tears streaming down my face—and I have longed with all my heart for Aslan's Country, a future yet to be when Immanuel shall come and ransom captive Israel that mourns in lonely exile. "How long?" I ask (e.g., Ps 13:1–2)—*Maranatha*, "Lord Jesus, come quickly" and restore all things to the purpose for which you created them (1 Cor 16:22; Rev 22:20).

The ancient church interceded for the righteous dead, James Ussher notes, for "the accomplishment of that which remained of their redemption: . . . their perfect consummation of bliss . . . in the Kingdom of heaven forever."[3] First, consummation prayer is not restricted to the living, but includes *the dead* as well. Such prayers, in fact, necessarily involve praying for the dead since consummation is not completed at death. While God has already inaugurated the kingdom and defeated death in the resurrection of Jesus, Allen Verhey says, "full participation in that triumph is still sadly not yet, even for the dead. The dead—no less than the living—have by God's grace already some share in it, but they too—no less than the living—must wait and watch and pray for God's final triumph."[4] The dead have not entered God's final kingdom—and so we pray that "with all who have departed this world . . . we may . . . receive the crown of life in the day of resurrection"[5] God's reign is not yet realized for any but is still awaited by all—and so in consummation prayers we are praying both for ourselves, the living, and for the dead. "Bring us with all the saints to feast at your table in heaven," the Anglican Eucharistic prayer asks, "bring us with all your saints into the joy of your eternal Kingdom."[6] Second, con-

---

2. Lewis, *Voyage of Dawn Treader*, 22, 213 and 244. Alcorn (*Heaven*, 461) also cites this scene.

3. Ussher, cited in Newman, "Tract 72," 25.

4. Verhey, *Christian Art of Dying*, 96, slightly modified.

5. Episcopal Church, *Book of Common Prayer*, 280.

6. Church of England, *Common Worship*, Eucharistic Prayer E and Episcopal

summation prayer is not restricted to the saved, but concerns *all the dead*, since the saved and unsaved alike will be swept up in the grand finale to history. I focus in this chapter, however, on completion of salvation for the blessed in heaven. Praying that God will hasten the resurrection and establish the kingdom has, Peter Marshall says, unimpeachable theological qualifications.[7] All branches of the church can accept its legitimacy. I begin with a historical overview of the concept of the final state; I then turn to theological analysis.

Consummation Prayers and the Future Consummation Requirement

Lashondra was a remarkable woman and a dedicated Christian. She led a life of love for God and service to others—everyone admired her kind, gentle, and generous spirit, her honesty and integrity. Through meditation on the stories of Scripture, Lashondra's life was informed by who Jesus was and how he lived. The Holy Spirit had impressed Christ's form upon her character so that she embodied the "fruit of the Spirit": love, joy, and peace. Two years ago Lashondra died. What we can pray for her depends on what happened to her when she died—the kind of heaven she entered.

Tom Wright contends that "heaven" is not the best word for the final state. In Greek philosophy the afterlife is disembodied spiritual survival—and "most Christians . . . express their future hope in terms of leaving this world and going to another one, called 'heaven'" as immaterial souls. But this is not the Christian vision of the life to come. "To be sure, God's people go to heaven when they die; they pass into God's dimension of reality." The intermediate hope of the blessed is *paradise*, a temporary place of restful happiness in the presence of God (2 Cor 5:8; Phil 1:23). But at the end of all things "the heavenly city comes down to earth" (Rev 21:1–5). The ultimate hope is the renewal of the entire cosmos, including bodily resurrection and the return of Jesus to a world made new.[8] Consummation prayers require a two-stage afterlife in which the last things are not present realities, but remain future events for the dead.

Church, *Book of Common Prayer*, 363.

7. Marshall, *Belief and Dead*, 182.

8. Wright, *Following Jesus*, 60. Also see *Surprised by Hope*, 5, 19, 26, 29 and *For All Saints*, 20.

While Lashondra entered joy, she did not enter *fullness* of joy; she experienced communion with Christ immediately after death, but her resurrection in God's new creation remains future. This two-stage afterlife is like an indirect flight with a layover and a final destination (leaving an unfinished future yet to come), not a one-stage direct flight (where we experience complete salvation immediately at death).[9] "We look forward in two ways," Dorothy and Gabriel Fackre say, "long-range and short-range." The last things concern the final future, the end of history—the next-to-last things concern "life after death but before the consummation of all things."[10]

Consummation prayers assume the *future consummation requirement*. To consummate something means to bring it to a conclusion or end, to completion, perfection, and fulfillment in every respect; consummation is the action of completing, accomplishing, or finishing something.[11] The final completion of God's redemptive plan either happens privately and individually for each person at the time of their death or is a public, collective, cosmic event that occurs at the end of history. If final fulfillment is accomplished for Lashondra at death, if she dies right away into the last things, then we cannot offer consummation prayers since they can make no difference in her condition. But if she is in an intermediate state awaiting final consummation then prayer makes sense since she has not already achieved all the happiness there is to achieve. Consummation prayer requires that the future be consummation-incomplete, that things are not in their final state, that eschatological events still have to occur. Consummation will only be complete when God's plan for history and individuals is finished—when Christ returns, the dead are raised, evil defeated and the eternal kingdom established on a renewed earth. Lashondra has not yet experienced these things. Because final consummation

---

9. This analogy comes from Alcorn, *Heaven*, 43 and Walls, *Heaven, Hell and Purgatory*, 30. Brown (*Ransom of Soul*, 12 and 18) points out that the focus in the early church was on the "Big Future" (the final state of a new heaven and earth, resurrection and the transformation of creation). Tertullian, for example, believed that martyrs enter heaven directly at death, while ordinary Christians enter a realm of waiting souls, resting in a shaded place of joyful refreshment (*refrigerium*). By the Middle Ages, however, the focus was on the "little future"—the intermediate state and the long, painful journey of the individual soul through purgatory.

10. Fackre, *Christian Basics*, 125–26.

11. *Oxford English Dictionary* online, Entry 39989.

lies ahead, Jürgen Moltmann says, Christians are "people-in-waiting"—and she, like us, is waiting for full redemption.[12]

An Overview of Beliefs on Heaven

Randy Alcorn points out that we equivocate, using one word to refer to two different realities—the heaven that is now and the heaven that will be. *Present heaven* (the transitional place, existing alongside the world right now, where we go when we die and where we await final consummation—the intermediate state) and *future heaven* (the permanent place, not yet existing, where we will live forever with God and each other after resurrection—the final state) are different realities.[13] Consummation prayers concern future heaven—so it will be helpful to have some understanding of what future heaven is like. What are we praying for when we petition for final consummation, for future heaven?

Biblical teaching about heaven is imprecise rather than systematic. Since its language is often symbolic and metaphoric, we should be careful about interpreting it literally. The *Catechism of the Catholic Church* cautions that the "mystery of blessed communion with God . . . is beyond all understanding and description" and reminds us that "no eye has seen, nor ear heard, nor the human heart conceived, what God has prepared for those who love him" (1 Cor 2:9).[14] "What we will be has not yet been revealed," St. John (1 John 3:2) says, and so we must always be reserved and modest about what we do not know. We should distinguish the core view of heaven (described in abstract terms like "beatific vision" or *theosis*—a condition of unbroken communion with God) from the embellished view (concrete metaphors such as garden, city, banquet, or marriage).[15]

12. Moltmann, *Theology of Hope*, 53.

13. Alcorn, *Heaven Workbook*, 32. "In the present heaven, we'll be joyfully in Christ's presence but looking forward to our bodily resurrection and permanent relocation to the new earth. Though a wonderful place, the present heaven is not the place God promises for us to live forever. God's children are destined for life as resurrected beings on a resurrected earth."

14. Roman Catholic Church, *Catechism of Catholic Church*, Section 1027, 268.

15. I draw the "core-embellished" distinction from Griffiths, "Purgatory," 427. Scripture uses poetic metaphor to picture eternity as a banquet hall (Isa 25:6; Matt 8:11; Luke 14:15–24), a wedding reception (Matt 25:1–13; Rev 19:7–9), a magnificent temple (Rev 4–5), a glorious city and garden *paradise* (Rev 21–22). See Webb, *Good Eating*, chapter 7 on what we do and do not know concerning heaven.

Biblical Words for "Heaven"

The biblical terms translated as "heaven" are *shāmayim* (Hebrew) and *ouranos* (Greek), and each has a double meaning.[16] First, they have an astronomical sense; the atmosphere surrounding the earth—the sky and the realm of the sun, moon, and stars—is called heaven (e.g., Deut 4:19; 11:11; Ps 147:8). Second, they have a theological sense. Ancient Near Eastern cultures had a three-story universe consisting of distinct realms, one above the other: heaven (the realm of God), earth (the realm of the living), and the netherworld (*sheol* or *hades*—the realm of the dead). Both Hebrew and Christian Scriptures portray heaven as being up; God looks down from heaven (e.g., Ps 53:2) and Jesus descended from and ascended to heaven (e.g., Eph 4:8–10; Acts 1:11), where he now lives and reigns and from where he will return to establish God's new age (Phil 3:20). The afterlife location of the righteous is never called "heaven" in the Bible. The one exception is Elijah's bodily translation to heaven (2 Kgs 2:1)—and the closest St. Paul comes is stating that after death "we have a building from God . . . , eternal in the heavens" (2 Cor 5:1). The term *paradise* (Greek, *paradeisos*) is a Persian loanword designating an enclosed garden. It entered Jewish literature in the third century BCE and became associated with eschatological images of Eden restored (Isa 51:3; 58:11; Ezek 31:8–9). The term is used three times in Christian Scripture (Luke 23:43; 2 Cor 12:4; Rev 2:7) where, Wright says, it refers to the intermediate resting place of the righteous like Lashondra—not their eternal abode.[17]

Creeds and Confessions on Heaven

Heaven has never been a subject of significant theological controversy, and so historic ecumenical creeds and denominational confessions say little about its nature. The Apostles' Creed simply affirms "the resurrection of the body and the life everlasting," as does the Nicene Creed: "we look for the resurrection of the dead and the life of the world to come." The creeds do not use the term "heaven."

The classic Roman Catholic statement defining heaven as beatific vision is Pope Benedict XII's *Benedictus Deus* of 1336. After death the

---

16. See Bartelmus, "Samayim"; Traub, "Ouranos"; Reddish, "Heaven"; Wright, "Heaven"; Charlesworth, "Paradise" (both articles).

17. Wright, *Surprised by Hope*, 150.

saints "see the divine essence with an intuitive vision and even face to face. ... By this vision and enjoyment [they] are truly blessed and have eternal life and rest."[18] The Protestant confessions accepted, without debate, scholastic teaching on heaven.[19] The *Augsburg Confession* states that after death the godly enjoy "everlasting joys."[20] The *Second Helvetic Confession* says that "the faithful go directly to Christ" where, the *Heidelberg Catechism* adds, they "praise God ... forever."[21] The *Westminster Confession* declares that the righteous dead "behold the face of God, in light and glory"—and following final judgment experience "fullness of joy."[22]

Contemporary doctrinal standards offer slightly more detail. The *Catechism of the Catholic Church* states that the saved "live for ever with Christ ... [where] they 'see God as God is,' face to face. ... This communion of life and love with the Trinity ... and all the blessed is called 'heaven.'" Final consummation involves a new creation where "God will have God's dwelling among men ... [and] those who are united with Christ will form the community of the redeemed."[23] The Episcopal Church catechism says that at the end of history God will "raise us from death in the fullness of our being, that we may live with Christ in the communion of

---

18. Pope Benedict XII, cited in U.S. Lutheran-Catholic Dialogue, *Hope of Eternal Life*, 94-95. In medieval Roman Catholicism there was disagreement about whether the blessed experience the beatific vision prior to resurrection. Most patristic theologians believed that—apart from the martyrs—the faithful departed had to wait for the beatific vision until the end of history. In the twelfth and thirteenth centuries Scholastic theologians like Aquinas taught that in the intermediate state disembodied souls attain supreme happiness and do not await something more final; resurrection will increase the extent, but not the intensity, of happiness. Monastic contemplatives like Bernard of Clairvaux, by contrast, emphasized the corporate aspect of salvation; only when the community of saints is complete will full joy be achieved—it is not received at death. Pope John XXII asserted that the blessed do not enjoy the beatific vision until resurrection. His successor, Pope Benedict XII, declared in *Benedictus Deus* that the saints receive complete fulfillment by seeing God immediately at death (or after perfection in purgatory). This position—believers enjoy full happiness before resurrection—became official doctrine for Roman Catholics.

19. As McDannell and Lang (*Heaven*, 150) point out, "in the sixteenth century, western Christianity divided not over the image of heaven but over getting there." The Reformers' main change was to reject purgatory and deny that Blessed Mary has royal status as *Regina Coeli*, Queen of Heaven.

20. *Augsburg Confession*, Article 17.

21. *Second Helvetic Confession*, chapter 26 and *Heidelberg Catechism* Question 58.

22. *Westminster Confession*, chapters 32 and 33, 81-84.

23. Roman Catholic Church, *Catechism of Catholic Church*, Sections 1023-24, 267 and 1042-47, 272-73.

the saints . . . in the joy of fully knowing and loving God and each other." In the meantime, the dead are "in God's presence" where they "grow in God's love."[24] Other statements of faith have similar teaching.

Historical Images of Future Heaven

The modesty of doctrinal statements on heaven, Jerry Walls says, allows "room for speculation within certain bounds."[25] Heaven has been described, Colleen McDannell and Bernhard Lang observe, in a variety of ways. "For some, life everlasting will be spent on a 'glorified' earth. Others think of heaven as a realm outside of the universe as we know it. There are those who predict an eternal life focused exclusively on God. Still others describe individual friendship and marriage."[26] Historical depictions do not distinguish present and future heaven—they focus on future heaven where we will spend eternity.

Among ancient civilizations, only Egypt believed in immortality in an idealized afterlife country. Israelite and Mesopotamian religions had no concept of heaven as a place where the dead go; after death individuals enter *sheol*, the dark and silent underworld. Exilic Jewish eschatology focused on the restoration of Israel as a nation—and belief in a personal afterlife originated in the post-exilic context of oppression and martyrdom. Early Greeks like Homer believed that the dead descend to *hades*; later tradition held that they reside in an idyllic earth—the Elysian Fields. Orphic religion—and its philosopher, Plato—taught that at death the soul enters an immaterial, timeless, and changeless realm beyond the sensible world. Philo of Alexandria integrated Platonic otherworldliness—survival as disembodied souls—into Jewish eschatology.

By the time of Jesus belief in life after death was widespread. The Pharisees affirmed bodily resurrection and the renewal of Israel in a transformed earth. Jesus' teaching about the kingdom of God indicates that it is fully consummated in the future; the dead, he acknowledges, will "rise again . . . on the last day" (John 11:24). In St. Paul's writing hope is directed toward the eschatological events of *parousia* and resurrection

---

24. Episcopal Church, *Book of Common Prayer*, 861–62.

25. Walls, *Heaven*, 9.

26. McDannell and Lang, *Heaven*, xxii. This overview draws on Casey, *Afterlives*; Hawkins, *Undiscovered Country*; Hebblethwaite, *Christian Hope*; McDannell and Lang, *Heaven*; McGrath, *Brief History of Heaven*; Russell, *History of Heaven* and *Paradise Mislaid*.

(Acts 23:6; 24:15; 26:6–7)—"hope of eternal life" (Titus 3:7) and "the day of our Lord Jesus Christ" (e.g., Phil 1:6,10), his second coming to judge the world and establish a kingdom of righteousness. St. John says that we will see and be like Christ when he appears (1 John 3:2); his heavenly vision describes ceaseless worship given to God by all creation (Rev 4:1—5:14) and the holy city where God dwells with redeemed humanity (21:1—22:5).

Richard Bauckham points out that "eschatological expectations . . . take the form either of perfected versions of the life experienced in this world . . . or of a radically different kind of world. . . . [The] major eschatological images which typify the more this-worldly and the more otherworldly forms of hope are the Kingdom of God and the vision of God."[27] Irenaeus of Lyons and Origen of Alexandria picture heaven as a glorious material world in which the pleasures of this life, cut short by martyrdom, return. The early Augustine of Hippo, by contrast, envisions a purely spiritual heaven centered on the vision of God, without other relationships or activities.[28] Renewed earthly life or timeless spiritual existence—these patristic options have remained the two basic accounts of future heaven. These conceptions correlate with two models outlined by McDannell and Lang. The first is theocentric—a heaven very different from this life, focused exclusively on contemplation of God. The second consists of what Alcorn calls "multifaceted joys"—a heaven that has much in common with this life, involving reunion with loved ones, human activities, and natural wonders.[29]

The Middle Ages featured two versions of theocentric spiritual heaven. Scholastic theologians describe beatific vision (intellectual knowledge of God) while monastics describe marriage-like union (passionate intimacy with God). Thomas Aquinas defines the essential element of

---

27. Bauckham, "Eschatology," 207. "A transcendent eschatology . . . introduces a radical discontinuity between history and the new creation, where a more immanent eschatology envisages continuity between historical progress and its ultimate result." If God will destroy the world and the body and only save the soul, this implies that God only cares about spiritual reality, not the material order (human culture and all of nature).

28. Augustine was influenced by the neo-Platonic dualism of Plotinus. As we detach from earthly desires we move, by degrees, toward union with the One. Shortly after his baptism he and his mother had an ecstatic vision where they ascended, step by step, beyond the physical world until they encountered God privately and intellectually (*Confessions*, 170–72).

29. Alcorn, *Heaven*, 176.

heaven as seeing God—"the vision of God in God's essence."[30] The Protestant Reformers, rejecting the human delights of Renaissance heaven, reaffirm an afterlife in which—as Martin Luther writes—"we will have enough to do with God. . . . This will be our very dear preoccupation."[31] John Calvin agrees: "to be in *paradise* and live with God is not to speak to each other and to be heard by each other, but is only to enjoy God."[32] Roman Catholic Reformers also describe a theocentric heaven; Pierre Nicole, for example, says that "God alone will be the possession of the elect, God alone their bliss. . . . It will be impossible for them to love and desire anything besides God"—and so the saints will "live in an eternal solitude with God alone," experiencing rest, contentment and praise.[33] Twentieth-century neo-orthodox theologians like Karl Barth describe heaven in minimalist terms as encounter with a wholly other God.

Earthly *paradise* visions of future heaven, by contrast, are multifaceted. The mature Augustine describes a heaven of human community—and Giles of Rome sees it as *societas perfecta*, harmonious social life in which, Bonaventure adds, "love will . . . be extended to all the saints."[34] In reaction to an ascetic afterlife absorbed with God, Renaissance scholars and artists (like Fra Angelica) depict heaven as a city, busy with flourishing relationships, cultural activities, and courtly splendor. Jonathan Edwards expects union with those we love as well as with the patriarchs, fathers, and saints. The Romantic poets and artists as well as Emmanuel Swedenborg imagine an anthropocentric heaven with elements of this world—family reunions, romantic love, and personal satisfactions; so do nineteenth-century writers such as Elizabeth Stuart Phelps, author of *The Gates Ajar*. Popular contemporary books and films depict heaven in

---

30. Aquinas, *Summa Theologica* Vol. 3, Supplement to the Third Part q 92, 2957. Aquinas acknowledges that heaven includes both a primary object (happiness deriving from the vision of God) and a secondary object (happiness deriving from human relationships).

31. Luther, cited in McDannell and Lang, *Heaven*, 153 and 148.

32. Calvin, cited in McDannell and Lang, *Heaven*, 155.

33. Nicole, cited in McDannell and Lang, *Heaven*, 170. Puritan Richard Baxter (cited in McDannell and Lang, *Heaven*, 172) also stressed a heaven where, while human relationships continue, "all the glory of the blessed is comprised in their enjoyment of God, and if there are any mediate joys there, they are but drops from this."

34. Augustine, *Confessions*, 170–74 and Bonaventure, cited in Hawkins, *Undiscovered Country*, 74.

rich detail: individuals retain their personalities, friendships resume, and earthly activities continue.[35]

I turn now from historical description to theological reflection. Consummation prayer is for the arrival of future heaven, which should be understood in terms of the kingdom of God—God's uncontested rule over creation.

The Kingdom of God as Final Consummation

"The Kingdom of God," Moltmann says, "is the quintessence of Christianity's eschatological message."[36] When we pray that Lashondra experience final consummation we are praying for the establishment of God's ultimate reign. But what is the kingdom? When will it be realized—in present history or in a future age? Where will it be located—on earth or in another realm?

What Is the Kingdom of God?

The kingdom of God refers to God's rule over creation. It is what Marcus Borg calls a religious-political metaphor indicating what life would be like on earth if God were king and the rulers of this world were not.[37]

Hebrew Scripture (e.g., Ps 24 and 93) portrays God as King reigning over Israel and the nations. The Israelite monarchy was established to ensure stable leadership but, following the golden age of David and Solomon, became politically oppressive and economically exploitative. Disappointment with the monarchy gave rise to messianic expectation—the hope that God would restore the Davidic throne with a righteous king (e.g., 2 Sam 7), end oppression, and institute justice (e.g., Isa 9:6–7). Exile and occupation heightened hope for the "Day of the Lord"—a dramatic intervention of God in history that will include both judgment and restoration.[38] At that time, the prophet Zechariah (14:9) declares, "the Lord will

---

35. See, for example, Alexander, *Proof of Heaven*; Burpo and Vincent, *Heaven Is For Real*; Malarkey, *The Boy Who Came Back from Heaven* (now exposed as a fraud); Piper, *Ninety Minutes in Heaven*. Nineteenth- and twentieth-century philosophy, science, and liberal Protestantism have been skeptical about heaven—see Russell, *Paradise Mislaid*.

36. Moltmann, *Coming of God*, 6.

37. Borg, *Heart of Christianity*, 132.

38. See Allison, "Day of Lord" and Hiers, "Day of Lord."

become King over all the earth"; evil will be defeated and *shālōm*—social peace, individual prosperity, physical health, and harmony in nature (Isa 2:1–5; 11:1–9; 35:1–10)—established. The Jews, Wright says, had "a great narrative of hope"—the God who made the world, bringing order out of chaos, and who rescued Israel, enslaved in Egypt, will come with power to rule in "everlasting dominion" (Dan 7:14) over the world.[39]

Jews of Jesus' day, controlled by a foreign nation, did not think that exile was over. At the heart of his public career was the announcement by word and deed that "the kingdom of God is at hand" (Mark 1:14–15). It was the subject of his parables, the point of his miracles and the center of his prayer—"your kingdom come" (Matt 6:10). Jesus understood God's reign as both present and future—God is becoming King here and now in his work[40] and will do so fully at the end of history.[41] Jesus is the Davidic King through whom God is coming to rule God's world. The first Christians believed that through resurrection and ascension "all authority in heaven and on earth" has been given to Christ (Matt 28:18)—and the

---

39. Wright, *Simply Jesus*, 35. Also see Arnold, "Old Testament Eschatology."

40. Jesus begins his ministry by announcing that "the time is fulfilled, and the kingdom of God has come near" (Mark 1:15)—and, asked when it was coming, answered "the kingdom of God is among you" (Luke 17:20–21). From prison John the Baptizer sent messengers to determine whether Jesus was the Messiah or not. Jesus responded by pointing to the signs of the age of salvation that he was performing: "the blind receive their sight, the lame walk, the lepers are cleansed, the deaf hear, the dead are raised, the poor have good news brought to them" (Luke 7:18–23). When the Pharisees alleged that Jesus' exorcisms were inspired by the devil, he replied: since "it is by the Spirit of God that I cast out demons, . . . the kingdom of God has come to you" (Matt 12:22–28). "Tax collectors and prostitutes *are going* [not will go] into the kingdom of God ahead of you," Jesus warns the religious leaders (Matt 21:31). St. John's Gospel stresses that eternal life is possessed now, the blessings of the future experienced in the present, by those who believe in Jesus (3:36; 5:24, 40; 6:40, 47, 54, 68; 10:10).

41. Jesus' eschatological discourses (e.g., Matt 24–25) assume future consummation and he states at the Last Supper that he will "never again drink of the fruit of the vine until that day when I drink it new in the kingdom of God" (Mark 14:25). His prayer also assumes future consummation. Lane (*Keeping Hope Alive*, 86; slightly modified), comments: "the first petition 'hallowed be Thy name,' is the immediate context of the second petition, 'Thy Kingdom come.' To sanctify the name of God . . . was to call forth the glory of God by defeating the Gentiles and regathering the scattered tribes of Israel. This eschatological thrust of the first petition is continued in the second petition. To pray 'Thy Kingdom come' is to request in an abstract way that God would come as King to restore Israel and to reign over God's people. The two petitions taken together have a clear eschatological orientation to them and as such indicate an expectation by Jesus of a future . . . Kingdom of God."

apostolic affirmation that "Jesus is Lord" (Acts 10:36; Rom 10:9; 1 Cor 12:3; Phil 2:11; 1 Tim 6:15) means that Caesar is not.[42] Christ's present lordship over history (Eph 1:20–22; cf. Phil 2:9–11; Col 1:15–18; 2:15) is contested by other "principalities and powers" (Eph 6:12)—but his future rule at "the day of our Lord Jesus Christ" (e.g., Phil 1:6,10) will be uncontested. St. John's apocalypse depicts God ruling and ends with God on the throne of the universe (Rev 20:11). "The early Christian writers," Wright says, "believed themselves to be living between Jesus' accomplishment of the reign of God and its full implementation."[43]

Hebrew and Christian visions are blended together by Charles Jennens—the librettist of George Frideric Handel's oratorio *Messiah*—in its depiction of Jesus' enthronement.[44] Psalm 2 was an installation song for the kings of Israel. After noting that powerful empires resist God's rule, a word of eschatological hope is given: "I will make the nations your heritage, and the ends of the earth your possession" (v. 8). Centuries later, St. John wrote to Christians undergoing persecution by Rome. The promise is identical: God will defeat evil, be enthroned as King, and bring the entire creation under righteous rule. "Hallelujah! for the Lord God omnipotent reigneth. The kingdom of this world is become the Kingdom of our Lord and of his Christ: and he shall reign for ever and ever! King of Kings and Lord of Lords, Hallelujah!" (Rev 19:6; 11:15; 19:16). This is the object of consummation prayer—our ultimate hope will be fulfilled in God's reign of peace and justice. We ask that Lashondra, with all of us, experience that soon.

When Is the Kingdom of God?

Post-exilic Jewish hope included both prophetic (present) and apocalyptic (future) elements. *Prophetic eschatology* was focused, Owen Thomas says, on "the restoration of the Davidic monarchy in a time of peace and plenty."[45] With conquest and occupation by foreign powers, prophetic hope faded and was replaced by apocalyptic hope. *Apocalyptic eschatol-*

---

42. See Borg, *Heart of Christianity*, 131–36 and Borg and Crossan, *First Paul*, chapter 4.

43. Wright, *How God Became King*, 162. Also see Rowland, "Eschatology of New Testament Church."

44. See Bullard, *Messiah*, 113–23.

45. Thomas, *Introduction to Theology*, 153.

ogy assumed two separate ages—the present evil age and the future good age; only a dramatic intervention by God will end human history, defeat evil and institute the kingdom. Dermot Lane comments: "whereas the prophetic tradition . . . looked to a time within history when God would establish peace and justice among the nations as well as harmony with nature, apocalyptic literature looked to a time outside of history when God would grant the fullness of salvation to the people of Israel" and the whole cosmos.[46]

There are three basic interpretations of the timing of the kingdom.[47] *Futurist eschatology* asserts that consummation will occur in the future at the second coming of Christ. According to Johannes Weiss and Albert Schweitzer, Jesus considered the kingdom to be entirely future—imminent, but never fulfilled. Futurist eschatology is apocalyptic: only a crisis, a radical break, will bring God's reign—beyond history, in eternal time. The kingdom is not here at all. *Realized eschatology* claims that the kingdom has fully arrived in the first coming of Christ. According to C. H. Dodd, fulfillment occurs in the present as believers are transferred into the realm of salvation brought by Jesus. Rudolf Bultmann demythologized eschatology by dropping all future reference and making eternal life a current existential reality, a quality of life in the present. Realized eschatology is prophetic: there is no further consummation in the future, only the slow expansion of God's rule in the world right now—within history, in present time.[48] The kingdom is here fully. *Inaugurated eschatology* holds that the kingdom is partly fulfilled within history and completely fulfilled beyond history. It has two stages—one present and one future; the first coming of Christ inaugurated it and the second coming will consummate it. In a famous World War II analogy, Oscar Cullmann

---

46. Lane, *Keeping Hope Alive*, 77. Prophetic eschatology assumes the historical fulfillment of God's will involving human participation. Apocalyptic eschatology sees no hope for the kingdom to emerge in this life; it can only break in from outside.

47. Modern eschatology, Moltmann (*Coming of God*, 6) comments, concerns the tension between futurist eschatology (where the end of all things lies wholly in the future) and presentist eschatology (where it has entirely already come and is present). These views can be reconciled by "distinguishing in temporal terms between that which is 'now already' present and that which is 'not yet' present."

48. Thomas, *Introduction to Theology*, 153 and 155. Bultmann says there is no future consummation because the kingdom of God is an internal reality experienced personally and existentially in this life. Eschatological events are moments of ultimate decision resulting in a present experience of renewed life. Dodd adds that there is no future consummation because the kingdom of God is an external reality expressed socially and politically in this life.

distinguishes D-day (the landing of Allied forces in Europe) from VE-day (the time of final victory and Germany's unconditional surrender).[49] The historical kingdom is already (now) and the eternal kingdom is not yet (to come).

Jesus' return in power and glory is called the *parousia* (Matt 24:3; 1 Cor 15:23; 1 Thess 5:23; 2 Thess 2:1; 2 Pet 1:6; 1 John 2:28). The Greek word means "presence" and is similar to *epiphaneia* (epiphany, "appearing"—1 Tim 6:14; 2 Tim 4:1, 8; Titus 2:13).[50] In Roman times the emperor would travel to various cities. "The word for such a visit," Wright says, "is 'royal presence' [*parousia*]. . . . Just as Caesar might one day visit a colony . . . , so the absent but ruling Lord of the world [will] one day appear and rule in person within this world."[51] At his return Jesus will end sin and wrong and consummate God's reign of justice and peace. "Without the second coming," Wright asserts, Christian faith "is reduced to . . . a private spirituality with a vague and uncertain personal hope, but with no prospect at all of a world radically transformed by Jesus as its rightful Lord."[52] While we do not know when, where, or how Christ will

---

49. Cullmann, *Christ and Time*, 141. "Just as the 'Victory Day' does in fact present something new in contrast to the decisive battle already fought at some point or other of the war, just so the end which is still to come also brings something new. To be sure, this new thing that the 'Victory Day' brings is based entirely upon that decisive battle, and would be absolutely impossible without it." As Robinson (*In the End*, 72) says: "the eclipse of the old order is yet only partial, but the sun has begun to move across its disc."

50. See Oepke, "Parousia"; Rowland, "Parousia" (both articles).

51. Wright, *Surprised by Hope*, 129. This undermines the notion of a "rapture"—removal from this wicked world to a spiritual heaven. St. Paul says that believers will "meet the Lord in the air" (1 Thess 4:17). Hoekema (*Bible and Future*, 168) comments: the Greek word "*apantesis* ['to meet'] is a technical term used . . . to describe a public welcome given by a city to a visiting dignitary. People would ordinarily leave the city to meet the distinguished visitor and then go back with him into the city." St. Paul's meaning, then, is that "believers are caught up in the clouds to meet the Lord as he descends from heaven, implying that after this joyful meeting they will go back with him to the earth." This is the exact opposite of popular rapture teaching. Also see Verhey, *Christian Art of Dying*, 201 and Wright, *Surprised by Hope*, 119–36.

52. Wright, *Simply Jesus*, 201. Theologians have debated when Christ's second coming will occur in relation to his earthly one thousand year earthly reign, the millennium. Currie (*Born Fundamentalist*, 181) summarizes the three basic positions. "*Post-millennialists* believe that the Church must usher in a time of peace and holiness for one thousand years before Christ will come again; thus his second coming will be post (after) millennial. . . . *Ammillennialists* believe that the Christian Church is the millennium. . . . We are in the millennium now. Christ set up his Kingdom at his first coming." This is the view held by Roman Catholics and mainline Protestants.

appear, we know that—in the words of the Nicene Creed—"he will come again in glory . . . and his Kingdom will have no end."

"The fundamental assertion of eschatology," Thomas says, "is that the God who is creator . . . and who has . . . purposes for creation . . . will . . . fulfill these purposes and that this fulfillment will be the end of history."[53] Without future events consummation prayer has no reference or purpose; it is consistent with both futurist and inaugurated eschatologies, but incompatible with realized eschatology.

Where Is the Kingdom of God?

While only the *timing* of the kingdom is relevant to consummation prayer, I briefly discuss the *location* of future heaven. We are persons who always exist in material bodies—so neither present nor future heaven constitute disembodied existence in an immaterial realm.[54] Space and time are necessary to account for afterlife bodies. While both heavens are physical realities they are different locations. Present heaven is separate from this earth, a dimension of space, time, and matter existing alongside the natural world.[55] Future heaven, however, will be on this earth—renewed.

At the center of Raphael's fresco *The School of Athens* stands Plato, pointing upward to the divine heavens (the transcendent and eternal realm), while Aristotle gestures horizontally to the surrounding human earth (the visible and changing world). This classic

---

"*Pre-millennialists* believe that Christ's second coming will occur immediately prior to the thousand years of peace and holiness; thus his coming will be pre (before) millennial. . . . After the millennium God will end history, and eternity will begin." This is the view of most conservative Protestants and is almost exclusively a recent North American phenomenon. Currie (187) points out that numbers in the Bible should be interpreted symbolically, not literally. "One thousand is the result of multiplying ten times ten times ten: ten cubed. Ten is the number of completion or perfection. Ten years cubed symbolizes God's Kingdom lasting until it was . . . perfectly completed."

53. Thomas, *Introduction to Theology*, 167 and 156. Brunner (cited in Hebblethwaite, *Christian Hope*, 137) states that "faith in Christ without the expectation of *parousia* is like a flight of stairs that leads nowhere." Christian theology is incomplete—in fact, it is incoherent—without final consummation.

54. For explanation and defense of this claim see Volume 1, chapter 6.

55. Lest this seem incredible, scientists believe that reality includes many more dimensions than we currently imagine. Present heaven may be a parallel universe, a space-time world that is equally real to the one we are in but with which we cannot interact (see Habermas and Moreland, *Beyond Death*, 440 and Roberts, *Exploring Heaven*, chapter 2).

divide—otherworldliness and this-worldliness, apocalyptic and prophetic, timeless spiritual existence or renewed earthly life—separates conceptions of future heaven. As we have seen, the Hebrew prophets and early Christians envisioned living in an earthly *paradise*, but by the Middle Ages "Platonic shrinkage"—to use Wright's phrase—shifted hope from a cosmic eschatology of God's kingdom on earth to a personal eschatology of salvation in spiritual heaven.[56] Christopher Rowland summarizes: in

> the earliest phase of the Christian doctrine of hope ... an earthly Kingdom of God was earnestly expected.... Over the first centuries, there was a diminution in the hope of the establishment of God's Kingdom on earth and a greater emphasis on the transcendent realm as the goal of the Christian soul.... A focus on heavenly eschatological goals eventually took precedence over the earthly eschatology as the dominant doctrine.[57]

The problem is that this "separate realm" view spiritualizes consummation and sees salvation gnostically—as deliverance from space, time, and matter. And it contradicts Scripture, since both Hebrew (Isa 65:17; 66:22) and Christian (2 Pet 3:13; Rev 21:1–2) texts depict bodily life on a transformed earth. As Kendra Hotz and Matthew Matthews put it, "Christian hope longs not for a flight of our souls from our bodies to a purely spiritual realm that replaces the present creation; rather, we long for the 'new creation' that embraces and restores the goodness of the present material

---

56. Wright, *How God Became King*, 232.

57. Rowland, "Eschatology of New Testament Church," 68–69. "Early Christian hope differs quite markedly from how it appeared in later Christian tradition, for [it was] concerned with a hope for this world rather than some transcendent realm." "A this-worldly promise ... represents a markedly different kind of eschatology from the mainstream Christian tradition in the centuries after Augustine: a hope for this world rather than some transcendent realm. This exemplifies a fundamental division within the Christian world ... and concerns whether Christians believe that the Kingdom of God involves a hope for the transformation of this world and its structures." Thomas (*Introduction to Theology*, 163) points out that "a unique feature of early eschatological teaching was the widespread affirmation of millennialism, the idea that when Christ returns he will reign on earth ... for a thousand years before the final fulfillment. After the third century ... this idea faded.... One of the causes of its fading was the influence of Middle Platonism with its teaching on the immortality of the soul and its concern with the journey of the soul to heaven." Western theology has misunderstood God's purpose for the world as a whole, Wright (*Surprised by Hope*, 5, 19, and 80) says: "the influence of Greek philosophy has been very marked, resulting in a future expectation that bears far more resemblance to Plato's vision of souls entering into disembodied bliss than to the biblical picture of new heavens and new earth."

order."[58] Wright agrees: "the ultimate future . . . is not about people leaving 'earth' and going to 'heaven,' but rather about the life of 'heaven' . . . coming down . . . to earth. . . . To make 'the Kingdom' a heavenly rather than an earthly reality is to miss one of the central points" of Scripture.[59] Final consummation is the renewal of the space-time world—the redeeming of God's good creation, not its replacement. "God's rule will be established in the earth," Verhey simply says, "not in some spiritual, or heavenly or other world."[60]

In the biblical story the Creator does not remain detached from creation but enters into it, making it God's dwelling. Israel experienced this indwelling in the temple—and in Christ God's indwelling took on human flesh (John 1:14; Col 2:9). At the end of history God will come to live with us on the new earth (Rev 21:2–3), just as Jesus lived with us on the present earth.[61] Jesus' resurrection exemplifies what Alcorn calls the "prin-

---

58. Hotz and Matthews, *Shaping Christian Life*, 74. Lewis portrays the new creation in *Last Battle* (178–95): the old Narnia is destroyed and a new world reborn—a new world that is in fact Narnia again, but its mountains are higher and its colors more intense.

59. Wright, *For All Saints*, 59–60; cf. *Surprised by Hope*, 80. It might be objected that while the Bible indicates that heaven will be on a material earth, it will be a brand new one. The *annihilationist view* claims that the present earth will be done away with and replaced by a new earth that is fundamentally different. St. Peter (2 Pet 3:10, 12–13; cf. Isa 51:6; Matt 4:29; Rev 21:1) says that at the day of the Lord "the heavens will be set ablaze and dissolved, and the elements will melt with fire." Al Wolters (cited in Hoekema, *Bible and Future*, 279) suggests a connection with Malachi 3:2–3: the day of God's coming "is like a refiner's fire" that will purify rather than demolish the entire cosmos. The *transformational view* holds that the new earth will be a healed and restored version of this earth. Several reasons suggest that creation will be transformed rather than annihilated. First, Hoekema (280) points out that the Greek word in 2 Peter 3:13 and Revelation 21:1 translated as "new" is *kainos*, not *neos*. "The word *neos* means new in time or origin, whereas the word *kainos* means new in nature or quality." This indicates a creation that, while superior in character, is continuous with the present earth. Second, St. Paul argues that some day "creation itself will be set free from its bondage to decay and will obtain the freedom of the glory of the children of God" (Rom 8:19–22), which suggests that the present earth will be restored from corruption rather than a totally different cosmos created. Third, "if God would have to annihilate the present cosmos," Hoekema (281) notes, "Satan would have won a great victory. For then Satan would have succeeded in so devastatingly corrupting . . . the present earth that God could do nothing with it but to blot it totally out of existence. But Satan did not win such a victory."

60. Verhey, *Christian Art of Dying*, 187.

61. See Volume 1, chapter 8. St. Paul (Eph 1:10) states that God has "a plan for the fullness of time, to gather up all things in [Christ], things in heaven and things on earth." Alcorn (*Heaven*, 103) comments that in the original creation heaven and

ciple of redemptive continuity"—God does not demolish the original creation and start over from scratch with a fresh creation that is entirely different.[62] Just as the resurrection body—in Thomas Oden's words—"is not a different body, but a different form of the same body," so the new creation is not a different creation, but a different and renewed form of this present creation.[63] The reality for which consummation prayers ask is not spiritual existence in a disembodied heaven but resurrected existence in a perfected world. That is what we pray for Lashondra.

Final Consummation and the Incomplete Nature of Present Heaven

Some theologians believe in immediate consummation at death with no intermediate state. But Scripture and tradition teach—and consummation prayer requires—a two-stage hope: as Wright puts it, "first, death and whatever lies immediately beyond; second, a new bodily existence in a newly remade world."[64]

Future consummation is *ancient theology*, Frederick Lee points out: "it was commonly believed in the first ages of the Church that the souls of all just men . . . were placed in some special locality . . . of rest and refreshment, distinct from [future] heaven, but yet the prelude to . . . it."[65] Future consummation is also *consensus theology*.

---

earth are distinct. "Heaven is God's home. Earth is our home. Jesus Christ, as the God-human, forever links God and humankind, and thereby forever links heaven and earth." In the final consummated state what is now divided—heaven and earth—will be joined into integrated reality that is home to both God and humanity.

62. Alcorn, *Heaven*, 114.

63. Oden, *Life in Spirit*, 402. Polkinghorne (*God of Hope*, 116) agrees: the "continuity between the old and new creations lies in the fact that the latter is the redeemed transform of the former. The pattern for this is the resurrection of Christ, where . . . the Lord's risen body is the eschatological transform of his dead body. This implies that the new creation does not arise from a radically novel creative act *ex nihilo*, but as a redemptive act *ex vetere*, out of the old." Wright (*Simply Jesus*, 203) says, "God will do for the whole cosmos, in the end, what God did for Jesus at Easter: the risen Jesus . . . is the prototype of the new creation." "The transition from the present world to the new one," he adds (*Surprised by Hope*, 122), is "a matter not of the destruction of the present space-time universe but of its radical healing."

64. Wright, *Surprised by Hope*, 41.

65. Lee, *Christian Doctrine*, 66.

1. Protestants believe it. The intermediate state is, Calvin says, a condition of both blessedness and anticipation "where in glad expectation [the dead] await the enjoyment of promised glory."[66] While at peace with Christ (2 Cor 5:8; Phil 1:21–23), present heaven is incomplete: because the saints "wait for something which they see not, and desire what they have not . . . , their peace is imperfect. . . . Their desire is always moving onward till the glory of God is complete, and this completion awaits the judgment day."[67] John Wesley also distinguishes two afterlife stages: "*paradise* is only the porch of heaven. . . . It is in heaven only that there is fullness of joy."[68]

2. Roman Catholics believe it. Joseph Ratzinger says: "there is an 'intermediate state' of being with Christ, something to be expected immediately after death. . . . The resurrection [is] . . . a further stage, as yet unrealized and so the proper object of fresh expectation." Two points are clear, he concludes: "[1] Human beings live on 'with the Lord' even before the resurrection. [2] This living on is not yet identical with the resurrection which comes only 'at the end of days' and will be the full breaking in of God's lordship over the world."[69]

3. Eastern Orthodox believe it. "For . . . the saints," Andrew Louth says, "blessedness will not be complete until the consummation of all human life at the last judgment."[70] The dead are with Christ, but their happiness is incomplete.

Wright summarizes: consummation

> is still in the future. This is the official view of all mainstream orthodox theologians, Catholic and Protestant, East and West. . . . The use of the word "heaven" to denote the ultimate goal of the redeemed . . . is severely misleading and does not begin to do justice to the Christian hope. . . . The ultimate destination

---

66. Calvin, *Institutes*, Book 3.25.6, 998. Richard Baxter (cited in Roberts, *Exploring Heaven*, 188) defines heaven as "the perfect, endless enjoyment of God by the perfected saints . . . , to which [they] arrive at death, and . . . most fully after the resurrection and final judgment."

67. Calvin, cited in McDannell and Lang, *Heaven*, 204.

68. Wesley, cited in Bloesch, *Last Things*, 142. Progressive evangelicals (like Bloesch, Hoekema, and Walls) assert this, as do conservative evangelicals (like Alcorn).

69. Ratzinger, *Eschatology*, 168 and 246–47 respectively. The two stages constitute "a single, albeit phased, hope." Roman Catholic magisterial teaching emphasizes a two-stage destiny after death (see Phan, "Roman Catholic Theology," 217–20).

70. Louth, *Introducing Eastern Orthodox Theology*, 146.

is not "going to heaven when you die" but being bodily raised into the transformed, glorious likeness of Jesus Christ.... If we want to speak of "going to heaven when we die," we should be clear that this represents the first, and far less important, stage of a two-stage process. Resurrection isn't life after death; it is life *after* life after death.[71]

The final consummation for which we pray and for which Lashondra waits is yet to come.

Present heaven—where the blessed exist between death and resurrection—is *temporary*. Jesus states that there are many "dwelling places" in the Father's house (John 14:2). Wright comments: the Greek word "*monai*, is regularly used ... not for a final resting place but for a temporary halt on a journey that will take you somewhere else in the long run." When Jesus says to the dying thief "today you will be with me in *paradise*" (Luke 23:43), Wright adds, the word "is ... not a final destination but the blissful garden, the parkland of rest and tranquility, where the dead are refreshed as they await the dawn of the new day."[72] The intermediate state, where Lashondra is now, is a transitional state between life on this earth and resurrection on the renewed earth.

Present heaven is *incomplete*. In St. John's apocalyptic vision (Rev 6:9–11) the martyrs cry "how long?" as they await ultimate redemption. "They are at rest," Wright observes, "but they are not yet enjoying the final bliss which is to come."[73] There are three reasons why. First, the intermediate state is incomplete because final consummation requires individual resurrection. For dualists who believe in a disembodied intermediate state, final happiness requires a complete human being composed of both body and soul. Aquinas says that because "the blessedness of the saints will involve not only glory of soul but of body as well, ... the holy souls already in heaven still await the glorification of their bodies." As a result, "hope [for something more is] in the blessed" dead. For materialists who believe in an embodied intermediate state, final happiness requires a further transformation of the body. Resurrection does not happen in death but is a future event. Second, the intermediate state is incomplete because final consummation is communal. Aquinas states that "beatitude [is] not only for oneself but for others"—and so "hope

---

71. Wright, *Surprised by Hope*, 168–69; emphasis in original.
72. Ibid., 150.
73. Wright, *For All Saints*, 24.

can be found in the blessed."[74] As Wright puts it: "until all God's people are safely home, none of them is yet fulfilled." Because the blessed do not reach fulfillment without us (Heb 11:40), they have not "experienced the completeness of redemption." "They won't," he adds, "until we all do."[75] While there is happiness before the resurrection, there is a fuller happiness afterwards when the communion of saints is made whole. "The hope for resurrection," Verhey says, "is the hope not just for the new creation of a solitary individual but for the new creation of persons-in-relation, the re-creation of community."[76] Third, the intermediate state is incomplete because final consummation is cosmic. The very last thing is the renewal of heaven and earth when "creation itself [is] set free from its bondage to decay" (Rom 8:21). Finality, Moltmann says, means "the cosmic *shekinah* of God"—God dwelling in a transformed earth.[77] Final consummation for individuals like Lashondra, all of humanity, and the entire cosmos are integrated—one cannot happen without the others.

Concluding Remarks: Consummation Prayers As Prayers of Hope

Consummation prayers require—in Anthony Hoekema's words—"that believers will go to heaven when they die . . . [and] that they will be happy during the intermediate state between death and resurrection. . . . But their happiness will be provisional and incomplete. For the completion of their happiness they await the resurrection of the body and the new earth which God will create as the culmination of God's redemptive work."[78] The Christian Reformed Church's contemporary confession puts it well.

> With tempered impatience, eager to see injustice ended, we expect the Day of the Lord. And we are confident that the light which shines in the present darkness will fill the earth when Christ appears. Come, Lord Jesus! Our world belongs to you.

---

74. Aquinas, *Summa Theologiae*, Vol. 33, 2a2ae q18 a2, 33. For discussion of dualist and materialist anthropologies see Volume 1, chapter 6.

75. Wright, *For All Saints*, 24 and *Surprised by Hope*, 169. Allison ("Eschatology of New Testament," 297) agrees: the fact that general resurrection is collective "means that no one is fully redeemed until everyone is redeemed, and that the story of the individual is not complete until the larger human story is complete."

76. Verhey, *Christian Art of Dying*, 192.

77. Moltmann, *Coming of God*, xiii.

78. Hoekema, *Bible and Future*, 274.

CONSUMMATION PRAYER FOR ALL THE DEPARTED 43

> ... We long [and pray] for that day when Jesus will return as triumphant King, when the dead will be raised, ... [when] every challenge to God's rule and every resistance to God's will shall be crushed, [when] God's Kingdom shall come fully and our Lord shall rule forever.... With the whole creation we wait [and pray] for the purifying fire of judgment [when] ... God will heal our hurts, end our wars and make the crooked straight. ... [Then] God will be all in all, righteousness and peace will flourish, everything will be made new.... Hallelujah! Come, Lord Jesus.[79]

The liturgical year ends on the last Sunday before Advent with the Feast of Christ the King. It celebrates and prays for the end of the story, the final consummation of all things—the future hope of bodily resurrection and the renewal of heaven and earth when, in the words of the collect, God "will restore all things in your well-beloved Son."[80] The reading from the book of Daniel portrays the coming kingdom with strange dreams and visions. Two in particular depict a series of four worldly kingdoms as elements of a statue (chapter 2—gold, silver, brass, and clay) and as various beasts (chapter 7—a lion, bear, leopard, and ten-horned creature). These earthly kingdoms are replaced by a kingdom not of human origin; in Daniel 2 a stone hewn from the mountainside is hurled at the statue, destroying it—while in Daniel 7 the power of the beasts is taken from them and given to a divine-human figure. "I saw one like a human being coming with the clouds of heaven. ... To him was given dominion and glory and kingship, that all peoples, nations and languages should serve him. His dominion is an everlasting dominion that shall not pass away, and his kingship is one that shall never be destroyed" (Dan 7:13-14).[81] Revelation 1:7-8 repeats these words: "to him be glory and

---

79. Christian Reformed Church, "Our World Belongs to God," Sections 6 and 56–58, 1021 and 1037–38, order slightly altered.

80. Episcopal Church, *Book of Common Prayer*, 236.

81. Barron ("Daniel and the New Kingdom") emphasizes that this text had extraordinary influence on early Christians as a template for understanding the significance of Jesus. First-century Jews had seen four great kingdoms emerge—Babylon, Persia, Greece, and Rome each rise and fall in succession. And they knew that they were living 500 years after the exile. The prophet Jeremiah had predicted the restoration of Israel after seventy years of captivity—years which Daniel defines as "weeks of years" (or 70 times 7, about 500 years). This is why Messianic expectation was particularly fervent at the time of Jesus. And then comes a charismatic prophet from the hills of Galilee proclaiming that the kingdom of God is arriving and—at his trial—directly citing Daniel 7 in establishing his identity. Early Christians understood Jesus as the

dominion forever and ever. . . . Look! He is coming with the clouds" (cf. Matt 26:64 and Luke 21:27).

Wright argues that ending the church calendar with the Feast of Christ the King distorts the gospel; "it implies that Jesus Christ becomes King at the end of the sequence, the end of the story" and suggests that the future over which he rules is a heavenly, not an earthly, realm. This is radically misleading since the kingdom has already begun. Jesus' public career was all about God's reign—his healings and meals enacted and announced that through him Israel's God was claiming the whole world as God's own. And among his followers, "confessing that 'Jesus is Lord' [Acts 10:36; Rom 10:9; 1 Cor 12:3]—meaning . . . that Caesar wasn't—was basic, bottom-line Christianity right from the start." Wright's point is that Christ is already ruling—while the Feast of Christ the King suggests that he will only reign at some point in the distant future and only over an immaterial realm. The church already acknowledges the risen Christ as true King of the world on Ascension Day—so there is no need for an additional feast of his kingship at year's end.[82]

Wright, however, sets up a false dilemma by suggesting that the two feasts—Ascension and Christ the King—contradict each other. They are not, in fact, mutually exclusive; proclaiming Christ as *already* King and awaiting Christ as *not yet* King are perfectly compatible. The Feast of Christ the King does not imply that his reign is strictly future and merely spiritual. It reminds us, instead, that the kingdom is—in Wright's own words—both a "present reality" and a "still-future hope." And it teaches us that we must give "allegiance to Jesus as Lord in the teeth of the claims of earthly rulers, systems, and philosophies" to be followed and obeyed.[83] "This day reminds us what the Christian thing is all about," Robert Barron points out; "that Jesus really is the King, the Lord of our lives, that we belong utterly to him." Because Jesus is already reigning he must be Lord of everything, of our entire existence, public and private, social as well as personal. Since Christ is Lord of the totality of life, we must not sequester him in a small corner of reality or pay attention to him only a few minutes every Sunday. Instead, we must make him sovereign over every aspect of life—otherwise we are not taking Christ the King seriously and are

---

human-divine figure who succeeds a series of fallen earthly kingdoms and establishes the kingdom of God.

82. Wright, *For All Saints*, 65, 57 and 67.

83. Ibid., 70 and 67.

merely fooling around with Christianity.[84] This awareness is fostered by consummation prayer.

God has not yet returned the whole word to God's original intentions; final redemption remains incomplete and has not yet occurred for anyone—including the dead. We do not experience final consummation in death because we are not saved apart from other people and all of creation. Only those who hold that the last things occur directly and entirely at death, who make no distinction between present heaven and future heaven, deny the necessary requirement of consummation prayer. And so we pray—Wright says—"that [the departed] may come to the fulfillment of God's complete purposes," that they experience resurrection when all creation is restored and God's reign fully comes in an earthly *paradise* (not a spiritual heaven).[85] Because Lashondra has not yet achieved supreme happiness, we can pray for an improvement in her condition—the completion of God's will for her. The Church of England Commission on Doctrine recommends consummation prayers for all the faithful departed and for particular persons: "may God in God's infinite love and mercy, bring the whole Church, living and departed in the Lord Jesus, to a joyful resurrection and the fulfillment of God's eternal Kingdom" (or "may God . . . bring N., together with the whole Church . . .").[86] "Send forth your Spirit, O Lord," we pray, "and renew the face of the earth" (Ps 104).

Josef Pieper says that "prayers of petition [are] nothing other than the voicing of hope."[87] Paul O'Callaghan agrees: "we petition God for what we are entitled to hope for from God."[88] Consummation prayers express hope that human existence is a comedy ending in joy and happiness, that—in the words of Julian of Norwich—"all shall be well, and

---

84. Barron, "What Does it Mean to Say that Christ is King?" As Abraham Kuyper (cited in Bratt, *Abraham Kuyper*, 488) says, "there is not a square inch in the whole domain of our human existence over which Christ, who is sovereign over all, does not cry 'Mine!'"

85. Wright, *For All Saints*, 24.

86. Archbishops' Commission, *Prayer and Departed*, 51. We pray for consummation in the hymns of Advent—"Come, thou long-expected Jesus" and "O come, O come, Emmanuel"—and in other gospel hymns: "Lord, haste the day when the faith shall be sight / the clouds be rolled back as a scroll / the trump shall resound, and the Lord shall descend" (Horatio Spafford, "It Is Well with My Soul") or "finish, then, thy new creation" (Charles Wesley, "Love Divine, All Love's Excelling").

87. Pieper, *On Hope*, 70.

88. O'Callaghan, *Christ Our Hope*, 219.

all shall be well, and all manner of things shall be well."[89] They express hope for the renewal of all things (Matt 19:28)—joyful resurrection and life in communion with God and one another in, as the Church of England Eucharistic prayer says, "the eternal victory of the Lamb's high feast." As we pray for consummation we come to believe in its reality and to desire its occurrence—and to incorporate hope for God's kingdom into our ways of thinking, feeling, and acting. Praying for completion of God's purposes means investing ourselves in ways of living that are congruent with the values of the coming kingdom—working for "that day when your Kingdom comes and justice and mercy will be seen in all the earth"—so that this present world becomes the beginning of that future world.[90] Not to pray for consummation of eschatological events is to despair—to believe that human existence is a tragedy ending in ruin and disappointment. As we encounter the brokenness of our world and the wreckage of individual lives, Barbara Brown Taylor says, it is a hard thing to believe in the promise that everything will turn out just fine in the end.[91] Consummation prayer counteracts this pessimism as we wait for what Bruce Cockburn calls God's "Festival of Friends."[92] It guards against despair and cultivates hope in God's eternal kingdom—so that, like Reepicheep, we long with all our hearts for Aslan's Country and, in the words of the Episcopal prayers, "look forward to that day when suffering is ended, and all creation is gathered in your loving arms."[93] Not to pray for consummation of eschatological events is also to forget or deny that petitionary prayer can hasten the kingdom, that the timing of future consummation depends partly on human action—that our acts and prayers can advance or hold back the fulfillment of God's purpose.[94]

Since Lashondra's final consummation is still future, consummation prayer for her makes sense—and since change and continuing progress

89. Julian, cited in Hick, *Death and Eternal Life*, 156.
90. Church of England, *Common Worship*, Eucharistic Prayer E.
91. Taylor, *Gospel Medicine*, 44.
92. Cockburn, "Festival of Friends."
93. Church of England, *Common Worship*, Additional Eucharistic Prayer Two.
94. See O'Callaghan, *Christ Our Hope*, 61 and 225. The eschatological future is indefinite—its timetable and details are yet to be determined by God and can be influenced by prayer. St. Peter (2 Pet 3:12) commands us to be persons who are "waiting for and *hastening*" [the Greek word *speudotas* means "to speed" or "urge on"] the final events, the coming of the day of God. Payne ("2 Peter," 1569) comments: "this is a striking suggestion, implying that human beings can in some way speed up God's plans."

occur in present heaven where she grows in love of God, growth prayers for her also have a point. That is the topic of the next chapter.

chapter 3

GROWTH PRAYER FOR THE BLESSED DEAD

*Infinite God,
we commend to your mercy the blessed who have died,
that your will for them—never-ending growth
in your love—may be fulfilled.*

AMEN.

MOM AND I WERE in her living room talking about my dad—looking at a watercolor of his boyhood farm (painted by my skilled brother John) and saying how much we still miss him a decade after his death. We paused, silent in our shared memories, tears brimming our eyes. Finally mom broke the stillness—in a low, wistful voice she said: "I wonder what heaven will really be like." Silence again, both of us lost in thought. I reached for her hand. "You often tell me that, after fifty years of happy marriage, you and dad were still learning and being surprised by new things about each other. Your love was never static, never stagnant, but always dynamic and growing. Maybe," I mused, "heaven is like that—continually growing to know, love, and enjoy God more and more." Her answer was instantaneous: "I like that." Another pause—"I really do."

The Episcopal Church catechism explains that we pray for the faithful departed "because we trust that in God's presence those who have chosen to serve God will grow in God's love, until they see God as God is."[1] Consummation prayers focus on future expec-

---

1. Episcopal Church, *Book of Common Prayer*, 862.

tation—the final completion the blessed await when they will see God as God is. Growth prayers, by contrast, focus on present experience—the condition they enjoy now as they are filled with God's love. Growth prayers require an *intermediate state*—a present heaven where the faithful departed await final consummation. This state must be conscious; if the dead are unconscious then growth prayers make no sense since they do not now exist as persons with awareness. When conceptualizing the intermediate state two variables are involved. In terms of *content*, present heaven is either theocentric or multifaceted. Theocentric heaven is exclusive and individualistic: the focus is on God alone in a private, spiritual relationship. Multifaceted heaven, by contrast, is inclusive and communitarian: the focus is on worshipping God, enjoying fellowship with one another, and engaging in meaningful activities. In terms of *process*, present heaven is either static or dynamic.[2] Theocentric heaven can be either a static beatific vision of God or dynamic growth in God; multifaceted heaven, however, is necessarily dynamic. There are, then, three possible models of present heaven: it is

1. a static theocentric state,
2. a dynamic theocentric state, or
3. a dynamic multifaceted state.

Options 2 and 3 allow growth prayer; if heaven is progressive development we can pray that the blessed experience an increase of bliss. Option 1 does not; if heaven is static perfection then growth prayers make no sense since the condition of the dead is unchanging. Growth prayers require a *dynamic intermediate state* involving progress toward ever-fuller perfection. Growth prayers, like consummation prayers, are fully in line with Scripture and tradition; they do not raise the controversial theological questions that purification and salvation prayers do. In this chapter I again reference Lashondra—the faithful Christian woman from the last chapter. What do we pray for her right now concerning her present experience?

---

2. It is possible that the intermediate state is static and the future state dynamic or *vice versa*. My own view is that both are dynamic.

Growth Prayer and the Continuing Progress Requirement

Most biblical depiction concerns future, not present, heaven. Early Israelite religion had no concept of heaven or a two-stage afterlife—only of *sheol*, the realm of the dead. Post-exilic beliefs about personal survival emphasize the *eschaton* (the last things, when the righteous shall rise to everlasting life—Dan 12:2), not the para-*eschaton* (the next-to-last things, the intermediate state between death and resurrection). Palestinian Judaism had more clearly formed beliefs. In Jesus' parable (Luke 16:19–31) the dead Lazarus appears to be in a state of joy, and the good thief is promised that he will be with Jesus immediately after death (Luke 23:43). St. Paul assures believers that the Christian dead are in a period of "sleep" awaiting resurrection (1 Thess 4:13–18)—they are in the presence of God, "with Christ" and "at home with the Lord" (2 Cor 5:6–8; Phil 1:23) in an open-ended process of being "transformed . . . from one degree of glory to another" (2 Cor 3:18).[3] St. John's vision describes conscious martyrs awaiting vindication in present heaven (Rev 6:9–11). These texts, which are open to differing interpretations, give little detail about the intermediate state. The creeds and doctrinal statements also say little about present heaven; the Episcopal Church catechism, for example, simply states that between death and resurrection the dead are "in God's presence" where they "grow in God's love."[4]

Growth prayers assume the *continuing progress requirement*: the spiritual development of the blessed is not finalized at death. Their individual histories are growth-incomplete—in heaven they continue to develop in knowledge and love of God. "Fulfillment will not happen," John Polkinghorne and Michael Welker say, "in a timeless moment of illumination but through an everlasting exploration of the riches of the divine nature."[5] In present heaven, John Wesley adds, the "holy souls who have been discharged from the body . . . will be continually ripening for [future] heaven, will be perpetually holier and happier, till they are received into 'the Kingdom prepared for them from the foundation of the

---

3. In Scripture the word "sleep" is simply a common synonym for "death"; it need not imply unconsciousness. It might be objected that in 2 Corinthians 3:18 St. Paul is not speaking of the dead but of the living. However, I believe that extending his meaning to the dead is theologically appropriate.

4. Episcopal Church, *Book of Common Prayer*, 862.

5. Polkinghorne and Welker, "Introduction," 13.

world' [Matt 25:34]."[6] Progressive development is also presupposed in the Anglican burial office: "grant that, increasing in knowledge and love of you, they may go from strength to strength in the life of perfect service in your heavenly Kingdom."[7] A growth-open future is necessary if prayer for the continual advancement of the faithful departed is to make sense.

Continuing progress assumes the *dynamic afterlife requirement*: the post-mortem condition of the dead is changing rather than unchanging. The intermediate state is—to repeat—either

1. a static, passive state of being beyond time in which change cannot occur or
2. a dynamic, active process of becoming within time where change happens.[8]

The *static state* view describes a present heaven where individuals exist in one timeless moment that always remains the same, an unchanging present without temporal succession. Heaven is a state of restful contemplation in God's presence. People "become disengaged and time stands still," Lisa Miller jests. "Nothing happens.... Everybody's ... totally blissed out."[9] Without time there is no progress, only passive, changeless experience. If heaven is growth-complete and individual histories are finished, if Lashondra's current experience is static, then growth prayer for her is pointless.

The *dynamic change* view describes a present heaven where events occur successively and unfold progressively, one after another. Heaven is a process of movement toward increasing participation in God's life. Development is change through time, and so a dynamic heaven is necessarily temporal. Hendrikus Berkhof says that in heaven (both present and future) we will "live again in the succession of past, present and future, but in such a way that . . . , though always progressing, we are always at our destination."[10] David Brown agrees: heaven is "an endless process of development . . . in terms of our ever-increasing understanding of God.

---

6. Wesley, cited in Chapman, "Rest and Light Perpetual," 40.

7. Episcopal Church, *Book of Common Prayer*, 489.

8. Nichols (*Death and Afterlife*, 171) puts the options concerning afterlife time simply: "heaven must be an eternal process of development or must be an eternal timeless moment." See Volume 1, chapter 7.

9. Miller, *Heaven*, 209.

10. Berkhof, cited in Alcorn, *Heaven*, 269.

... Heaven [is] an endless voyage of discovery ... that inevitably involves change for us, rather than [being a] static condition."[11] We are essentially temporal beings for whom change is necessary; we must experience any life as temporal process and so cannot exist in a timeless heaven. And the activities of heaven—worship, relationships, work, and leisure—are essentially temporal events, which involve duration and take place in succession. Heaven has a developing history in time; the dead remain beings in time, experiencing a flow of constantly-changing moments, a sequence of events (not a simple, timeless, ever-present moment). Heaven is not, John Meyendorff says, "a static contemplation of divine 'essence,' but a dynamic ascent of love, which never ends, because God's transcendent being is inexhaustible, and always contains new things to be discovered through the union of love."[12] Heaven is infinite progress toward an infinite God (which requires time and change), not a timeless, changeless beatific vision. If Lashondra's situation is growth-incomplete and temporal—a condition in which change happens, where spiritual progress occurs as she actively participates more and more in God's life—then growth prayers for her have a point.

Theological Conceptions of Present Heaven

In theocentric heaven the blessed are focused entirely on God. Western and Eastern Christianity diverged historically in their depictions of it: for the West, beatific vision involves static contemplation of God—while for the East *theosis* means perpetual progress toward marriage-like union with God. Thomas Aquinas' still and immobile heaven is the opposite of Gregory of Nyssa's developmental heaven of endless growth.[13] Multifaceted heaven, by contrast, is not focused exclusively on contemplation of God but also involves reunion with loved ones and human activities.

---

11. Brown, "No Heaven without Purgatory," 449.
12. Meyendorff, *Byzantine Theology*, 219.
13. See Walls, "Heaven," 403. This is not quite accurate concerning the West—while Scholastic theologians emphasized an intellectual and static beatific vision, monastic spirituality described loving and dynamic union with God.

Option 1: Present Heaven as Static Beatific Vision

In heaven we encounter God, seeing God face to face (Rev 22:4; cf. 1 Cor 13:12; 1 John 3:21). Since the Middle Ages the Roman Catholic Church has called this the "beatific vision"—which etymologically means "happy-making sight." Augustine of Hippo declares that "we shall see God forever, we shall love God without satiety, we shall praise God without wearying. . . . We shall be still and see, we shall see and we shall love, we shall love and we shall praise."[14] Our eternal destiny, Aquinas says, consists of "perfect union of the soul with God, insofar as it enjoys God perfectly, seeing God and loving God in perfection."[15] John Calvin agrees: "as partakers in heavenly glory we shall see God as God is."[16]

Medieval theologians classified work as either contemplative (focused on eternal heavenly things) or active (focused on transient earthly things)—and considered contemplative religious callings superior to active mundane callings. This distinction influenced conceptions of heaven. Aquinas describes a beatific vision consisting of intellectual understanding of God—a non-sensory, intuitive knowledge of God's essence that is communicated directly to the spirit.[17] He follows Aristotle, who held that, since reason is our best capacity, ultimate happiness is cognitive. God's own activity is pure self-contemplation, and in thinking on God human beings most closely approximate the divine.[18] The greatest happiness,

---

14. Augustine, *City of God*, Book 22.30, 1088–91.

15. Aquinas, *Summa Theologica* Vol. 3, Supplement to the Third Part, q 92, 2957. The traditional view of beatific vision draws on St. Paul's statement that now we know God in part, seeing God reflected in created things—but then we will have direct knowledge of God as God is (1 Cor 13:12). The vision of God is unmediated through any created thing and, since it surpasses natural human powers, requires supernatural illumination, the *lumen gloriae*—the "light of glory" that elevates our minds and wills so that we know and love God perfectly.

16. Calvin, *Institutes*, Book 2.14.3, 485.

17. The beatific vision as defined by Pope Benedict XII is glossed by Lane (*Keeping Hope Alive*, 139): the souls of the just "see the divine essence with an intuitive vision [one not derived from reasoning] and even face to face [nothing stands between God and the person] without the mediation of any creature by way of object of vision [no finite created thing serves as a medium through which, as in this life, God is known]; rather the divine essence immediately manifests itself to them plainly, clearly and openly, and in this vision they enjoy the divine essence [God is revealed as God really is]."

18. Aristotle, *Metaphysics*, 1072b20–30, 205. Also see Casey, *Afterlives*, 289 and Zagzebski, "Heaven."

Aquinas inferred, involves the highest operation of the mind—meditation on God as God really is. In heaven attention is devoted to God alone as the exclusive source of joy; "there is no room," John Casey says, for "human society, conversation, and recreation which stands outside the beatific vision. This is the heaven anticipated in the whole Catholic tradition of monasticism . . . and asceticism."[19]

Aquinas' heaven is static. Plato claimed that change involves imperfection (movement from less perfect to more perfect or *vice versa*) and so a perfect afterlife must be changeless. Aquinas located heaven in the stillness of the divine world—the empyrean, the "fiery place" of pure light, which is God's dwelling—beyond the circling of the earth and celestial planets. Heaven involves no action except mental activity: "all the occupations of the active life will cease," he says. "Only the occupation of the contemplative life will remain."[20] The beatific vision constitutes a passive experience, a total absorption in intellectual awareness of God occurring in a timeless and motionless realm. Such a static condition is inconsistent with growth prayer. While we can offer prayers of thanksgiving that Lashondra has entered joy, we cannot offer petitionary prayers for growth since they can make no difference in her condition.

Contemporary Western scholars understand the beatific vision as love and knowledge and praise of God. The Roman Catholic International Theological Commission states that the beatific vision consists in friendship with the Trinity—for which the language of "seeing God" is metaphor. The *Catechism of the Catholic Church* equates "seeing God as God is, face to face" with entering the "communion of life and love that is the Trinity."[21] In Hebrew Scripture seeing God face to face means in-

19. Casey, *Afterlives*, 291; cf. 258–60 and 290. Also see Cosden, *Heavenly Good of Earthly Work*, 32, 41 and 61. This is not entirely accurate. Aquinas thinks that while the love of friends is not essential to heavenly happiness—only the vision of God is—love of other human beings results from love of God.

20. Aquinas, cited in O'Callaghan, *Christ Our Hope*, 174. In Ptolemaic cosmology the universe consists of concentric spheres, with earth at the center and, in ascending order, the planets circling it. Beyond them are the fixed stars—and past the outermost sphere of the cosmos, the divine world, without space, time, or materiality. It is composed of two levels: the empyrean (the "fiery place" of pure light—from the Latin *pyr*, "fire") is the dwelling place of angels and the redeemed—and the "heaven of heavens" is the abode of God. See Russell, *History of Heaven*, 22–23 and McDannell and Lang, *Heaven*, 8of. Aquinas (*Summa Theologica* Vol. 3, Supplement to the Third Part, q 91 a2, 2950–53) held that in *future* heaven the transformed universe will be timeless and unchanging; the earth and all heavenly bodies will stand still.

21. International Theological Commission, "Some Current Questions," 235 and

timacy with God (Exod 33:11); it is like the deep joy of looking into the face of a loved one. Bernard of Clairvaux held that in heaven we partake of the divine nature as "glowing iron becomes indistinguishable from the fire." Florentin Boudreaux comments: if

> you thrust a piece of iron into the fire, it soon . . . becomes red and hot, like the fire. It is thus made a partaker of the nature of fire, without, however, losing its own essential iron-nature. This illustrates what takes place in the beatific vision. . . . [The person] . . . becomes bright with God's brightness, beautiful with God's beauty, pure with God's purity, happy with God's . . . happiness, and perfect with God's divine perfection. . . . [The person] has become a partaker of the "divine nature," while [retaining their] created nature and personal identity.[22]

Present heaven is more than being statically in God's presence; it is being progressively filled with God's life. Understanding heaven as personal sharing in the community of love which is God's being brings the Western symbol (beatific vision) and the Eastern symbol (*theosis*) together—and is compatible with growth prayer.

Option 2: Present Heaven as Dynamic Growth toward God

Plato believed that, because the soul is divinely created and pre-exists its placement in a physical body, it desires to return to God. Philo of Alexandria held that the spiritual life is a series of steps as the soul ascends to God. Plotinus of Rome taught "deliverance from the things of this world" and "escape in solitude to the Solitary." As the soul detaches from earthly desires it moves, by degrees, toward union with the One.[23] This neo-Platonic idea of the homeward journey of the soul to God influenced patristic views of heaven as ceaseless growth, constant ascent to unity with God in love. Irenaeus of Lyons argues that our knowledge of God

---

Roman Catholic Church, *Catechism of Catholic Church*, Sections 1023–24, 267.

22. Bernard, cited in Russell, *History of Heaven*, 117 and Boudreaux, "Happiness of Heaven," 9. Bernard also offers another image of heavenly union—what happens when a drop of water is poured into wine and assumes the wine's color and taste (U.S. Lutheran-Catholic Dialogue, *Hope of Eternal Life*, 84).

23. Plotinus, cited in McDannell and Lang, *Heaven*, 57. For details on what early Christians believed about the last things see Daley, *Hope of Early Church*. For more on the history and development of deification in Christian tradition, including its roots in Greek philosophy, see Christensen and Wittung, *Partakers of Divine Nature*.

will never be complete: "God must always be the greater, going above and beyond everything, and not only in this world but also in the future one, so that God might always remain the Teacher, while humanity, as the pupil, might always learn from God." In heaven we will "always go on toward God."[24] Origen of Alexandria says that those who seek God "always walk and always move on, and the further they go, so much more does the road still to walk grow long and stretch out endlessly."[25] Colleen McDannell and Bernhard Lang note that while Scholastic theologians describe beatific vision (an intellectual heaven whose goal is knowledge of God), monastic spirituality emphasizes "beatific lovemaking" (an intimate heaven aimed at union with God). Bernard of Clairvaux, Angela of Foligno, and Hildegard of Bingen, for example, picture heaven as courtly love—mystical marriage between God and the soul.[26] Dante Alighieri's *Paradiso*, Casey says, symbolizes ascent toward God. "The blessed are seen expanding their love more and more, through an ever-growing concentration on God. . . . [As] each soul's understanding of the divine nature deepens and increases . . . [so] does the love and happiness of every soul."[27] Calvin suggests that at least the intermediate state is progressive: the saints' "desire is always moving onward till the glory of God

---

24. Irenaeus, cited in Ferguson, "God's Infinity and Man's Mutability," 60 and Irenaeus, cited in Balthasar, *Dare We Hope*, 130. Also see Daley, *Hope of Early Church*, 31–32.

25. Origen, cited in Daley, *Hope of Early Church*, 50.

26. McDannell and Lang, *Heaven*, 106. Also see Russell, *History of Heaven*, 117 and 144. Marriage mysticism is traceable back at least to Origen, who in *Homilies on the Song of Songs* writes of God as the Bridegroom coming to him (see Pope Benedict XVI, *Fathers of Church*, 29).

27. Casey, *Afterlives*, 282–83. Dante's *Paradiso* offers, perhaps, the greatest portrait of heaven in human literature. It symbolizes Aquinas' theology of the ascent of the mind toward God. In heaven the saved grow in love as their understanding of God expands. Dante's levels are based on medieval cosmology; in *Inferno* the pilgrim descends downward to the center of hell, while in *Paradiso* he ascends upward through the planets to the highest heaven. In each sphere he meets souls awaiting resurrection, each with a different level of bliss corresponding to their ability to understand and love God. As they approach heaven, the pilgrim's guide, Beatrice, leaves him and joins the blessed in a rose-shaped amphitheater below the empyrean. The pilgrim continues on, meeting the three apostles—St. Peter, St. James, and St. John—as well as Mary, the Mother of God, and Christ himself. Finally, he enters God's heaven, a place of blinding light shining in three circles—and experiences the beatific vision of the Trinity, "the Love that moves the sun and the other stars." Dante's highest heaven of pure light, paradoxically, is beyond space and time. See Casey, *Afterlives*, chapter 12 and Russell, *History of Heaven*, chapters 11 and 12.

is complete, and this completion awaits the judgment day."²⁸ Jonathan Edwards also envisions heaven as dynamic: "as [those in heaven] increase in the knowledge of God ..., the more they will see of God's excellency; and the more they see of God's excellency ..., the more they will love God; and the more they love God, the more delight and happiness ... will they have in God." In heaven "the saints will be progressive in knowledge to all eternity"—"there is eternal progress with new beauties always being discovered."²⁹ Joseph Addison, too, endorses a heaven of perpetual progress: like two nearly-parallel lines, God and the soul "draw near to one another for all eternity, without a possibility of touching."³⁰ Because there is an infinite amount about God to learn and love, in heaven we are always growing, always moving. In C. S. Lewis' picture of heaven "the further up and the further in you go, the bigger everything gets"—it is "the Great Story" where "every Chapter is better than the One before" and always involves "a perpetual increase in beatitude."³¹ Heaven, Rowan Williams says, "is an endlessly unfolding story ... growth without a final horizon."³²

Gregory of Nyssa developed a dynamic eschatology in which *theosis* (participation in the divine life) involves *epectasis* (continual advancement in knowing, loving, and enjoying God—a journey and ascent toward true life both here and hereafter). In commenting on the *Song of Songs*, he likens the soul's pursuit of God to the constant yearning of lovers. As a bride's love "progresses, her desire grows with each step. And, because there is always an unlimited good beyond what [she] has attained, she always seems to be just beginning her ascent." Like my

28. Calvin, cited in McDannell and Lang, *Heaven*, 204.

29. Edwards, cited in Alcorn, *Heaven*, 199, 319, and 320.

30. Addison, cited in McDannell and Lang, *Heaven*, 206. Isaac Watts (cited in McDannell and Lang, *Heaven*, 208) also questioned the idea that heaven is simply a place of rest: "we cannot suppose that spirits of just men shall be eternally confined to a sedentary state of inactive contemplation."

31. Lewis, *Last Battle*, 207 and 211 and *Letters to Malcolm*, 108. The refrain "further up and further in" repeats (176, 181, 185, 192, 196, 198, 201–3). The new Narnia is, in fact, a series of different level Narnias, "world within world, Narnia within Narnia"—"like an onion, except that as you continue to go in and in, each circle is larger than the last" (*Last Battle*, 207). A similar thought is found in *Prince Caspian* (141): "Aslan," said Lucy, "you're bigger." "That is because you are old, little one," answered he. "Not because you are?" "I am not. But every year you grow, you will find me bigger." Williams (*Lion's World*, 121–22) comments: "the more we develop, the more there is to see and know of God. . . . We shall be constantly growing into [God], without end."

32. Williams, *Lion's World*, 130–31.

parents' marriage, heaven, both present and future, is open-ended—there is always more of God to know and love. "The soul that looks up towards God ... constantly experiences an ever-new yearning for that which lies ahead, and her desire is never given its full satisfaction. Hence she never ceases to 'stretch herself forth to those things that are before' [Phil 3:13], ever passing from her present stage to enter more deeply ... into the stage which lies ahead."[33] In *Life of Moses*, Gregory argues that as Moses ascends Mount Sinai, each summit is the point of departure for a new height; he "continually climbed to the step above and never ceased to rise higher, because he always found a step higher than the one he had attained."[34] In the same way, the person in heaven grows continually into fuller participation in God. This growth is never completed because desire for God "is intensified by the soul's very progress towards it. And this is the real meaning of seeing God: never to have this desire satisfied.... And so no limit can be set to our progress towards God."[35]

God's nature requires a progressive heaven. God is infinite and human minds are finite—and so we never reach some maximal state of spiritual development. Since God, Gregory says, "has no limit, the participant's desire ... has no stopping place but stretches out with the limitless"; we will never run out of new aspects of God to understand, love, and enjoy.[36] Edwards agrees: heaven is "a never-ending, ever-increasing discovery of more and more of God's glory with greater and greater joy in God." There will never come a time when there is "no more glory for the redeemed to discover and enjoy."[37] In addition to being infinite, God is active. The Trinity is not static immobility but eternal movement—*perichōrēsis*, a dance, a "gushing forth of love" (to use Jeffrey Burton Russell's words).[38] Since heaven, Anthony Thiselton says, "constitutes a mode of existence characterized by the Holy Spirit, [it] will be ongoing, moving

---

33. Gregory, *Commentary of Song of Songs*, 119 and 223–24. *Theosis* is a unity of will—assimilation and conformity of the human will to the divine will—not a unity of substance; this is how we participate in God's nature. Pope Benedict XVI (*Fathers of Church*, 74) comments: "Gregory uses an ... image already present in Paul's letter to the Philippians: *epekteinomenos* (Phil 3:13), that is, 'I press on' toward what is greater. ... The perfection which we desire to attain is not acquired once and for all; perfection means journeying on."

34. Gregory, *Life of Moses*, II.227, 114.

35. Ibid., II.239, 116.

36. Ibid., I.7, 31.

37. Edwards, cited in Alcorn, *Heaven*, 320.

38. Russell, *History of Heaven*, 149.

ahead, dynamic and on-the-move. It will be more like a flowing stream . . . than a lake." He adds: "we must exclude any notion of [heaven] as static perfection. It will reflect the character of the living, ongoing God, and of the dynamic, ever-fresh movements of the Holy Spirit. We shall not be like those forever 'frozen' in the last shot of a film."[39]

Human nature also requires a progressive heaven. Our characters are developmental—we are never in a state of being where we remain the same, but are always in a process of becoming. Persons, Gregory says, "cannot exist without change." We have an ever-increasing capacity for more of God: like an expanding balloon, the soul is "a container which always becomes larger with the addition of what is poured into it."[40] While "eating an abundance extinguishes the appetite," when seeking God "surfeit is never found. . . . The enjoyment . . . does not cut off the desire . . . but rather nourishes the longing."[41]

Karl Rahner worries that if heaven is an "ever continuing . . . succession in time" then the blessed are "doomed always to roam, without ever finally arriving anywhere."[42] But the fact that we never arrive at our destination but are always on the way towards God does not mean that we experience *subjective* frustration and disappointment in heaven. "What Moses yearned for," Gregory says, "is satisfied by the very things which leave his desire unsatisfied."[43] In heaven we are not like an addict who, indulging her habit, experiences a vicious cycle of craving. Instead, we are like the bride whose "desire grows as she goes on to each new stage of development" in love with her spouse.[44] A mountaineer who reaches a summit is not frustrated to find unexplored ranges opening up but desires to climb even higher. "Our thirsting will be satisfied," Gregory the Great says, "yet having been satisfied, we shall thirst."[45] Berkhof agrees: "though always progressing, we are always at our destination."[46]

---

39. Thiselton, *Life After Death*, 128 and 111; cf. 209.

40. Gregory, cited in Ferguson, "God's Infinity and Man's Mutability," 68 and Gregory, *Soul and Resurrection*, 87; slightly modified. God, Pope Benedict XVI (*Fathers of Church*, 74) says, "continually stretches the soul's possibilities to make it capable of ever greater goods."

41. Gregory, cited in Ferguson, "God's Infinity and Man's Mutability," 72.

42. Rahner, *Theological Investigations*, Vol. 19, 171.

43. Gregory, *Life of Moses*, II.235, 115.

44. Gregory, *Commentary on Song of Songs*, 190.

45. Gregory the Great, cited in Russell, *History of Heaven*, 96.

46. Berkhof, cited in Alcorn, *Heaven*, 269.

Nor does the fact that we are continually developing mean that our blessedness is *objectively* imperfect. The Church of England Commission on Doctrine points out that prayers "for light and peace [do not] imply a present lack. We may always pray for an increase in what is currently being enjoyed."[47] John Kronen and Eric Reitan explain that, because of the gap between God and human beings, "endless growth is the 'best state' which the saved can enjoy."[48] Polkinghorne concurs: perfection is not static immobility (like a statue) but progressive development (like music)—"dynamic becoming is the form of perfection appropriate to creatures of our kind."[49] Change does not, as Plato thought, imply imperfection; instead, Gregory says, "this is true perfection, never to stop growing towards what is better."[50] This does not mean that as we progress we become better off. Aquinas' argument concerning resurrection makes the point. Since ultimate happiness requires a complete human being, a disembodied intermediate state soul—which is only part of a person—cannot enjoy complete perfection. When, at the resurrection, the soul regains a body, its happiness will increase—not in intensity but in extent (since, as Christopher Brown puts it, "there is more of [a person] to enjoy God after than before the general resurrection").[51] Aquinas denies that joy in the intermediate state is imperfect; it is, rather, perfect blessedness, even though the resurrection state will be more perfect. Russell explains: "this difference of degree in perfection is consistent with Aquinas' ontological scale, in which things may be perfect according to their status but less perfect than something above them."[52] Consider, for example, how individuals develop across the lifespan; an infant and an adult are both perfect for their stage of development—and yet they are growing and changing. In the same way, a growing relationship with God in heaven does not imply inferior and superior stages. As Thiselton notes, "the stage

47. Archbishops' Commission, *Prayer and Departed*, 20.
48. Kronen and Reitan, *God's Final Victory*, 69–70.
49. Polkinghorne, *God of Hope*, 143; also 15, 117, 120, and 135.
50. Gregory, cited in Ferguson, "God's Infinity and Man's Mutability," 73.
51. Brown, "Friendship in Heaven," 239. The Aquinas passage is *Summa Theologiae*, Vol. 16, 1a2ae q4 a5, 101–7. In Boundreaux's ("Happiness in Heaven," 35) words, the joy "which has been concentrated in the soul alone overflows to the body."
52. Russell, *History of Heaven*, 138. Thus "the beatitude of the soul separated from the body is perfect for the status of separated souls but less perfect than the perfection of soul and body rejoined." While Aquinas' argument assumes a dualistic anthropology, materialists can make a parallel argument: only when our intermediate state bodies are transformed into perfectly glorified bodies do we reach a fuller joy.

beyond the perfect is not more perfect but equally perfect . . . for the next stage."[53]

Finally, the fact that heaven is continual development means that immortality will not be tedious, a place where—Peter Hawkins says—we are "bored silly." Bernard Williams argues that happiness is necessarily temporary—and so heaven, while initially happy, eventually becomes boring.[54] John Martin Fischer responds by distinguishing between self-exhausting pleasures and repeatable pleasures. Riding a motorcycle for an instrumental reason—to overcome fear, for example—is self-exhausting; once the activity is done and the goal met, the pleasure is over. Riding a motorcycle for intrinsic enjoyment, however, can be repeated again and again—as can kayaking the river, playing the guitar, drinking fine wine, or making love with a spouse. Because they involve new dimensions, the enjoyments of heaven are repeatable—pleasures we never tire of.[55] We will never be bored since there are endless aspects of God to discover.

The soul in heaven, Gregory asserts, "makes its way upward without ceasing"—"the one who is rising towards God constantly experiences the continual incitement towards further progress."[56] Since participation in God is, in Everett Ferguson's words, always a movement, never an attainment—we can pray for Lashondra's continued growth and endless exploration of God.[57] As the Church of England Commission on Doctrine points out, we "may always pray for an increase in what is currently being enjoyed."[58]

Option 3: Present Heaven as Dynamic Multifaceted Activity

Many theologians find the traditional theocentric heaven of undivided attention to God alone problematic. In both Aquinas' static beatific

---

53. Thiselton, *Life After Death*, 209–10. If the earlier was less perfect than the later, he points out, then "a perfect baby could never develop into a perfect boy or girl, or eventually into a perfect man or woman."

54. Hawkins, *Undiscovered Country*, 75 and Williams, "Makroupolos Case." See Walls, *Heaven*, 196–97 and *Heaven, Hell and Purgtory*, 218–19.

55. Fischer, "Why Immortality is Not So Bad." See Talbott, "Heaven and Hell in Christian Thought," section 5.2.

56. Gregory, *Life of Moses*, II.226, 113 and Gregory, cited in Ferguson "God's Infinity and Man's Mutability," 73.

57. Ferguson, "God's Infinity and Man's Mutability," 67.

58. Archbishops' Commission, *Prayer and Departed*, 20.

vision and Gregory's dynamic beatific development there is no room for human relationships and meaningful activity outside of God. Owen Thomas points out that theocentric heaven has been "interpreted in an individualistic and intellectualistic way which does not do justice to the other symbols"—banquet and marriage, garden and city—which suggest relationships and activity.[59] Dermot Lane shares this concern: making God the exclusive centerpiece of heaven "reduces eschatology to a private relationship between the individual and God" and results in "neglect of the social and cosmic implications of eschatology."[60] Multifaceted models hold that in heaven we will love and worship God, fellowship with each other, and engage in significant activities. Heaven—both present and future—is not a still, unmoving place, Tom Wright says, but "a vibrant and active human life."[61]

We are *spiritual beings*—so adoration of God is one of the primary activities of heaven. In St. John's vision all the company of heaven worship God, singing "you are worthy . . . to receive glory and honor and power" (Rev 4:10–11; cf. 5:12–13). The blessed do not simply contemplate God passively; instead, Augustine says, they "praise without wearying."[62] Each person is unique, Lewis observes; "your soul has a curious shape because it is a hollow made to fit a particular swelling in the infinite contours of the divine substance. . . . For it is not humanity in the abstract that is to be saved, but you—you, the individual reader, John Stubbs or Janet Smith. . . . Your place in heaven will seem to be made for you and you alone, because you were made for it—made for it . . . as a glove is made for a hand." And so, Lewis goes on, "each of the redeemed shall forever know and praise some one aspect of the divine beauty better than any other creature can."[63]

We are *social persons*—so heaven is not hermits in monastic isolation but contains a variety of relationships. The *imago dei* is relational: we are made, not for independent existence, but for interdependent relationships. As Boudreaux puts it, "we are social beings by nature . . . and we are never in our normal state except when in communion with

---

59. Thomas, *Introduction to Theology*, 169.

60. Lane, *Keeping Hope Alive*, 139. Moltmann (*Sun of Righteousness*, 133) complains that the idea that the blessed in heaven know God directly, unmediated by created things, is "extremely hostile to creation."

61. Wright, *Surprised by Hope*, 20.

62. Augustine, *City of God*, Book 20.30, 1088.

63. Lewis, *Problem of Pain*, 135 and 137–38.

our fellow human beings."[64] Heaven consists, Augustine says, of mutual love, "a life of enjoyment of God and of one's neighbor in God"—and is pictured as a joyful communal feast (Isa 25:6; Matt 22:1–14; Rev 19:9).[65] The social joy of heaven includes two types of interpersonal relationships: general communion with all the saints ("the bride of Christ"—Rev 21:2, 9) and reunion with people we know and love here on earth (as St. Paul comforted the Thessalonian believers who feared that their dead would miss heaven—1 Thess 4:13–18).[66] We enjoy God in community with others, not in an isolated personal experience—and the enjoyment of God is heightened by being shared with all the blessed.[67]

We are *active agents*—so heaven will be a place of creative and joyful activity. We must not, Boudreaux says, "imagine that the vision of God will so completely absorb and monopolize every [human] faculty, that . . . we will become motionless and inactive as a statue. . . . Our union with God . . . , far from suspending . . . the activities of our nature, will increase and perfect them."[68] Alexander Hodge agrees: in heaven "there must be the exercise of all the faculties. . . . The reason, the intellectual

---

64. Boudreaux, "Happiness of Heaven," 41.

65. Augustine, *City of God*, Book 19.13, 870–72. We are united, O'Callaghan (*Christ Our Hope*, 175–76) says, "not only with God in Christ, but also with the rest of humanity."

66. Even theocentrists such as Richard Baxter (cited in Alcorn, *Heaven*, 342) allow natural love in heaven: "I know . . . that it is the presence of God that makes heaven to be heaven. But yet it much sweetens the thoughts of that place to me that there are there such a multitude of my most dear and precious friends in Christ."

67. While nothing besides God is necessary for perfect joy, other things—including human relationships—do play a role in it. Aquinas thinks embodiment is necessary for supreme happiness, and so the soul's joy increases after resurrection. In the same way, while an individualistic heaven would be happy, a social heaven is happier. As the pleasure of a visit to the Grand Canyon is enhanced by being shared with other people, so the private enjoyment of God is not as extensive as it would be if shared with friends also enjoying it. Seeing God in solitary fashion is less good than seeing God in the community of saints. Heaven, then, is not a private encounter with God but includes, Aquinas (cited in Brown, "Friendship in Heaven," 233) says, "the pleasant companionship of all the blessed, a companionship that is replete with delight."

68. Boudreaux, "Happiness of Heaven," 32–34. "We are active by nature," he adds. "Action . . . , both of mind and body, is a law of our being, which cannot be changed without . . . destroying, our whole nature. . . . In heaven we shall be far more active than we can possibly be here . . . ." "A lot of people think of heaven as perpetual retirement with nothing to do," Connelly (*Promise of Heaven*, 22) observes—like attending a boring church service forever. "But that is not the picture the Bible paints. Rest? Yes. Retirement? Never!"

curiosity, the imagination, the aesthetic instincts, the holy affections, the social affinities, the inexhaustible resources of strength and power native to the human soul must all find in heaven exercise and satisfaction."[69] While heaven will involve leisure, rest, and contemplation, Arthur Roberts suggests that we will engage in two forms of activity: work (instrumental activity done as a means to something else) and play (intrinsic activity done for its own sake).[70] Both the prophet Isaiah (60:1–14) and St. John (Rev 21:24) picture heaven as an urban metropolis bustling with cultural activity. The holy city is inhabited by "a great multitude ... from every nation, from all tribes and peoples and languages" (Isa 60:16; Rev 7:9–10). This multicultural community of Hausas and Mexicans, Koreans and Navajos, Finns and Iraqis will bring into heaven their unique gifts of food and clothing, their activities of music and dance.[71] While this depiction concerns future heaven, its notion of activity may apply to present heaven as well.

It might be objected that social relationships and human activities make heaven simply a continuation of this life rather than a radical break. In reply, the principle of redemptive continuity indicates that while there is discontinuity, there must be significant continuity as well. As Polkinghorne says, without continuity, heaven lacks connection to the story of this world—and without discontinuity, it merely repeats the story of this world.[72] Because of the types of beings we essentially are—conscious, embodied, temporal, active, relational—the afterlife must be similar in many ways to this life. Heaven is not, Sidney Callahan states, "a totally alien new place apart from all the people and things that have made us what we are and that we have loved."[73] Growing worship and love of God, growing friendship with the saints, growing creative activity are the essence of present heaven. Growth prayer asks an increase of joy for Lashondra in each domain.

69. Hodge, cited in Alcorn, *Heaven*, 99.

70. Roberts, *Exploring Heaven*, chapter 7.

71. See Mouw, *When Kings Come Marching In*. Into God's city the good things of human civilization are gathered, cleansed of evil and transformed into instruments of blessing. The scope of divine redemption includes commerce, technology, education, recreation, art, and politics. "The 'stuff' of human cultural rebellion will nonetheless be gathered into the holy city . . . . God will redeem all of these things, harnessing them for service in the city" (18). Weapons of war, for example, will be turned into agricultural implements (Isa 2:4).

72. Polkinghorne, *God of Hope*, xxiii; cf. 15.

73. Callahan, *With All Heart and Mind*, 192.

It can also be objected that social relationships and human activities dilute our focus on God alone. Take social relationships. "It might seem," Paul O'Callaghan writes, "that if the love of God in heaven becomes an all-consuming passion, love for others should by right be eliminated or severely diminished."[74] Our love for God will empty us, leaving nothing for others. Loving God and loving neighbor, however, is not a zero-sum game in which the gain of one means the loss of the other. To love God, Marcus Borg says, is not to love God alone but also to love that which God loves—the neighbor and all creation. Joseph Ratzinger agrees: loving people "is not by way of competition with [loving God] but, on the contrary, is its very consequence."[75] There is no false dichotomy between loving God and loving other people; instead, to love neighbor, both Hebrew (Deut 6:5 and Lev 19:18) and Christian (Matt 22:37–39) Scriptures assert, is to love God. When love is shared it does not divide—it multiplies. As my later children Sarah and David entered my life I did not love Becky, my eldest, less. Instead, my love increased to include each new child as they came along; each is fully loved, not one-third loved. O'Callaghan observes: to view "the love of God in competitive terms does not take into account the fact that the love with which we love God merges with the love of neighbor."[76] There is no conflict between worshiping God and relating to others in heaven.

Aside on Growth Prayer for People with Disabilities

I conclude with thoughts that illustrate heavenly growth in a unique way. My son David, now in his twenties, is developmentally disabled as the result of a prenatal brain injury that adversely impacts his communication and adaptive functioning in all areas. He does not read, is completely non-verbal, cannot understand the nature and consequences of significant choices, and requires assistance with every aspect of daily living.[77] What can I hope for David in the world to come? Can I hope that

---

74. O'Callaghan, *Christ Our Hope*, 178.
75. Borg, *Heart of Christianity*, 34 and Ratzinger, *Eschatology*, 235.
76. O'Callaghan, *Christ Our Hope*, 178.
77. David is not, of course, simply a collection of disabilities. He also has numerous virtues (a memory to envy and a kind heart incapable of prejudice—he takes far more joy in giving presents than in receiving them and has never met a "stranger," someone he simply dislikes) and abilities (he rides his recumbent tricycle hundreds of miles each summer, stocks shelves at our local food pantry, loves airshows, and is

he will be cognitively typical or should I expect that he will continue to be impaired? And what can I pray for people with disabilities—physical, sensory, and intellectual—who have already entered God's presence?

The *elimination view* claims that people with disabilities will be healed in heaven. This position is implied by the biblical argument for healing in general.[78] To the Israelites God promised "I am the Lord who heals you" (Exod 15:26), "who heals all your diseases" (Ps 103:3; cf. 41:3 and 147:3). The prophets proclaim that in the life to come "the eyes of the blind shall be opened, and the ears of the deaf unstopped; then the lame shall leap like a deer, and the tongue of the speechless sing for joy" (Isa 35:5–6; cf. 29:18). Jesus' healings demonstrate God's defeat of the destructive powers of evil—that "the kingdom of God has come" (Matt 12:22–29; cf. Luke 10:8–9). When John the Baptizer doubted Jesus' identity, healings were given as proof—"the blind receive their sight, the lame walk, the lepers are cleansed, the deaf hear" (Matt 11:4–5). Pseudo-Justin—a mysterious fourth-century writer using the name of Justin Martyr—draws the obvious conclusion: "if on earth [Christ] healed . . . sickness of the flesh and made the body whole, how much more will he do this in [heaven], so that the flesh shall [be] perfect and entire."[79] Augustine believed that in the heavenly body "anything . . . that is deformed . . . will be restored in such a way as to remove the deformity."[80] Wesley says that those with cognitive deficits—"weakness or slowness of understanding, dullness or confused of apprehension, incoherence of thought"—will be "perfectly freed [when] the spirit returns to God."[81]

---

surprisingly adept at crokinole—a board game in which players take turns shooting discs across the playing surface). His *joie de vivre*—his cheerful enjoyment of life—and abounding love for family and friends are an example to all who know him.

78. See Kelsey, *Healing and Christianity*. I assume that disability is the result of sin, not creation. Disabilities are objectively disadvantageous since they interfere with typical functioning; they are not simply neutral differences like eye color. Disability is caused both by biological malfunction and social non-accomodation. The storyline of Scripture supports healing and elimination of disability in heaven. 1. In the beginning God created all things good. We are meant to enjoy full bodily functioning without disease or impairment. 2. Then sin entered creation—and now the world is not the way it should be. The fall results in illness and dysfunction, which are detrimental to human flourishing. 3. God acts to restore wholeness—including physical health and mental function—to what is broken.

79. Pseudo-Justin, cited in Davis, *Risen Indeed*, 109.

80. Augustine, *City of God* Book 13.19, 532 and Book 22.19, 1060; cf. 22.20, 1064.

81. Wesley, cited in Yong, *Theology and Down Syndrome*, 265–66.

The *retention view* claims that people with disabilities will not be healed in heaven. Amos Yong rejects "the traditional image of the [life to come] as a disability-free *paradise*" and defends "a disability-inclusive eschatological vision." Like Christ's nail-scarred hands, "the [afterlife] body does not . . . have to be free of the marks of . . . present impairments."[82] People with disabilities will flourish in heaven, not because they are physically healed, but because the social stigmas and physical barriers that segregate and hamper them are removed. The retention view is suggested by biblical imagery indicating that people with disabilities will exist in heaven just as they are. "I am going to . . . gather them," Jeremiah (31:8; cf. Mic 4:6–7; Zeph 3:19) announces, "among them the blind and the lame." In Jesus' parable of the eschatological dinner, when the invited guests refuse to attend, the host tells his servant to "bring in . . . the crippled, the blind, and the lame" (Luke 14:1–23).[83] The retention view also has philosophical support. The afterlife must preserve individual identity. An essential property is one that a person must have while an accidental property is one that they happen to have but could lack. "Some impairments," Yong says, "are so identity-constitutive that their removal would involve the obliteration of the person as well."[84] If disability is essential to David's identity, then without it he would be a different person.

The retention view and the elimination view can be reconciled in the following way: in heaven disabilities are retained in the short run, but eliminated in the long run. There is a parallel here with purgatory. Just as morally imperfect believers enter the afterlife sinful but do not remain that way (they undergo a gradual process of moral transformation), so people with disabilities enter the afterlife impaired, but do not remain

---

82. Yong, *Bible, Disability and Church*, 118 and 122.

83. It might be objected that Yong has misunderstood these prophetic visions. In the Bible sickness and disability language often functions as metaphor for sin, and these images symbolize the redemption of exiled Israel (not of impaired individuals) and warn that the unrighteous will enter the kingdom of God ahead of pious people. Even if the prophets and Jesus are teaching about disability inclusion, we cannot assume that because people with disabilities are present in heaven that they are never healed. See my "Hope for Heavenly Healing," forthcoming in *Journal of Disability and Religion*.

84. Yong, *Bible, Disability and Church*, 121. "Congenital conditions like dwarfism, Down syndrome, autistic spectrum disorder, and other types of learning and developmental disabilities are arguably of this sort. But there are also sensory impairments that people live with over the course of their lives which become identity-constitutive, such as blindness or deafness." See Volume 1, chapter 6 for a discussion of the metaphysics of identity.

that way (they experience a gradual process of healing). Instantaneous healing at death would annihilate the disabled person by abruptly removing properties by which they are, at least partly, defined—but slow changes which are gradually assimilated into physical or mental functioning over time do not.[85]

It might be objected that if disabilities are identity-constituting then they are truly essential to the disabled person's existence—and so can never be removed, even gradually. Since personal properties come on a spectrum of importance, however, determining which are essential and which are accidental is difficult. Perhaps disability traits—like sinful vices—are not permanently identity-constituting (at every stage of a person's existence) but only temporarily identity-conferring (at a particular stage of existence). Disabling properties, while substantial, may be contingent and accidental rather than necessary and essential. If so, then they can be removed without eliminating the person. As long as these changes are gradual, they do not threaten identity.

It might also be objected that Scripture teaches instant transformation. St. Paul, for example, states that at the last trumpet "we will all be changed, in a moment, in the twinkling of an eye" (1 Cor 15:51–52). His reference, however, is restricted to the change from a mortal earthly body to an immortal resurrection body. Beyond that, it says nothing about the nature or speed of the transformations experienced in heaven.

Finally, it might be objected that Jesus did what I say cannot be done: he performed instantaneous identity-preserving healings. Jesus instantly healed the permanently disabled without disrupting identity—everyone recognized the man born blind after his dramatic cure, in fact that was part of the controversy (John 9). This suggests that immediate elimination of disabling traits in heaven is possible (which undermines the argument that removing them must, of necessity, be gradual). This raises complex issues, but let me briefly outline a way forward. First, it is important to determine exactly what kinds of conditions Jesus healed. Most were sicknesses (the woman with hemorrhages—Matt 9:20–22), sensory disabilities (blind Bartimaeus—Mark 10:46–52; cf. Matt 9:27–30 and John 9), physical disabilities

---

85. What Hershenov ("Metaphysical Problem") calls "the last state requirement" claims that a person can exist again only if they return as they last existed (just like a baseball game, delayed by rain in the sixth inning, must resume in the sixth inning, not the second). This means that a frail eighty-year-old will be resurrected as a frail eighty-year-old, not as a vigorous thirty-year-old. The "gradual assimilation requirement" states that instant changes threaten identity, but slow changes—which are gradually integrated into physical or mental functioning over time—do not.

(the crippled man whose friends removed the roof and the paralytic at the pool of Bethesda—Mark 2:1–12 and John 5:2–9), and mental illnesses due to demon possession (the Gerasene demoniac—Mark 5:1–20). It appears that Jesus did not heal anyone with developmental disabilities. Second, we must determine what kinds of conditions are identity-conferring. Tim Stainton suggests that physical and sensory disabilities are weak-identity characteristics; these traits, like that of "being the middle child," are accidental features of the person and so are not identity-constituting. Intellectual disabilities, by contrast, are strong-identity characteristics which cannot be eliminated without eliminating the person who has them. Physical disabilities, it seems, are less identity-conferring than cognitive ones.[86] Personal identity concerns the persistence of personality across time, and so is largely (but not exclusively) cognitive; physical disabilities, while they complicate functioning, do not alter overall personality structure like psychological disabilities do. This is why mental disabilities constitute identity in ways that bodily disabilities do not—and why the former, but perhaps not the latter, are only consistent with gradual elimination. Removing them abruptly, as Yong says, "threatens the continuity between [disabled people's] present identities and that of their afterlife bodies."[87] But mental disabilities can be removed gradually because, while they shape identities in substantive rather than incidental ways, they are not absolute or essential, but relative or accidental, traits.

Gregory of Nyssa's dynamic eschatology of everlasting progress in the ascent toward God, an eternal journey of transformation from perfection to perfection, suggests how disabilities are gradually healed in heaven.[88] David will not be left out on account of his disability—and yet dysfunction ultimately has no place in God's heaven. In order to preserve identity, David will enter heaven disabled, but will not stay that way. As he ascends more and more toward completion in God, his disabilities will be progressively healed until one day he will be disability-free. In heaven what Jürgen Moltmann calls "spoiled lives" will develop fully, growing

---

86. Stainton, cited in Yong, *Theology and Down Syndrome*, 334. Also see McMahan's ("Radical Cognitive Limitation") argument that physical limitations do not disrupt higher human goods in ways that psychological limitations do, since various cognitive capacities are necessary for intimate personal relationships, acquisition of knowledge, and achievement of difficult goals.

87. Yong, *Theology and Down Syndrome*, 269, slightly modified; also see 269–70 and 334–35.

88. Ibid., 274–92. I take Gregory's argument further than Yong does.

to completion and perfection as they "become the person God meant them to be."[89] We can, then, pray for people with disabilities in heaven, that God's healing grace gradually eliminate their impairments—that the eyes of the blind see, the ears of the deaf hear, the lame leap like deer, the tongues of the speechless sing for joy, and the minds of the slow know and understand. Similar prayers can be offered for babies who die in infancy—that they gradually grow to maturity in God's presence.

Concluding Remarks: Growth Prayers as Prayers of Hope

Growth prayers require a dynamic afterlife of continuing progress, endless movement into fuller participation in God. Our future life, John Hick says, will be "a state of being intensely alive in an existence which is both perfect fulfillment and yet also endless activity and newness."[90] If present heaven is theocentric, then it is ongoing development in knowing and loving God. If present heaven is multifaceted, then it is infinite growth in worshipping God, enjoying relationships, and engaging in meaningful activities. Whether theocentric or multifaceted, the intermediate state must be dynamic for growth prayers to make to sense. This infinite process of growing requires that there be time and change in heaven, an eternity that is—Anthony Hoekema points out—an "endless timeline," a heaven that is not timeless but has temporal sequence and eternal duration.[91] Heaven, Edwards says, is progressive: "how happy is that love, in which there is an eternal progress in all these things: wherein new beauties are continually discovered, and more and more loveliness, and in which we shall forever increase in beauty ourselves; where we shall be made capable of . . . giving, and shall receive, more and more endearing expressions of love forever."[92] Alfred Taylor agrees: heaven is a forward-moving life because "the blessed . . . always have new discoveries awaiting them, more to learn than they have already found out of . . . God." It is "a land where charity grows, where each citizen learns to glow more and more with an understanding love, not only of the common King, but of their fellow citizens."[93] Sam Storms, perhaps, best sums up continuing development:

89. Moltmann, *Coming of God*, 116–17.
90. Hick, *Center of Christianity*, 112.
91. Hoekema, *Bible and Future*, 305.
92. Edwards, cited in Alcorn, *Heaven*, 345.
93. Taylor, cited in Hebblethwaite, *Christian Hope*, 223.

we will constantly be more amazed with God, more in love with God, and thus ever more relishing God's presence and our relationship with God. . . . We will never finally arrive, as if upon reaching a peak we discover there is nothing beyond. Our experience of God . . . will deepen and develop, intensify and amplify, unfold and increase, broaden and balloon.

Or—changing metaphors—"the happiness of heaven is not like the steady, placid state of a mountain lake where barely a ripple disturbs the tranquility of its water. Heaven is more akin to the surging, swelling waves of [a river] at flood stage."[94] Alcorn, too, gives a good analogy: after Christopher Columbus discovered the New World, Spain minted coins with the Latin slogan *plus ultra*—"more beyond." A dynamic heaven will always involve *plus ultra*—there will always be more to discover about God and each other. We never plateau, but continue to develop and love with growing intensity.[95] Or, as Casey simply states, "heaven is not a final coming to rest, . . . a state of eternal stillness. Heaven is a state of eternal progress toward [God], not of having finally arrived."[96]

Josef Pieper says that "prayers of petition [are] nothing other than the voicing of hope."[97] O'Callaghan agrees: "we petition God for what we are entitled to hope for from God."[98] Growth prayers express hope, Wright says, that those in present heaven "be refreshed, and filled with God's joy and peace."[99] They express hope that the blessed, in union with God and each other, are "transformed . . . from one degree of glory to another" (2 Cor 3:18). This is what we pray for Lashondra. As we pray for heavenly growth we come to believe in its reality and to desire its occurrence—and to incorporate a growing relationship with God and other people into our ways of thinking, feeling, and acting in this life. Praying for spiritual development in service of God means practicing spiritual disciplines that form such a relationship now.

Consummation prayers are focused on expectation of future heaven while growth prayers concern experience of present heaven. Growth prayers express hope that God will bless the faithful departed with greater degrees of joy and further growth in grace. Growth prayers should not be

94. Storms, cited in Alcorn, *Heaven*, 179 and 425.
95. Alcorn, *Heaven*, 441.
96. Casey, *Afterlives*, 349.
97. Pieper, *On Hope*, 70.
98. O'Callaghan, *Christ Our Hope*, 219.
99. Wright, *For All Saints*, 39. Also see *Surprised by Hope*, 272.

theologically divisive since there is good reason to think that the life to come is one of continuing development in love of God and others who love God. In the next two chapters I move to more controversial prayers.

chapter 4

PURIFICATION PRAYER FOR THE IMPERFECT DEAD

Holy God,

we commend to your mercy the imperfect who have died,
that your will for them—characters which are able to love
wholly—may be fulfilled.

AMEN.

AN EVANGELICAL CHRISTIAN STUDENT, Dave, and I were standing in the college hallway talking theology. Skeptical of my faith, he asked "Professor, are you saved?" "No"—I stated baldly. He frowned—"really?" "Well," I laughed, "salvation has past, present, and future aspects." Protestant tradition taught me that I am saved from the penalty of sin, I am being saved from the power of sin, and I will be saved from the presence of sin. And we have theological words—justification, sanctification, glorification—that label each dimension. "So," I said to Dave, "I'm not saved yet—I am being saved." A smile—"that's a fair point," he conceded.[1] Our conversation reminded me of something Robert Fulghum writes: "Americans . . . prefer definite answers . . . Yes or no. No grays please. In Indonesia there is a word in common use that nicely wires around the need for black and white. *Belum* is the word and it means 'not quite yet.' . . . 'Do you speak

---

1. I later read that theologian H. Richard Niebuhr replied the same way to a street evangelist who asked him if he was saved. "I was saved on Calvary. I am being saved by faith right now. I shall be saved when the Kingdom finally comes." Salvation is in three tenses—past, present, and future. See Fackre, *Christian Basics*, 92.

English?' *Belum*. Not quite yet. 'Do you have any children?' *Belum*." Are you saved? *Belum*. Not quite yet.[2]

Prayer for individuals in purgatory is a charged issue that has divided the church. In Roman Catholicism prayer for the dead only benefits those in purgatory; prayer for the blessed in heaven already enjoying the vision of God is pointless and prayer for the unsaved in hell who are beyond hope is of no use. It has been difficult for Protestants to separate purgatory from its medieval abuses. In this chapter I explain and defend purgatory, the necessary assumption of purification prayer. My argument relies on doctrines widely accepted by theologians—and thus is conservative in its foundations. I begin by clearing up some misconceptions.

First, we should distinguish what Paul Griffiths calls the *core view* of purgatory from the *embellished view*.[3] While official Roman Catholic teaching is reserved and minimal, popular understandings of purgatory are more elaborate. The core view has two elements:

1. purgatory exists (as an after-death process of sanctification that prepares us for heaven—the Latin word *purgare* means to "make clean" or "purify") and

2. the prayers of the church help those in purgatory.

The embellished view of artists and writers adds sensational details—that it involves physical torment by literal fire, for instance.

Second, we should distinguish the *satisfaction* view of purgatory from the *sanctification* view. Tom Wright asserts that "there is one doctrine of purgatory, that taught by Rome, and [non-Catholics] reject it."[4] This is flatly false. There are two doctrines of purgatory. In the satisfaction theory the purpose of purgatory is to remove guilt by paying for sins which are not repented of before death—while in the sanctification theory the purpose of purgatory is to complete the process of moral transformation which is necessary for eternal fellowship with God. Protestants need not find the latter conception problematic.

Purification prayers require a *conscious intermediate state* where the imperfect departed await entry to highest heaven; if they are unconscious then such prayers make no sense since they do not now exist as persons. Purification prayers also require a *dynamic intermediate state*—existence

---

2. Fulghum, *It Was On Fire*, 189.
3. Griffiths, "Purgatory," 427.
4. Wright, *For All Saints*, 28.

in time where change can happen. This chapter is aimed primarily at Protestants and—since its content is more controversial, is argued in more detail.

Purification Prayer and the Perfect Holiness Requirement

Gary sincerely believed the gospel and tried in some ways to follow God's call on his life—but he was, overall, a bitter, angry, and unpleasant person. He was cantankerous, critical, mean-spirited, and bad-tempered; his harsh words and actions left a trail of hurt and pain, particularly in his children. God's love was not formed in him (Gal 4:19); he did not reach the full stature of Christ (Eph 4:13) by living no longer for himself but for God and neighbor (2 Cor 5:15). Two years ago Gary died—hard and stubborn, selfish and unloving. Given that heaven is a holy city (Rev 21:2) where only righteousness dwells (2 Pet 3:13) and that Gary died without perfect holiness, what can we pray for him? That depends on what happened to him when he died.

The inner life of the triune God is one of persons in communion, and heaven is intimate community modeled on these relationships. God proclaims to Israel that "as a young man marries a young woman, so shall your builder marry you" (Isa 62:5). As long as we are focused on ourselves, we cannot participate fully in God's relational life. "The principle occupation of heaven," Richard Swinburne says, "is the enjoyment of the friendship of God." This means that "the only people who will be . . . in heaven will be people with a certain character, . . . that of perfect goodness."[5] This necessary condition of union with God is the *perfect holiness requirement*—which is a *perfect love requirement* since we must be able to love whole-heartedly in order to live within the divine life. Gary was not a perfect lover at the time of his death—and he cannot enter heaven selfish and unholy. Self-centeredness impedes intimacy with God; it must be purged away before Gary can meet Christ in his glory. If the afterlife is sanctification-complete—if Gary's moral development is concluded at death when he is instantly transformed by God—then purification prayers for him are pointless. But if the afterlife

---

5. Swinburne, "Theodicy of Heaven and Hell," 41 and 43–44. Because heaven is a home for good people, only people of a certain sort are suited to live there.

is sanctification-incomplete—if there is time beyond death in which his perfecting continues, then purification prayers for Gary make sense.[6]

A Brief History of Purgatory

The ancient church never mentioned a place called purgatory, but did accept a process of purification after death for imperfect Christians.[7] Among the church fathers the idea of a cleansing fire, perhaps meant metaphorically rather than literally, was widespread. The martyrs go straight to heaven, while other Christians—especially those who weakened under persecution—experience an intermediate state of purification, what Origen of Alexandria calls a "place of instruction"—"a classroom or school of souls" where punishment is "applied with the object of healing."[8] The church fathers distinguished the wise or cleansing fire (which purifies believers and, many thought, occurs at the last judgment) from the avenging or punishing fire (which destroys non-believers in hell). As conversions increased after the end of persecution, there were more questions: can the deathbed repentance of a sinner deserve immediate heaven? Can a just God condemn sinful *Christians* to hell or allow *sinful* Christians into heaven?[9] The theology of purgatory, the Roman Catholic International

---

6. Hick, *Death and Eternal Life*, 461, 460, and 458.

7. This was perhaps influenced by Palestinian Judaism; the Rabbinic school of Shammai taught that "in judgment there are three kinds of people: some are destined for eternal life, those completely impious for eternal shame and dishonor; the in-betweens (neither entirely good nor entirely bad, an intermediate place) descend into the *gehenna* to be . . . purified; then they rise and are saved." Rabbinic text, cited in O'Callaghan, *Christ Our Hope*, 289. In the second century Clement of Alexandria identified three classes of people: the unconverted (unenlightened pagans), the converted but immature (simple-minded believers) and the mature Christian (who is perfect in knowledge and virtue). See Christiansen, "John Wesley," 222.

8. Origen, *De Principiis*, 2.11.6, 299 and 2.10.6, 296. See Eno, "Fathers and Cleansing Fire" and Bloesch, *Last Things*, 148–51. The fathers believed that to enter heaven one must pass through the fiery sword of the angels guarding *paradise* (Gen 3:24). Other passages mentioning fire and cleansing—which suggested to them a smelter removing the impurities of sin—were also thought relevant (e.g., Isa 4:4; Mal 3:2–3).

9. See Brown, *Ransom of Soul*, 53–61, 209. Augustine and other church fathers faced a problem after the Constantinian shift flooded the church with sinners. Most Christians are neither heroic saints nor hardened rebels—they are ordinary sinners in an officially-established church. What is the afterlife fate of average sinners who comprise a grey zone between martyrs and reprobates? Augustine recognized a threefold division of the dead: the "altogether good" who immediately entered heaven, the "altogether bad" who went directly to hell, and the "not altogether good or bad" who

Theological Commission says, "began to develop in the third century in the case of those who had been restored to peace with the Church without having made the full penance before death."[10]

Augustine of Hippo believed that some post-mortem punishments are purifying. Some "who endure temporal pains after death . . . will receive forgiveness in the world to come for what is not forgiven in this."[11] In order to discourage moral laxity, he rejected "Christian universalism" (the idea that all the baptized would be saved regardless of how wicked their lives had been) and restricted purification to Christians who were repentant and slight sinners, excluding those who abandoned Christ by a life of sin. These are people "who have been reborn in Christ and whose life . . . has not been so evil that they are judged unworthy of such mercy and yet not so good that they are seen to have no need of it."[12] Gregory

---

comprised a majority in the church after it "swallowed Roman society whole" (53). This eventually resulted in the three-fold division of the afterlife—heaven, hell, and purgatory. Many were sure that afterlife rituals could save sinners, but Augustine was not so sure; he rejected, for example, images of Christ as an otherworldly emperor using his imperial prerogative to show mercy and remit sin. Only light sinners among the "not altogether good or bad" could be helped by almsgiving, prayer, and celebration of the Eucharist. Fearful of encouraging moral laxity (63–64, 111–13), Augustine refused to give clear, reassuring answers regarding the afterlife fate of the average sinner. But his own anti-Pelagian emphasis on sin logically implied purgatory (85). Where Pelagius believed that Christians could live free of sin, Augustine insisted that we sin daily. These small sins accumulate, "built up like a coral reef by a deposit of thoughts and deeds" (209; cf. 100) and require daily penance. Pelagius claimed two groups—sin-free saints bound for heaven and impious rebels destined for hell. But Augustine's belief that we sin constantly in this life required three groups: great saints, great sinners, and a middle zone made up of most people in a church of the "not altogether good or bad." Some small, unconscious daily sins are not removed in this life through penance; this created a need for afterlife purgation which was necessary to rescue average sinners from the harsh dualism of Pelagius (106). While Augustine was silent on the mechanics of purgatory and prayer for the dead, the afterlife came to be seen as fearful and foreboding—and the journey of the soul to heaven required all the prayer it could get (164).

10. International Theological Commission, "Some Current Questions," 232. The debate about re-admission to the church of the *lapsi*—"fallen" Christians who did not behave properly when put to the test—divided theologians into laxists (who restored believers with few conditions) and rigorists (who granted forgiveness only after exemplary repentance). See Pope Benedict XVI, *Fathers of Church*, 37.

11. Augustine, *City of God*, Book 21.13, 990–91.

12. Ibid., Book 21.24, 1003. Augustine (*Confessions*, Book 9.35, 177) prayed for his mother after her death, expressing confidence in her salvation but acknowledging her need of forgiveness for "sins" and "debts" she was guilty of since her baptism. See Daley, *Hope of Early Church*, 138 and Atwell, "Aspects in Augustine's Thought."

the Great agreed that "there must be a cleansing fire . . . because of some minor faults that may remain to be purged away." He, too, limits this to the "slight transgressions" of those who "sinned through ignorance, and not through malice." Gregory emphasized that the prayers of the church, and especially "the holy Sacrifice of Christ . . . brings great benefits to souls . . . after death, provided their sins can be pardoned in the life to come."[13] Gregory's theology inspired the medieval doctrine of purgatory and intercessory masses for the dead.

While the Eastern church continued to believe in posthumous sanctification, by late antiquity in the West the satisfaction view of purgatory was in place. The sacrament of penance was developed to solve a problem: baptism washes us clean of original sin and prepares us for heaven—but if we sin after baptism then we lose salvation. Rebaptism is not possible, and so penance is necessary to cleanse the soul and fit it once more for heaven.[14] If satisfaction through penance is not completed in this life, then it must be completed in the next. Purgatory was defined as dogma in 1254 when Pope Innocent IV gave it official approval; it was reaffirmed by the Second Council of Lyons (1274), the Council of Florence (1439), and the Council of Trent (1563).[15] Some, however, envisioned purgatory less as penalty than as a process of moral growth. Catherine of Genoa,

---

13. Gregory the Great, *Dialogues*, Book 4.41–42 and 57, 248, 250 and 266. See Atwell, "From Augustine to Gregory the Great."

14. In Roman Catholic theology there are two types of forgiveness for sins: forgiveness through baptism for unbelievers and forgiveness through penance for baptized believers.

15. *Pope Innocent IV* (cited in Le Goff, *Birth of Purgatory*, 283–84): "The souls of those who die after receiving penance but without having had the time to complete it, or who die without mortal sin but guilty of venial sins or minor faults, are purged after death . . . . In the temporary fire, sins, not of course crimes and capital errors, which could not . . . have been forgiven through penance, but slight and minor sins, are purged." *The Council of Lyons* (cited in Le Goff, *Birth of Purgatory*, 285): "Those who fall into sin after baptism must not be rebaptized, but . . . through a genuine penitence they obtain pardon for their sins. That, if truly penitent, they die in charity before having, by worthy fruits of repentance, rendered satisfaction for what they have done by commission or omission, their souls . . . are purged after their death, by purgatorial or purificatory penalties." *The Council of Florence* (cited in O'Callaghan, *Christ Our Hope*, 294): "If truly penitent people die in the love of God before they have made satisfaction for acts and omissions by worthy fruits of repentance, their souls are cleansed after death by cleansing pains; and the suffrages of the living faithful avail them in giving relief from such pains." And the *Council of Trent* (Session 25, 'Decree Concerning Purgatory'): "There is a purgatory, and . . . the souls there detained are aided by the suffrages of the faithful and chiefly by the acceptable sacrifice of the altar."

for example, emphasized the joy and hope experienced in purgatory as the rust of sin is consumed and replaced by the love necessary for what we most desire—oneness with God.[16] Dante Alighieri's purgatory, while painful, is also a place of contentment where individuals climb the terraced sides of a mountain—each dedicated to removing one of the seven deadly sins, a particular failure of love—that rises up into light.[17] The doctrine eventually gave rise to abusive *quid pro quo* practices where time suffering in purgatory was shortened by prayers and indulgences. This caused protest—first from the Eastern Orthodox and then the Protestant Reformers. The Second Vatican Council, while not using the word "purgatory," "proposes again the decrees of . . . the Council of Florence and the Council of Trent."[18]

In summary, the Eastern Orthodox Church has always believed in a post-mortem process of sanctification, the Roman Catholic Church has taught satisfaction in a place called purgatory, and Protestants have generally rejected both.

The Bible and Purgatory

Protestants make two objections concerning the biblical credentials of purgatory—that it is not found in Scripture and that it contradicts Scripture.

Concern 1: The Bible Does Not Teach Purgatory

The first, less serious objection is that purgatory is not found in Scripture (particularly the passages cited by Roman Catholics). 2 Maccabees 12:39–45 reports that, during the war for Jewish independence, Judas Maccabeus found idolatrous emblems under the clothing of fallen comrades. He immediately "turned to supplication, praying that the sin that had been committed might be wholly blotted out"—in this way "he made atonement for the dead." While the writer believed that sins could be forgiven after death, this text says nothing about post-mortem purification—and its value depends on its canonical status, a question on which the churches disagree. In 1 Corinthians 3:10–15 St. Paul reminds apostles

---

16. Catherine of Genoa, *Treatise on Purgatory*.
17. See Hawkins, *Undiscovered Country*, 50–62.
18. Second Vatican Council, *Lumen Gentium*, Chapter 7.49–51.

that their work "will be revealed with fire"—good quality work will "receive a reward" while poor quality work will be "burned . . . ; the builder will be saved, but only as through fire." Scholars comment that the fire 1. is the revealing fire of the last judgment (it occurs on "the Day"), not a cleansing fire between death and resurrection, 2. does not purify persons but tests actions (including good actions that do not need cleansing), and 3. refers to faithfulness in ministry on the part of evangelists rather than the general deeds of ordinary believers. This text does not imply different posthumous fates for good and bad Christians. Matthew 12:32—where Jesus says that "whoever speaks against the Holy Spirit will not be forgiven, either in this age or in the age to come"—suggests to some that sins can be pardoned in the afterlife. It cannot happen in heaven because there is no sin there, and it cannot happen in hell because there is no forgiveness there—and so it must happen in purgatory. But since the parallel passages (Mark 3:29; Luke 12:10) indicate that the sin against the Holy Spirit is "never" and "not" forgiven, Jesus' point is that labeling good as evil and rejecting him, who is filled with the Spirit, is an eternal sin. This saying does not concern purgatory. Nor does Matthew 5:25–26—when you are "thrown into prison . . . you will never get out until you have paid the last penny"—which is part of Jesus' teaching about anger and hatred in this life. Other texts cited as proof (like Isa 4:4 or Mal 3:2–4) also say nothing about purgatory.

Roman Catholic theologian Zachary Hayes acknowledges that "there is no clear textual basis in Scripture for the . . . doctrine of purgatory."[19] But silence is not decisive since beliefs that go beyond what the Bible says are legitimate so long as they are implied by it—or at least do not contradict it. "The fact that purgatory is not explicitly present in Scripture," Jerry Walls says, "is not enough to settle the issue. . . . The deeper issue is whether it is a reasonable inference from important truths that are clearly found there. If theology involves . . . disciplined speculation and logical inference, then the doctrine of purgatory cannot simply be dismissed on the grounds that Scripture does not explicitly articulate it."[20] I argue that purgatory is a logical extension of biblical truth.

---

19. Hayes, "Purgatorial View," 107. The reason there is no mention of purgatory, Nichols (*Death and Afterlife*, 173) suggests, is that the first generation of Christians expected the return of Jesus within their lifetime and so did not develop elaborate doctrines about an intermediate state.

20. Walls, "Purgatory for Everyone," 3. Nichols (*Death and Afterlife*, 174) agrees: the lack of reference to purgatory does not settle the matter since "it is not the case that

Concern 2: The Bible Rejects Purgatory

The second, more serious objection is that purgatory contradicts biblical teaching in two ways. First, Donald Bloesch claims, purgatory is "a spirituality of works-righteousness that rests upon the attaining of merit rather than justification by free grace.... The implication is that Christ's sacrifice is insufficient to cleanse from all sin and that his work of reparation needs to be completed by works of penance on the part of believers who have not broken free from all sin."[21] While a punishing purgatory aimed at pardon is inconsistent with biblical teaching that salvation is by grace through faith in Christ's sacrifice alone, however, a purifying process aimed at moral transformation is not.

Second, Wright argues that purgatory is incompatible with Jesus' promise to the good thief "today you will be with me in *paradise*" (Luke 23:43) and St. Paul's teaching that to depart this life is to be with Christ (2 Cor 5:8; Phil 1:23). 1 Corinthians 3:10–15 indicates, not that there are two groups of dead believers, saints in heaven and souls in purgatory, but that at death all the saved immediately enter heaven, some gloriously, others barely.[22] This concern is answered, however, when purgatory is understood, not as a lesser hell or a third place between heaven and hell, but as a lesser heaven. David Vander Laan suggests that heaven has different levels; since "God's presence is ... a kind of spiritual communion, a relationship of love and delight, ... it is the sort of thing that comes in degrees."[23] The Episcopal Church catechism teaches that we pray for the dead because "we trust that in God's presence those who have chosen to serve God will grow in God's love, until they see God as God is."[24] All departed believers are with God; those who are perfected in love see God fully while those with imperfect character enter the purgatorial level—what Edward Pusey calls the "vestibule of heaven"—where they enjoy communion with God, albeit incompletely. As they grow in love for God, they move to the beatific vision level—what C. S. Lewis calls

---

everything Christians believe [such as the doctrine of the Trinity] is found explicitly in Scripture." Also see Hayes, "Purgatorial View," 101–8 and Volume 1, chapter 1.

21. Bloesch, *Last Things*, 151.

22. Wright, *For All Saints*, 21–25 and *Surprised by Hope*, 169.

23. Vander Laan, "Sanctification Argument for Purgatory," 336. Also see Walls, *Purgatory*, 89.

24. Episcopal Church, *Book of Common Prayer*, 862.

"deep heaven"—where they see God as God is.[25] The names "heaven" and "purgatory" imply that they are separate places. They are, instead, different stages of one place. In the remainder of this book the word "heaven" refers to the beatific level. What we pray for the imperfect like Gary is purification in a part of heaven.

The doctrine of purgatory, while not taught in Scripture, is not contrary to it. I now turn to the logic of purgatory—how it can be inferred from the Bible. I begin by returning to the distinction between two very different theories of purgatory.

Purgatory Defined

Justin Barnard says that "on the satisfaction model, what gets purged . . . is the penalty for sin. . . . By contrast, what gets purged in the sanctification model is the disposition to sin."[26] Edward Hardy puts it this way: satisfaction purgatory is a prison where we are punished to satisfy divine justice while sanctification purgatory is a hospital where our characters are perfected in love.[27]

The Satisfaction Model: Purgatory as Legal Prison

The satisfaction view of purgatory is retributive. It has, Walls says, a backward-looking purpose involving punishment to pay the penalty for

---

25. Pusey, cited in Liddon, "Life of Pusey." Lewis (*Great Divorce*, 67) says: "ye had better not call [purgatory] Heaven. Not Deep Heaven . . . . Ye can call it the Valley of the Shadow of Life." As Currie (*Born Fundamentalist*, 132–33) indicates, there are two parts to heaven: "one part for those who can see God—the pure—and one for those who can't—the less than perfectly pure. . . . Purgatory is like the entrance or vestibule to heaven." Modern writers, in order to not reify a mystery, often describe purgatory as a process rather than a place. This distinction, however, is incoherent. Individuals always exist some*where* after death; they have a physical location, and therefore purgatory must be somewhere. See Cooper, *Body, Soul and Life Everlasting*, 88.

26. Barnard, "Purgatory and Dilemma of Sanctification," 326. Judisch ("Sanctification, Satisfaction, and Purpose of Purgatory") argues that the two models are identical when properly understood. Some theologians have a mixed model of purgatory that combines satisfaction and sanctification, but for simplicity's sake I will only discuss the two main views of purgatory.

27. Hardy, "Blessed Dead," 165. Lewis (*Letters to Malcolm*, 108) distinguishes the medieval Roman Catholic view of purgatory as a place of retributive punishment (which the Reformers correctly rejected) from the "right view" which sees it as a place of purification.

past sins.[28] In Roman Catholic theology the concept of satisfaction assumes a distinction between guilt (which is forgiven when we repent) and punishment, of which there are two kinds: eternal and temporal.[29] Confession and priestly absolution remove guilt and eternal punishment; part of temporal punishment is also remitted by priestly action, while part requires personal satisfaction (acts which pay the debt of remaining punishment). If adequate satisfaction is not made in this life then it must be done in purgatory. "One remains a debtor for the punishment," Thomas Aquinas says, which "must . . . be purged after this life before they achieve the final reward. This purgation . . . is made by punishments . . . which satisfy the debt."[30] *God* forgives guilt, but *we* must make works to satisfy divine justice—and purgatory pays debts of punishment not paid in this life.

The problem with this view is that, according to Scripture, Christ alone makes complete satisfaction for sin. "The blood of Jesus . . . cleanses us from all sin" (1 John 1:7) and since "in him we have redemption, the forgiveness of sins" (Col 1:14), "there is therefore now no condemnation for those who are in Christ Jesus" (Rom 8:1). At the Council of Florence, Eastern Orthodox archbishop Mark of Ephesus denied the distinction between guilt and punishment, and insisted that no punishment remains for sins which are forgiven. "God . . . after God has forgiven [a sinner] . . . immediately delivers him from punishment also."[31] Martin Luther declares that purgatory "conflicts with the chief article that only Christ, and

---

28. Walls, *Purgatory*, 59.

29. God forgives guilt but, being just, must still punish sin. Moses, while remaining in God's favor, was punished for his disobedience by being forbidden to enter Canaan (Num 20:11–12), and King David's sins of adultery and murder were punished even though they were already forgiven (2 Sam 12:13–15). In Roman Catholic theology venial sins require a temporal punishment only, while mortal sins require both eternal and temporal punishment. Eternal punishment is paid by Christ; temporal punishment is paid by us through penance and purgatory.

30. Aquinas, *Summa Contra Gentiles*, 4.91.6. Also see *Summa Theologica* Vol. 3, Supplement to the Third Part, Appendix 2 a1, 3022: "if justice demands that sin be set in order by due punishment, it follows that one who after contrition for his fault and after being absolved, dies before making due satisfaction, is punished after this life."

31. Mark, cited in Seraphim Rose, *Soul After Death*, 213. "If the offense to God leads to punishment, then when the guilt is forgiven . . . , the very consequence of the guilt—punishment—of necessity comes to an end." Also see Vassiliadis, *Mystery of Death*, 444–47 and Meyendorf, *Byzantine Theology*, 220–21. At the Council of Florence the Eastern Orthodox rejected Roman Catholic insistence on 1. an actual place 2. for punishment 3. by fire.

not the works of men, are to help souls."[32] John Calvin rejects purgatory because in it "expiation of sins is sought elsewhere than in the blood of Christ.... For what means this purgatory... but that satisfaction for sins is paid by the souls of the dead.... But... the blood of Christ is the sole satisfaction for the sins of believers."[33] Protestants like Wright agree: "the idea that Christians need to suffer punishment for their sins in a post-mortem purgatory... reveals a straightforward failure to grasp the very heart of what was achieved on the cross."[34] Eastern Orthodox theologian Timothy Ware sums it up well: "it makes no sense to say that [someone in purgatory] is undergoing punishment for sins that God in God's mercy has already forgiven."[35]

The Sanctification Model: Purgatory As Moral Hospital

Imperfect believers like Gary do not need further punishment—but they do need further cleansing. Ware says that "someone who dies in a state of genuine repentance, but who is in other respects ill-prepared to come face to face with God, may well require... purification after... death."[36] In the sanctification view, purgatory is restorative: it has a forward-looking purpose—to fit us for communion with God by removing sinful, self-centered dispositions and replacing them with holy, other-centered ones.

In contemporary Roman Catholicism, Terence Nichols notes, purgatory is understood "more as a state of growth and purification of love after death rather than a state of paying penalties for... sins."[37] Take Karl Rahner, for example: "what is... removed by this purification is an internal state produced... by sins committed during life and not yet

---

32. Luther, *Smalcald Articles*, 2.2.12. *Defense of the Augsburg Confession* (Article 6.42–43) states that "the death of Christ is a satisfaction not only for guilt, but also for eternal death.... How monstrous... it is to say that the satisfaction of Christ redeemed from the guilt, and our punishments redeem from eternal death."

33. Calvin, *Institutes*, Book 3.5.6, 676. He, too, rejects the distinction of penalty and guilt: "if we are delivered from guilt through Christ the penalties that arise from it must cease" (*Institutes*, Book 3.4.30, 658).

34. Wright, *For All Saints*, 30.

35. Ware, "One Body in Christ," 185.

36. Ibid., 185.

37. Nichols, *Death and Afterlife*, 172. As Rowell (*Hell and Victorians*, 178) says, "an emphasis on punishment for sin, and satisfaction... has largely been replaced by a purgatory whose chief characteristic is the slow and painful removal of a bad disposition."

completely eradicated by turning to God and being forgiven." The person in purgatory "does not . . . assert that they love God with all their heart, that their whole existence is integrated into this love: they admit that in them are . . . a mass of instincts . . . of which it . . . cannot be said that they are all completely integrated into the personal decision" for God. Purgatory completes "the integration of one's whole being into the love of God."[38] It is a "process of maturation . . . in which [a person's] basic decision [for God] permeates the whole length and breadth of their reality," their whole existence at all levels.[39] Protestants who defend purgatory have a sanctifying view,[40] as do the Eastern Orthodox.[41] The sanctification model, unlike the satisfaction model, is fully compatible with the doctrine of justification by grace through faith. In the rest of this book the word "purgatory" refers to sanctification in a part of heaven.

Defending Purgatory

Set out formally in logical steps, the theological argument for purgatory is this:

1. Heaven—full union with God—requires perfect holiness (an ability to love with all our hearts).

2. Perfect holiness is not achieved *before death* (few people reach moral perfection in this life).

---

38. Rahner, *Theological Investigations* Vol. 19, 182, 184, and 187.

39. Rahner, *Foundations of Christian Faith*, 442. Ombres (*Theology of Purgatory*, 51, 24, 67–68, and 85–86) emphasizes "a less legalistic or punitive understanding of purgatory." A "conversion in the center of the person" does not mean that the disposition to sin is cancelled out or that their moral transformation is thorough. Those in purgatory "are being . . . reconstituted wholly for God" in a process of "healing, restoration and reordering." Lane (*Keeping Hope Alive*, 146–47), Ratzinger (*Eschatology*, 230) and Roman Catholic Church, *Catechism of the Catholic Church* (Sections 1030–32, 268–69) also emphasize sanctification.

40. See Barnard, "Purgatory and Dilemma of Sanctification"; Hick, *Death and Eternal Life*, 455; Lewis, *Letters to Malcolm*, 107–9 and *Screwtape Letters*, 148; Moltmann, "Is There Life After Death?" 247–52; Olson, "Is There a Protestant Purgatory?"; Pinnock, "Response to Hayes," 130; Polkinghorne, "Eschatology: Some Questions," 39–41; Rowell, *Hell and Victorians*, 90–115 and 153–79; Walls, *Heaven*, chapter 2, "Purgatory for Everyone"; *Purgatory* and *Heaven, Hell and Purgatory*, chapter 4.

41. See Louth, *Introducing Eastern Orthodox Theology*, 154–55; Vassiladis, *Mystery of Death*, 444–47 and Ware, "One Body," 183–87.

3. Perfect holiness is not achieved *at the moment of death* (God cannot give us a radically-altered nature at the moment of death in some instant, magic sanctification).

4. Therefore, perfect holiness is achieved *after death* (there is a process of moral growth after death by which we are transformed into the kind of persons who can be united with God).[42]

All Christians accept premises 1 and 2; premise 3 is the controversial one.

Heaven Requires Perfect Sanctification Holiness

Love binds God together as Three and One—and we are made in the image of the God whose essence is self-giving love. The doctrine of creation implies that "the whole purpose for which we exist," as Lewis says, "is to be . . . taken into the life of God." God's love is not a one-way street running from God to us; instead, God wants mutual love in which we give love back to God.[43] God is perfectly holy—and in order to enter God's presence we, too, must be perfectly holy.[44] The Bible speaks of two types

---

42. Judisch, "Sanctification, Satisfaction, and Purpose of Purgatory," 170. This argument is implicit in Aquinas (*Summa Contra Gentiles*, 4.91.6), although he overlooks the possibility of instant transformation. To the vision of God "no [person] can be elevated unless it be thoroughly and entirely purified [premise 1]. . . . But by sin the soul is unclean in its disordered union to inferior things. . . . It does at times happen that . . . purification is not entirely perfected in this life, one remains a debtor for the punishment [premise 2]. . . . They must, then, be purged after this life before they achieve the final reward. . . . Therefore, if the souls of the good have something capable of purgation in this world, they are held back from the achievement of their reward while they undergo cleansing punishments. And this is the reason we hold that there is a purgatory [conclusion]." Kant (cited in Day, *Hope*, 40), too, recognizes the necessity of posthumous moral development: "on the basis of [a person's] previous progress from the worse to the morally better . . . one may hope for a further uninterrupted continuance of this progress . . . beyond this life."

43. This wording comes from Stassen and Gushee, *Kingdom Ethics*, 330 and Lewis, *Mere Christianity*, 141.

44. God's holiness is both *metaphysical* (God's being is separate from and exalted above creation—Isa 57:15) and *moral* (God's character is free from all sin—Isa 5:16; Hab 1:13). "God is light and in him there is no darkness at all" (1 John 1:5). The covenant required Israel to be "a people holy to the Lord" (Deut 26:19; cf. Lev 19:2). The psalmist (24:3–5; cf. 15:1–2) says: "who shall ascend the hill of the Lord? And who shall stand in his holy place? Those who have clean hands and pure hearts." Jesus declared that "the pure in heart . . . will see God" and commanded us to "be perfect, . . . as your heavenly Father is perfect." Unless you are righteous, he warns, "you will never enter the kingdom of heaven" (Matt 5:8, 20, 48). 1 Peter (1:15–16) emphasizes that

of holiness—justification holiness (forgiveness—being declared holy) and sanctification holiness (transformation—being made holy). Which type of holiness—reckoned or actual—does heaven require? The answer grows out of our understanding of the nature of salvation—which in turn comes from our understanding of sin.

Human sinfulness has two dimensions, and God's salvation deals with both.[45] Sin creates a problem between us and God objectively. We are guilty and condemned, deserving of punishment. Justification removes sin's penalty and puts us right with God. Justification is a legal category; it means to be pronounced not guilty in a court of law. But sin is also a problem within us; it makes us self-centered subjectively. We are depraved and spoiled, closed in on ourselves and unable to love others. Sanctification frees us from sin's power and puts us right within. Sanctification is a moral category; it refers to personal renewal, a real change of character as we become God-centered and not self-centered. Where justification is external righteousness credited to us (Rom 4:5; Gal 3:6), sanctification is internal righteousness created in us as we put off the old self and put on the new (Eph 4:22–24; cf. Rom 6:10–13; Col 3:5, 8, 12), die to sin and live to righteousness (1 Pet 1:15–16; 2:1, 24). Where justification is passively received by faith alone, sanctification is actively achieved by moral effort (assisted, of course, by divine grace, which is always primary). Where justification is a one-time event that happens instantly and is complete, sanctification is progressive, having degrees, as we gradually grow into salvation (1 Pet 2:2) and become increasingly conformed to the image of Christ (2 Cor 3:18; Gal 4:19).

Here is the important point: being justified does not entail being sanctified. We must, Lewis says, have the "twist in the central man straightened out"—but a "conversion in the center of the person," Robert

---

"as he who called you is holy, be holy yourselves in all your conduct, for it is written, 'You shall be holy, for I am holy.'" "Do you not know," St. Paul (1 Cor 6:9; cf. 3:16–17; 9:24—10:13) warns, "that wrongdoers will not inherit the kingdom of God?" The author of Hebrews (12:14), too, tells us to "pursue . . . the holiness without which no one will see the Lord." In his vision of restored Israel, Isaiah (35:8) says, "a highway shall be there, and it shall be called the Holy Way; the unclean shall not travel on it"—and St. John (Rev 21:27) indicates that "nothing unclean will enter" the New Jerusalem.

45. See Volume 1, chapter 8. Aquinas (*Summa Contra Gentiles*, 4.72.3) says that sin has two consequences. "The damages into which [a person] has been led by sin" are 1. that the individual "incurs the guilt of punishment" as well as experiencing 2a. "the disordering of the mind" (being "turned away from the incommutable good—namely, God—and . . . turned toward sin") and 2b. the "weakening of the natural good" (being "rendered more prone toward sinning and more reluctant toward doing well").

Ombres notes, does not mean that the disposition to sin is cancelled out or that love has permeated the entire character.[46] It is a myth, Brennan Manning says, that "once converted, fully converted"—that forgiveness makes us sinless.[47] Forgiveness does not change us so that we perfectly love God and other people. A bad-tempered husband does not stop being mean and angry just because his wife forgives him for mistreating her. He still needs moral reform—to have his character flaws repaired so he can love her and be in relationship with her.[48] In the same way, a change in God's attitude to us does not automatically change our characters, removing selfish dispositions and conferring loving ones—and so forgiveness does not adequately prepare us for union with God. Sin not only damages relationship with God, it also deforms the sinner's character—so even after guilt is forgiven, the effects of sin remain in the will. Owen Thomas writes: "while God freely forgives the penitent sinner, God does not and cannot . . . enter into fellowship with them in their sinful state. First they must be made holy and righteous by the infusion of love. The mere imputation of righteousness" is not enough.[49] Or as David Currie

---

46. Lewis, *Mere Christianity*, 87 and Ombres, *Theology of Purgatory*, 24.

47. Manning, *Ragamuffin Gospel*, 27.

48. This example comes from Walls, *Heaven, Hell and Purgatory*, 111. As Ratzinger (*Eschatology*, 219 and 226; cf. 231) says, "one's fundamental life decision" for God may be "covered over by layers of secondary decisions"; as a result, it "needs to be dug free." There is a "difference between someone's valid fundamental decision, whereby he is accepted in grace [justification], and the . . . permeation of the effects of that decision throughout the being of the whole person [sanctification]." Ford ("Prayer and Departed Saints") puts it well: "when we commit sin, we inflict wounds upon ourselves. . . . Sin can leave long-lasting scars even after God's forgiveness is granted and accepted. The effects of sustained sin . . . do not simply vanish when we accept God's forgiveness. . . . Only through an ongoing life of faith in Christ do we gradually become cleansed and healed . . . from these wounds of sin. This happens as we gradually become more and more suffused with God's . . . love." Our ingrained inclinations go deep into our being—and they remain after we are "born from above" (John 3:3) and become a "new creation" (2 Cor 5:17). It requires time and effort to root out and "put to death" (Rom 8:13) this complex network of habits and attitudes (Mulholland, *Invitation to Journey*, chapter 10).

49. Thomas, *Introduction to Theology*, 134. Willard (*Divine Conspiracy*, 36–48) rejects the idea that forgiveness is all there is to being a Christian—"that you can have a faith in Christ that brings forgiveness, while in every other respect your life is no different from that of others who have no faith in Christ at all." Too many Protestants, he worries, emphasize justification by grace in a way that has nothing to do with the kind of persons we are. "Perhaps there has occurred a moment of mental assent to a creed . . . and forgiveness floods forth. An appropriate amount of righteousness is shifted from Christ's account to our account in the bank of heaven, and all our debts are paid.

puts it: "our faith does not just cover up our rebellious wills so we can slip into heaven."[50] While grace brings both pardon and healing, Walls says, "the heart of salvation is to change us so we gladly love and obey God. This is how we are united to God in a relationship of mutual love. . . . The element of forgiveness, although crucial, is secondary to this."[51] Justification holiness, then, is not sufficient for Gary to be in union with God; sanctification holiness is also necessary. Love, Pope Benedict XVI says, "is the ladder that leads to God"; only if we love can we enter relationship with another.[52] "Love creates a fellowship," Stephen Webb states, "and only those who are able to respond to love by loving in return can enter into that fellowship."[53] Love-holiness must be integrated into Gary's character so that it permeates the entirety of who he is.

These two truths are the biblical and theological foundation of purgatory.

Our guilt is erased" and we are saved—despite Jesus having no real impact on our character and our behavior. In this false view the essence of salvation—justification—is strictly external and located wholly in God; it is not about personal transformation. Many Christians, Pope Francis says (*Name of God is Mercy*, 26 and 144), treat sin as a stain to be removed, "something that you can have dry-cleaned so that everything goes back to normal." Instead, sin is a wound to be healed—salvation is "not like taking your clothes to the dry cleaner." In justification "God forgives our sins, which God truly blots out; and yet sin leaves a negative effect on the way we think and act." Sanctification "reaches the pardoned sinner and frees them from every residue left by the consequences of sin, enabling them to act with charity, to grow in love, rather than to fall back into sin."

50. Currie, *Born Fundamentalist*, 123; cf. 44 and 109–26. Where Protestants see the mind as the essential part of a person that must be redeemed (and thus emphasize faith alone), Roman Catholics see the will (and so emphasize faith coupled with works). Both theologies assert that we are saved by grace. Also see Kreeft and Tacelli, *Handbook of Apologetics*, 320–321 on faith and works.

51. Walls, *Heaven*, 50. As Bloesch (*Essentials of Evangelical Theology*, Vol. 2, 228) puts it, "we are given a title to heaven (by justification)" and "fitness for heaven (by sanctification)." The conservative Protestant faith of my childhood suggested, by implication at least, that—as Currie (*Born Fundamentalist*, 121) puts it—when we die Jesus will ask us "why should I let you into heaven?" "Judgment will be a quiz in which the correct answer gets you in and the wrong one forces you out." Or in McLaren's (*Last Word*, 188) words, "on judgment day, all God will care about is opening up our skulls and checking in our brains"—as in folders from a file cabinet—"to see if we had the right notion of salvation by grace through faith in there somewhere" or if "there's some residue in there of having said the sinner's prayer." For more on holiness as the ability to 1. love 2. wholly, see Appendix Note 2.

52. Pope Benedict XVI, *Fathers of Church*, 76.

53. Webb, *Good Eating*, 250.

1. Heaven is *theosis*: participation in the relational life of God (2 Pet 1:4). The essence of heaven is self-giving love.
2. Sharing in the divine life requires sanctification holiness: the ability to love God (and neighbor) wholeheartedly. Becoming like God is becoming righteous and holy.

These doctrines are non-controversial.

We do Not Die Perfectly Holy

When is perfect holiness achieved? There are three possibilities:

1. before death during this life,
2. at the moment of death, or
3. after death in the next life.

The first option is empirically false. It is an observable fact that at death most believers' ability to love is fragmentary; they are in right standing with God (their sins are forgiven), but are not ready for eternal life with God (their characters remain self-centered).[54] That leaves two options: purification at or after death. *How* is perfect holiness achieved? There are two possibilities: we are either purified

a. by a direct act of God or

b. by our own free choices as we cooperate with divine grace.

The "how" and "when" questions are connected: either

2a. we are instantly sanctified by a unilateral act of God at the moment of death or

3b. we are gradually sanctified by our own free choices in the period after death.

We do Not Become Perfectly Holy at Death

Protestants have typically believed the first option (2a)—at death God abruptly transformed Gary into a morally perfect person without his cooperation. Luther says that at "our dissolution [the Holy Spirit] will

---

54. Barnard, "Purgatory and Dilemma of Sanctification."

accomplish [perfect holiness] altogether in an instant." Death "makes an end of sins and vices" and "cuts our sin clean away from us."[55] Calvin, while not explicit about direct sanctification, implies it since the faithful "immediately after death enjoy blessed repose."[56] John Wesley maintains that God automatically transforms our character at "the instant of death, the moment before the soul leaves the body."[57] Charles Hodge argues that just as God can immediately heal someone physically, bypassing the normal gradual process of healing, so God can instantly purify our characters at death. "The Protestant doctrine," he concludes, "is that the souls of believers are at death made perfect in holiness."[58] Some contemporary Roman Catholic theologians also suggest that purification occurs in the experience of dying itself.[59]

Wright asserts that at death we are instantly transformed by a unilateral act of God. "Although during the present life we struggle with sin, and may or may not make small and slight progress towards genuine

---

55. Luther, *Large Catechism*, The Creed Section 57–59 and Luther, cited in Kerr, *Compend of Luther's Theology*, 241. The *Formula of Concord* (Epitome 1, chapter 10, Book of Concord) agrees that "separation [from sin] will take place completely through death, at the resurrection."

56. Calvin, *Institutes*, Book 3.5.10, 684—because they are already perfect our prayers confer no benefit upon them. The *Heidelberg Catechism* (Questions 62 and 57) states that the "soul after this life shall be immediately taken up to Christ," as does the *Second Helvetic Confession* (chapters 9 and 26): "the faithful, after bodily death, go directly to Christ, and, therefore . . . what some teach concerning the fire of purgatory is opposed to the Christian faith." The *Westminster Confession* (chapter 32.1, 81–82) agrees that at death the souls of the elect "immediately return to God" where they are "then made perfect in holiness." The Church of England *Homily on Prayer* (19.3) also implies that God transforms our character into sinless perfection at the moment of death: "the soul of [the saved] passing out of the body, goeth straighways . . . to heaven. . . . The only purgatory, wherein we must trust to be saved is the death and blood of Christ."

57. Wesley, cited in Walls, *Purgatory*, 48.

58. Hodge, cited in Walls, *Purgatory*, 43. Bloesch (*Last Things*, 152) says that death has sanctifying power: perfect holiness "is consummated at death or in the very brief transition from death to *paradise*."

59. Rahner (*Theological Investigations*, Vol. 19, 186) wonders if sanctification is "realized in the very event of death. . . . Why could not . . . the event of purification be identified with the depth and intensity of the pain that the person experiences in death itself?" Ratzinger (*Eschatology*, 231) states that at final judgment "encounter with the Lord . . . is the fire that burns away our dross and re-forms us to be vessels of eternal joy." Ladislaus Boros claims that as the individual turns toward God at the moment of death there is a cleansing that purifies them through and through (see LaDue, *Trinity Guide*, 60).

holiness, our remaining propensity to sin is finished, cut off, done with all at once, in physical death." He cites a number of texts which, he claims, indicate that "bodily death itself actually puts sin to an end"—Romans 6:7, for example: "whoever has died is freed from sin."[60] Regardless of a believer's degree of sanctification, God gives them a completely loving character at death, thus instantly preparing them to enter God's presence. The biblical texts offered by Wright, however, simply do not say that the death of the body gets rid of all that is self-centered. Nor does belief in progressive sanctification after death contradict these verses. In Romans 6:6–7 St. Paul states that baptism unites us to Christ's death (thus separating us from a sinful way of living) and resurrection (thereby creating a new quality of life). Baptism does not eradicate our sinful nature, however, since he goes on to urge moral effort to behave in keeping with the new life of righteousness, not the old life of sin (6:12–13). Nowhere in this discussion of baptism does St. Paul imply that bodily death instantly transforms our characters. The same goes for Colossians 2:11–13, which indicates that at baptism we put off the sinful nature which acts against God. He is not talking about physical death at all, but about regeneration to a new way of living in this life. Wright's argument for instant sanctification is unconvincing.

Anthony Thiselton suggests that "the Holy Spirit [conveys] holiness to the Christian in [death] itself, rather than in a long process of purification in purgatory." What causes this instantaneous transformation is the change of environment from earth to heaven. "Holiness under the conditions of this world, where God can be seen only by faith, and where temptations abound, differs from holiness when we come face to face with God, leave temptations and earthly attractions behind, . . . and are totally open to the power of the Holy Spirit."[61] Thiselton's argument is

60. Wright, *For All Saints*, 29–32. The biblical texts are John 11:25–26, 13:10 and 15:3, Rom 5:2, 6:6–7, and 8:10–11, Col 2:11–13, and 1 John 1:7. Also see *Surprised by Hope*, 170: "as the Reformers insisted, bodily death itself is the destruction of the sinful person. . . . Death itself gets rid of all that is still sinful . . . . There is nothing then left to purge." This view is also defended by Jonathan Edwards (cited in Walls, *Heaven*, 58 and 53): at death "the saved soul leaves all its sin with the body; when it puts off the body of the man, it puts off the body of sin with it. When the body is buried, all sin is buried forever" and "at death the believer not only gains a perfect and eternal deliverance from sin and temptation, but is adorned with a perfect and glorious holiness. The work of sanctification is then completed, and the beautiful image of God has then its finishing strokes by the pencil of God, and begins to shine forth with a heavenly beauty."

61. Thiselton, *Life After Death*, 128. He continues (137): "holiness indeed requires a long period of growth and time within the conditions of this world. But the perfect

problematic, however, since sinful actions are not simply a function of environment. The sources of behavior are both outside us in the circumstances we encounter and inside us in the dispositions of our hearts and minds.[62] While heaven changes the external factors in behavior, it does not change the internal ones (just like getting a problem drinker away from taverns does not eradicate his desire for alcohol). Change of environment, while necessary for perfect holiness, is not sufficient—in addition we need deep psychological adjustment; the layers of selfish habits which have worked their way into the inner structure of our characters must be removed. Thiselton's argument for instant purification is also unconvincing.

There is no necessary connection, Walls notes, between the moral and the bodily—and so death can no more remove pride than old age removes greed. "Sins are not cured merely by dropping our old bodies and receiving new ones." Sin is not left behind when the earthly body is left behind because sin is located in the mind and will, not the body.[63] Death itself, Gregory of Nyssa says, does not "cleanse us from the remains of the fleshly glue" of vice.

> If one should become completely carnal in his mind, devoting all the activity and energy of his soul to the will of the flesh, such a man even when he gets out of the flesh is not separated from its experiences. Those who spend most of their time in evil-smelling places, even if they go out into the fresh air, are not cleansed from the unpleasantness which has adhered to them from prolonged contact. In the same way, even when the transition has been made to the invisible . . . life, the lovers of the flesh would doubtless be unable to avoid bringing with them some of the fleshly odor.

---

vision [and] presence of God . . . suggest that it is otherwise in the conditions of the post-resurrection world." Kronen and Reitan (*God's Final Victory*, 13–14 and 28–29) claim that the beatific vision is the only thing that can eradicate sin and rightly order our love to God alone.

62. Baumeister and Heatherton ("Self-Regulation Failure") note that two components contribute to behavior—latent inner motivations (stable inclinations) and activating outer stimuli (events that trigger these inclinations and create an impulse to act).

63. Walls, "Purgatory for Everyone," 9 and *Heaven, Hell and Purgatory*, 137–38. "Separating a sinful spirit from a corruptible body will not automatically make it pure" (*Purgatory*, 50). Locating sin in the physical body, he says ("Purgatory for Everyone," 9), is a form of gnosticism.

Purification after death is a gradual process, Gregory says, like a refiner's fire or squeezing mud off a rope. "Wrapped up as it is in material and earthly attachments, [the person in purgatory] struggles and is stretched. ... What is alien to God has to be scraped off forcibly because it has ... grown onto the soul."[64] Three additional reasons cast doubt on immediate moral transformation—and thus support gradual sanctification.

Sanctification Is Essentially Cooperative

Justification, an instantaneous event, is God's act alone—but sanctification, a gradual process, requires active cooperation between us and God. Instantaneous divine transformation would make us passive in the process of sanctification. In order to be our own, moral goodness must be chosen by us, not done for us—and because we are free beings, God does not automatically make us holy without our own participation.[65] If God were to perfect Gary immediately and unilaterally, then he would inherit a ready-made moral character, not one that is truly his own.[66]

Walls suggests a second way in which purgatory requires free choice. What needs healing are not just character defects within individuals but broken relationships between people. Perpetrators must accept responsibility for wrongful actions and develop empathy for those they have hurt, and victims must change how they think about, feel toward and treat those who have hurt them. We must actively participate in these processes of repentance, forgiveness, and reconciliation; they cannot "be accomplished in a way that bypasses the free cooperation of the persons involved."[67]

It might be objected that even sanctification purgatory is a form of works-righteousness which contradicts salvation by grace. This is not

---

64. Gregory of Nyssa, *Soul and Resurrection*, 76 and 84.

65. This, Currie (*Born Fundamentalist*, 124) points out, is the role of works in salvation—works transform our character. Salvation is by grace through faith coupled with works (Jas 2:14–16); both faith and works are the result of divine assistance—grace. Sins not only offend God, they also destroy the sinner's character. "Confession and God's forgiveness can and do take care of the offense toward God, but the [person's] character is still damaged.... Works mold our character over time. They slowly erase the imperfections ... that make it easier to sin again." At death our guilt is forgiven, but our character imperfections remain—requiring post-mortem purging.

66. This argument is made in Brown, "No Heaven without Purgatory."

67. Walls, *Purgatory*, 120.

true. The fact that we are actively involved in developing virtues of love—whether in this life or the next—does not mean that holiness is achieved by our own unassisted efforts. "We are God's workmanship" (Eph 2:10 *NIV*)—we work our own salvation, St. Paul says, only because of the primacy of grace, because God is at work within us (Phil 2:12–13). Walls comments: "to pit purgatory against grace is to fail completely to grasp that purgatory itself is very much a matter of grace. To draw this contrast is to ignore the fact that grace is much more than forgiveness, that it is also sanctification and transformation. . . . Purgatory is nothing more than the continuation of the sanctifying grace we need."[68]

Sanctification Is Essentially Developmental

Moral development is, by its very nature, a progressive process that occurs incrementally and so takes time; it is not a momentary event. Just like losing weight or learning a foreign language do not happen over night, so character change happens in small degrees, not giant leaps. We are by nature habit-formers, Aristotle says, and so moral growth involves habituation—doing something repeatedly until it becomes second nature. Traits "are completed through habit. . . . We become just by doing just actions, temperate by doing temperate actions, brave by doing brave actions."[69] Virtues like love are developed by repeated actions that engrave specific attitudes and responses into a person's character. These inclinations come to determine their personality more and more, eventually eliminating all other dispositions. Love becomes fully who they are—and so the perfect will never sin because they are set in their ways.[70]

---

68. Ibid., 174. "God's grace is precisely what . . . enables our transformation." Grace is not "exclusively a matter of forgiveness" ("Purgatory for Everyone," 10). Ratzinger (*Eschatology*, 231) agrees: purgatory "does not replace grace by works, but allows the former to achieve its full victory precisely as grace." Purgatory "would contradict the doctrine of grace only if penance [and sanctification] were the antithesis of grace and not its form."

69. Aristotle, *Nicomachean Ethics* 1103a16–1103b21, 18–19. Also see 1103a16–1103b21, 19: "virtue [and vice] of character . . . results from habit. . . . Virtues [and vices] . . . we acquire just as we acquire crafts. . . . We become builders, for instance, by building, and we become harpists by playing the harp. Similarly, . . . what we do in our dealings with other people makes some of us just, some unjust. . . . To sum it up in a single account: a state [of character] results from [the repetition of] similar activities."

70. "By our choices," Swinburne ("Theodicy of Heaven and Hell," 47–48) says, "we shift the range of possible choice. By good choices this time there come within our

Repentance, Lewis says, "means unlearning all the . . . self-will that we have been training ourselves into."[71] For Gary, stripping away selfishness—both in this life and the next—is a gradual process, not a point-in-time event. Aquinas notes that sinful habits adhere to us because they have become engraved in our characters—and the more adhesive the sin, the longer and harder to remove. "Some . . . sins cling more persistently than others, according as the affections are more inclined to them, and more firmly fixed in them. And since that which clings more persistently is more slowly cleansed, it follows that some are . . . in purgatory longer than others."[72] Swinburne makes the same point: there is "a certain stickiness about character, for character is a matter of what [we] do naturally. If someone has made themselves the sort of person who does something naturally, to do anything else is going to be unnatural—to start with. A change will need time and energy."[73] The degree and length of purification is proportional to the seriousness of sin and the hold it has over a person's character. Immediate transformation violates the inherently developmental nature of the self, which requires time to change deep habits. Because we are beings who exist in time—David Brown asserts—"there is no way of rendering . . . an abrupt transition in essentially temporal beings conceivable."[74] In addition, the healing of broken relationships

---

range possibilities for greater good next time, and some evil choices are no longer a possibility. . . . If [we] systematically resist desires of a certain kind, [we] will gradually become the kind of person to whom such desires do not occur." Sinless Christians in heaven have perfectly integrated characters where all their beliefs and desires fit together. Pawl and Timpe ("Incompatiblism, Sin and Free Will in Heaven") and Brown ("Making the Best Even Better") discuss an apparent problem—that the redeemed in heaven are free but nonetheless cannot sin.

71. Lewis, *Mere Christianity*, 59. He adds (*Screwtape Letters*, 31 and 60) that virtues must go beyond simply being approved in the mind; they must "reach the will and [be] embodied in habits." We must convert thoughts into actions, imagination, and affection into deliberate choices of will.

72. Aquinas, *Summa Theologica* Vol. 3, Supplement to the Third Part, Appendix 1 q2 a6, 3021. The term "adhesive" comes from Walls, *Purgatory*, 73. Augustine (*Enchiridion* 18.69, 47) agrees that time in purgatory depends on the degree of hold sin has on the character: "some of the faithful [will] be saved by . . . purgatorial fire, in proportion as they have loved the goods that perish, and in proportion to their attachment to them."

73. Swinburne, "Theodicy of Heaven and Hell," 47–48 and 45.

74. Brown, "No Heaven without Purgatory," 450–51. "No clear sense attaches to the claim that a human being could become instantaneously virtuous, morally perfect, and so, if God is to respect our nature as essentially temporal beings, God must have allowed for . . . purgatory to exist."

happens gradually, not all at once; repentance, forgiveness, and reconciliation are not instantaneous events but ongoing processes that take time.

It might be objected that purgatory encourages moral laxity and makes this life not serious. As Peter Hawkins puts it, "people could be lulled into thinking that they could put off until tomorrow—after death—the repentance they failed to do today."[75] This was why Augustine and Gregory the Great limited purgatory to those with slight sins (and excluded those with serious sins, who were damned eternally). We must, however, take our choices seriously since there is moral continuity between our actions in this life and our destiny in the next. Whenever we act we are never just doing, but are always becoming—how we live shapes us into certain sorts of persons, and our afterlife destinies are extensions of the characters we have chosen in this life. As Lewis puts it:

> every time you make a choice you are turning the central part of you, the part of you that chooses, into something a little different from what it was before. . . . With all your innumerable choices, all your life long you are slowly turning this central thing either into a heavenly creature or into a hellish creature: either into a creature that is in harmony with God, and with other creatures and with itself, or else into one that is in a state of war and hatred with God, and with its fellow-creatures and with itself.[76]

The more we sin here, the more deeply-entrenched our sinful characters become—and the more difficult and painful and lengthy our transformation in purgatory.[77] We will be purified for heaven one way or another, Gregory of Nyssa points out, "either by our effort in this life or by the purification hereafter." And so "we who are living in the flesh ought as much as possible to . . . release ourselves from [the hold of sin] by the life of virtue, so that after death we may not need another death to cleanse us from the remains of the fleshly glue."[78] Because habits build a force in our lives that are hard to overcome and because our habits of life here follow us into the afterlife, purgatory should encourage, not discourage, holy living, inspiring moral rigor, not moral laxity. In fact, rather than *purgatory* promoting moral laziness, it may be the other way around: if we will

---

75. Hawkins, *Undiscovered Country*, 47. The same objection is made to escapable hell; I discuss it in chapter 5.

76. Lewis, *Mere Christianity*, 86.

77. Walls, *Purgatory*, 98.

78. Gregory, *Soul and Resurrection*, 77 and 75–76.

be instantly and automatically perfected by God at death, why work at developing holiness in this life? Perhaps this is part of what kept Gary from working out his own salvation, his own perfect holiness, in this life.

Only Gradual Sanctification Preserves Identity

Immediate transformation provided by God would disrupt the continuity of personal identity—the property of remaining the same through change. Identity over time requires the existence of a single individual with a continuous history. A person at one time is identical to a person at another time if proper psychological continuity links them.[79] The connection between these two persons is preserved by gradual change but destroyed by abrupt change. If a newborn baby was instantaneously transformed into an elderly senior, the two individuals would not be the same person. In the same way, if at death God immediately eliminates Gary's sinful character and gives him loving dispositions all at once, then the man who lived on earth and the man who exists after death are not the same person since their moral characters share little in common (just like if Adolf Hitler took a pill that immediately gave him the virtues of Francis of Assisi). Gradual sanctification, by contrast, allows new habits and dispositions to be integrated over time into the structure of our psychology. Slow changes maintain identity because the individual at different stages of moral development—the earlier imperfect person and the later perfect one—are connected together as a single person.[80]

---

79. For analysis of personal identity see Volume 1, chapter 6.

80. If God miraculously made widespread changes to a person's character, this would transform them into someone else. They would become an artificial creation of God that lacks continuity and identity with the prior individual (see Baggini, *Pig Wants to be Eaten*, 262–64). This argument is made in Barnard, "Purgatory and Dilemma of Sanctification" and in Walls, *Purgatory*, chapter 4 and *Heaven, Hell and Purgatory*, 126–38. The Hitler example comes from Adams, "Divine Justice, Divine Love," 25. Character change and moral transformation must meet the assimilation requirement. "Assimilation," Hershenov ("Metaphysical Problem," 33) says, "has to do with how an entity integrates new [character traits] with its old. Not any kind of [trait] replacement will preserve the existence of the entity in question." Acceptable trait "replacement is determined by what is the norm for the type of entity in question." We are, Zimmerman ("Christians Should Affirm Mind-Body Dualism," 321) adds, successive entities that gain and lose traits—both physical and psychological—over time. Kagan (*Death*, 130–31) comments: "we can still say it's . . . the same evolving personality, so long as there's a pattern of overlap and continuity. . . . New goals get added, some goals get lost. New beliefs get added, some beliefs get lost. There might be few, if any, beliefs, desires

I conclude that premise 3 is true; after death imperfect persons like Gary experience gradual purification rather than an instantaneous leap from imperfection to perfection. As Arthur Chambers says, "there is no more reason for thinking that the work of perfecting can be brought about suddenly by the disrupting hand of death than there is for supposing that the cracking of the shell will make the newly-hatched chick a full-grown fowl."[81] Perfect holiness does not happen instantly and cannot be done for us by God. We are essentially free beings (who must choose character change for ourselves) and essentially temporal beings (who grow morally through an incremental process of habituation).[82] Since Gary did not become perfectly holy in this life and since he cannot be abruptly sanctified by a unilateral act of God at the moment of death, he must be gradually sanctified by his own free choices in the period after death.

---

or goals that make it all the way through. But so long as there's the right pattern of overlap and continuity, we have the same personality." Someone's character immediately after death will be identical to the character they had at death; there will be complete overlap. As time in purgatory goes on it will continue to change and evolve as it did in this life—becoming less and less like the sinful selfish character that remained at death. We can change a great deal and still be the same person if we change gradually rather than instantly. But if large parts of our character—sinful beliefs and desires—are eliminated all at once, then we do not survive. This argument was anticipated in 1836 by Isaac Taylor (cited in McDannell and Lang, Heaven, 283) who speculated that the soul enters the afterlife in the same state as it leaves this life, since any drastic change would mean annihilation of one person and the creation of a different one.

81. Chambers, cited in McDannell and Lang, Heaven, 285.

82. Sanctification is an essentially social process. Becoming loving occurs in the company of other people; it is not something we can accomplish alone. As Hick (Death and Eternal Life, 269) points out, "we are essentially social creatures, existing and developing as persons in interaction with other persons." The social nature of morality and the interpersonal nature of virtuous character mean that neither is possible in solitude. Turning away from self-centeredness toward other-centeredness means facing situations of moral choice and repeatedly choosing others over self. In addition, because purgatory means the healing of broken relationships it involves communication and interaction with others over time. This requires an environment conducive to moral development: a temporal, dynamic, embodied state in which we can give and receive love in relationship with other persons. Body and mind sin together. Since the body was an instrument for committing sin, purification in purgatory must include the body as well as the mind. Purgatory, then, is public and social, not private and solitary.

Concluding Remarks: Purification Prayer as Prayers of Hope

The question every theology must answer, Walls says, is "what happens to [someone] who dies in a state of grace but who is not sufficiently purged of . . . sins?" What happens to people like Gary who accept the truth about God and themselves and plead by faith the mercy of God for salvation through Christ's atonement—but who die before their characters have been made perfect? This is the problem purgatory solves.[83]

Sin cuts us off from relationship—and the holiness heaven requires is sanctification holiness (actual transformation of character), not simply justification holiness (a legal declaration of a change in status or attribution of an alien righteousness that belongs to someone else). As Walls says, "we need more than forgiveness and justification to purge our sinful dispositions and make us fully ready for heaven."[84] We are made to be drawn into the dynamics of the inner life of God, the relationships that constitute God's nature. Salvation is—as the Syriac tradition presents it—healing from the wound of sin, the permanent, ongoing process of learning to love God and other people over self; it is not a one-time event of belief and conversion. Heaven is a place for perfect lovers—those who are, in Hans urs Von Balthasar's words "congealed in goodness" and so able to participate in the fellowship of the Trinity.[85] At death believers

---

83. Walls, *Purgatory*, 47 and wording from "Purgatory for Everyone," 2. This fact—that we die both righteous and sinners—means that "some version of purgatory is a theological necessity for any adequate Christian scheme of thought. For ultimate salvation requires that one be fully purged of all sin, and justification and regeneration, the initial components of salvation, do not fully accomplish this. . . . The 'remains of sin' must be dealt with in some fashion, and the question of when and how this occurs cannot be evaded" (*Purgatory*, 36–37).

84. Walls, *Purgatory*, 174.

85. On the Syriac tradition, see Pope Benedict XVI, *Fathers of Church*, 119. Balthasar, *Dare We Hope*, 145. We should understand salvation and the requirements for entering heaven, Borg (*Meeting Jesus Again*, 136) says, in transformational terms (becoming compassionate as God is compassionate) rather than fideistic terms (believing things about Jesus). Willard (*Divine Conspiracy*, 36–48) claims that both conservatives and liberals disconnect saving faith from moral character: "to the right, being a Christian is a matter of having your sins forgiven. . . . To the left, you are Christian if you have a significant commitment to the elimination of social evils." Neither group emphasizes personal transformation or discipleship, becoming Christlike. Conservatives, in particular, agree that—"forgiveness of sin because of transferred merit, with the resultant admission to heaven after death"—is the essence of salvation; it is a "forensic or legal condition rather than a vital reality of character" and eternal destiny, getting into heaven, is the sole target. But we get a totally different picture of salvation, Willard asserts, if we regard having life from the kingdom of God now—as suggested

like Gary remain self-centered—and so need a period of growth until the ability to love permeates their whole being. The purpose of purgatory is to complete the process of being made holy; it is not a prison where he obtains forgiveness but a hospital where he is healed. As Anne Lammott writes, "when we appear before God, God will say 'I love you very much. I forgive you all your crap. Now go clean up your mess, and then come into heaven, because lunch is waiting." Or, as Lewis puts it, "our souls demand purgatory, don't they? Would it not break the heart if God said to us, 'It is true . . . that your breath smells and your rags drip with mud and slime, but we are charitable here . . . . Enter into the joy'? Should we not reply, 'With submission, sir . . . , I'd rather be cleaned first.' 'It may hurt, you know'—'Even so, sir.'"[86] Purgatory is painful, Sidney Callahan suggests, because we "experience the pain, torment and trouble that our weaknesses and mean-spirited cruelties have visited upon other persons."[87]

Purgatory is a logical implication of understanding salvation as moral renewal, in which we take part, that enables us to love God perfectly. Pope John Paul II summarizes:

> purgatory is the process of purification for those who die in the love of God but who are not completely imbued with that love. . . . We must be purified if we are to enter into perfect and complete union with God. Jesus Christ, who became the perfect expiation for our sins and took upon himself the punishment that was our due, brings us God's mercy and love. But before we enter into God's Kingdom every trace of sin within us must be eliminated, every imperfection in our soul must be corrected. This is exactly what takes place in purgatory.[88]

---

by the words and actions of Jesus—as the goal.

86. Lamott, *Grace*, 108 and Lewis, *Letters to Malcolm*, 108.

87. Callahan, *With All Heart and Mind*, 193.

88. John Paul II, cited in Judisch, "Purgatory and Dilemma of Sanctification," 167. Nichols (*Death and Afterlife*, 164; cf. 172–75) agrees: "if Jesus meant what he said ("Be perfect . . . as your heavenly Father is perfect," Matt 5:48) and we have to be perfect in love to enter into the fullness of God's presence, that is, into heaven, then either most of us will not make it into heaven at all or there must be opportunity for us to complete the process we have begun in this life of dying to self and growing into the love of God. . . . Most people at the end of this life have not totally rejected God (and so do not belong in hell) nor have they become perfect in love of God and neighbor (and so do not merit immediate entrance into the fullness of heaven). Most of us are in between. . . . Those of us whose love of God and neighbor is imperfect will need after death a time of purification or of growing into the full love of God and neighbor. Perhaps God

This process is both painful (since learning the truth about ourselves and our failures and stripping off self-centered attitudes hurts) and joyful (since we are with God, preparing for the deeper union our hearts desire).[89] Purgatory, Hawkins says, is

> the serious business of rebirth. . . . Rather than being a penitentiary . . . , purgatory is a hospital for the healing of brokenness. It is . . . a conservatory where soloists become a chorus and where speakers develop a use for "we" and "us" instead of only "I" and "me." . . . Purgatory is a naturalization center where refugees from earth . . . learn how to become citizens of the City of God.

Self-centeredness "is a sickness to be cured"—and so purgatory "is all about . . . the experience of becoming new," about re-ordering disordered love and exchanging virtues for vices.[90]

Prayer in the communion of saints is one way in which Christians help each other. Michael Root argues that "the true nub of the issue [of praying for individuals in purgatory] is ecclesiological, concerning the role of the Church in aiding the individual Christian in the struggle with sin and its consequences."[91] If we were isolated individuals before God, then becoming holy would be a solitary effort and prayer for those in purgatory useless. But since we are members of a corporate body with responsibilities to each other, and since death does not sever the spiritual union of the saved, each can be helped by the others. Just as we pray for each other's sanctification now, so the prayers of the living assist those who have died.

Josef Pieper says that "prayers of petition [are] nothing other than the voicing of hope."[92] Paul O'Callaghan agrees: "we petition God for what we are entitled to hope for from God."[93] Purification prayers express hope

---

could purify our love instantly so that this state would require no time, but that is not how we grow. We typically need time to receive and absorb the fullness of God's love."

89. Lewis (*Voyage of Dawn Treader*, chapter 7) depicts the pain of stripping off old habits in the "undragoning" of Eustace. While suffering is not the purpose of purgatory, purification normally involves suffering. The pain of moral growth is not arbitrary punishment but is intrinsic (just like the pain of having a tooth pulled); becoming loving is uncomfortable for selfish persons (Lewis, *Letters to Malcolm*, 109). See Walls, "Purgatory for Everyone," 10.

90. Hawkins, *Undiscovered Country*, 52–55.

91. Root, cited in Wainwright, "Saints and Departed," 85.

92. Pieper, *On Hope*, 70.

93. O'Callaghan, *Christ Our Hope*, 219.

that those who die imperfect complete the process of sanctification, that the selfishness which remains in their characters is purified, that they are perfected in their ability to love and soon come to complete union with God. Our prayer is that they be made holy and blameless, that God "sanctify them entirely" (1 Thess 5:23)—and is patterned after Psalm 51.[94] We ask that the imperfect have "a broken and contrite heart," a full awareness of sin (v. 17). We ask God to "purge them . . . , and they shall be clean; wash them, and they shall be whiter than snow"—to "create in them a clean heart," to "put a new and right spirit within them" (vv. 7, 10). We pray that in God's presence they grow in God's love until it permeates all layers of their personality and they see God as God is, entering the joy of deep heaven. In praying for them, we also pray Anselm of Canterbury's prayer for ourselves: "O Lord, draw my whole self into your love. . . . Let your love seize my whole being; let it possess me completely." Let me be transformed from love of self to love of God and neighbor.[95]

Since Gary died without having completed the sanctification process, and since being made ready for a heaven of perfect love requires his cooperation with God's grace, purification prayer for him has a point. In the next chapter I move beyond prayers for the faithful departed to salvation prayer for the unsaved dead.

---

94. See Ombres, *Theology of Purgatory*, 72–73.
95. Anselm, cited in Doctrine Commission, *Mystery of Salvation*, 108.

chapter 5

SALVATION PRAYER FOR THE UNSAVED DEAD

Loving God,
we commend to your mercy the unsaved who have died,
that your will for them—repentance, forgiveness, and new life—
may be fulfilled.

AMEN

Energized discussion was already underway when I entered the classroom. Students were talking about the news report—which was awful. A nineteen-year-old man, stone drunk, had run a red light in Chicago at high speed, T-boning another car. The crash killed parents and grandparents, leaving two young children orphans and alone in the world. Anger was all over talk radio and private conversation—and now here in my classroom. I set down my lecture notes and cup of coffee and listened in. Soon I was leading the charge. "We should be outraged. Lock him up and throw away the key. The loser's callous indifference to human life demands justice. Teach him a lesson." Having vented our feelings, the class sank into silence. And then her hand went up—the shy student who seldom spoke up, but when she did you had better listen. "I get what you're saying," she began; "what he did is horrible and inexcusable. I, too, am angry. He must be punished. And I feel really sad for the victims." She paused; we sensed that more was coming, and were not disappointed. "But," she continued, "I also feel immense sadness for that young man, the driver. What has gone so wrong in his life that by age nineteen he is an alcoholic with a prior drunk driving conviction? What was his childhood like? Was he loved or rejected? And now he's ruined his life forever." Silence quilted the room as her question hung over us. She had turned the kaleidoscope and we now saw a different picture; the young man's story had taken on new and more complex dimensions. How should we respond? With justice? With care? With both, perhaps?[1] Later I was to ask myself—is God more like me (operating from a firm sense of anger and justice that wants to punish) or more like my student (who feels, thinks, and acts by compassion and mercy that wants to restore)? Well, consider.

Last summer I saw God. Traffic had slowed both ways as a doe, followed by her fawn, crossed the busy four-lane highway. Mom was safely in the tall grass at the side of the road and heading into the woods when she realized that baby was not with her. The fawn, lost and disoriented, had turned down the middle of the highway, frantically searching this way and that—unable to find either mom or its way to safety. Cars, trucks, and motorcycles were now stopped, people hushed as they watched. Then came the holy moment: momma deer saw her baby in danger, left the protection of the forest, and ventured into the open highway. She trotted to its side and led it into the trees. Tears filled my eyes as I recalled the words of revival songwriter Ira Sankey: "There were ninety and nine that safely lay in the shelter of the fold; but one was out on the hills . . . away from the tender Shepherd's care. 'Lord, Thou hast here thy ninety and nine—are they not enough for thee?' But the Shepherd made answer, 'This of mine has wandered away from me; and although the road be rough and steep I go to the desert to find my sheep.'"[2] For the biblical God ninety-nine out of one hundred is not enough; God will not be satisfied until every last person is safely home (Matt 18:10–14).

---

1. Gilligan (*In a Different Voice*) suggests that men and women think in different ways about ethics. Men appeal to impersonal principles that show concern for humanity in general (an ethic of justice based in logic) while women focus on caring relationships that treat individuals in a personal way (an ethic of care based in emotion). Psychologists have conducted hundreds of studies on gender, emotion and morality—and research reveals some differences between men and women. We all need both virtues, of course; the prophet Micah (6:8) reminds us that the Lord requires us to do justice and to love kindness.

2. Sankey, "Ninety and Nine"—the words were written by Elizabeth Clephane. This is the God depicted in Francis Thompson's poem 'Hound of Heaven.' "Surely goodness and mercy pursue me," Brueggemann (*Collected Sermons*, 114) translates Psalm 23:6. "God's friendliness and kindness . . . run after us and chase us down, grab us and hold us. The verb 'follow' is a powerful, active verb. We are being chased by God's powerful love."

Prayer for the unsaved dead is for those in hell. As the logical complement of heaven, hell is a necessary part of Christian theology. We can refuse relationship with God, and hell is what happens when we do. As with heaven and purgatory, we should distinguish the core view of hell (as separation from God) from the embellished view (as depicted, for example, in Hieronymus Bosch's terrifying images of a torture chamber inhabited by devils and monsters). The traditional model, Jonathan Kvanvig notes, has four elements.[3] First, the retributive punishment thesis: the purpose of hell is to pay back to the wicked the penalty of sin they deserve. Second, the no-escape thesis: the sentence of hell is irreversible, and since its inhabitants cannot get out, people remain there eternally. Third, the actual occupants thesis: hell has inhabitants; because some people are there, hell is not empty. Fourth, the conscious existence thesis: those in hell suffer—certainly pains of loss (the spiritual pain of separation from God) and perhaps pains of sense (the physical pain symbolized by fire).

Revised views of hell reject one or more features of the traditional view. *Choice models* deny the retributive punishment thesis; in free will theories the suffering of hell is self-imposed, not inflicted by an angry God. "People are in hell because they choose it," Clark Pinnock and Robert Brow state; "none are sent there against their will."[4] God does not exclude the unsaved from heaven; they exclude themselves. Separation from God is the natural consequence of living a self-centered life. *Escapism* denies the no-escape thesis. While hell exists and might be eternally populated, any of the unsaved can leave hell and enter heaven. Death

---

3. Kvanvig, "Hell," and *Problem of Hell*.

4. Pinnock and Brow, *Unbounded Love*, 88. Lewis (*Great Divorce*, 75) agrees: "all that are in hell, choose it. Without that self-choice there would be no hell." In Dante's *Inferno* hell is not external punishment but a natural consequence which enacts the character of the sinner. The punishments are not arbitrary but inherent in the sinful acts; the greedy, for example, push heavy weights while the gluttonous wallow in muck. The problem of hell is a version of the problem of evil and the free will defense of hell is patterned after the free will theodicy of evil. God cannot leave us free and guarantee we will not do evil—nor can God leave us free and guarantee we will not refuse salvation. But free will is a necessary means to important goods that cannot be achieved without it. Free will both explains evil in this world and hell in the next. All versions of hell face what Sider ("Hell and Vagueness") calls the "vagueness problem." It is possible that two individuals who are nearly identical in moral character differ in their afterlife destinies. People are seldom either saints or wicked; instead of a clear line, there is middle ground, since almost all of us have both good and evil elements in our characters.

is not a deadline beyond which salvation is impossible.[5] *Universalism* denies the actual occupants thesis. While hell initially has inhabitants, it will ultimately be empty since at some point every person will repent and turn to God. *Conditional immortality* (or annihilationism) denies the conscious existence thesis. Instead of having indestructible souls, we are created mortal—and so all persons cease to exist at death. Rather than giving them new life only to make them suffer forever, God simply leaves the wicked in non-existence.[6]

Christians—even those who pray for the dead—have seldom prayed for the unsaved in hell. "The Church offers no prayers for the damned," the Roman Catholic International Theological Commission bluntly states.[7] It is, by contrast, long and widely held in the Eastern Orthodox churches that prayer can assist the unsaved dead (but how it does so is unsettled). "According to Orthodox teaching," Hilarion Alfeyev says, "it is possible to be freed from the torments of hell; the practice of praying for the departed and even 'for those in hell' at Pentecost vespers is based on this."[8] There are good reasons to pray for the unsaved in hell. Salvation prayer assumes that human choices are responsible for hell and that escape from hell is possible. Escapism and universalism should be clearly distinguished. Universal salvation entails posthumous salvation; if all are saved, and if many are not saved in this life, then they must be saved after death. But posthumous salvation does not entail universal salvation; an escapable hell may never be empty since some may refuse grace

---

5. The term "escapism" comes from Buckareff and Plug, "Escaping Hell."

6. To be clear, there are complexities here. In the first place, there are two forms of annihilationism—the form of which I speak (in which humans are by nature mortal—while God gives everlasting life to believers, God leaves the unsaved in non-existence) and the view that God resurrects the wicked, punishes them in hell, and after an appropriate time burns them into extinction. In the second place, while annihilationists regularly identify their view with conditional immortality, there are reasons to question that identification. First, annihilationism is compatible with the classical doctrine of the natural immortality of the soul. While the soul is in-itself immortal, God could extinguish it if God so chose. Second, those who believe in conditional immortality can affirm eternal hell. They could argue that the soul, left to itself, would die—but since divine retribution requires that sin be punished forever, God keeps the soul in existence forever so that it can be punished forever. In other words, while most annihilationists affirm conditional immorality and most believers in eternal hell deny it, there is no essential reason why either camp needs to do this. Thanks to my editor Robin Parry for pressing me on this point.

7. International Theological Commission, "Some Current Questions," 238.

8. Alfeyev, "Eschatology," 115.

forever. Salvation prayer does not require universalism, only escapism; if it is even possible that the unsaved can repent and leave hell, then we should pray for them. Salvation prayers assume a *conscious intermediate state* where the unsaved departed are separated from God; if they are unconscious then salvation prayers make no sense since they do not now exist as persons. Salvation prayers also assume a *dynamic intermediate state*—existence in time where change can happen. This chapter defends escapism; it is the longest because it argues in a thorough way for significant revision of historical practice.

The Open Death Requirement

Carlos actively resisted God his whole life. He was more than an atheist who did not believe; as an anti-theist he actively opposed Christian faith. Carlos was a self-centered person through and through—pride, envy, greed, and lust defined his character. He lived by deception and exploitation, using other people for his own selfish goals, without concern for their needs or wishes. He did all this with few misgivings of conscience. Two years ago Carlos died. What can we pray for him? That depends on what kind of hell he entered.

Prayer for the unsaved like Carlos asks that they escape hell and enter heaven. Death is either salvation-closed or salvation-open. Spiritual destiny is either fixed at death (when all opportunity for repentance ends) or is not fixed at death (which means forgiveness is still available). Thomas Aquinas states that the unsaved dead can "in no fashion whatsoever . . . escape [suffering] and find refuge in beatitude. . . . It is [not] possible for the damned to consider blessedness as still open to them." If "the damned are entirely excluded from grace" then escape from hell is not possible and prayer for Carlos is pointless.[9] In order for such prayer to make sense the *open death requirement*—death is not a point of no return beyond which salvation is impossible—is a necessary assumption. If Carlos has a way out of hell into heaven then praying for him has a point.

---

9. Aquinas, *Summa Theologiae*, Vol. 33, 2a2ae q18 a3, 37 and Aquinas, cited in Walls, *Purgatory*, 196. In *Summa Theologica* Supplement to the Third Part, q 69a3, Aquinas discusses whether souls in hell are able to leave.

Two Objections to Open Death

I begin with two objections that, if true, immediately foreclose escapism— that it is incompatible with Scripture and with established church teaching.

Open Death and the Bible

It might be thought that the finality of death is clearly taught in Scripture. In Luke 16:26 the rich man is told by Abraham, "between you and us a great chasm has been fixed, so that those who might want to pass from here to you cannot do so, and no one can cross from there to us." This parable does teach the general truth of rewards and punishments after death, but we must be careful not to infer too much from its details—especially since the point of both stories in Luke 16 concern the just use of wealth, not personal eschatology.[10] Hebrews 9:27 states that "it is appointed for mortals to die once, and after that the judgment." The traditional interpretation is that there are no more chances for salvation after death, but the verse simply does not teach that. It does say that we have only one earthly life and that judgment follows death; but it does not say what the purpose or result of judgment is, that God's love stops reaching out to the unsaved, or that they cannot repent beyond the grave.[11] The same is true for 2 Corinthians 5:10—"all of us must appear before the judgment seat of Christ, so that each may receive recompense for what has been done in the body." While choices for or against God during this life are important, time in the body is not decisive for a person's spiritual destiny.[12] In John

---

10. Wright (*Surprised by Hope*, 176) says that this parable "use[s] stock imagery from ancient Judaism, such as 'Abraham's bosom,' not to teach about what happens after death but to insist on justice and mercy within the present life."

11. Neuhaus (*Death on Friday Afternoon*, 52) says "it seems doubtful that [Hebrews 9] is intended as a schedule, stating in a punctiliar way a sequence of events. Not too much weight should be placed on what is, after all, a subordinate clause in a passage making the point that Christ had to die only once for our sins."

12. There is an intrinsic relationship between our actions in this life and our destiny in the next. Heaven is not an arbitrary reward nor hell an arbitrary punishment for how we live this life. Rather, how we live shapes us into certain sorts of persons, and so our afterlife destinies are extensions of the characters we have chosen in this life. Casey (*Afterlives*, 349) says the predominant love in our lives makes us the person we are—and at death we become our love of self or our love of God. The afterlife—both heaven and hell—is the fulfillment of choices made in this life, not extrinsic reward or punishment.

5:28–29 Jesus says that "the hour is coming when all who are in their graves ... will come out—those who have done good, to the resurrection of life, and those who have done evil, to the resurrection of condemnation." We are told here about judgment, but are not told that it brings eternal damnation or that the state of being condemned constitutes God's *final* dealing with the unsaved.[13]

Perhaps, however, while not directly stated, the closed view is implied by biblical descriptions of the post-mortem condition as eternal or everlasting. Jesus (Matt 25:46) states that the wicked "will go away into eternal punishment but the righteous into eternal life," and St. Paul (2 Thess 1:9) warns that evildoers will experience "eternal destruction." If punishment is everlasting or eternal, then death is closed and escape from hell impossible. Three responses are in order.

First, the Greek adjective translated "eternal" or "everlasting" is *aiōnios*—which derives from the noun *aiōn*, meaning "age" or "period of time." In both Hebrew and Christian Scriptures eternity, in the sense of unending time, applies to God alone. When used in eschatological contexts, however, it means "pertaining to an age"—specifically, the age to come (since Jewish apocalyptic thought divided time into two eras—present and future). "*Aiōnios* is a qualitative rather than a quantitative word," Randolph Tasker notes.[14] In Jesus' sayings and St. Paul's letters eternal life is the *quality* of life that characterizes God's coming new age; in the same way, R. T. France states, eternal punishment "is punishment which relates to the age to come rather than punishment which continues forever."[15] It is often argued that hell must be eternal in order for heaven to be eternal. The blessedness of the righteous and the torment of the wicked are two parallel but opposite realities, as Ilaria Ramelli puts it. Jesus states that the sinful go to eternal punishment (Matt 25:41) and the just to eternal life (Matt 25:46). Both punishment and beatitude must be

---

13. See Bonda, *One Purpose of God*, 121.

14. See Sasse, "Aion" and Tasker, *Gospel according to St. Matthew*, 240. "'Eternal life' is the life that is characteristic of the age to come.... Similarly, 'eternal punishment' in [Matt 25:46] indicates that lack of charity ... will be punished in the age to come. There is, however, no indication as to how long that punishment will last.... It would certainly be difficult to exaggerate the harmful effect of [the] unfortunate mistranslation of 'eternal' as 'everlasting.'" Thiselton (*Life After Death*, 152) adds that no biblical text mentions the duration of hell.

15. France, *Gospel of Matthew*, 966–67. "The assumption that 'eternal' is a synonym for 'everlasting' ... depends more on modern English usage than on the meaning of *aiōnios*, which ... [is] related to the concept of the two ages."

eternal in the same way since both are declared to be *aiōnios*; if the misery will cease then the joy must also cease. This argument, however, is based on a misunderstanding of the word's meaning. It ignores, Ramelli points out, that "in the phrases *kolasis aiōnios* and *zōe aiōnios* the adjective does not mean 'eternal' but 'of the world to come.'" The phrases "eternal punishment" or "eternal destruction" thus cannot serve as proof-texts for the closed view of death. As Ramelli concludes, "the passages in which the doctrine of eternal damnation is grounded are highly controversial in their translation and interpretation."[16]

Second, escapism is consistent with eternal hell (if *aiōnios* did mean "continuing forever").[17] On the traditional view hell is everlasting punishment for past sins committed during earthly life. This, however, would be unfair: just punishment is proportionate to a crime's seriousness, but the temporary sins of this life do not deserve everlasting punishment.[18] So if hell is eternal, it must be in response to continuing sin in the next life. Suppose, at the start of a family gathering, I send my daughter to her room for fighting with her cousins—telling her "when you can act nicely, you may come out." I do not want her to be grounded very long, and I regularly knock on her door to invite her out—but she may become stubborn, refuse to apologize, and miss the entire party. It is her present choices that keep her in her room, not her past act of disobedience. In the same way, hell could be eternal, not because someone's sins on earth merit everlasting punishment, but because after death they continue forever to reject God and to suffer separation from God forever as a continuing consequence. Escapism is compatible, then, with eternal hell.

Third, even if posthumous salvation did have problem texts, this would not be devastating since all theological positions have difficult

16. Ramelli, *Christian Doctrine of Apokatastasis*, 731 and 821. The noun *aiōn* refers to an interval of time, not an absolute unending eternity—and the adjective *aiōnios* concerns *future*, otherworldly fates that belong to the coming aeon, not *eternal* punishment and reward (see pages 25–34, 187, 543, 551–53, 670, 706, 767). *Aiōnios* refers to a future aeon in contrast to the present aeon. The adjective *aidios* (translated "everlasting") never refers to punishment in the next world; only heavenly life is so described. Also see Ramelli and Konstan, *Terms for Eternity*.

17. See Seymour, *Theodicy of Hell*, chapter 3.

18. Early church theologians recognized the proportionality problem. Origen, for example, states that infinite suffering is incompatible with finite sin since "it would be absurd if a judge inflicted eternal punishments to a soul that sinned for three years, or more, or less." Justice requires punishment to be commensurate with the sinner's sin, Theodore of Mopsuestia says. "How can one continue to speak of justice if punishment has no limit?" (cited in Ramelli, *Christian Doctrine of Apokatastasis*, 353 and 553).

biblical passages to explain. Every thinking Christian—not just escapists—is in the same situation of having to reinterpret doctrines for which there is apparent biblical support.[19] Affirming the Bible's authority, Tom Wright says, "is precisely not to say, 'we know what Scripture means and don't need to raise any more questions.' It is always a way of saying that the Church in each generation must make fresh . . . efforts to understand Scripture more fully . . . , even if that means cutting across cherished traditions."[20]

Open Death and Church Tradition

It might be argued that open death, even if compatible with Scripture, contradicts Christian tradition. All major doctrinal statements since the fifth century affirm closed death.[21] None of the early councils describe

---

19. Talbott (*Inescapable Love of God*, 47–48) points out that there is biblical support for each of three inconsistent propositions:
1. God wants to save all persons (1 Tim 2:4; 2 Pet 3:9),
2. God can achieve God's purposes (Ps 115:3; Isa 46:10–11) and
3. some sinners will never be reconciled to God (Matt 25:46; 2 Thess 1:9).

The upshot, he says, is that "every reflective Christian . . . must reject a proposition for which there is at least some . . . biblical support." Augustinians reject statement 1: while God's providential love is universal, God's saving love is restricted to the elect. Non-Augustinians reject statement 2: while God's saving love is unlimited, God's redemptive power can be frustrated by free human choices. Universalists reject statement 3: God's love and power cannot be thwarted and so all persons will ultimately be saved. All three theological systems are in the same situation of having to reinterpret a proposition for which there is apparent biblical support.

20. Wright, *Last Word*, 91. The history of interpretation creates what Thistelton ("Can Hermeneutics Ease Deadlock?," 152) calls a "horizon of expectation" that conditions how we understand biblical texts. Certain readings of Scripture seem natural simply because we have heard them repeated so often that we are habituated to understanding the text that way. But tradition is not infallible and has little force is mistaken.

21. The sixth-century *Athanasian Creed* (in Episcopal Church, *Book of Common Prayer*, 865) states "they that have done good shall go into life everlasting; and they that have done evil into everlasting fire"—and the 1215 *Fourth Lateran Council* (Canon 1) declares eternal punishment. Luther and Calvin accepted traditional teaching on hell and damnation. The Lutheran *Augsburg Confession* (chapter 17) declares that "at the consummation of the world Christ will appear for judgment, and will raise up all the dead; . . . ungodly men and the devils He will condemn to be tormented without end" and "condemn[s] the Anabaptists, who think that there will be an end to the punishments of condemned men and devils." The Reformed *Second Helvetic Confession* (chapter 26) says "unbelievers are immediately cast into hell from which no exit is opened for the wicked by any services of the living." The Church of England *Homily*

everlasting punishment, however, and escapism has been a live option from the time of the church fathers. David Powys identifies three broad eras of Christian thought concerning the fate of the wicked: diversity, uniformity, and diversity.[22]

Era 1: there was *ancient diversity* on the question of hell. Jeffrey Trumbower observes that the closed view "was slow to develop and not universally accepted in the Christian movement's first four hundred years. . . . Many early Christians . . . [allowed] for the possibility of posthumous salvation for non-Christians." Apocryphal texts concerning prayer for the salvation of those in hell suggest that many in the early church did not believe the fate of the unsaved to be fixed forever at death.[23] Three figures, Powys says, represent the diversity of early views. Irenaeus of Lyons believed in *conditional immortality*. Human beings are not, as Plato thought, naturally immortal; instead, after judgment new life is conferred

---

on Prayer: "after bodily death 'every mortal man dieth either in the state of salvation or damnation . . . [;] the soul of man passing out of the body, goeth straightways either to heaven, or else to hell, whereof the one needeth no prayer, and the other is without redemption"), the *Westminster Confession* (chapter 33: "the wicked . . . shall be cast into eternal torments, and be punished with everlasting destruction from the presence of the Lord") and the Roman Catholic Church, *Catechism of the Catholic Church* (Article 1035, 270: "the teaching of the church affirms the existence of hell and its eternity. Immediately after death the souls of those who die in a state of mortal sin descend into hell, where they suffer the punishments of hell, 'eternal fire'") all teach eternal punishment of the wicked. Human destiny is determined by the life lived on earth; death is the firm boundary of salvation beyond which a person's fate is sealed.

22. Powys, *Hell*, Part 1.

23. Trumbower, *Rescue for Dead*, 3. See Volume 1 chapter 2. Apocryphal tales like *The Acts of Paul and Thecla* and *The Passion of Perpetua and Felicitas*—in which dead persons are rescued by prayer—suggest an open view of death. So did the various "descent" traditions and Origen's speculation concerning the restoration of all things at the end of history. Some church fathers defended "Christian universalism" (the salvation of all baptized Christians) while others accepted "universalism proper" (the salvation of all persons). Ramelli's volume *Christian Doctrine of Apokatastasis* is the most comprehensive and systematic study of universal restoration, a major soteriological doctrine in ancient Christianity. She presents its history in numerous thinkers and analyses its development over eight centuries from the very beginning of Christianity to late antiquity and the early Middle Ages. The abiding issues are present in these early debates, arguments and assumptions concerning the hermeneutics of biblical interpretation, the interaction of philosophy and Scripture, the scope of God's salvific purpose and Christ's redemptive sacrifice, the nature of God's justice and mercy, the essence of good and evil, the psychology of sin, the purpose of punishment (retributive or corrective), the tension between grace and free will, the metaphysics of body and soul, the relationship of time and eternity. These theoretical questions appear over and over in the course of church history, and they frame the debate today.

by God on the righteous, while the wicked cease to exist. Gregory of Nyssa believed in *universal salvation*. After death the unrighteous experience remedial punishment which will result in repentance for all. Augustine of Hippo believed in *continuing punishment*. The non-Christian dead are in eternal conscious torment, and nothing can affect the finality of their fate; their punishment is not corrective, but retributive.[24] Where Irenaeus and Augustine saw death as closed, Gregory believed it to be open. *Apokatastasis* (the total abolition of evil and the restoration of every person to God) was a major doctrine in early Christianity. It was not held by a few isolated individuals but enjoyed widespread support up to the end of the fourth century.[25]

Era 2: there was *medieval and Reformation uniformity* on the question of hell. A harsh doctrine of unending punishment developed when the end of persecution produced a morally lax church in which Christian discipleship lost its spiritual vigor. Augustine's positions on closed death and eternal damnation became official doctrine in the West because of political interference in theological decisions. Roman Emperor Justinian I determined Origen of Alexandria's speculation concerning *apokatastasis* to be in error—and convened the Fifth Ecumenical Council which declared posthumous and universal salvation heretical.[26] "As an orthodox

---

24. Ramelli (*Christian Doctrine of Apokatastasis*, 659–676) points out that Augustine (cited at 664), in his anti-Manichean phase, supported the theory of universal restoration. "The goodness of God orders and leads all the beings that have fallen until they return [and] are restored to the condition from which they have fallen." Augustine eventually repudiated *apokatastasis*—which he acknowledged was embraced by the vast majority of Christians in his day—as heresy; he called its supporters 'the merciful' since they rejected eternal punishment (*City of God*, Book 21.17 and 18, 995–998).

25. See Ramelli, *Christian Doctrine of Apokatastasis*, 817–23. *Apokatastasis* was defended by the likes of Bardaisan, Origen, Pamphilus, Methodius, Eusebius, Macrina the Younger, Gregory of Nyssa, Gregory Nazianzus, Evagrius, Diodore and Theodore, Pseudo-Dionysius, Ephrem the Syrian and several other Syriac writers, Maximus the Confessor, and John Eriugena.

26 Things are actually more complex than this statement lets on. Justinian did think *apokatastasis* an error and he did convene the Fifth Ecumenical Council—however, its output in relation to *apokatastasis* is contested. The council issue concerned Christological heresy and no mention was made of *apokatastasis* in its main documents—but an appendix containing a series of anathemas was later added to the proceedings, statements that drew on the conclusions of a local council some years earlier that Justinian had overseen. Many scholars maintain that *apokatastasis per se* was not condemned in these anathemas, only a problematic version of it. Ramelli (*Christian Doctrine of Apokatastasis*, 658 and 724–38) argues that the condemnation of Origen probably never occurred formally—and if it did, was the result of both political pressure and a

theology came to be crystallized," Thomas Talbott says, "it was as much a product of imperial politics as it was of theological debate or biblical exegesis." This fact, he argues, gives reason "for not identifying the Christian faith too quickly with what we now call orthodox Christian doctrine."[27]

Era 3: there is *modern diversity* on the question of hell. Both before and after the Reformation hell was understood as unending punishment. A few sixteenth-century Anabaptists taught universalism—and in seventeenth-century England there was occasional dissent against eternal damnation.[28] In the eighteenth-century Friedrich Schleiermacher pointed out an absurd implication of hell: the happiness of the redeemed would be ruined by awareness of and sympathy for the unsaved. Heaven is not possible if hell exists—and so all must be saved if any are to enjoy the bliss of heaven.[29] Discussion of the fate of non-believers dominated

---

long series of theological misunderstandings, even ignorance and deliberate alteration of his works. If universalism was declared heretical then that may settle the debate for many Roman Catholics and Orthodox—but if it was not then there is space for further ecumenical discussion. See Kimel, "*Apocatastasis*: The Heresy that Never Was." Thanks to my editor Robin Parry for this historical clarification.

27. Talbott, *Inescapable Love*, 17–22. It is common to suppose "that those with the strongest arguments—exegetical, historical, and theological—typically . . . prevailed in the early church councils. But . . . the truth is very different from that: those who prevailed were those with the civil authorities on their side" (16).

28. See Walker, *Decline of Hell*.

29. Kreeft and Tacelli (*Handbook of Apologetics*, 271 and 305) who reject the argument state it well. Suppose you go to heaven and your loved one goes to hell. Either you know they are are in hell or you do not. If not, then your heavenly happiness is founded on ignorance. If so, either this knowledge will disturb your joy or it will not. If it does not then you have stopped loving the other person; you have become cold and unloving, and thus are not good. If it does, then you keep loving them but are not happy. So if hell exists then heaven is either ignorant, unloving or unhappy. Therefore hell cannot exist. This argument reverses the traditional claim that the blessed will rejoice at the misery of the damned. Images of God and the saved laughing at the unsaved suffering torment in hell are deeply contradictory—indeed heretical—to the God found in Scripture. Talbott (*Inescapable Love*, chapter 8 and 193–95) and Kronen and Reitan (*God's Final Victory*, 80–89) reiterate Schleiermacher's argument that hell makes heaven impossible. If eternal hell exists and if heaven is perfect bliss, then those in heaven—who possess perfect love and therefore love the unsaved—will know of and grieve over their suffering. Craig ("Talbott's Universalism") claims that God could conceal the truth of hell from those in heaven. Talbott, Kronen, and Reitan reply that this is both logically impossible (because heaven involves social relationships and so the blessed would both notice the absence of the unsaved and feel unhappy about their misery) and morally impermissible (since it would require everlasting divine deception and would, in addition, make God's victory over evil hollow and the enjoyment of heaven a false happiness).

nineteenth-century theology; conditional immortality, escapism, universalism, and eternal hell all had prominent defenders—as they do today.[30] Richard Bauckham says that "common to almost all versions of the 'wider hope' [is] the belief that death [is] not the decisive break which traditional orthodoxy had taught. Repentance [and] conversion . . . are still possible after death."[31]

Eastern Christianity—while having strong advocates of closed death like John Chrysostom—has been more open to salvation after death.[32] In the ancient church there were various "descent" traditions, based on the obscure passages (1 Pet 3:18–21; 4:6) concerning Christ's presence in the realm of the dead between his death and resurrection. Early literature describes Christ harrowing hell—smashing its gates, conquering the devil, liberating its occupants, and leading them to heaven.[33] The

---

30. Many theologians are annihilationists. See Date, *Rethinking Hell*; Edwards and Stott, *Essentials*, 312–29; Fudge, *Fire That Consumes*; Mealy, *End of Unrepentant*; Pinnock, "Annihilationism" and "Conditional View"; Wenham, "Case for Conditionalism"; Wright, *For All Saints*, 42–46 and *Surprised by Hope*, 175–83. Many other theologians, both Protestant and Roman Catholic, are hopeful universalists—Karl Barth and Emil Brunner (Reformed), Hans Urs von Balthasar and Karl Rahner (Roman Catholics), J. A. T. Robinson, John Hick, and Jürgen Moltmann (Protestant), and a few evangelicals like Gregory MacDonald.

31. Bauckham, "Universalism," 29. For more on the why belief in eternal hell declined see Appendix Note 3.

32. Chrysostom, who defended closed death and eternal hell in the Eastern church, was the parallel figure to Augustine in the West. He (cited in Daley, *Hope of Early Church*, 105–8) writes: "here one can appeal to the Emperor for clemency—but there, never! They will not be released, but will remain, roasting and in such agony as cannot be expressed." Ramelli (*Christian Doctrine of Apokatastasis*, 549–57) argues that Chrysostom was ambiguous on the question of universal salvation. His references to hell's eternality have a hortatory—an exhorting or urging—purpose: to deter moral laxity. In his homiletic and pastoral context, threats of fear were an expedient rhetorical device designed to frighten people from sinful behavior. And yet Chrysostom encourages prayers and almsgiving, which he emphasizes can free the dead from post-mortem punishment. "Not . . . in vain [do we] make mention of the departed . . . and approach God in their behalf, beseeching the Lamb who . . . takes away the sin of the world . . . that some refreshment may thereby ensue to them. . . . For if the children of Job were purged by the sacrifice of their father, why do you doubt that when we too offer for the departed, some consolation arises to them? . . . Why therefore do you grieve . . . when it is in your power to gather so much pardon for the departed? (*Homily on First Corinthians*, Part 2, Homily 41.8, 592–93). Chrysostom likely accepted "Christian universalism"—salvation of all the baptized—and may have extended salvation to all humanity.

33. In the fourth century the first reference to the descent appeared in the Athanasian and Apostles' Creeds. Discussion appears in Origen, Cyril of Alexandria, Cyril of

Western church restricted the group saved to righteous Israelites, but the Eastern church—according to Alfeyev—taught "that Christ granted to all the possibility of salvation."[34] The liturgy of Holy Saturday proclaims that hell, while real, is finite and temporary: "hell reigns, but not forever, over the race of mortals; for you, O Mighty One . . . shattered with your life-giving hand the bars of death, and proclaimed to those who slept there from every age . . . redemption."[35] The descent to *hades*, Alfeyev says, is an integral part of Eastern Orthodox soteriology. "The death sentence passed by God does not mean that human beings are deprived of hope for salvation because, failing to turn to God during their lifetimes, people could turn to God in the afterlife, having heard Christ's preaching in hell."[36] Hell is not an autonomous realm abandoned by God but remains filled with Christ's presence, which saves all who repent from all generations. This does not imply universal salvation since those who clearly reject God's love remain in hell. Nor is escapism the consistent teaching of the Eastern church.[37]

"It is a mistake to [think] that 'hell' has always denoted everlasting punishment in 'orthodox' theology," Anthony Thiselton states. "Eternal punishment, rather than being '*the* orthodox view of the Church,' simply covers its widespread acceptance . . . as the dominant view of the western

---

Jerusalem, John Chrysostom, and Ephrem the Syrian (see Ramelli, *Christian Doctrine of Apokatastasis*, 331–32).

34. Alfeyev, *Christ Conqueror of Hell*, 208. Also see Alfeyev, "Eschatology" and Kukota, "Christ, Medicine of Life." Theological poetry and liturgical texts describe Christ's victory which leaves hell bare and desolate. The icons of the resurrection depict Christ raising Adam and Eve—who are seen not as concrete individuals but as symbols of the entire human race whom Christ leads to heaven.

35. Cited in Alfeyev, *Christ Conqueror of Hell*, 192.

36. Alfeyev, *Christ Conqueror of Hell*, 212. Where the Roman Catholic Church teaches that the descent was a unique and unrepeatable event, the Eastern Orthodox Church considers Christ's victory valid for all times and generations. Roman Catholic Church teaching on the descent is summarized in Roman Catholic Church, *Catechism of Catholic Church*, Article 631–37, 164–65.

37. See La Due, *Trinity Guide*, 131. Louth ("Eastern Orthodox Eschatology," 242) says that according to some "after death the soul is unchangeably set in accordance with the fundamental orientation of its longing." Both Florovsky (*Creation and Redemption*, Vol. 3, 254–65) and Vassiliadis (*Mystery of Death*, 506–37) argue that even though Christ made a heaven of *hades*, hell remains eternal. Larchet (*Life After Death*, 215) claims that sinners can be delivered from hell only in the time before Christ's second coming.

Church."[38] And *even if* tradition was uniformly against open death, established church teaching is not infallible. There is good reason to revise the traditional view—and such revision denies no central element of faith. To paraphrase Gregory MacDonald: the only major Christian doctrine salvation prayer rejects "is the teaching that those in hell have passed beyond the point of no return; and . . . this belief is quite detachable from the web of Christian belief. . . . Although it is a widely held doctrine, it is peripheral in its structural role in Christian theology. It can be removed and replaced without doing harm."[39] Closed death is neither the plain teaching of Scripture nor uniform church teaching—open death, Jerry Walls says, is not "a theological novelty."[40] I now turn to positive arguments for open death.

Defending Open Death

Death is salvation-closed, Aquinas says, for two reasons:

1. God no longer desires to save the dead and so withdraws grace, and
2. the unrepentant dead are no longer able to change their wills.[41]

In order for death to be salvation-open Aquinas must be wrong on both counts:

1. God must never stop offering salvation, and
2. individuals must never lose their freedom to respond.

These two conditions—the permanence of grace and free will—constitute the salvation-open view of death.[42] I explain and defend each in turn.

---

38. Thiselton, *Life After Death*, 145–49; emphasis added.

39. MacDonald, *Evangelical Universalist*, 167. Kreeft and Tacelli (*Handbook of Apologetics*, 282-285) contend that disbelief in hell entails multiple consequences that destroy the Christian faith. While belief in no hell may do so, belief in escapable hell does not.

40. Walls, *Heaven, Hell and Purgatory*, 205.

41. Aquinas, cited in O'Callaghan, *Christ Our Hope*, 207: "the damned are entirely excluded from grace. Therefore they will not be able to change their will for the better."

42. Technically, Aquinas need only be wrong on the first idea, that the unsaved are excluded from grace. The sole reason he gives for why they cannot repent after death is that God's love for them ends. Human freedom does not end for additional reasons—thus all that is needed to refute his argument is to show that God's love and offer of salvation never end. If divine grace continues after death, that fact by itself—on

The Unending Divine Love Requirement

Andrei Buckareff and Allen Plug summarize the argument for escapism: since "all of God's actions are just and loving . . . we should expect that God would make provision for people to convert in the *eschaton* and that the opportunities for persons to convert should not be exhausted by a single post-mortem opportunity."[43] It might be thought that, while *God's love* does not end at death, *chances for salvation* do—that God continues to love the unsaved but closes to them the possibility of salvation. This—however—is not possible since the former entails the latter. To love someone is to will their good, to want what is best for them, to actively promote their welfare, to help meet the needs which are necessary for their flourishing and without which they experience serious harm. Because we have been created for fellowship with God and find there our supreme happiness, relationship with God is essential for every person's well-being. To be permanently separated from God is to find ourselves condemned to frustration and suffering.[44] Death, St. Paul assures us, cannot separate us from the love of God (Rom 8:38–39)—so if God loves the unsaved dead, then God must desire their ultimate fulfillment and offer them posthumous salvation. Unending divine love has both biblical and theological support.

The Bible Affirms Unending Divine Love

We must read the Bible, Brian Daley says, with "a love-centered hermeneutic" which affirms that God loves each person with infinite love and desires the salvation of all.[45] The Hebrew word *āhab* (translated "love") suggests strong emotional attachment and desire to be with—and the word *chesed* refers to God's steadfast faithfulness. While human love

---

Aquinas' analysis—is all that is necessary for posthumous salvation to be possible. Nor does salvation prayer require that either divine love or human freedom continue forever—only that they continue past death. Even if either or both end at some post-mortem point, we can never know when that point is for any unsaved individual and so should always pray for them.

43. Buckareff and Plug, "Value, Finality and Frustration," 78.

44. Adams ("Problem of Hell," 304) defines an evil as "horrendous" if suffering that evil means that within a person's experience good is defeated. Earthly life followed by separation from God is an instance of horrendous evil. For an unredeemed person, any temporal happiness enjoyed here will be wiped out by eternal suffering.

45. Daley, "Old Books," 65. See Benedict XVI, *Fathers of Church*, 86.

is unreliable and vacillating—we fall in and out of love—God's love is constant and eternal, an unswerving loyalty and unfailing commitment that persists beyond betrayal and always offers forgiveness.[46] "I have loved you with an everlasting love; therefore I have continued my faithfulness to you" (Jer 31:3). "The steadfast love of the Lord never ceases; his mercies never come to an end" (Lam 3:22). God's "steadfast love endures for ever" (Ps 136; cf. 103:17). "The mountains may depart and the hills be removed, but my steadfast love shall not depart from you" (Isa 54:10). In Christian Scripture the word *agapē* is used to describe God's love. It means selfless, sacrificial, unconditional love—self-giving devotion that is passionately concerned for and committed to the well-being of the other person. God's very nature is love (1 John 4:8) and God loves the world (John 3:16).[47] God, St. Paul (Rom 8:31) asserts, is for us, not against us. God is for us period, not for us if . . . ; God is for all of us, not just some of us; and God is for us permanently, not temporarily. St. Paul's hymn of praise heaps word upon word in an attempt to express God's lavish, inexhaustible love (Eph 2:4–7): "God, who is *rich* in mercy, out of the *great love* with which he loved us even when we were dead through our trespasses" has shown us "the *immeasurable riches* of his *grace* in *kindness* toward us." God "desires everyone to be saved" (1 Tim 2:4) and is "not wanting any to perish, but all to come to repentance" (2 Pet 3:9; cf. Matt 18:14).

The God depicted in Scripture is a God who will not let us go, who never gives up on sinners. Divine persistence is pictured in the life of the prophet Hosea (1:14—2:23; 11:1–9), who still desired relationship even when his wife turned to other lovers. Jesus says that, like a shepherd looking for the very last sheep, God actively pursues every person and will not rest *until* they are won back (Matt 18:10–14). William Willimon comments: "Jesus seeks . . . as long as it takes, . . . not only in life but also in death."[48] God is like a heartsick father anxiously scanning the horizon as he awaits the return of a lost son (Luke 15:11–32); his longing for recon-

---

46. See Wallis, "Ahabh" and Zobel, "Hesed."

47. See Stauffer, "Agape." It might be objected that these passages refer to those in the covenants of Israel and the church. Yet God's indiscriminate love is seen from Jonah's mission to foreign Nineveh to Christ loving gentile sinners, indeed the whole world (John 3:16), enough to die (Rom 5:6–8)—and Scripture explicitly proclaims that God does not want any to perish (2 Pet 3:9) but desires everyone to be saved (1 Tim 2:4).

48. Willimon, *Who Will Be Saved?* 84.

ciliation did not falter when the boy cut off contact and moved far away. As Pope Francis says, "in the parables devoted to mercy, Jesus reveals the nature of God as that of a Father who never gives up until he has forgiven the wrong and overcome rejection with compassion and mercy."[49]

The Lord is compassion and love, and every person rests within the wings of God's embrace, within the gracious care of the One who created them. "You are precious in my sight, and honored, and I love you," God declares (Isa 43:4). All people, living and dead, are bathed in the love that flows from God's friendly heart.[50] Even those who have excluded themselves from God's presence are precious to God, and death does not end God's work for their salvation since "love never gives up [but] keeps going to the end" (1 Cor 13:8, *The Message*).

Theological Reflection Supports Unending Divine Love

There are four questions concerning the availability and extent of salvation.

1. Does God love every person and want them to be saved? Augustinianism says no and non-Augustinianism yes.[51]

2. Is saving grace available outside the Christian church to those who do not hear and believe the gospel? Exclusivism says no and inclusivism yes.

3. Is salvation possible beyond this life for those who die in sin? Closed-death theology (non-escapism) says no and open-death theology (escapism) yes.

4. Will all persons be saved? Separatism says no and universalism yes.

---

49. Pope Francis, "Misericordiae Vultus," in *Name of God is Mercy*, 116.

50. This phrase "God's friendly heart" comes from the film *Luther* (2003). "The love of God exists even for those who are not disposed to receive it," Pope Francis (*Name of God is Mercy*, 17) says; "they are all loved by God, they are sought out by God."

51. Augustinianism (or in Protestant theology, Calvinism) states that while God's providential love is universal, God's saving love is particular; it is restricted to the elect whom God purposed to save and for whom Christ died. Non-Augustinianism (or in Protestant theology, Arminianism) affirms that while God offers salvation to all, we must respond to grace and believe the gospel in order to be saved.

By considering what is wrong with Augustinianism and exclusivism we can also see what is wrong with closed death.

Imagine three scenarios regarding my children. First, if I loved Becky and Sarah but not David then I would not be truly loving. Second, if I loved my daughters completely (meeting their every desire) but loved my son partly (only providing for some of his needs) then I would not be truly loving. Third, if I loved all three, but only until age eighteen (when, having crossed the line from childhood to adulthood, I told them to leave and never come back) then I would not be truly loving. In each case I fall short of full parental love. Perfect love is an essential property that defines the identity of God, not an accidental quality that God just happens to have. God cannot not love perfectly—and so God loves inclusively (all persons are given equal opportunity to be saved), maximally (all persons are given optimal opportunity to be saved), and eternally (persons are given endless opportunity to be saved).

Divine mercy has been the central teaching of Pope Francis' papacy. Mercy is "God's identity card," he says. "Mercy is the first attribute of God. The name of God is mercy." The mercy of God "is God's loving concern for each one of us. God . . . desires our well-being, and . . . wants to see us happy, full of joy and peaceful." Because God is love, God "embraces, . . . welcomes [and] leans down to forgive." God—being compassionate—does not want anyone to be lost, and this means that "we are loved forever despite our sinfulness. . . . Mercy will always be greater than any sin," so "no one can put a limit on the love of the all-forgiving God."[52]

> No one can place a limit on divine mercy because its doors are always open. . . . The mercy of . . . God knows no bounds and extends to everyone, without exception. . . . From the heart of the Trinity . . . the great river of mercy swells up and flows unceasingly. It is a spring that will never run dry . . . because the mercy of God never ends.[53]

No one falls outside God's tender love, ever. Francis imagines this God like a weary mother "exhausting herself with work [in order] to bring home food to her drug-addicted son. She loves him, in spite of his mistakes."[54]

God's goodness cannot allow the predestination of some to damnation and others to salvation—God did not create anyone with a purpose

---

52. Pope Francis, *Name of God is Mercy*, 9, 85, 8–9, 119, 106, and 86.

53. Pope Francis, "Misericordiae Vultus," in *Name of God Is Mercy*, 146–49.

54. Pope Francis, *Name of God is Mercy*, 88.

of misery, but for joy. "How could we even imagine, without grave blasphemy," John Cassian asks, "that God does not want all humans to be saved, but only some instead of all? Should some perish, these would perish against God's will." Christ's superabundant grace "calls everyone without exception" and is "always available."[55] Nor does God's love—which is active benevolent concern that desires and seeks our highest well-being—make salvation depend on hearing the gospel and believing in Christ. Salvation is either found only through explicit belief in the gospel in this life or it is not. If the first disjunct is true, then God demands the impossible—belief in a Jesus of whom many people cannot possibly hear—and so does not really want everyone to be saved. If saving grace is available only to those who encounter the gospel in this life, then—as Karl Rahner says—"the overwhelming mass of [humanity] . . . are . . . excluded from the fulfillment of their lives and condemned to eternal meaninglessness."[56] Believing the gospel is not possible for the unevangelized and so—because God does love all persons and want them to be saved—the second disjunct must be true: grace is available apart from conscious faith in Christ. Put another way, either explicit belief in the gospel is not necessary for salvation (and people can be saved through implicit faith as shown in sincere moral action and religious piety in this life) or, while belief must be explicit, it is not necessary during this life (and people can believe when they are evangelized beyond death).

The perennial heresy, Talbott says, is to limit divine love.[57] Augustinianism and exclusivism deny that God loves inclusively or maximally; they are false because they limit God's love to certain people (the elect or the evangelized), excluding the rest. Closed death denies that God loves eternally; it is false because it limits God's love for sinners to this life but not the next. Just as it is impossible for God to love only some people but not others, so it is impossible for God to love only before a certain time but not after. Time-limited love is simply not perfect love. As Talbott says, "that God should will some good for each [person] during . . . seventy years of life on earth is hardly evidence of love, not when that seventy years is followed by an eternity of separation. . . . The claim that [God] loves a person for a while and then ceases to love that person

---

55. Cassian, cited in Ramelli, *Christian Doctrine of Apokatastasis*, 682–83.

56. Rahner, *Theological Investigations* Vol. 6, 391. See my "Broad Inclusive Salvation."

57. Talbott, *Inescapable Love*, 123. Also see Gulley and Mulholland, *If Grace is True*, 94–103.

makes no sense at all."[58] Augustinianism, exclusivism, and closed death are all equally mistaken: none endorses a perfectly loving God who truly desires the best for all human persons.

The key issue in closed death, as with Augustinianism and exclusivism, concerns the character of God. If God's love is perfect, then it cannot be temporary—which means that death is not an absolute limit on salvation. Rob Bell states sharply that if death is closed then "God becomes somebody totally different the moment you die. . . . A loving heavenly father who will go to extraordinary lengths to have a relationship with [someone] would, in the blink of an eye, become a cruel . . . tormenter who would ensure that they had no escape from an endless future of agony."[59] To make death a deadline when God withdraws grace, Frederick D. Maurice says more measuredly, is to "throw an atmosphere of doubt on the whole question whether God loves God's creatures [and] desires their salvation."[60] Martin Luther flirted with escapism: "God forbid that I should limit the time of acquiring faith to the present life. In the depth of divine mercy there may be opportunity to win it in the future."[61] Even some evangelicals, like Donald Bloesch, accept posthumous salvation as a logical implication of divine love. "God loves all and pursues all into

---

58. Talbott, "Doctrine of Everlasting Punishment," 21 and 26; emphasis in original. Macquarrie (*Christian Hope*, 127) says, "if God is the God of love revealed in Jesus Christ then death will not wipe out God's care for the persons God has created." Lamont ("Justice and Goodness of Hell," 166) thinks that because God is "perfectly loving . . . to every person in need of grace God *at some time* offers that person grace." This, of course, is logically compatible with God cutting grace off at death. Open death requires a stronger claim—"that for every person in need of grace, God *always* offers that person grace"—which Lamont does not think perfect love requires. Lamont's claim that God is "perfectly loving" is inconsistent—however—with his claim that God only offers grace "at some time." The argument I develop in this chapter refutes Lamont's claim and shows why offering grace for a limited time is inconsistent with God being perfectly loving, why time-limited love cannot be perfect love.

59. Bell, *Love Wins*, 173–74, slightly modified. Bell adds: "if God can switch gears like that, switch entire modes of being that quickly, that raises a thousand questions about whether a being like this could ever be trusted, let alone be good. Loving one moment, vicious the next. Kind and compassionate, only to become cruel and relentless in the blink of an eye." Walls (*Purgatory*, 137) concurs: "if God is willing to accept any repentance in this life, one wonders why God would not accept sincere repentance after death, if indeed God truly desires to save all persons." Exclusivism is false because it makes salvation depend on the circumstances of one's birth—and closed death is false because it makes salvation depend on the time of one's death (Walls, *Hell*, 87).

60. Maurice, "Word 'Eternal,'" 17–18.

61. Luther, cited in Bloesch, *Last Things*, 146.

the darkness of ... hell. ... God's love will not let us go—even when we use our freedom to resist this love. The future is open rather than closed, for even beyond ... death God's grace is at work"—and this implies "the possibility of deliverance beyond the grave (post-mortem salvation)."[62]

Let me put the argument in a more philosophical way. Clement of Alexandria claims that "God being *good*, and the Lord *powerful*, God saves with ... an equality which extends to all that turn to God, whether here or elsewhere. For it is not here alone that the active power of God is ..., but it is everywhere and always at work."[63] The argument—based on God's two primary traits—is logically straightforward:

1. God wants to open death (because God is love God desires the salvation of every person, including the dead).
2. God can open death (because God is powerful there is no moral or metaphysical impediment to God offering salvation to the dead).
3. If God wants to open death and can open death, then God does open death.
4. Therefore, God opens death—hell can be escaped.

Statement 3 is obviously true—desire and ability are individually necessary and jointly sufficient conditions for action. If God wants to do something and has the power to do it, then God does it. So if God does not open death, then there are only two possible explanations—either statement 1 is false (God does not want to open death) or statement 2 is false (God is not able to open death). Either answer is troublesome.[64]

---

62. Bloesch, *Last Things*, 240. "Divine perseverance," he says (13; cf. 40), "holds that God in God's love does not abandon any of God's people to perdition but pursues them into the darkness of ... hell, thereby keeping open the opportunity for salvation." "The reality of hell must be taken seriously," he (*Last Things*, 218) insists, "but this is not a hell outside the compass of God's love." Divine "grace can penetrate the barrier of death and reclaim those who are now lost"—and so judgment is not the last word (147); "even when one is in hell one can be forgiven" (227).

63. Clement of Alexandria, *Stromata*, 6.6, 492; slightly modified.

64. What might be called the "problem of closed death"—a version of the problem of evil—plagues traditional theology. As Rowell (*Hell and Victorians*, 125, slightly modified) puts it: if death is closed then either "God ceases to love those whom God once loved" or "the power of sin in the lost is so great that it is capable of defeating the love of God." The problem consists in a trilemma of three contradictory statements.

1. God, being perfectly loving, wants to offer posthumous salvation by making death open.
2. God, being truly powerful, can offer posthumous salvation by making death

Neither respect for human freedom nor the demands of justice require God to close death. Nor is time stronger than God—as Clarence Jordan pointedly says:

> maybe God is in hot pursuit of us; we've been thinking of giving our heart to Christ. We're thinking so hard on it we're driving along and we don't hear the whistle of a freight train. And *bam* . . . it just smashes us to pieces. And God said, "You know, I almost had him. That freight train beat me to him." What kind of a God is that? A God whose purposes can be voided by a freight train?[65]

God has the desire and the ability to offer posthumous salvation—and so death is open.[66]

---

open.

3. God does not offer posthumous salvation but makes death closed.

The three propositions are inconsistent, so we can affirm any two only if we deny the third. *On the one hand*, 2 and 3 are compatible if we deny 1: God is able to offer posthumous salvation but does not want to. Instead, God wants to give dead sinners the punishment they deserve. But—MacDonald (*Evangelical Universalist*, 32) claims—"there is no obvious reason why God would draw the point of no return at death (or anywhere at all). There is, however, a good reason for thinking that God would not—namely, God is loving, gracious, and merciful." *On the other hand*, 1 and 3 are compatible if we deny 2: God wants to offer posthumous salvation but is unable to because of human freedom or the demands of retributive justice. It is hard to see, however, what metaphysical constraint or moral obligation would prevent God from offering grace after death. At death God loses neither the desire nor the power to save the damned. Since 1 and 2 are both true, 3—closed death—is the proposition that should be rejected. Put differently, Augustinianism asserts that God can save all but will not; non-Augustinianism asserts that God wants to save all but cannot; universalism asserts that God wants to and can save all—so will.

65. Jordan, cited in Gulley and Mulholland, *If Grace is True*, 122.

66. Dante (*Purgatorio*, 3.119–23, in *Divine Comedy*, 210–11) claims that God is more generous, not more punitive, than we think. His proof is that repentance of terrible sins in the last seconds of life saves—and his example is Manfred, son of Emperor Frederick II. In his final moments, bleeding to death from wounds sustained in battle—as he tells it—"I gave my soul to God who grants forgiveness willingly. Horrible was the nature of my sins, but boundless mercy stretches out its arms to anyone who comes in search of it." Dante depicts several others who repented late—all of whom demonstrate God's eagerness to accept repentance, no matter how flawed. Reflecting on this, Walls (*Heaven, Hell and Purgatory*, 189–92 and *Purgatory*, 129–37) presses the question: why do seconds count? Why would a loving God always accept repentance at the last possible moment of this life but never accept repentance in the next life? Lewis (*Problem of Pain*, 85) also marvels at God's humility in being willing to accept repentance as a last resort—and Pope Francis (*Name of God is Mercy*, 51 and 29; cf.

Death is not only open—it is *permanently* open. Salvation is a standing offer; God leaves the choice open at every moment after death, so it is never too late to decide for God. Temporarily open death would make salvation a limited-time offer (since at some point God withdraws grace and closes death). The same logic that supports open death requires permanently open death—temporarily open death is no more compatible with perfect divine love than closed death is.[67]

Wrath and Judgment Do Not End Divine Love

Escapists are often accused of not taking human sin and divine wrath seriously. "There is evil and it will pay," an acquaintance once told me; "that's why hell is eternal." This argument, however, assumes a false dilemma: *either* God is hard on sin (and death is closed) *or* death is open (and God is soft on sin). But punishment and love are not mutually exclusive: God can both be hard on sin and leave death open. It simply does not follow that if God punishes sin and if evil will pay, then death is closed and hell inescapable.

A biblical theology must take God's anger at human sin seriously. Hebrew history is filled with harsh judgment—God destroys the world by a flood, burns Sodom with fire, kills Nadab and Abihu for false sacrifice, allows adversity after entry into Canaan, punishes King David's adultery and sends Israel into exile. In the early church Ananias and Sapphira die because of their sin (Acts 5:1–11). The prophets predict the "Day of the Lord" when God will judge Israel and the nations (e.g., Amos 5:18–20). Jesus warns his hearers to "flee from the wrath to come" (Matt 3:7; cf. John 3:36) and gives vivid descriptions of exclusion from God's kingdom in *gehenna* (Mark 9:43–48; Matt 8:12). St. Paul declares that "the wrath of God comes on those who are disobedient" (Eph 5:6; cf. Rom 1:18)—they "will suffer the punishment of eternal destruction" (2 Thess 1:9). St. John's apocalyptic vision depicts judgment where evildoers are "thrown into the lake of fire" (Rev 20:15; cf. 14:10–11).

---

xix and 34) argues that God is "ready to welcome any person who takes a step or even expresses the desire to take a step that leads home." God is "looking for the smallest opening."

67. See Appendix Note 4 for additional defense of permanently open death.

Divine anger is not only real—it is good.[68] God is committed to setting the world right, and this means eliminating evil and injustice. Bell puts it well: "when we hear people saying they can't believe in a God who gets angry—yes they can. How should God react to a child being forced into prostitution? How should God feel about a country starving while warlords hoard their food supply? What kind of God wouldn't get angry at a financial scheme that robs thousands of people of their life savings?"[69] Wright observes that

> throughout the Bible ... God's coming judgment is a good thing, something to be celebrated, longed for, yearned over [e.g., Ps 98: 9–10].... In a world of systematic injustice, bullying, violence, arrogance and oppression, the thought that there might come a day when the wicked are firmly put in their place and the poor and weak are given their due is the best news there can be. Faced with a world in rebellion, a world full of exploitation and wickedness, a good God *must* be a God of judgment.[70]

---

68. Divine wrath, Marshall (*Beyond Retribution*, 171 and 173) says, "designates God's fervent reaction to human wickedness. God's refusal to tolerate, compromise with or indulge evil ... is not a ... case of ill temper on God's part but a measured commitment to act against evil and injustice in order to contain it and destroy it." Without anger, Tasker ("Wrath," 1341) states, "God would cease to be fully righteous and God's love would degenerate into sentimentality."

69. Bell, *Love Wins*, 38. He adds: "every oil spill, every report of another woman sexually assaulted, every news report that another political leader has silenced the opposition through torture, imprisonment and execution, every time we see someone stepped on by an institution or corporation more interested in profit than people ..., we shake our fist and cry out 'Will somebody please do something about this?'" I am always struck that after the public reading of lessons like Amos 8:4–7 (where God promises judgment on those oppressing the needy) or Psalm 7:1–10 (which calls God to rise up in wrath), the congregation responds "thanks be to God." Ramelli (*Christian Doctrine of Apokatastasis*, 705–6) points out that the church fathers who supported universal salvation also warned that sinners will receive the punishment they deserve. Due retribution, however, does not preclude or contradict eventual salvation.

70. Wright, *Surprised by Hope*, 137, emphasis added. "The Psalms and the prophets," Lewis (*Reflection on Psalms*, 9–11) points out, "are full of the longing for judgment, and regard the announcement that 'judgment' is coming as good news.... They look forward to 'judgment' because ... they have been wronged and hope to see their wrongs righted." The righteous cry "how long?" as they await justice (Ps 35:17; Hab 1:2; Luke 18:1–8; Rev 6:10). Reversal is the joyful theme of Mary's song of praise (Luke 1:50–53).

Evil must be defeated before God's purposes can be realized—and so, Stephen Davis says, "the wrath of God is our only hope."[71]

We must not, however, separate divine justice from divine love. Since God's nature is love, everything God does—including anger and punishment—flows from love. Peter Kreeft and Ronald Tacelli point out that "Scripture never says 'God is justice,' but it does say 'God is love.'" Love is more primordial than justice—"love is God's essence, justice is one of its works."[72] "God's mercy and justice are not distinct attributes that... push God in opposite directions, thereby creating a conflict within God," Talbott emphasizes. "To the contrary, God has but one moral attribute and that is loving-kindness—[and] mercy and justice are different expressions of the one attribute."[73] Pope Francis agrees: "mercy is not opposed to justice but rather expresses God's way of reaching out to the sinner, offering them a new chance to ... convert and believe." Indeed, "God's justice is God's mercy."[74] Judgment is how love shows itself if it is rejected. Consider the history recounted in 2 Chronicles 36:14–23.[75] Israel, having been called into relationship with Yahweh, was "exceedingly unfaithful." In response, God "sent persistently to them by his messengers, because he had compassion on his people." When Israel still refused God's love, "the wrath of the Lord... became so great that there was no remedy." The people were taken captive and the temple destroyed. God's love, however, is not suspended or withdrawn—and judgment is followed by restoration. Cyrus the Persian returns the exiles to Jerusalem and rebuilds the temple.

Since God's call to salvation is present in judgment, hell is not retributive (vengeful punishment meant to give sinners their just deserts)

---

71. Davis, "Hell, Wrath and Grace of God," 92.

72. Kreeft and Tacelli, *Handbook of Apologetics*, 292.

73. Talbott, *Inescapable Love*, 146 and 117–18, slightly modified); cf. 71–72 and 106. For more on the relationship of justice and love and biblical conceptions of justice see Appendix Note 5.

74. Pope Francis, "Misericordiae Vultus," in *Name of God is Mercy*, 141. He adds (78–80; cf. 119–20 and 142–43) that "with mercy and forgiveness, God goes beyond justice, God subsumes it and succeeds it in a higher event in which we experience love." The fact that mercy surpasses justice is seen in the message of the prophet Hosea (11:5–9). "When there is mercy, justice is more just, and it fulfills its true essence. This does not mean that we should ... let those who have committed serious crimes loose. It means that we have to help those who have fallen to get back up." The goal is rehabilitation, not retribution.

75. See Barron, "*Hesed* All the Way Through."

but corrective (healing punishment meant to reform them).[76] In Hebrew Scripture the word *chēmā* (translated "wrath") derives from a stem meaning "fire" or "burning." "*Chema* is not permanent," Thiselton notes, "it can be 'turned away.' . . . Although it often brings punishment . . . it may also have a remedial purpose."[77] In Christian Scripture the word *kolasis* ("punishment"—Matt 25:46; 2 Pet 2:9; 1 John 4:18) indicates that the goal of hell is corrective. The word is an agricultural term which means to prune the branches of a tree so it can flourish; it "is never used," William Barclay says, "of anything but remedial punishment."[78] Since God strikes in order to heal (Isa 19:22), God's wrath is a saving wrath, and so hell is not an end but a means to an end—salvation. Many in the ancient church saw post-mortem punishment as—in Clement of Alexandria's words—"salvific justice." All early supporters of posthumous salvation agreed on the necessity of punishment first; evil will be punished, but these punishments are educative, rather than retributive. Only after punishment,

---

76. Travis (*Christ and Judgment*, 8) says that "the emphasis on restorative justice is not on 'paying back' the offender, but on positively 'putting right' what has gone wrong between the offender and the victim." Nussbaum ("Transitional Anger") argues that retribution makes no sense, since inflicting pain on an offender does not constructively address the victim's injury. Doing something unwelcome to a perpetrator as payback does not set wrong right—it does not bring dead people back to life, heal broken limbs or undo sexual violations. The retaliatory project—striking back and injuring an offender—does not take away the injury of the victim. It does not counterbalance, reverse or annul the harm, it does not cancel or repair the damage. The idea that payback restores is a fantasy. This does not mean that punishment is useless, but it does mean that the goal of punishment must not be retributive but reformative—that aims at improving the offender and thereby vindicating the victim.

77. Thiselton, *Life After Death*, 159–60. Also see Fensham, "Crime and Punishment." The Hebrew word stem *slm* means "to compensate" or "to restore the balance." The stem *ykh* can refer to punishment, but its usual meaning is "to reprove." The stem *ysr* can be used for legal punishment also has the sense of educational instruction and parental correction. The stem *nqm* when used of punishment inflicted by God on the wicked, means "to vindicate."

78. Barclay, cited in Talbott, *Inescapable Love*, 91. In Christian Scripture the only words that clearly mean punishment are *timoria* and *kolasis*; *timoria* is synonymous with *kolasis*, the usual word for punishment (Matt 25:46; Acts 4:21; 22:5; 26:11; Heb 10:29; 2 Pet 2:9; 1 John 4:18). Schneider ("Kolazo, Kolasis," 814) says that *kolasis* means to cut short, to lop off, to trim—with the purpose of fostering growth. Also see Talbott, "Pauline Interpretation," 47 and Fensham, "Crime and Punishment." It is true that in classical Greek *kolasis* is used to refer to corrective punishment, but by the time of Jesus its usage is less straightforward. The Septuagint uses it as a generic word for punishment—so the word may, but need not, suggest corrective punishment. Thanks to my editor Robin Parry for pointing this out to me.

indeed only through it, can salvation come. They believed punishment will have an end, not that it will not take place—they denied its eternity, not its reality. Once the evil in a person is destroyed, they are restored to God. Open death and posthumous salvation, then, do not contradict deserved justice and punishment.[79]

God's judgment saves both victims and perpetrators. As Jürgen Moltmann says, it "brings justice for the victims and puts the perpetrators right. . . . The victims of sin and violence will receive justice. They will be raised up, put right, healed and brought into life. The perpetrators of sin and violence will receive a justice which transforms and rectifies."[80] Victims are freed from evil suffered—they are vindicated and restored; perpetrators are freed from evil committed—they are forgiven and transformed.

The fact that God judges in order to save means that judgment is penultimate rather than final. Scripture confirms this. "His anger is but for a moment; his favor is for a lifetime" (Ps 30:5). "For a brief moment I abandoned you, but with great compassion I will gather you. In overflowing wrath for a moment I hid my face from you, but with everlasting love I will have compassion on you" (Isa 54:7–8). "You shall no more be termed Forsaken, and your land shall no more be termed Desolate; but you shall be called My Delight Is In Her, and your land Married" (Isa 62:4). "The Lord will not reject forever. Although he causes grief, he will have compassion according to the abundance of his steadfast love" (Lam 3:31–33). Forgiveness is the defining trait that distinguishes *Yahweh* from the other gods: "who is a God like you, pardoning iniquity and passing over . . . transgression . . . ? He does not retain his anger forever, because he delights in showing clemency" (Mic 7:18). "You are a gracious God and merciful, slow to anger, and abounding in steadfast love, and ready to relent from punishing" (Jonah 4:2; cf. Exod 34:6–7; Ps 103:8–9; Joel 2:13). The prophet Hosea pictures God, not as a harsh judge, but as a parent who cannot let go of a wayward child. Having pronounced sentence (11:5–7), God draws back—"how can I give you up, Ephraim? How can I

---

79. See Ramelli, *Christian Doctrine of Apokatastasis*, 543 and 556. Saying that sinners will be punished after death does not mean saying they will be punished eternally. Pseudo-Dionysius (cited at 705), in encouraging prayer for the dead, tells priests *not* to pray that the wicked not receive punishment, *but* that after punishment they enter heaven. See Alfeyev ("Eschatology," 116–18) on Isaac the Syrian's teaching concerning universal salvation through punishment. See Appendix Note 5 for more on ancient church views of punishment.

80. Moltmann, *Sun of Righteousness*, 137. Also see *In the End*, 53, 56, 61, and 68.

hand you over, O Israel? . . . My heart recoils within me; my compassion grows warm and tender. I will not execute my fierce anger . . . and I will not come in wrath" (11:8–9). Throughout the Bible we see this pattern of reversal—judgment followed by salvation. Israel was exiled but then returned to the land—"He who scattered Israel will gather him" (Jer 31:10; cf. Mic 3:9–4:5). The nations will be destroyed and then saved—even the evil city Sodom (Ezek 16:53–55) and Israel's enemies Egypt and Assyria (Isa 19:16–25; 34:1–4; 45:20–25) are restored. God has cut Israel off in order to produce repentance, after which it will be grafted back in (Rom 9–11)—and eschatological punishment of the nations (Rev 20:10–15) is followed by restoration (21:24–27).[81] We can infer from these texts that the unsaved dead are still fiercely loved by God and that punishment is not God's final purpose.

"The road to mercy leads through the judgment," Jan Bonda says. "God has not imprisoned [the unsaved] . . . with the intention of leaving them in that state, but rather of leading them back to obedience and to be merciful to them."[82] Allen Verhey agrees: "the world will not be put right without judgment. But on the far side of that judgment the mercy of God will restore and renew 'all things.'"[83] Because posthumous salvation occurs through judgment, not apart from it, escapists do not minimize the gravity of human sin and the necessity of divine justice. They do not ignore the 'hard virtues' of holiness, justice and punishment in favor of the 'soft virtues' of love, mercy and forgiveness.[84]

The Unending Human Freedom Requirement

God's love continues past death—but this fact by itself is not sufficient for posthumous salvation. For that, a second condition is necessary:

---

81. For detailed discussion see MacDonald, *Evangelical Universalist*, chapters 3, 4, and 5.

82. Bonda, *One Purpose of God*, 193.

83. Verhey, *Christian Art of Dying*, 200; slightly modified.

84. The language of hard and soft virtues comes from Habermas and Moreland, *Beyond Death*, 287. Origen, who believes in universal salvation, acknowledges that God may need to use drastic remedies to heal sinners. This is not done "out of hatred for the wicked, returning them evil for evil in retribution"—he says—but "the rage of God's vengeance aims at purifying souls" (cited in Ramelli, *Christian Doctrine of Apokatastasis*, 186–88). See Appendix Note 6 for why it is the other way around—why those who believe in eternal hell are the ones who water down the gravity of judgment, ending up with a trite and tame hell.

human freedom must also continue past death. Since "the doors of hell are locked on the inside," as C. S. Lewis says, the unsaved can choose to repent or not—and those who do leave hell.[85]

Human freedom can be understood in two ways. *Compatiblism* holds that a person's action is free if it is caused by their own beliefs and desires and not by some form of external control. Actions can be determined by prior causes yet still be free. *Libertarianism* defines an action as free if the person can either do or not do it, if they can make a different choice than the one they actually make. Freedom means being able to choose between genuine alternatives—and what a person decides is not predetermined. When we are free we choose based on reasons—the mind determines what is good and the will follows it. We cannot choose what we have no reason to choose and we will choose what we have every reason to choose.[86] A choice view of hell assumes libertarian freedom—and libertarian freedom requires various conditions. First, competence—an ability to understand information, deliberate alternatives, and choose a course of action. Second, knowledge—facts about available options and the consequences of each. Third, voluntariness—absence of force from both external factors (such as other people) and internal factors (such as disabling emotional states).[87] Roman Catholic theology teaches that mortal sins—which separate us from God eternally—must meet three

---

85. Lewis, *Problem of Pain*, 115. Lewis allegorizes escapism in *Great Divorce*: from hell the unsaved take day excursions by bus to the border of heaven—where they can stay if they are willing to forgo their sins.

86. Kronen and Reitan (*God's Final Victory*, 132–36) call this rational freedom—and see it as an alternative to compatiblism and libertarianism. Our freedom is libertarian—involving the ability to choose other than we do—only when conflicting motives pull us in different directions. But when we have uniform motives—every reason to do an action and no reason not to—then that choice becomes inevitable and other choices impossible (in which case rational freedom is compatiblistic). I treat "rational freedom" as a species of libertarian freedom. Smith (*Imagining the Kingdom*, 79–84) sees the concept of habit as a way to avoid both libertarian freedom and mechanical determinism. "I'm not an unconstrained 'free' creature 'without inertia'; neither am I the passive victim of external causes and determining forces." Instead, my choices are influenced by unconscious dispositions that have become second nature to me.

87. In order to be responsible for an action, Washburn (*Philosophical Dilemmas*, 312–13) says, four factors are necessary: 1. cause (a person's action causes something to happen); 2. intention (a person means to do the thing in question, they do it on purpose); 3. sanity (a person is able to understand the nature of what they are doing); and 4. free choice (a person is not forced to act as they do). It can be difficult to know whether the factors are present or not—but if any one is missing, then the person is not responsible but has an excuse.

conditions, each of which is necessary. First, its object must be a grave violation of God's law (as specified in the Ten Commandments, for example). Second, it must be done with full knowledge of the sinful character of the act, of its opposition to God's law. Third, the sin must be committed with deliberate consent, as a conscious personal choice of evil. Someone is guilty of mortal sin, then, when they fully consent with their will to do what they consciously realize is a serious offence to God.[88] While pseudo-choice can occur under conditions of impairment, deception, and compulsion, genuine choice requires full mental abilities, truthful knowledge, and no controlling influence.[89]

Traditional theology asserts that, even if posthumous grace is offered, the unsaved cannot respond because freedom ends at death when the will is confirmed in good or evil. "Beyond death no more decisions altering the course of one's existence can be made," Ladislaus Boros says. "Death makes human decisions irrevocable. One's decision as concerning God now becomes final, permanent, unchangeable."[90] Two reasons—both flawed—are given for thinking that the will of the unsaved dead is fixed in sin and can no longer repent.[91]

---

88. See Roman Catholic Church, *Catechism of Catholic Church*, Sections 1857–60, 455. We lose the possibility of communion with God, O'Callaghan (*Christ Our Hope*, 184) says, if we sin in a "clear-minded" and "responsible" way.

89. The degree of competence, knowledge, and voluntariness required varies with the amount of risk the decision involves—and so a high degree of risk such as eternal damnation requires a high level of freedom.

90. Boros, cited in Hick, *Death and Eternal Life*, 236. Some scholars claim that our fundamental option, the choice for or against God, is the culmination of small decisions continuously made across our entire life—while others assert that in the act of dying a person determines their eternal destiny once and for all. Boros' final option theory is a synthesis of open and closed death. We are given a final opportunity for salvation *at* death (when we encounter Christ, gain full knowledge of the truth and irrevocably decide our eternal fate), but no chance for repentance *after* death. Even those who have lived a life without faith can be saved at the last moment when the final choice is presented. See Hick, *Death and Eternal Life*, chapter 12; La Due, *Trinity Guide*, 57–61; O'Callaghan, *Christ Our Hope*, 267–69; Sanders, *No Other Name*, 164–67.

91. For two metaphysical arguments for why human freedom ends at death see Appendix Note 7.

The Decisive Earthly Choice Argument for Lost Freedom

People have the chance to choose salvation *before* death—a common argument goes—and thus lose their freedom to do so *at* death. Bradley Sickler claims that "God [has] given everyone, even the most remote tribes, enough light to see that God exists, and to see . . . the sort of life God calls them to. What they have is short of the full revelation of God in Jesus Christ, but it is enough to make an informed choice between living with God or apart from God."[92] Freedom ends at death, John Lamont argues, because the unsaved make their moral intentions clear when they sin "with full knowledge [of the mind] and consent of the will."[93] James Cain agrees: death is closed "for anyone who in this lifetime is capable of fully functioning as a genuine moral agent"—who freely and knowingly chooses to live apart from God.[94]

The decisive earthly choice argument is unsound since its premise—every person in this life has the opportunity necessary for choosing their eternal destiny—is not plausible.[95] Damnation requires a *decisive* choice against God, Walls says. Such "a choice [is] made with deliberation and

---

92. Sickler, "Infernal Voluntarism," 165 and 171. Murray ("Heaven and Hell") claims that God makes it perfectly clear to all persons that the purpose of life is to become lovers of God rather than lovers of self. Everyone—even those who do not hear the gospel—has, through general revelation, sufficient knowledge for salvation.

93. Lamont, "Justice and Goodness of Hell," 161 and 167–68. A single unrepented sin "constitutes the rejection of friendship with God" and "produces a permanent attachment to evil. . . . Those souls who die with a will attached to sin continue in their attachment to sin forever."

94. Cain, "Why I am Unconvinced," 135. Davis ("Hell, Wrath and Grace of God," 102) holds that while death may be open for some, there is no "'second chance' for those who have freely and knowingly chosen to live apart from God."

95. Jesus himself acknowledges this: Tyre and Sidon would have repented had they had the evidence provided to Chorazin and Bethsaida (Matt 11:21). *Exclusivists* cannot plausibly claim that all have opportunity to believe the gospel—many live in times and places where they cannot hear, and infants, children, and people with developmental disabilities are unable to respond. Sickler ("Infernal Voluntarism," 164) admits that "anyone who believes heaven is only accessible to those who have heard and responded to the gospel of Jesus Christ must also believe that untold millions—even billions—of people will die without even a chance at salvation." Nor is it at all plausible that those who have not heard would not have believed even if they had. (That Molinist "solution" to the problem of damnation is offered by Craig, "No Other Name." For more on Molinism and salvation, see Appendix Note 8.) Even *inclusivists*—who allow that salvation does not require conscious faith in Christ—cannot realistically think that all who live sinful rather than righteous lives had a full opportunity, through their moral actions, to choose for or against God.

understanding of what is involved."[96] This requires optimal conditions—that grace is offered in such a way that the person has every possible opportunity to repent. "A negative response to God is decisive only if one persists in rejecting God in the most favorable circumstances."[97] In this life, however, sinners are in unfavorable circumstances. No one freely and knowingly, clear-mindedly and responsibly, chooses damnation; refusal of God is due, instead, to impairment, ignorance, and bondage.[98]

Choice against God in this life does not meet the competence requirement. Human freedom resembles that of immature children, not that of mature adults. Because our freedom is impaired, Marilyn Adams contends, we are "no more competent to be entrusted with our . . . eternal destiny than a two year old . . . is to be allowed choices that could result

---

96. Walls, "Eternal Hell and Christian Concept of God," 274. The argument is simple:

1. Because God is loving, all persons receive optimal grace (God does all God can do to save them short of overriding their freewill).
2. Some do not receive optimal grace in this life.
3. Therefore, some receive optimal grace in the next life (death is open and posthumous salvation is possible).

Punt (*So Also in Christ*, 60–61 and 83) agrees that only those who consciously, willingly, and obstinately refuse revelation in the gospel, creation, and conscience are lost.

97. Walls, *Hell*, 89–90. It is "a settled response which is made by one fully informed of the Christian faith. Such a response would not be haphazard, superficial or prone to change in shifting circumstances or with awareness of new information. Such a response could be described as a rooted disposition." Also see *Heaven, Hell and Purgatory*, 199–203 and 208–11. Geach (*Virtues*, 45–46), too, rejects the idea that someone "can fail to achieve their last end by force of circumstances, through no fault of their own. . . . The teaching of faith is that every person has a genuine chance of a salvation—sufficient grace, in theological jargon—and nobody is forced to miss his last end" through situations beyond their control.

98. Lewis (*Screwtape Letters*, 49, 54–56) suggests that ordinary sinners proceed to hell without great crimes. Through a series of trivial choices people "however slowly, head right away from the sun on a line which will carry them into the cold and dark." The "sleeping worms" of gradual decay cause sinners to become "weak and fuddled." The senior devil advises the junior: "you will say that these are very small sins; and doubtless, like all young tempters, you are anxious to be able to report spectacular wickedness. But do remember, the only thing that matters is the extent to which you separate the [person] from [God]. It does not matter how small the sins are, provided that their cumulative effect is to move the [person] away from the Light and out into the Nothing. Murder is no better than cards if cards can do the trick. Indeed, the safest road to hell is the gradual one—the gentle slope, soft underfoot, without sudden turnings, without milestones, without signposts."

in death or serious physical impairment." A loving mother would not let her child put his hand in a fire out of respect for the child's "free will."[99]

Nor does rejection of God meet the knowledge and voluntariness requirements. Augustine emphasizes that "we sin from two causes: either from not seeing what we ought to do, or else from not doing what we have already seen we ought to do. Of these two, the first is ignorance of the evil; the second, weakness."[100] People seldom choose wrong for the sake of wrong; instead, they think they are doing good or they yield to powerful temptation. All practical decisions, Plato says, are determined by beliefs about what is good. A person who concludes that a particular action is best will do it, so when we choose wrong we do so believing it somehow to be good.[101] Wrong choices are due to ignorance. They are also due to weakness of will. A person who lacks self-control, Aristotle says, is unable to do the good they know they should do. Although they understand right from wrong, distorted desires, strong passions, and entrenched habits defeat their willpower and better judgment.[102] Sinners are unfree in both ways; they seldom, if ever, function as genuine moral agents choosing with full knowledge of the mind and consent of the will.

99. Adams, "Problem of Hell," 313 and Murray, "Heaven and Hell," 312. Also see Walls, *Heaven, Hell and Purgatory*, 75. Because sinners are not competent, their "choices" can be overridden by God for their own good, Adams says.

100. Augustine, *Enchiridion*, 22.81. "Sin . . . breeds sin," Lewis (*Problem of Pain*, 104) states, "by strengthening sinful habit and weakening the conscience." "Nonsense in the intellect" and "corruption in the will"—he adds (*Screwtape Letters*, 118), are the roots of sin.

101. Ethical intellectualism is the view that evil is chosen due to faulty evaluation—we do bad because it looks attractive and is thought to be good. "Men err," Plato says in *Protagoras* (357d and 358d, 185–86), "in their choice of good and evil, from defect of knowledge," and thus "no man voluntarily pursues . . . that which he thinks to be evil." Aristotle (*Nicomachean Ethics* 1147a12–18, 104) agrees that strong temptation can make a person unable to think straight and may even drive deep convictions from conscious awareness. Wrongdoing is the result of ignorance and deception; because it is caused by mistaken judgment, it is not free. See Ramelli, *Christian Doctrine of Apokatastasis*, 123 and 387–88.

102. A weak person, Aristotle (*Nicomachean Ethics* 1150b20–1151a21, 110–11) says, lacks self-control and is unable to do the good that they know they should do. Plato (*Republic* 590c, 262) agrees that in some people "the best part of [the] soul is naturally weak and cannot rule the animals within." We sin because our wills are enslaved by passions—and so wrongdoing is not free. Sinful choice, Willard (*Divine Conspiracy*, 341) says, is the result of "patterns of wrongdoing . . . that govern our lives because of our long habituation to a world alienated from God." This is the "indwelling sin"—the automatic responses of thinking, feeling, and acting—described by St. Paul (Rom 7:17) that makes us "slaves of sin" (John 8:34; Rom 6:16).

Decisive choice against God in this life is not possible because of these salvation inhibitors.[103] *Ignorance* (being blinded by the god of this world—2 Cor 4:4) confuses our knowledge of the good so we act in self-deception and illusion. Those who reject God do so in ignorance of both where true happiness lies and of the awful nature of separation from God. Because "hell is a horror inconceivable to those who choose it," Charles Seymour says, "we are not really choosing hell when we reject God in this life, for we have no clear idea what hell is like."[104] Raymond VanArragon agrees: "an appropriate degree of knowledge and awareness is a necessary condition for free choice; but it seems doubtful that anyone who chooses to close the door on God forever will have a sufficient grasp of what she is rejecting, and even more doubtful that she could appropriately comprehend the monumental character of her choice."[105] *Weakness* (being slaves to sin—Rom 6:16) impairs our ability to choose the good; instead, we act in the grip of social forces and personal habits we cannot control. Rejection of God, Clement of Alexandria claims, does not arise out of a free will but from an enslaved will, one that is immersed in sinful passions. A person can become, Richard Swinburne says, "so mastered by his desires that he loses all ability to resist them." Rejection of God in this life, then, is caused by faulty beliefs (which misrepresent alternatives) and by faulty desires (which control choices)—and so is not genuinely free.[106]

We must not, MacDonald warns, "overplay human hostility toward God."[107] Most sinners are not hardened rebels who consciously reject God; instead, they are too caught up in other things to care about God. Sinners misjudge sin to be good—a way of creating a happy life, of satisfying the restlessness they feel as spiritual beings. "The man at the brothel door," G. K. Chesterton observes, "is looking for God"—his action is rooted in restlessness (he is on a spiritual quest, attempting to overcome loneliness), not rebellion (he is not inwardly shaking his fist at God).[108]

---

103. This term comes from Kronen and Reitan, *God's Final Victory*, 142.

104. Seymour, *Theodicy of Hell*, 136. Lewis (*Screwtape Letters*, 13) says that while everything is "hazy" in the mind now, hell provides a "peculiar kind of clarity."

105. VanArragon, "Is it Possible to Freely Reject God Forever?" 32.

106. Clement, cited in Ramelli, *Christian Doctrine of Apokatastasis*, 123; Swinburne, "Theodicy of Heaven and Hell," 48–49, slightly modified and Kronen and Reitan, *God's Final Victory*, 133–34.

107. MacDonald, *Evangelical Universalist*, 165.

108. Chesterton, cited in Mouw, *Distorted Truth*, 46. Sinners are—to use a word from my evangelical youth—"lost." It is a good description. They do not know where

Sinning is a largely automatic response that happens without reflection, that does not—Dallas Willard says—"run through our conscious mind or deliberative will. . . . It is rare that what we do wrong is the result of careful deliberation" and intentional choice. Instead, "habits are the primary form in which human evil exists in practical life."[109] Scripture portrays even the most extreme acts—the crucifixion of Jesus ("they do not know what they are doing"—Luke 23:34) and Saul's violent persecution of the church ("I . . . acted ignorantly in unbelief"—1 Tim 1:13)—as sins of ignorance rather than intentional wickedness.[110] Thiselton points out that—given the social context of individual choice—sinners are victims, not free choosers.

> Humans may be imprisoned by their historical finitude. . . . Society and their situation in history have foreclosed certain options. A thoroughly "rationalist" or evidentially "scientific" society may make Christian belief more difficult, and this becomes . . . a force of oppression. . . . To be born outside of the heritage of the Christian Church or a Christian family is thereby to be exposed to the dominating and oppressive structures of "principalities and powers," whether in the form of aggressive secularism or religious paganism. . . . Humankind is more like oppressed victims than those who freely choose to do . . . evil acts.[111]

Moltmann agrees that freedom operates "only 'with limited liability' and greatly 'diminished responsibility'"—"inner forces and outward circumstances . . . make . . . people the slaves of evil," individuals "who are bound to do what they do without any freedom of their own."[112]

---

they are going; instead of being hostile and opposed to God, they are neither for nor against God.

109. Willard, *Divine Conspiracy*, 343–44. As my colleague Timothy Linehan (who reminded me of Willard's writing) rhetorically asks, "when was the last time you consciously, deliberately, decided to sin?" We rarely do wrong as a result of careful thought; instead, we sin as a matter of routine behavior.

110. The goats in Jesus' parable of judgment (Matt 25:44) are surprised at the verdict of condemnation—as are those who say "Lord, Lord," expecting a favorable reception but receiving judgment (Matt 7:21–23).

111. Thistleton, *Life After Death*, 182.

112. Moltmann, *In the End*, 58–59 and 72. Ciurria ("Moral Responsibility") argues that "moral responsibility ain't just in the head." She rejects psychological internalism (the idea that moral responsibility is determined solely or primarily by internal intentional states) in favor of psychological externalism (the idea that moral responsibility depends largely on historical and environmental factors). Pope Francis (*Name of God*

It is not possible to decisively reject God in this life since earthly choices do not meet the conditions of genuine freedom. Therefore, Karl Rahner says, we should not think "that with the death of a person . . . freedom is . . . inevitably at an end." Instead, there are "opportunities and scope for . . . post-mortal . . . freedom to someone who had been denied [it] in . . . earthly life."[113] We might, in fact, turn the traditional argument backwards. For many individuals the afterlife, instead of ending freedom will bring freedom for the first time. Only after death, when their minds are enlightened and their wills liberated from sinful passions, are the unsaved free.[114]

But even if all persons *do* have a full opportunity for salvation, why assume that they are given only one opportunity—this life? Perhaps to make earthly life significant, to encourage moral rigor. Closed death gives urgency and meaning to our choices here and now since this is the only time when we can respond to God. As the Roman Catholic theological commission puts it, "since we have only one lifetime in which the gift of divine friendship . . . is offered . . . , the serious nature of our life is obvious. Decisions we make now have eternal consequences."[115] Gary Habermas and James Moreland agree: eternal hell means that "our choices really matter. They affect us . . . in this life and beyond."[116] Open death—by contrast—encourages moral laxity; if individuals can repent after death, then there is no need to believe and live an upright life now. Because

---

is Mercy, 72) agrees that sin is often due to external life circumstance.

113. Rahner, *Theological Investigations*, Vol. 19, 190–93. Many have "never reached finality as a result of self-fulfillment in freedom"; there exist "human beings for whom there is not an absolute decision for or against God in a particular life" (181).

114. See Thistleton, *Life After Death*, 183. Also see Sanders, *No Other Name*, 193–94. In hell sinners are illuminated from minds blinded by deception and healed from wills enslaved to passions. Instruction develops minds that know God and liberation creates wills that love God; the result is that all sinners voluntarily and freely choose God in the end. This analysis has roots far back in ancient Christianity (see Ramelli, *Christian Doctrine of Apokatastasis*, 365, 425, 502, and 823).

115. International Theological Commission, "Some Current Questions," 236. Ancient supporters of universal salvation worried about encouraging moral laxity. Some, such as Origen, kept it secret, only teaching it to the spiritually mature in order to prevent sloth—others, like Gregory of Nyssa, with the aim of diverting people from sin, emphasize how terrible and long post-mortem punishment can be. Justinian's motivation for condemning the salvation of all is pastoral—since those who preach it "make people lazy in fulfilling God's commandments." See Ramelli, *Christian Doctrine of Apokatastasis*, 70, 434 and 730–31.

116. Habermas and Moreland, *Beyond Death*, 293.

choices build character and turn us into certain types of persons—however—there is an intrinsic relationship between our actions in this life and our destiny in the next. Posthumous salvation, while possible, is not easy or automatic. "The more we sin and persist in our rebellion," Walls says, "the more complicated will be our repentance"—and so the possibility of reversing decisions in the next life "does not trivialize this life and make it insignificant."[117] In addition, he points out, if *post-mortem* repentance trivializes this life then so does *deathbed* repentance. If we can delay salvation until the last moment of life—which all Christians allow—this, too, makes previous choices less serious.[118]

"The fragile and . . . shadowy freedom we know during earthly life"—to use Joseph Ratzinger's words—"is too feeble and limited to support the weight of an everlasting and irreversible destiny."[119] Even if the unsaved do have a full chance for salvation in this life it does not follow that they have no further chances in the next. That my grounded daughter could leave her room before seven o'clock, when dinner is served, does not mean she cannot come out at eight o'clock for desert. There is no *logical* connection between 1. full freedom before death and 2. no freedom after death. Perhaps, though, there is a *psychological* connection. Sin, Paul O'Callaghan says, "hardens with time, in such a way that the one who commits it becomes closed to repentance, and eventually becomes virtually incapable of it."[120] I now consider that argument.

---

117. Walls, *Purgatory*, 147. Lewis (*Mere Christianity*, 117) says that "good and evil both increase at compound interest. That is why the little decisions you and I make every day are of such infinite importance." Hick (*Death and Eternal Life*, 456) says that the fact that our choices have urgency "does not . . . necessitate the doctrine of one short life followed by an eternity in heaven or hell."

118. Walls, *Heaven, Hell and Purgatory*, 194. This also refutes Boros' final option theory—that those who have lived a life without faith can be saved when they encounter Christ in the moment of death.

119. Ratzinger, *Eschatology*, 208. Ratzinger is here citing the views of others, such as Boros and Rahner, not affirming this as his own opinion.

120. O'Callaghan, *Christ Our Hope*, 213. Swinburne (*Providence and Problem of Evil*, 143 and 145) says that "we are so made that we gradually form our characters—either so that we become naturally good (prone to do the good . . .) or so that we naturally yield to bad desires such that they acquire permanent mastery over us." We have the ability to "mould our characters so as to fix them permanently" including "so immunizing ourselves to any moral influence that we no longer have the possibility of forming a good character . . . , lose the power to choose between alternatives . . . [and] are no longer able to choose . . . the good of the beatific vision."

The Hardened Character Argument for Lost Freedom

Habermas and Moreland state that

> character is shaped moment by moment, day by day, in the thousands of little choices we make. Every day our character is increasingly formed, and in each choice we make we either move toward God or away from God. As our character grows, some choices become possible and others impossible. The longer one lives in opposition to God . . . the harder it is to choose to turn that around.[121]

When a person's character has become engulfed by sin, change is practically impossible.

Choices over time make us into certain kinds of persons, and as habit-formers we are able to destroy our own freedom. Sinning blinds our minds and enslaves our wills; as we become set in our ways we narrow the range of choices open to us and find ourselves with fewer options—finally forming characters that no longer desire God and from which freedom has been eliminated. "There is continuity forming in the life of each person," Walls says, and "those who remain in sin come increasingly to be in its power." As "we move further and further from God we become more and more hardened in sin" and "less and less likely to repent and be reconciled to God."[122] Once "evil is present through and through a personality, and there is no place left for good even to get a foothold," then—even if God leaves death salvation-open—a person is not free to choose it. "Evil gains sufficient potency that the possibility of repentance is all but foreclosed." Such a person is "thoroughly immune to the grace of God" and, since their character is firmly fixed and frozen in sin, cannot repent.[123] "It is good that God should allow people the choice of forming their characters in such a way as not to be open to future change," Swinburne adds. "For if God refused to allow someone to develop an irreformably bad character, that would be depriving her of an ultimate choice of the sort of person she is to be."[124]

---

121. Habermas and Moreland, *Beyond Death*, 301.

122. Walls, "Heaven and Hell," in *OHPT*, 505.

123. Walls, *Hell*, 119, 120, and 124. "One can [sin] to the point that his character is thoroughly formed by evil. In such a condition, . . . a person no longer feels any desire to respond to God or do the good" (131). We can develop patterns of behavior that dominate us more and more and from which we cannot escape.

124. Swinburne, *Providence and Problem of Evil*, 121.

Michael Murray thinks that hell is inescapable because freedom ends abruptly *at* death when we become completely set in our ways. Walls thinks that, while post-mortem repentance is possible, freedom can be gradually lost *after* death.[125] Davis agrees: posthumous grace is offered, but some of the unsaved will refuse. "Their hostility [to God] will grow; their hearts will grow ever harder. . . . Perhaps God never gives up on people, but some folks seem to have hardened their hearts to such a degree that they will never repent and turn to God."[126]

While there is no doubt that we are habit-formers, it is hard to see why hardened character eliminates freedom either at or after death. Empirical observation suggests that habit formation does not produce completely-determined characters. We do not lose freedom even if we narrow our choices substantially; acting against settled inclinations, while hard, is not impossible. A smoker, alcoholic, or gambler always has the choice to take the difficult steps to undo their addiction—and even sinners habituated to evil do not lose freedom to turn to God. Think of the cruel Ninevites (Jonah 3) and the wicked 'good thief' (Luke 23:39–43). There is also a theological reason for thinking that human freedom never ends.

Perfect holiness, I argued in chapter 4, means that love completely permeates our character so that we only desire God. As Clyde Ragland says, perfection "consists in psychic integration around a single goal, and this is what the blessed enjoy in heaven."[127] When love is integrated into every level of our personality we lose our ability to choose evil. Total sinfulness is the reverse of perfect holiness. By repeated choices we can form characters, Walls claims, so integrated into sin that evil "involves one's whole person [. . . and] is fully endorsed at every level of who we are." Once evil completely permeates someone's character and extinguishes

---

125. Murray, "Heaven and Hell," 296; Walls, *Purgatory*, 144.

126. Davis, "Hell, Wrath and Grace of God," 96 and 102. Pusey (cited in Liddon, "Life of Pusey," 4–5) agrees: "freewill implies the power . . . to persevere in choosing amiss" until evil "pervade[s] and disorder[s] the whole being" and the person cannot repent." For freewill defenses of hell see Davis, "Universalism, Hell and Fate of Ignorant"; Walls, *Hell*, chapter 5; Wright, *For All Saints*, 42–46 and *Surprised by Hope*, 175–83.

127. Ragland, "Love and Damnation," 217. Swinburne ("Theodicy of Heaven and Hell," 40) says that "a man will only be fully [perfect] if he has no conflicting wants; if he is doing what he wants to be doing and wants in no way to be doing anything else." This is why the blessed cannot sin in heaven; they have no motive to ever sin again once they experience union with God as the greatest good.

all desire for God, they are no longer able to choose salvation.[128] Jeffrey Burton Russell adds that evil constitutes the identity of a totally sinful person—and so cannot be eliminated without eliminating the person themselves. "While in theory it is possible to remove evil from a subject [thoroughly formed by evil], in practice such a process would destroy the intricate wholeness of the personality. If . . . Nero were burned clean of his evil, it would not be . . . Nero . . . who would be saved."[129]

No one—however—can ever develop a character that is fully bad, where evil has infiltrated and consumed every level of their being. The image of God, which includes free will, can be blurred—but not cancelled—by sin. While perfect holiness can be attained, total sinfulness cannot. Sinfulness, moreover, is not identity-conferring; while substantial, vices (just like the disability traits discussed in chapter 3) are contingent rather than necessary elements of personality, and so can gradually be removed.[130] Those in heaven have characters that are purely good and from which evil has been entirely eliminated; their characters are permanently fixed. There is a difference, however, from those in hell. God made us as spiritual beings, and so our hearts are uneasy until they find peace in God. Desire for God can never be entirely eliminated from anyone's character; the unsaved can never be psychologically integrated around the single goal of evil but will always feel some pull toward God because they are naturally inclined to God.[131] Freedom to accept or reject God

128. Walls, "Eternal Hell and Christian Concept of God," 274. Also see Swinburne, "Theodicy of Heaven and Hell," 47–48.

129. Russell, *History of Heaven*, 75. Similar identity concerns arise around disability (chapter 3) and vice (chapter 4).

130. Ramelli (*Christian Doctrine of Apokatastasis*, 147, 156, 358, 684–85, 820) indicates that the church fathers who supported universal salvation did not see evil as part of created and innate human essence but as something acquired by actions. We are sinful in our *wills*, not our *natures*—and so "the seeds of virtue," John Cassian (cited at 684) contends, "are impossible to destroy." Theologians from Origen and Gregory of Nyssa to Rahner and Hick argue that human orientation to God is part of created human nature, an aspect of the image of God existing in every person. While this natural tendency toward God can be *obscured* by sin, it cannot be *cancelled* (820).

131. Indeed, if anyone ever would eventually achieve this integration of their whole existence into evil, then they would annihilate themselves by ceasing to be a spiritual being—and would thus become non-human. Wright (*Surprised by Hope*, 181–82) suggests this possibility—once desire for God is entirely extinguished, the person ceases to exits. As Lewis (*Problem of Pain*, 113–14) says, "what casts itself into hell is not a man: it is 'remains.' To be a complete man means to have the passions obedient to the will and the will offered to God: to have been a man—to be an ex-man or 'damned ghost'—would presumably mean to consist of a will utterly centered in

belong to different orders. John Sachs explains: "human freedom's 'no' to God cannot be simply a parallel alternative to a 'yes' to God. . . . Human freedom is created for one end alone: God. . . . Therefore . . . human freedom can attain real finality only when it reaches the definitiveness for which it is specifically created."[132] Human nature has an inherent bias to choose rather than reject God; as Ragland puts it, "our desire for God is necessary to our nature: no pattern of voluntary choice can eradicate it. . . . [This] ineradicable human longing for God [ensures] both the existence of some freedom and the perpetual possibility for repentance, even in the most thoroughly vicious person."[133] We remain free as long as we are separated from God; but once we choose God, our *telos* is completed and our wills become fixed and closed. "Human freedom becomes finally and irrevocably definitive only in God," Sachs says. "As long as human freedom . . . rejects God, it would fail to attain that . . . finality for which it was destined."[134]

One more point. Suppose, against my argument, that the unsaved *do* become unfree—then God can remove salvation inhibitors. God can eliminate ignorance by letting them experience the awful consequences of separation from God—until they see clearly that sin brings misery and that God is the true source of joy. God can remove bondage by gradually working grace into their characters, releasing the unsaved from behavior patterns that they cannot control.[135] Once all impediments to free choice are removed they will again be able to choose God.

---

itself and passions utterly uncontrolled by the will." Walls (*Purgatory*, 171) agrees: "a person can so resist God . . . that he loses all personality and reduces himself to mere ashes or remains" without a "spark of humanity."

132. Sachs, "Current Eschatology," 247. Lane (*Keeping Hope Alive*, 164) agrees: "the human capacity to say 'No' or 'Yes' to God is not an equal or neutral capacity. Instead . . . human freedom is weighted . . . in the direction of choosing God." Sachs and Lane are paraphrasing Rahner's (*Foundations of Christian Faith*, 435–36) claim that statements about heaven and hell are not parallel. Rahner (*Theological Investigations*, Vol. 17, 192) suggests that hell is an extension of purgatory. "Purgatory could be understood as providing an opportunity for those who did not reach a final personal decision in this earthly . . . life." Lewis (*Great Divorce*, 67) suggests the same: "if they leave that gray town behind it will not have been Hell. To say that any leaves it, it is Purgatory."

133. Ragland, "Love and Damnation," 219. Ratzinger (*Eschatology*, 155) agrees: refusing God is against our essence and therefore cannot be eliminated.

134. Sachs, "Current Eschatology," 248.

135. Balthasar (*Dare We Hope?* 219–20) says that "grace can steal its way into souls and begin to spread itself out there more and more. The greater the area becomes

It might be objected that such intervention by God is morally impermissible since it destroys human autonomy. Walls worries that the only way for God to convince stubborn sinners that God is the source of true happiness is "by making those who rebel against God ever more miserable and tormented." But great suffering undermines free choice since "there is a limit to what any finite person can bear without simply being forced to give in."[136] By removing salvation inhibitors—however—God restores, rather than destroys, genuine freedom. Divine intervention, Adams asserts, is "agency-enabling" rather than "agency-obstructing." Talbott agrees: God is "able to . . . remove the ignorance, the illusions, the bondage to unhealthy desires—without in any way interfering with human freedom."[137]

Summary on Open Death

Lamont claims that "sinners are punished for rejecting God by God's rejecting them."[138] There are two problems with this argument. First, the premise—that sinners reject God—is false. Imagine a woman badly hurt in her youth by a judgmental church that disowned her when, unmarried, she became pregnant—or a man, raised in a thoroughly secular family,

---

that grace thus occupies . . . , the more improbable it becomes that the soul will remain closed to it. . . . The more that grace wins ground from the things that had filled the soul before it, the more it repels the effects of the acts directed against it. And to this process of displacement there are, in principle, no limits." John Cassian (cited in Ramelli, *Christian Doctrine of Apokatastasis*, 684) argues that if God finds a person's attitude "lazy and cold, God moves our hearts with healthy exhortations, by which good will is either renewed or formed in us."

136. Walls, "Eternal Hell and Christian Concept of God," 276; also see *Heaven, Hell and Purgatory*, 78–82. Murray ("Three Versions of Universalism") argues that God's refusal to take no for an answer is a form of harassment that is incompatible with free choice. Like someone choosing unhealthy food, God forces the unsaved to try again—until they finally submit and choose what is good for them, even though they do not want to. Murray's argument is critiqued by Kronen and Reitan (*God's Final Victory*, 170–77).

137. Adams, *Horrendous Evils*, 157 and Talbott, "No Hell," 283. The ancient theologians of *apokatastasis* believed that all sinners will freely choose God after illumination and purification in hell. Divine assistance does not undermine or eliminate human freedom in the next life any more than it does in this life. God's help does not make sinners repent by dominating their wills; instead, it enables them to choose salvation freely.

138. Lamont, "Justice and Goodness of Hell," 67.

who is busily engaged in the pleasures and problems of life.[139] Both have little use for God and are unable to take the gospel seriously. "When we hear that a certain person has 'rejected Christ,'" Bell says, "we should . . . ask, 'which Christ?'"—a distorted one or the real one? "Think about the many who know about Christians only from what they've seen on television and so assume that Jesus is antiscience, antigay, standing out on the sidewalk with his bullhorn, telling people they're going to burn forever?"[140] Davis makes the same point: "some who hear the gospel hear it in such a way that they are psychologically unable to respond positively. Perhaps they heard the gospel for the first and only time from a fool or a bigot or a scoundrel. Or perhaps they were caused to be prejudiced against Christianity by skeptical parents or teachers."[141] Such persons have not rejected God in a clear-minded and responsible way. Second, the conclusion—that rejected grace is withdrawn—is false and, in any case, does not follow from the premise. It assumes, Philip Gulley and James Mulholland point out, that our attitude to God determines God's attitude to us. Suppose my teenage daughter, upset with me, screams "I hate you." In fact, she does not, but is simply frustrated and angry. But even if she really did hate me, that would not change my love. To her "I hate you" I reply "your hate can't change my love." If we could sin ourselves out of God's love then grace would be contingent on our response and would not be unwavering *chesed* and steadfast *agape*.[142]

The claim that sinners reject God is false since it violates the necessary conditions of human freedom—and the claim that God rejects sinners is false since it violates the necessary conditions of divine goodness. Death is open both from God's side and from the sinner's side. We can and should, then, pray salvation for Carlos and all the unsaved dead. But is there reason to think that posthumous salvation is more than a theoretical possibility? Can we confidently believe that salvation prayers will be answered?

---

139. Lewis' (*Screwtape Letters*, 10, 95, 97) imaginary devil says that his goal is to "fuddle" sinners, to "wrap a darkness" about their thoughts, "darkening [the] intellect" by keeping their focus on ordinary life.

140. Bell, *Love Wins*, 7.

141. Davis, "Universalism, Hell and Fate of Ignorant," 183–84.

142. See Gulley and Mulholland, *If Grace is True*, 110–11 and Robinson, *In the End*, 93.

Why We Can Honestly Pray for Universal Salvation

Escapism does not contradict posthumous salvation pessimism (that most, perhaps all, of the unsaved do not repent and remain in hell forever) or entail posthumous salvation optimism (that many, perhaps all, choose salvation and leave hell). But while pessimism is possible, it is not plausible. Posthumous salvation pessimism offers us a tragically defeated God since most unsaved persons experience eternal separation from God. Posthumous salvation optimism and universalism, by contrast, picture a creation that is not an ultimate disaster but one in which God's purpose in making human persons is achieved. Three lines of argument indicate that salvation prayer will be answered.[143]

First, the Bible describes the *eschaton* in terms of victory and triumph. There is tension between the antithesis texts (which warn of a final separation of saved and lost—e.g., Matt 25:31–46) and *apokatastasis* texts (which declare the ultimate restoration of all people to God—e.g., Eph 1:10). The antithesis statements must be read within the context of the *apokatastasis* statements (since only they are consistent with a loving and powerful God who judges in order to save).[144] The Hebrew prophets foretell a day of in-gathering when all people in all nations—including Israel's enemies, Egypt and Assyria (Isa 19:18–25)—will know and worship Yah-

---

143. Origen (cited in Ramelli, *Christian Doctrine of Apokatastasis*, 185, slightly modified) argues that eternal hell constitutes a problem of theodicy: "if the God whom they call 'good' is good with all, surely God is good also with those who will perish. But then, why doesn't God save them? If God does not want, God will not be good; if God wants but cannot, God will not be omnipotent." Talbott (*Inescapable Love of God*, 47–48 and "Universalism and Greater Good," 102–5) puts it similarly:

1. God wants all people to be saved and
2. God can save all contradict
3. some are never saved (but experience eternal hell or are annihilated).

Put formally, the argument for universal salvation parallels the argument for open death:

1. God is love and purposes to save all.
2. God is powerful and can achieve God's purposes.
3. Therefore, all are saved.

144. There are various ways to reconcile the two sets of texts. Balthasar (*Dare We Hope*, 44–45) suggests that dual-outcome texts are pre-Easter while single-outcome texts are post-Easter. Hick (*Death and Eternal Life*, 248–49) suggests that dual-outcome texts are existential and moral warnings while single-outcome texts are theological descriptions. Since both texts are found in Scripture, the decision of which controls which is theological, not biblical.

weh. "I am coming to gather all nations and tongues, and they shall come and see my glory" (Isa 66:18)—"the Lord of hosts will make for all peoples [i.e., non-Israelites] a feast of rich food" (Isa 25:6) and "will change the speech of the peoples to a pure speech, that all of them may call on the name of the Lord and serve him" (Zeph 3:9; cf. Isa 43:5–7; Zech 2:11). Jesus declares, "I will draw all people to myself" (John 12:32).[145] St. Paul predicts a future in which "every knee should bend . . . and every tongue should [voluntarily and joyfully] confess that Jesus Christ is Lord" (Phil 2:10–11; cf. Isa 45:22–23).[146] St. Paul makes several parallel statements regarding "all" individuals dying in Adam and being made alive in Christ (1 Cor 15:22; cf. Rom 5:18 and 11:32)—through whom "God was pleased to reconcile to himself all things" (Col 1:16, 20).[147] God's goal is to gather all of creation into the life of God—that "God may be all in all" (1 Cor 15:28). Scripture speaks, Wright says, "of the great sweep of God's mercy, reconciling and freeing the whole cosmos. This doesn't sound like a small group of people snatched away to salvation while the great majority faces destruction."[148] Instead, all the ends of the earth shall see the saving power of God (Ps 98:3).

If hell is eternal, then God is not totally victorious over evil, which is not finally eliminated but becomes a permanent fixture enduring forever alongside God—"a corner of unredeemed reality in the new creation,"

---

145. Jesus says "I *will* [not "I will try to" or "might"] draw *all* [not "some" or "no"] people."

146. The verb "confess" means with praise and thanksgiving. Every knee without exception will bow voluntarily, not against their will. In St. Paul's writing, the notion of "confessing Jesus as Lord" always implies salvation and refers to joyful praise. Persons do not just submit to God—they willingly and happily submit. See Bonda, *One Purpose of God*, 220–29; Johnson, "Wideness in God's Mercy," 89–90; MacDonald, *Evangelical Universalist*, 98–100; Talbott, *Inescapable Love*, 64–68 and "Christ Victorious," 23–24.

147. As Talbott (*Inescapable Love*, 55) points out, in these universal statements, the scope of the first "all" determines the scope of the second. The second "all" is not more restrictive than, but is parallel to, the first. MacDonald (*Evangelical Universalist*, 79–88) agrees: the very same people who suffer from Adam's sin benefit from Christ's atonement—and so Christ's redemption is as wide as sin's corruption. Both reach every person since the same group is referred to in both statements.

148. Wright, *For All Saints*, 42. Neuhaus (*Death on Friday Afternoon*, 44–45) agrees: "the gospel is sometimes presented as though God is running a desperate rescue mission, saving a few survivors from the shipwreck of what had been God's hopes for creation. . . . God's plan is not to rescue a religious elite from an otherwise botched creation but to restore all things in Christ."

says Pinnock.[149] But since God will be all in all, no sin or rebellion will remain anywhere. If anyone—and certainly if most of the unsaved—remains in hell forever, then God's purpose in creating them (that they be united with God) is defeated rather than fulfilled. Imagine a mother with several children, some of whom reject her despite her best efforts at friendship. She dies without being reconciled to them. This mother's purpose *qua* parent—to have children to love and be loved by—partly fails.[150] Annihilation—permanent extinction of the wicked—is little better than eternal hell; it, too, constitutes a defeat of God's purpose to be in relationship with human beings. As "the destruction of . . . persons who . . . were created in the image of God," Talbott says, it "would leave a terrible stain and blemish on God's creation."[151] Both eternal hell and annihilation leave God's victory incomplete, as Barclay points out. "No father could be happy while there were members of his family forever in agony. No father would count it a triumph to obliterate the disobedient members of his family. The only triumph a father can know is to have all his

---

149. Pinnock, "Destruction of Finally Impenitent," 255.

150. If any are forever lost then "God confronts ultimate defeat in the souls of the damned" since "despite God's unrelenting love, God's efforts will be for naught. At least in some human souls, sin will prove more powerful than God" (Kronen and Reitan, *God's Final Victory*, 26). Thomas (*Introduction to Theology*, 168) agrees: "Aquinas asserts that God's purposes can be fulfilled even though some are condemned. God in God's love wills that all should be saved, but, because God's love is just and holy, some may be condemned. But this amounts to a failure of God's love and a failure in the fulfillment of God's purposes for God's creation." Buckareff and Plug ("Value, Finality and Frustration," 89–90) point out that whether God's purpose is frustrated by eternal hell depends on how we define God's purpose. They argue that God's purpose is successfully executed if escapism rather than universalism is true. Walls ("Eternal Hell and Christian Concept of God," 288) agrees: God is not defeated by eternal hell because, in creating free persons, God knowingly took the risk that some might forever refuse relationship with God. The success of God's plan does not depend on our response. This, I think, is false. Lewis (*Problem of Pain*, 115) rightly acknowledges that "it is objected that the ultimate loss of a single soul means the defeat of omnipotence. And so it does. In creating beings with free will, omnipotence from the outset submits to the possibility of such defeat. . . . The damned are . . . successful rebels to the end."

151. Talbott, *Inescapable Love*, 98. Ancient theologians who defended universal salvation also give a metaphysical reason for *apokatastasis*. Good and evil cannot exist co-eternally. "They ground their argument in a strong ontological monism: evil cannot be coeternal with the good, because the latter is God and only God/the Good is ontologically subsistent, whereas evil is a lack; it is a privation of Good and being." It is therefore doomed to eventually disappear (Ramelli, *Christian Doctrine of Apokatastasis*, 804–5; cf. 358).

family back home."[152] Julian of Norwich calls this God's "great work"—"God shall make all things well. . . . The blessed Trinity shall make well all that is not well."[153] Or, as Bell succinctly says, in the end "Love wins."[154]

Second, there is the relentless love of God who waits as long as repentance takes. As we have seen, the Hebrew prophets portray God as a lover who always goes the extra mile and who never gives up despite rejection and betrayal (Hos 1:14–23; 11:1–9; cf. Isa 49:5–16). Jesus depicts God as a hen eager to gather her brood safely under her wings (Matt 23:37), as a shepherd desperately looking for one lost sheep, as a woman turning her house upside down to find a missing coin, as a heartsick father anxiously awaiting the return of a wandering son (Luke 15). God's tireless love never deserts any person that God has made for union with God, and no human person can escape this love—even after death (Ps 139:7–12). The God who is nothing but giving and whose love never runs out pursues all persons with undying grace. Because "the name of God is mercy," Pope Francis says, "there are no situations we cannot get out of, we are not condemned to sink into quicksand, in which the more we move the deeper we sink. Jesus is there, his hand extended, ready to reach out to us and pull us out of the mud, out of sin, out of the abyss of evil into which we have fallen."[155]

Third, there is no logical motive for any person to freely and eternally resist God. According to separatists, sinners may become so entrenched in willfulness and pride that they forever refuse God's offer of salvation. This, however, is not plausible. "No one who truly understands God's grace will reject it," Gulley and Mulholland assert. "To do so would be a sign not of freedom but of insanity."[156] Ragland points out that "if the damned retain freedom, then they must retain reason, for it is a precondition of freedom."[157] Choosing freely means acting for reasons—and ra-

---

152. Barclay, cited in Bell, *Love Wins Companion*, 182.

153. Julian, cited in Ramelli, *Christian Doctrine of Apokatastasis*, 825–26. I leave it indeterminate whether all moral agents (including fallen angels and Satan) or only all human beings will be restored to God.

154. Bell, *Love Wins*.

155. Pope Francis, *Name of God is Mercy*, 85

156. Gulley and Mulholland, *If Grace is True*, 107. Kreeft and Tacelli (*Handbook of Apologetics*, 290) agree: "if hell is chosen freely, the problem . . . becomes not one of reconciling hell with God's love, but reconciling hell with human sanity. Who would freely prefer hell to heaven unless they were insane?"

157. Ragland, "Love and Damnation," 219.

tionality limits the range of possible choices a person can make. Imagine, Talbott says, a person who thrusts their hand into an open fire, screams in agony but does not withdraw it. Such a choice, if unmotivated by any reasons (such as trying to retrieve the device that would stop a nuclear weapon from detonating in a major city), is unintelligible. "If someone does something in the absence of any motive for doing it and in the presence of an exceedingly strong motive for not doing it, then he or she displays the kind of irrationality that is incompatible with free choice."[158] The unsaved in hell, like the person with their hand in the fire, have every reason to repent and no logical reason not to. The bitter consequences of rejecting God will eventually convince them that doing so cannot satisfy—despite whatever perverse pleasure rebellion brings—and they will freely turn to God. As John Hick says, "God does not have to coerce us to respond to God, for God has already so created us that our nature, seeking its own fulfillment and good, leads us to God."[159] Eternal choices against God can only be caused by salvation inhibitors which prevent free choice—but, Talbott notes, "once God has purged the individual of all ignorance and deception and bondage to desire, what motive for rejecting God would then remain?"[160] When my daughter in her room, who wants to be happy, realizes she is missing the party, she has every reason to change her attitude—at least eventually.[161]

158. Talbott, *Inescapable Love*, 184. Eternal hell involves the "rejection requirement": some will freely and forever reject God and thus separate themselves from God in hell. This claim is false: we are naturally oriented toward God as the ultimate source of happiness and have no motive to choose misery freely and forever. Hell brings home to sinners the reality of sin and gives them motive—God gives opportunity—to repent (see Talbott, "Universalism," 451 and "No Hell").

159. Hick, *Death and Eternal Life*, 252. Universal salvation does not conflict with free will because human beings are oriented to God by nature—but some will need a long time to repent.

160. Talbott, "Providence, Freedom and Human Destiny," 228. Talbott, in arguing that separation from God cannot be a free and rational choice, follows church fathers such as Origen and Gregory of Nyssa—and ultimately Plato. Gregory makes the same argument: God will "allow the human being to do whatever it wanted and taste all the evils it wished, and then learn from experience what it has preferred to [God], and then come back, with its desire, to its original beatitude, voluntarily" (see Ramelli, *Christian Doctrine of Apokatastasis*, 427; cf. 820). Sinners are persuaded, not compelled, to repent—they voluntarily submit to Christ once their minds are illuminated and wills purified. For more on universal salvation see Appendix Note 9.

161. Habermas and Moreland (*Beyond Death*, 302) object that if there is a second chance for salvation after death and the shock of judgment, then sinners are not really choosing heaven but choosing to avoid hell. This distinction, however, collapses. For

Choices against God can be either free or eternal, but not both. The unsaved dead, like Carlos, can reject God *eternally* only if they are acting in ignorance or bondage (and are thus not free). Or they can reject God *freely* (but only temporarily). What they cannot do is reject God both freely and eternally. God will eventually evoke a free response from all people.[162] Jesus' Parable of the Prodigal Son (Luke 15:11–32) indicates, Walls suggests, that "we can choose evil in the short run under the illusion that it will make us happy." The prodigal enjoyed his sinful lifestyle for a while. "However, the inevitable result of choosing evil is that it will make us miserable. The illusion that sin can make us happy will eventually be shattered as it was for the prodigal son when he found himself broke and alone, feeding the pigs." He then realized that it was better to go back home—and returned to the father who awaited him with open arms.[163] Since there are infinite chances for salvation after death, the unsaved may refuse God temporarily but not eternally.

Even if the strong claim that it is *impossible* to freely refuse God's love forever is mistaken, the weaker claim that it is *improbable* is obviously true.[164] God will never finally reject some persons by withdrawing grace and giving up trying to save them. And it is at the very least highly unlikely that any person will finally reject God, continuing to choose personal misery by refusing God's persuasive love. The hopeful view of hell—that the unsaved leave when they repent—means that we can

my daughter, choice 1 (to join the party) and choice 2 (to avoid missing the party) are one and the same. But even if sinners are simply choosing to avoid hell, that is enough for God. Manning (*Ragamuffin Gospel*, 189 and 195) points out that in Jesus' parable the prodigal son "stumbled home simply to survive," because he was bankrupt and disillusioned, not because he cared that "he had broken his father's heart." He came home "not from a burning desire to see his father, but just to stay alive." And yet there was "a light in the window and a 'Welcome Home' sign on the door."

162. Talbott thinks that God saves all by *using* freedom; Adams thinks God saves all by *overriding* freedom. I agree with Talbott; without being freely chosen, "love" is not love. Origen says that "no being is incurable for the One who has created it"—this contradicts Plato's assertion that incurable sinners remain in Tartarus forever. See Ramelli, *Christian Doctrine of Apokatastasis*, 153, 189, and 554.

163. Walls, *Heaven, Hell and Purgatory*, 76–77. Also see Pope Francis, *Name of God is Mercy*, xix.

164. Kvanvig ("Hell," 417–18) notes that universal salvation can be seen as either *contingent* (eternal hell is possible, but in fact no one remains there forever) or *necessary* (eternal hell—rejecting God freely and forever—is logically impossible). Walls (*Heaven, Hell and Purgatory*, 209) declares eternal hell to be an entirely contingent truth: it is possible that all could be saved. Eternal hell is not necessary (in order for God to be glorified by damning some persons, for example).

reasonably believe that our prayers for all of them, including Carlos, will be answered.

Separatists may not be convinced by this argument. But note: salvation prayer does not hinge on universalism, or even on posthumous salvation optimism, only on escapism—an open view of death. Edward Pusey—who defended everlasting hell—encouraged salvation prayer: "instead of being haunted with the thought ... 'was he saved?' ... we may commend our departed ones to their Father's care, sure that ... they are ... still under the shadow of God's hand, longing for their consummation both of body and soul."[165] Bloesch agrees: "what about prayers for the lost? We may hope for the final reunion of all souls and even pray for this." "It is not wrong to ask 'may God have mercy on their souls' if we fear that the deceased have separated themselves from the love of God."[166] Helmut Thielecke, too, says "nothing prevents one from beseeching in prayer that those who have rejected Christ might themselves not be rejected, that their histories might continue together with God in eternity, and that the boundlessness of eternal love should not draw back even before them."[167] Even Wright, who seems to allow for post-mortem salvation since "we can never say of anyone for certain, including Hitler and bin Laden, that they have gone so far down the road of wickedness that they are beyond redemption," should be open to prayer on their behalf.[168]

The Church of England Archbishops Commission recommends we pray: "God of infinite mercy and justice, who has made man in thine own image, and hatest nothing thou hast made, we rejoice in thy love for all creation and commend all men to thee, that in them thy will be done."[169] United Methodist Church funerals allow prayers for persons who did not profess Christian faith: "look favorably ... upon those ... who scarcely knew your grace. ... Grant mercy also to those who have departed this life in ignorance or defiance of you. We plead for them in the spirit of him who prayed, 'Father, forgive them, for they know not what they do.'"[170] The

---

165. Pusey, cited in Liddon, "Life of Pusey," 6.

166. Bloesch, *Last Things*, 149 and 167–68. We should pray for the dead, "even for those who are not yet bound to Christ in faith, on the grounds that the Spirit may well be at work in such prayers turning people to Christ for redemption" (166).

167. Thielecke, cited in Balthasar, *Dare We Hope?* 36.

168. Wright, *For All Saints*, 44.

169. Archbishop's Commission, *Prayer and Departed*, 55. The Episcopal Church Prayers of the People Form IV (*Book of Common Prayer*, 389) follows this wording.

170. United Methodist Church, *Service of Death and Resurrection*, 83.

Christian Reformed Church also has funeral prayers for those who lived openly sinful lives ("we place in your merciful hands N. . . . His/her life was filled with sin and struggle, but only you . . . perceive what mustard seed of faith . . . was hidden in his/her heart") and for those who were not known to be Christian ("we commend N. . . . to your merciful care, knowing that you . . . will do right").[171] And the Eastern Orthodox Church, in the prayers of Pentecost, ask "O Christ . . . , who hast descended into hell and shattered the eternal bars, revealing the way of ascent for those who dwell in that lower world . . . accept intercessory propitiation on behalf of those held fast in hell."[172] If post-mortem salvation is even possible, then we should pray for the unsaved—whether we are separatists or universalists.

Concluding Remarks: Salvation Prayer as Prayers of Hope

Tradition states that the non-Christian dead are beyond hope in unending conscious torment. "I am the way into eternal grief, I am the way to a forsaken race. . . . Abandon every hope, all you who enter" reads the sign above Dante Alighieri's inferno.[173] Jean-Paul Sartre's play on hell is titled *No Exit*. If there is no possibility of change after death then it is impossible for Carlos to be helped by prayer. But here is the problem, John A. T. Robinson says—"no Being who had an infinite concern for the salvation of every soul could possibly be conceived as saying in effect: 'unless you turn to me by the age of seventy . . . I cannot give you a further chance.' A God like that is either at the mercy of death [and so lacks power] or . . . is not the God of the parable of the prodigal son [and so lacks goodness]."[174] We cannot believe that there are no further chances for salvation after death without limiting the love of God. According to Karl Barth, Scripture "points plainly in the direction of a truly eternal divine patience and . . . universal reconciliation." While we must not "count on this," he adds,

---

171. Vander Zee, *In Life and Death*, 203–4. Technically, the first petition assumes closed death, asking God to reward implicit faith of this life. The second, however, is compatible with open death.

172. Cited in Ware, "One Body," 189–90.

173. Dante, *Divine Comedy*, 14. Kenneth Kantzer (cited in Talbott, *Inescapable Love*, 37) agrees: "the biblical answer [concerning afterlife destiny] . . . is a hard and crushing word, devastating to human hope."

174. Robinson, *In the End*, 44. Eternal hell, I have argued, contradicts God's love, justice and power as well as human freedom and sanity.

"we are surely commanded . . . to hope and *pray* for this."[175] If hoping and praying for universal salvation is a duty, then *ipso facto* hoping and praying for posthumous salvation is as well. When we hope for something we want it to happen and think that it may.[176] If sinners like Carlos can respond to God in a saving way in the afterlife, then we have every reason to pray for them.

"The question of the salvation of all humanity cannot be addressed theoretically," Alfeyev says; "it invites not speculation, but prayer."[177] Josef Pieper says that "prayers of petition [are] nothing other than the voicing of hope."[178] O'Callaghan agrees: "we petition God for what we are entitled to hope for from God."[179] Salvation prayers are prayers of hope—that the unsaved will respond to God's continuing offer of grace. We ask—to use Sidney Callahan's words—that the Holy Spirit's voice within the person, "which is already prompting and inviting from within," may "whisper more loudly." Not to pray for salvation is to despair—to expect that they are forever condemned.[180]

So what do we pray for the unsaved departed? James van Tholen offers words of counsel to those praying for a loved one who has refused God, words that apply equally to prayer for those in hell: "you should not let yourself believe . . . that they have wandered too far, that God will have no more to do with them, that [God] will give up on them."[181] And so we pray that the unsaved like Carlos be freed from ignorance and bondage, that they yield to God's persuasive love. We pray for them words from the liturgy of Ambrose of Milan: "bend down over their wounds and heal them, giving them a medicine stronger than their afflictions, a mercy greater than their fault."[182] We pray that, like the prodigal son in

---

175. Barth, cited in Bell, *Love Wins Companion*, 182. Rahner (cited in O'Callaghan, *Christ Our Hope*, 219) says that Christians "have . . . the sacred 'duty' to hope that the history of freedom will have, for themselves and for others, a happy ending." Balthasar (*Dare We Hope?* 211 and 213) agrees that we have "the obligation to hope for all" to be saved.

176. For an analysis of hope see Volume 1, chapter 9.

177. Alfeyev, "Eschatology," 118.

178. Pieper, *On Hope*, 70.

179. O'Callaghan, *Christ Our Hope*, 219.

180. Callahan, *With All Heart and Mind*, 186.

181. Van Tholen, *Where All Hope Lies*, 178.

182. Ambrosian Liturgy, cited in Pope Francis, *Name of God is Mercy*, 34. The actual wording is "you bent down over our wounds and healed us, giving us a medicine stronger than our afflictions, a mercy greater than our fault."

the far country, they come to their senses, return to the Father and share in the joys of heaven. We pray that the consequences of their continuing rebellion against God destroy whatever motive they have to refuse salvation—that their misery at being separated from God bring repentance and reconciliation. We pray the Roman Catholic Fatima Prayer: "O my Jesus . . . lead all souls to heaven, especially those most in need of thy mercy"—which is, of course, the unsaved dead.[183] At the very least, Geoffrey Rowell says, all Christians can offer this guarded petition: "if the departed person for whom I pray is in a state where they can be helped, then, O God, be gentle and merciful."[184]

God desires and works for the salvation of all—and we should pray in accordance with what God wills. Not to pray for those in hell is to be guilty of a real failure in the exercise of Christian hope and love. The Eastern Orthodox saint, Silouan of Athos, heard another hermit say with satisfaction, "God will punish all atheists. They will burn in everlasting fire." Silouan, with sorrow, answered, "love could not bear that. We must pray for all."[185]

Eschatology and the doctrines of heaven, purgatory, and hell—Walls says—are not only intellectually fascinating but existentially engaging as well.[186] We turn in the final chapters to consider how praying for the dead is spiritually forming for the living.

183. Fatima Prayer.

184. Rowell, *Liturgy of Christian Burial*, 78. As Richard Hooker (cited in Hebblethwaite, *Christian Hope*, 79) says, we can pray for God's "mercy upon all men."

185. Louth, *Introducing Eastern Orthodox Theology*, 159. Also see Alfeyev, "Eschatology," 118.

186. Walls, "Heaven and Hell," in *RCPR*, 645.

chapter 6

THE GENERAL SPIRITUAL VALUE OF PRAYING FOR THE DEAD

I MET THEM AT a rest stop in Michigan—the group of Aussie bikers with cooking utensils and camping equipment strapped on their Harley-Davidsons. We swapped a few riding stories before I noticed the stickers—one on each rearview mirror and taped low on the inside of the windshields. A message: *Keep Right* and an arrow pointing →. Knowing what they meant, I asked anyway. "Well, in Australia we drive on the left," the wiry bearded fellow explained. "It's easy to get distracted, to forget and revert to habit, especially when rounding corners. The stickers help us pay attention. They remind us to stay on the right side of the road. Make sense, mate?" Indeed.

Christians trying to live faithfully in a secular culture are like Australians driving in America. Society understands life without reference to God—and many believers unconsciously accept modern assumptions into their thinking.[1] We are "conformed to this world," St. Paul (Rom 12:1–2) says, and embrace the philosophical ideology of the dominant

---

1. We are born into a world, a poisonous atmosphere, which conditions our thoughts and actions in sinful and selfish ways; this happens unconsciously—we do not choose this condition, we are born into it. As an analogy, consider a "crack baby" born from the beginning of life with its mother's addiction to cocaine. This is the meaning of original sin—we breathe into our characters from the moment we are born dysfunctional ways of being in the world (Ps 51:5). Just like a "crack baby" needs medical help, so we need something we cannot do for ourselves, an outside intervention to save us—this is the meaning of grace and of being "born again" (John 3:3 *NIV*). See Barron, "*Vitae Spiritualis Ianua.*"

culture, which becomes the norm of the church. The solution is psychological restructuring—"being transformed by the renewing of our minds" and hearts. Like the Aussie bikers, we need regular reminders of Christian truth so we do not become engrossed in false cultural values. We must immerse ourselves in spiritual practices that cultivate distinctively Christian perspectives and behaviors. We forget who we are and must rediscover it—we surrender to culture, lose our Christian identity and must remember it so we live in line with the gospel.

Take one example. Christians should die differently than people without faith in resurrection. As he approached the end of his life, my father wanted no part of medically-futile treatment that would play god, waste resources, idolize physical existence, and keep him from his heavenly home. His only comfort in life and death—as the *Heidelberg Catechism* has it—was that he belonged in body and soul to his faithful Savior, Jesus Christ.[2] One morning we sat as a family, together with his doctor who had just pronounced a terminal diagnosis, praying in a hospital conference room. Dad requested his favorite song—and so we sang, weeping as we listened to his strong voice: "when I stand in glory, I will see his face; there I'll serve my King forever, in that holy place." Dad's final hope was not that science and technology would save him from death. Instead, formed by a lifetime of prayer, his final hope was in "the resurrection of the body and the life of the world to come."[3]

Previous chapters have examined why we pray for all the departed and what our petitions for them consist in. But now—to quote Tom Wright—"we must ask: so what?" Is all of this "simply a matter of tidying up our beliefs" about eschatology and prayer for the dead—"or does it have any practical consequences here and now?"[4] In the next two chapters I explain the spiritual value of praying for the departed—the impact that it has on individual discipleship and the mission of the church.

Petitionary prayer, Thomas Flint says, has two purposes: it is "circumstance-changing" and "consciousness-raising"—it affects God and it shapes us.[5] Prayer has a divine influence function—it sometimes causes God to act in ways that God would not have acted if not asked to do so.

---

2. *Heidelberg Catechism*, Question 1. "Whether we live or whether we die, we are the Lord's," St. Paul says (Rom 14:8).

3. Green, "There is a Redeemer" in *Sing: A New Creation*, Song 145 and Nicene Creed, in Episcopal Church, *Book of Common Prayer*, 328.

4. Wright, *Surprised by Hope*, 189.

5. Flint, *Divine Providence*, 223 and 220.

By influencing God to act on their behalf, prayer for the departed assists them and affects their present state.[6] It is now time to focus on the human formation function—how prayer affects the person who prays. Prayer in general is *consciousness-raising*. Because how we act is determined by what we believe and desire, and because cultural visions of life conflict with Christian truth, we need spiritual practices like prayer to reorient our hearts and minds so that we live as people who belong to God rather than to ourselves or mainstream culture. Walter Wink puts it well: prayer "is the field hospital in which the diseased spirituality that we have contracted from [society] can most directly be diagnosed and treated."[7] Prayer for the dead is *eschatological consciousness-raising*. Through it, Pope Benedict XVI states, we replace the "meager, misplaced hope that leads us away from God" with grand eschatological hope for the coming of God's kingdom.[8] In this chapter I discuss how prayer is spiritually forming and I suggest some spiritual benefits of praying for the dead in general. In the next chapter I explore how prayer for each group of the departed shapes specific attitudes and actions.

The Spiritual Value of Prayer in General

Christianity is fundamentally a way of life—living as citizens of God's kingdom, as "aliens and exiles" with a different set of allegiances than the world (1 Pet 2:11). In Christian tradition prayer, character, and behavior have been connected by the formula *lex orandi, lex credendi, lex agendi*— the rule of prayer is the rule of belief and the rule of action. I broaden the formula to include desire: how we pray shapes what we believe and desire and therefore how we act.

---

6. See Volume 1, chapter 5.

7. Wink, *Engaging the Powers*, 198.

8. Pope Benedict XVI, *Spe Salvi*, 17. Walls (*Purgatory*, 29) suggests that the Protestant ban on purgatory (and prayer for the dead) was a significant factor in secularization (living life without reference to God). Where such prayers cultivated a concern for the eternal world to come, abandoning them redirected interest, resources, and energy onto this world. Walls' focus is purgatory—but his point applies as well to prayer for the dead.

Right Action Requires Right Belief and Desire

In order to understand how prayer enables us to live as faithful Christians we need a theory of human action. A *deliberation model* of behavior sees actions as intentionally chosen. We face a choice, stop and think about each option, then consciously make a decision. While this model may describe how we resolve difficult dilemmas, according to a *disposition model* we usually act automatically, conditioned by unconscious habit rather than consciously-formed intentions. Instead of deliberating and deciding, our actions follow naturally from beliefs and desires that are deep in our characters.[9] The term "character" comes from the Greek word *charasso*, which means to engrave a mark on something like a coin. A person's character is a set of ingrained traits and dispositions—habitual ways of thinking, feeling, desiring, and acting. Having worked their way deep into the structure of our psychological lives, these stable inclinations result in automatic behaviors. In Hebrew and Christian Scripture the "heart" or "spirit" is the interior core of a person that, like a computer operating system, controls what we do. The root causes of behavior are desires and beliefs. When acting intentionally, a person wants to achieve some goal and thinks that a certain action will bring it about. My action of looking for an apple in the refrigerator, for example, is caused by my desire to eat an apple and my belief that apples are stored there. The desire provides motivation to act and the belief gives direction about how best to act. A person's character has a persisting structure of beliefs and desires which together create a readiness to act; they form the will, the executive center of the self.

We are thinking beings with *beliefs* in our heads. "A person's beliefs are their view of how the world is, their 'picture' or 'map' of how things

---

9. Take, for example, St. Peter: he had resolved to be loyal, but fear rose up from within, causing him to betray Jesus at trial (Matt 26:69–75). Contemporary psychology indicates that most of what we do is automated, coming from inclinations we follow without thinking. Sources are listed in my "Cultivating Character." Smith (*Imagining the Kingdom*, 8–9, 31–33, 53, 79, 86, and 141) agrees that our actions are based, not primarily on cognitive deliberation and conscious thought, but on acquired habit, unconscious desires, and pre-intellectual dispositions. The driving force behind behavior is a set of beliefs and desires operating beneath the level of conscious awareness—habits of intellect and affection which are formed by repeated practices and which prime us to act in certain ways. Character is this set of dispositions by which we construe—understand and navigate—the world; the inertia of habits which have become second nature incline us to act without thinking.

are," Richard Swinburne says, what they hold to be true about reality.[10] We act on the basis of our beliefs—if I believe that the dog is friendly, I approach it; if I think it vicious, I avoid it. This insight applies not just to specific ideas like "the dog is friendly," but to the complex web of assumptions that determines how we understand the world. "What occupies our minds," Dallas Willard says, "governs what we do. It sets the ... tone out of which our actions flow."[11] The Greek philosophers teach that wisdom (seeing the world aright) is necessary if we are to act correctly and that ignorance (distorted assumptions) produces poor choices. The psalmist (119:33–34) knew that beliefs determine behavior: "teach me, O LORD, the way of your statutes, and I will observe it to the end." Jesus says that "the one who hears the Word and understands it ... bears fruit" (Matt 13:23) and St. Paul asserts that those who "set their minds on the things of the flesh live according to the flesh" while "those who live according to the Spirit set their minds on the things of the Spirit" (Rom 8:5–7). We live as faithful Christians when our beliefs align with God's truth. But in a secular society we get pulled along with the flow of culture; Christian convictions are pushed off into one corner rather than integrated into all of life.

We are also loving beings with *desires* in our hearts. "A person's desires," Swinburne says, "are their natural inclinations to do things, experience things and have things—what they feel naturally inclined to do or seek."[12] Every intentional action, the Greek philosophers say, aims at something we think is good. Augustine of Hippo agrees: love—desire directed to specific things—is the basic power that moves all action.[13] We are influenced by "a picture of ... life that pulls us toward it"—James Smith comments—that makes us "value certain things, aim for certain

---

10. Swinburne, *Evolution of Soul*, 18, slightly modified; cf. chapter 14. Smith (*Imagining the Kingdom*, 34, 39, 51, 68, 87, and 93) identifies the cognitive determinants of behavior as "perceptions." Perceptions pre-load inclinations for acting; once we see a situation in a certain way we are primed to act in a certain way. If I think a poorly-performing student is lazy, I react in one way—but if I think they are learning disabled, I react in another way. Inclinations to act are activated through perceptions that color a situation for us so we naturally respond in particular ways.

11. Willard, *Divine Conspiracy*, 324.

12. Swinburne, *Evolution of Soul*, 18, slightly modified.

13. Desire, Augustine (*City of God*, Book 14.7, 557) says, is "love which strains after the possession of the loved object." See Aristotle, *Nicomachean Ethics* 1094a1–1094b12, 1–2.

goods, pursue certain dreams, and work on certain projects."[14] The psalmist (119:36–37) understood that desires determine behavior: "turn my heart to your decrees, and not to selfish gain. Turn my eyes from looking at vanities." Jesus teaches that "where your treasure is there your heart will be also" (Matt 6:21), and St. Paul recognizes that virtues are habits of right desire ("what the Spirit desires" is love, joy, and peace) and vices are habits of wrong desire ("the desires of the flesh" cause envy, greed, and anger—Gal 5:16–23; cf. Rom 7:14–25). Rightly-ordered love (*caritas*) desires God above all else, Augustine says, while wrongly-ordered love (*cupiditas*) seeks ultimate happiness in the goods of this world.[15]

Since there is a direct causal connection between them, *right acting requires right believing and desiring.* Christian people are called to live by the values of God's kingdom, but are not immune to acting on beliefs and desires that are alien to Christian faith. Two mutually incompatible orientations compete for our allegiance, Augustine says, the city of God and the city of the world; we experience the fundamental struggle between two loves, love of self (and earthly goods) and love of God.[16] Our hearts and minds, Smith points out, are a battle ground shaped by contradictory visions of human flourishing, by the cross-pressure of competing

---

14. Smith, *Desiring the Kingdom*, 81 and 25, slightly modified. Activities that are regularly repeated, like shopping at the mall or watching entertainment television, "point our love to ultimate visions of human flourishing." These micro-practices (Smith, *Imagining the Kingdom*, 110, 142) embed particular desires in our unconscious dispositions by "grabbing hold of our hearts and capturing [our] imaginations, shaping our loves and desires" (86)—and thereby determining our behavior.

15. We must, Augustine (*On Christian Doctrine*, Book 1.27, 530) says, know the value of what we desire. "He is a man of just and holy life who forms an unprejudiced estimate of things, and keeps his affections also under strict control, so that he neither loves what he ought not to love, nor fails to love what he ought to love, nor loves that more which ought to be loved less, nor loves that equally which ought to be loved either less or more, nor loves that less or more which ought to be loved equally." Benzoni ("Augustinian Understanding of Love") offers an important clarification: "*caritas* and *cupiditas* are not . . . to be simply distinguished as 'love of God' versus 'love of the world'; for *caritas* entails *proper* love of the world. *Cupiditas* is *improper* love of the world; it is seeking one's final happiness in the world rather than in God. *Caritas* is love of God, from which flows proper love of the world. . . . In *caritas*, we do indeed love God's creatures, but we love them with a love that is referred to God. We do not love them as the final end, the source of value, but as relative ends who receive their value from God."

16. Augustine (*City of God*, Book 24.28, 593) says that "the two cities were created by two kinds of love: the earthly city was created by self-love . . . , the heavenly city by the love of God."

construals of reality. As Christians living in secular society we simultaneously forge conflicting maps of the world—yet only one, culture or Christ, can be primary and controlling.[17] "Israel in every generation and circumstance is invited to other loyalties," Walter Brueggemann notes. "And of course it is not different in every circumstance and generation of the Church." Indeed, "the contemporary Church is . . . largely enculturated to the [social] ethos. Our consciousness has been claimed by false fields of perception."[18] Without knowing it, the assumptions of dominant culture (performance, possessions, and popularity) overwhelm Christian priorities (love of God and service to neighbor). As a result, many Christians become assimilated to culture; they think, desire, and act in ways that are incongruent with the gospel. Ronald Sider reports that, according to sociologists, "Christians are as likely to embrace lifestyles every bit as hedonistic, materialistic, self-centered, and sexually immoral as the world in general. . . . Whether the issue is marriage and sexuality or money and care for the poor, [Christians] today are living scandalously unbiblical lives" that are no different from their unbelieving neighbors.[19] Unless we are intentional about developing Christian dispositions, mainstream society will dictate our beliefs and desires and determine our choices.

Right Belief and Desire Requires Prayer

Culture shapes our hearts and minds away from God's kingdom and toward visions of human flourishing that are antithetical to it. To counteract the influence of culture we need what Richard Mouw calls

---

17. Smith, *Imagining the Kingdom*, 82 and 114.

18. Brueggemann, *Covenanted Self*, 65 and *Prophetic Imagination*, 1. Willard (*Divine Conspiracy*, 140) laments the fact that in much of the church having faith in Jesus is separated from learning how think and act as he did. Instead of combining faith and obedience, we subtract law from grace. Discipleship, he (282 and 301) says, means being an apprentice—"someone who has decided to be with another person . . . in order to become capable of doing what that person does or to become what that person is." The focus of discipleship is learning how to live our lives in God's kingdom, how to become like Christ in the whole of daily existence.

19. Sider, cited in Scazzero, *Emotionally-Healthy Spirituality*, 30–31. Lewis (*Screwtape Letters*, 43, 54, 47, and 108) says that "a moderated religion is as [bad] as no religion at all." We can embrace "externally the habits of a Christian" but retain a "spiritual state [that is] much the same" as that of secular culture. In this way a person can have "two parallel lives"—one secular and one (nominally, at least) Christian—that are inconsistent, in which Christianity does not flow over into daily life.

"exercises in corrective spirituality."[20] Conversion, Brueggemann states, means "transformed consciousness that results in an altered *perception* of world, neighbor and self, and an authorization to *live* differently in that world."[21] Prayer is one way we renew our minds (Rom 12:2), take every thought and desire captive to Christ (2 Cor 10:4–5) and set our hearts on God's truth (Col 3:2). Through this practice, Pope Benedict XVI says, we are "like the beloved disciple who rested his head against his Master's heart and there learned the way to think, speak and act."[22] Prayer is a consciousness-raising and thus a character-shaping practice.

Spiritual formation, Dietrich Bonhoeffer says, means "being drawn into the form of Jesus Christ, . . . being conformed" and molded to his character and conduct. He rejects "thinking in terms of two realms"—seeing Christian convictions and life in the world as mutually-exclusive opposites. Compartmentalizing our experience into sacred and secular limits Christ's lordship to our personal and private lives (our internal dispositions) and leaves our professional and public lives (our external actions) unaddressed by the gospel. Jesus, however, "demands undivided obedience."[23] Anthony Siegrist explains: we "cannot divide reality into two contradictory zones, one operating in obedience to Jesus and the other operating independent of Jesus' influence." Instead, the "disciples of Jesus must obey him in all circumstances of life."[24] This requires a break with the world. The Christian's relationship with society is mediated through Christ, Bonhoeffer says: "he is in the middle. He has deprived those whom he has called of every immediate connection to those given realities. He wants to be the medium; everything should happen only through him. He stands . . . between me and the world. . . . That is why there must be a break with the immediacies of life."[25] Siegrist explains again: "the decision for Christ in obedience is the decision to embrace a different version of reality altogether and thus to redefine our responsibilities in

---

20. Mouw, *Uncommon Decency*, 159. Brown (*Ransom of Soul*, 92) points out that the ancient Greek philosophers encouraged disciplines to make reality look different by telling themselves stories about the nature of things (life, death, honor, wealth). These counter-cultural stories were to subvert everyday common sense by turning conventional values on their head.

21. Brueggemann, *Biblical Perspectives on Evangelism*, 129; emphasis added.

22. Pope Benedict XVI, *Fathers of Church*, 102.

23. Bonhoeffer, *Ethics*, 93 and 58 and *Discipleship*, 135.

24. Nation, Siegrist and Umbel, *Bonhoeffer the Assassin?* 156.

25. Bonhoeffer, *Discipleship*, 93–94.

light of what is now seen to be real."[26] As Bonhoeffer himself knew, Jesus' call to follow disrupts allegiances with social realities that are contrary to the gospel—in his case, an authoritarian government concerned with the purity of the *volk* and territorial expansion through war.

Discipleship is the continuing formation of our lives into lives modeled on Jesus—into the virtues of faith, hope, love, patience, hospitality, forgiveness. Right acting requires right believing and desiring—and *right believing and desiring require spiritual practices like prayer*. We must, Don Saliers says, be "drawn into the way in which God views the world."[27] We cannot directly create new beliefs and desires just by choice, by logic, or willpower; we cannot wake up in the morning, Smith says, and simply decide "from now on I'll have Christian beliefs and desires."[28] We can, however, adjust them indirectly through spiritual practice. Aristotle observed that the only way to restructure our fundamental inclinations is by long habituation through repeated actions.[29] Pierre Hadot describes spiritual formation as work done by a person on themselves in order to turn themselves into a particular type of person.[30] The means of spiritual formation are spiritual practices—which Willard defines as activities of mind or body that are done deliberately and regularly in order to engrave specific dispositions into our characters.[31] We train ourselves through

26. Nation, Siegrist, and Umbel, *Bonhoeffer the Assassin?* 152.

27. Saliers, "Liturgy and Ethics," 181.

28. Smith, *Imagining the Kingdom*, 125 and 93.

29. Aristotle (cited in Sherman, "Habituation of Character," 246) says that "character . . . is that which is developed from habit; and anything is habituated [or trained] which . . . , through being changed repeatedly in a certain way by guidance which is not innate [but deliberate], is eventually capable of acting in that way."

30. Hadot, *Philosophy as Way of Life*, 126. A spiritual exercise is "a procedure or determinate act, intended to influence oneself, carried out with the express goal of achieving a determinate moral effect. . . . Spiritual exercises [are] *exercises* because they are practical, require effort and training, and are lived; they [are] *spiritual* because they involve the entire spirit, one's whole way of being" (21). Contemporary science indicates that consistent behavior creates physical changes within the information pathways of the brain. As habits formed by conscious activity become patterns established in the brain, they become second nature (Wright, *After You Believe*, 37–43).

31. Willard, *Spirit of Disciplines*, 67–69. A spiritual discipline, he (*Divine Conspiracy*, 353) adds, is "any activity within our power that we engage in to enable us to do what we cannot do by direct effort." The disciplines of abstinence (solitude, silence, fasting, chastity, frugality) "are designed to weaken or break the power of life engagements that press against our involvement in the Kingdom of God"—while the disciplines of engagement (worship, service, study, prayer) "are designed to immerse us even more deeply into that Kingdom" (357–64 and 418).

spiritual practice the way an athlete or musician does, cultivating particular ways of thinking and desiring until they become second nature. Prayer turns our hearts toward God—and as our beliefs and desires change, so do our actions. (By emphasizing human responsibility I do not mean to ignore the work of the Holy Spirit in moral growth; sanctification is always the result of both divine grace, which is primary, and human effort—Phil 2:12–13.)

Meditation—dwelling on something, holding it in consciousness—is the foundational spiritual discipline. "The Hebrew word *siach* means 'to muse,' 'go over in one's mind,' 'rehearse' (Ps 119:15, 23, 27, 48, 78, 148)," R. Paul Stevens comments. "*Hagah* means 'to mutter' or 'meditate.' It is used of the sound characteristic of the moaning of the dove or the growling of the lion over its prey." The Latin word for meditation means "to rehearse," and the Tibetan word for meditation means "familiarization."[32] As Christians, we are forgetful; we assimilate beliefs and desires from culture and neglect basic truths of faith, which recede from our consciousness. We become unconsciously habituated to disordered loves, to ways of life that contradict God's kingdom. We act without thinking, the engine of habit running quietly under the hood of our minds, because we have absorbed from society a false vision of what matters.[33] What we require, Willard says, is a "renovation of the heart."[34]

Forgetfulness can only be countered by reminder and repetition; what we pay attention to becomes more prominent in our hearts and minds. Moses warns the Israelites "take care and watch yourselves closely, so as neither to forget [God's truths] nor to let them slip from your mind all the days of your life"—"take care that you do not forget . . . but remember the Lord your God" (Deut 4:9 and 8:2, 11, 18). The people must "keep [God's words] in your heart" (Deut 6:6–8)—this constant awareness of God's truth would counteract the influence of pagan ideas. They must keep the Passover (Exod 13:3–10; 12:14) and set up memorial stones at Gilgal (Josh 4:1–24) in memory of the exodus from slavery and the crossing of the Jordan River. The virtuous person regularly meditates on God's truth (Ps 1:2), calling to mind the deeds of God (Ps 77:11–12) and keeping

---

32. Stevens, "Spiritual Disciplines," 935 and Dalai Lama and Groleman, *Disturbing Emotions*, 214.

33. Smith, *Imagining the Kingdom*, 81 and 142. Even if a person has been converted in their mind, Lewis (*Screwtape Letters*, 11) says, all their habits pull against Christian virtue.

34. Willard, *Renovation of Heart*.

their way pure by "guarding it according to your Word.... I treasure your Word in my heart, so that I may not sin against you" (Ps 119:9-11). The prophet Daniel (6:10), exiled in Babylon, prayed three times a day facing Jerusalem as a reminder of truths and values he would otherwise forget. In the upper room, after supper, Jesus took bread and wine and said "Take it. Eat it. Drink it. Don't ever forget. Instead, remember."[35] True disciples are those in whom the Word of Christ abides fully (Col 3:16); their faculties have been trained by practice (Heb 5:14) so that they have the mind of Christ (Phil 2:5; 1 Cor 2:16) and their whole life is oriented to imitating him. Because we are double-minded, seeing truth but then quickly forgetting (Jas 1:24), we need regular disciplines to keep us connected to God's perspective and to subvert cultural understandings of reality. God's "Word [must be] planted in you" (Jas 1:21 *NIV*); it must become part of our very being—something internal, not external, to us, written, St. Paul (2 Cor 3:3) says, "not on tablets of stone but on tablets of human hearts" (cf. Jer 31:33; Ezek 36:25-27; Heb 10:16). Regular prayer "is a form of remembrance," Michael Sells says. "It is meant to break into normal human preoccupations and reorient a person to matters of ultimate concern."[36] Through prayer we rehearse truth over and over again so that we internalize it. "I need the corrective vision of prayer," Philip Yancey says, "because all day long I . . . lose sight of God's perspective"; prayer "is the act of seeing reality from God's point of view."[37] Prayer, in the words of my parish priest, "changes out the messages in our heads" so that "I keep the Lord always before me" (Ps 16:8) and hear the voice of Jesus (John 10:27) in my busy and noisy world.

35. Evans, *Searching for Sunday*, 123 and 128.

36. Sells, *Approaching the Qur'an*, 39. Mindfulness (*taqwa*) and remembrance (*dhikr*) are core virtues of Islamic civilization. "The premise of the Qur'anic reminder is that the human being is by nature forgetful, and by habit and preoccupation caught up in the concerns of the world which hide the central reality of the moral imperative for generosity and justice. One form of reminder is the performance of the prayers, breaking the preoccupation of the day, ritually and regularly, to orient oneself toward the prophetic message . . . . The other form of remembrance is the repetition and recitation . . . of the basic message concerning the day of reckoning" (75). Yancey (*Prayer*, 166 and 181) notes that "in medieval times, and still today in monasteries, the chiming of a church bell would cause all who heard it to stop and say the prescribed prayer. It forced them to remember God." In Roman times "bells from the . . . forum tolled divisions in the day—at 6:00 a.m., 9:00 a.m., noon, 3:00 p.m., and 6:00 p.m. Devout Jews adopted this schedule for their daily prayers, and early Christians continued the practice"—which became the "prayer of the hours."

37. Yancey, *Prayer*, 24 and 29.

Scholar after scholar makes the point that prayer is corrective. Antti Alhonsaari says that by praying the believer is "repeatedly making himself see the world in a certain way . . . [and] is repeatedly bending his emotional life and his behavior to conform to this reality."[38] Jürgen Moltmann emphasizes that when we pray "we are seeking the reality of God, and are breaking out of the Hall of Mirrors of our own illusory wishes, in which we have been imprisoned." Prayer is "the beginning of a cure for the numbing addictions of the secular world"—and "the person who prays, lives more attentively."[39] Wright agrees that through prayer our beliefs and desires are "sorted out, straightened out, untangled." By praying "we are taking the first steps from the chaos of our normal interior life towards . . . order and clarity" that rightly orders our disordered loves.[40] The role of prayer, Brueggemann adds, is "to nurture, nourish, and evoke a consciousness and perception alternative to the consciousness and perception of the dominant culture."[41] "We must traffic incessantly in [the] narrative which God inhabits," he says, until it saturates our minds and we "switch worlds"—replacing old belief and desire patterns with new ones.[42] Spiritual practices like prayer—in the words of the Episcopal

---

38. Alhonsaari, cited in Tiessen, *Providence and Prayer*, 108.

39. Moltmann, *In the End*, 83–84.

40. Wright, *Lord and His Prayer*, 44. Guroian (*Incarnate Love*, 74) observes that faithful Christian living is grounded in prayer because without it we are "incapable of discerning between the world's standards and those which belong to the kingdom of God." O'Keefe (*Becoming Good*, 95) says that through prayer "the Christian understanding of self, others, and world . . . comes to provide the interpretive lens through which the world is viewed and understood." Saliers ("Liturgy and Ethics," 179–80) asserts that right living requires "a continual re-entry" into God's truth. Prayer supplies "a rehearsal of the narratives and a continual re-embedding of persons in the language of faith. . . . The Christian life is coming to understand who God is and what [God's] intentions for human beings are. . . . This coming to understand is precisely what [spiritual] practice provides." Spiritual practices, Smith (*Desiring the Kingdom*, 88) says, "function as counter-formation to the mis-formation" of secular culture. Willimon and Hauerwas (*Lord, Teach Us*, 19) declare that repetitive prayer is a practice in "bending our wants toward what God wants" so that we "become the people God has called us to be." While these authors are referring to worship, their words apply to prayer as well.

41. Brueggemann, *Prophetic Imagination*, 3. While Brueggemann is referring to worship, his words apply to prayer as well.

42. Brueggemann, *Biblical Perspectives on Evangelism*, 112 and "Preaching as Reimagination," 327. While Brueggemann is referring to worship and preaching, his words apply to prayer as well.

Church Collect of Purity—"cleanse the thoughts of our hearts" and shape our view of reality so that we live by Christian convictions.[43]

Being Christian is not something we settle into in static fashion; instead, we are always in an ongoing process of *becoming* Christian through the repetition of practices that—to use words from Julian Baggini— "stitches [faith] into the fabric of daily life."[44] Discipleship is the formation of character, of reforming our beliefs and desires—"breaking the habits of wrongdoing," Willard says, "that govern our lives because of our long habituation to a world alienated from God" and, positively, helping us acquire habits of goodness.[45] Prayer trains us, Smith says, to take the right things for granted; it habituates us to know and love what God wants for human beings and all creation. Prayer forms rightly-ordered desires by aiming our hearts and minds at the kingdom of God; it is a practice that over time gradually and unconsciously shapes our fundamental orientation to the world. Prayer is what Smith calls "perceptual training"—construal training—that enables us to see life in the right way and value the right things; its result is sanctified perception.[46] Where culture forms us in habits of egocentricity—a vision of life which revolves around self-gratification, in which we are the center of the universe—prayer calls us out of ourselves and into the life of God. Through it we clothe ourselves with the virtues of Christ (Col 3:12–15). Prayer, Smith goes on to say, is a counter-measure that corrects secular influences, a form of redemptive thinking and desiring. It is a reparative discipline that—through regular, repeated routines—rehabituates and reorders our minds and hearts with new habits of thinking and feeling that are indexed to the kingdom of God. We inherit from society certain ways of seeing the world; prayer is a way out of this socialization—it corrects our beliefs and desires so we construe the world in the right way, breaking the domination of cultural assumptions. Praying—and praying for the dead in particular—implants in us a vision of reality and a corresponding way of life, one attuned to the values of life characteristic of God's kingdom.[47]

---

43. Episcopal Church, *Book of Common Prayer*, 355. Tertullian asserts that "Christ is truth, not fashion"—and the word "fashion," Pope Benedict XVI (*Fathers of Church*, 12) notes, means "cultural fashion, current fads."

44. Baggini, *Virtues of Table*, 199; also see 277.

45. Willard, *Divine Conspiracy*, 341.

46. Smith, *Imagining the Kingdom*, 3–5, 34–36, 41, 81, 101, 140, and 153–56.

47. Ibid., 123, 148, 155, 164, and 178. Also see Ochs, "Morning Prayer."

Overall Spiritual Benefits of Praying for the Departed

With this model of how prayer in general shapes Christian consciousness, I now consider some ways in which prayer for the dead counters eschatological forgetfulness and fosters eschatological remembrance. Muslim daily prayers have a future focus; awareness of the "day of reckoning" when every person will give an account of their actions encourages moral vigilance in the present.[48] Regular prayer for the dead can serve a similar function for Christians by centering us on the meaning of death. How we approach death reflects what we believe. "We, the Church, need to recover the art of dying," Lauren Winner contends. "We need to reacquaint ourselves with death. We need to help people die well and mourn well."[49] By reminding us that God is victorious over death and will give life to our mortal bodies (Rom 8:11), prayer for the dead teaches us the meaning of death and how to practice it faithfully. It encourages us to reflect on our own death and live in its light, to die and grieve in hope of resurrection.

Praying for the Dead Corrects Forgetfulness of Death

There is a long tradition from antiquity to the present of meditation on death as a tool for effective living.[50] Contemporary culture, however, does not promote thinking about death; we find it deeply disturbing, and so divert ourselves by becoming absorbed in daily activities—work, entertainment, food, alcohol, and sex. "Being unable to cure death," Blaise Pascal says, we "have decided, in order to be happy, not to think about such things." We "go through life without giving so much as a thought to the final end of life . . . , thinking only of the happiness of the moment."[51] Seneca the Younger cautions—however—that "if your own frailty never occurs to you," you will "squander [time] as though you had a full and

---

48. The values presented in the Qur'an, Sells (*Approaching the Qur'an*, 16-17) says, ask the reader "a simple question: what will be of value at the end of a human life? The framework of this question is the concept of a . . . day of reckoning in which each human being will face what he or she has done and has not done. The premise . . . is that the human being avoids the ultimate question through self-delusion."
49. Winner, "Foreword," in Moll, *Art of Dying*, 11.
50. I develop this analysis in "Make Today Count."
51. Pascal, *Pensees*, 106 and 41, slightly modified.

overflowing supply."[52] Leo Tolstoy's novella *The Death of Ivan Ilyich* depicts a self-centered man who, while dying, discovers that the values on which he constructed his life—social approval, wealth, work, and pleasure—are "not the real thing." Ivan's story stands as a warning: if we deny death we will waste our lives—but if we remember that we will die we will understand what matters most: simple everyday pleasures, human relationships, and faithful discipleship.[53] Martin Heidegger states that we are radically contingent beings—beings-toward-death—who live every moment with the chance of extinction from this life. Feeling anxiety, we "cover up dying," live foolishly and die unprepared. We can, however, "live in the light of death." The realization that we are finite gives life urgency and makes authentic existence possible.[54]

The dead, Rob Moll says, "reflect our own future selves"—the persons we will one day be. Praying for them is a *memento mori*—"remember you must die"—exercise that helps us integrate death into our living.[55] It reminds us that we ourselves will someday be among the departed, that as we pray for them now, so others will pray for us. The purpose of *memento mori* is best expressed by Lucian of Samosata: "if only humans could get it straight from the beginning: that they're going to die; that, after a brief stay in life, they have to depart . . . , then they'd live more wisely and die with fewer regrets."[56] The Bible encourages *memento mori*: in the words of the Preacher (Eccl 7:2 *NIV*), "death is the destiny of everyone; the living should take this to heart"—and the psalmist reminds us that life is short, like a flower soon to vanish (90:5; 103:15-16) and so we should "count our days that we gain a wise heart" (90:12). Spiritual exercises for contemplating mortality were an important aspect of religious piety in the patristic, medieval, and Reformation church; they urged people to live a righteous life in preparation for death and judgment day. Thomas à Kempis advises: "be always ready, and live in such a manner that death

---

52. Seneca, *On Shortness of Life*, 5.
53. Tolstoy, *Death of Ivan Ilyich*, 128.
54. Heidegger, *Being and Time*, 298-99.
55. Moll, *Art of Dying*, 158. The Latin phrase *memento mori* originated in ancient Rome when, during a general's victory parade, his slave would accompany him, whispering the words as a warning against excessive pride at his achievements—in your hour of fame, remember that all the glorious figures of the past are dead and forgotten. Medieval and Renaissance artists often included a skull—sitting on a desk, for example—in their paintings and portraits. See Duclow, *"Memento Mori."*
56. Lucian, cited in Hadot, *Philosophy as Way of Life*, 246.

may not find you unprepared.... The hour of death will shortly come, and therefore take care how you conduct yourself."[57] Timothy Ware agrees: mindfulness of death "is not negative but affirmative; it does not make our earthly existence drab and colorless, but has precisely the opposite effect. Because we keep death in mind, thereby living each day in the eschatological Now, our daily words and actions acquire an eternal dimension that otherwise they would lack." Moltmann puts it simply: "the remembrance of death makes us wise for living."[58]

Pondering our own death through praying for the dead is a powerful force for spiritual growth because to do so is to confront the fundamental human question—how should I live? What is the meaning and purpose of life? Am I practicing love for God and service of neighbor so as to hear the words "well done...; enter into...joy" (Matt 25:21)? Some day—perhaps today—will be my last, and so "now is the acceptable time" to live faithfully (2 Cor 6:2), now "is . . . the moment for you to wake from sleep" (Rom 13:11). I should ask myself "what will Jesus see when he looks at my life?" Can I say, as Job (29:14–16): "I put on righteousness, and it clothed me; my justice was like a robe and a turban. I was eyes to the blind, and feet to the lame. I was a father to the needy, and I championed the cause of the stranger." Do I prioritize what God values by feeding the hungry and giving drink to the thirsty? Do I welcome strangers, clothe the naked, care for the sick, visit prisoners (Matt 25:35–36)? Prayer for the dead creates—in Gary Habermas' and James Moreland's words—a "top-down heavenly perspective" where we "strive first for the kingdom of God" (Matt 6:33) and invest our treasures in heaven (Matt 6:21), where we "set our minds on things that are above, not on things that are on earth" (Col 3:2; cf. Phil 3:19-20). Prayer centers our lives so we view everything from the perspective of eternity; it reminds us that we are strangers on earth, pilgrims seeking a better country (Heb 11:16). As we become heavenly-minded in a good way, "we can assess our current priorities, eliminate poor choices and begin . . . extending ourselves into projects more in keeping with our heavenly priorities." In the words of an

---

57. Kempis, *Imitation of Christ*, 63–65.

58. Ware, "One Body in Christ," 180 and Moltmann, *Coming of God*, 57. As missionary C. T. Studd puts it, "Only one life, 'twill soon be past. Only what's done for Christ will last." What is done for Christ is not restricted to "Christian activities" concerning church or spiritual practice, but is what advances God's kingdom in every aspect—our marriages and families, work and recreation, the spending of our money and how we vote.

Episcopal church collect, prayer for the dead gives us "grace to . . . desire what you promise; that, among the swift and varied changes of the world our hearts may surely there be fixed where true joys are to be found."[59]

Praying for the dead—especially for those we know who die suddenly or young—counters forgetfulness of death and creates a constant knowledge that life is brief, thereby encouraging personal examination and reordered priorities. They make us—in the words of the Episcopal burial prayers—"deeply aware of the shortness and uncertainty of human life" and enable us to live "in holiness and righteousness all our days" so that we die "having the testimony of a good conscience." Not knowing if our time will be long or short enriches the quality of our personal lives and sharpens our Christian discipleship. By reminding us that "in the midst of life we are in death," praying for the dead teaches us to measure our days and our choices so we live for what is truly important.[60] It purifies our priorities so we "seek the future city, the . . . heavenly Jerusalem," in Pope Benedict XVI's words, and "preserve the proper scale of values without ever submitting to the fashions of the moment."[61]

Praying for the Dead Corrects Fear of Dying

As we pray for the departed we learn not to deny death—or to defy it. We fear death because it is evil. "When I consider the brief span of my life, absorbed in the eternity of time which went before and will come after it," Pascal confesses, "I am terrified."[62] The way we understand death determines how we react to it. A secular worldview claims that this life is all there is, that death is the absolute end of human existence. If death is the end of everything then it is the ultimate evil to fear and fight. As C. S. Lewis' imaginary devil Screwtape writes, "human beings . . . tend to regard death as the prime evil and survival as the greatest good."[63] Death, St. Paul admits, is an "enemy" (1 Cor 15:26)—something real and frightening that negates the good gift of life, destroys personal meaning, and separates us from those we love. But death—which "has been swallowed

---

59. Habermas and Moreland, *Beyond Death*, 353 and Episcopal Church, *Book of Common Prayer*, 219.

60. Episcopal Church, *Book of Common Prayer*, 504 and 492.

61. Benedict XVI, *Fathers of Church*, 98.

62. Pascal, *Pensees*, 74.

63. Lewis, *Screwtape Letters*, 131.

up in victory" (1 Cor 15:54)—is also a friend which brings us home to God. In the biblical worldview death is a transition to a new and better life. As Frederica Mathewes-Green puts it: "someday, time will run out . . . and I will go in a box. The box has a trick bottom; I tumble through it into something beyond words."[64] Victor Hugo puts it equally well: "the tomb is not a blind alley—it is a thoroughfare. It closes with the twilight to open with the dawn."[65] Bonhoeffer agrees: death is "the gateway to our home, to the tent of joy, to the eternal realm of peace"—the final "station on the road to freedom." As he said leaving his prison cell to be executed for acting against the Nazi government, "this is the end—but for me, the beginning of life."[66] Through his resurrection, the author of Hebrews says, Jesus "destroyed the one who has the power of death . . . and freed those who all their lives were held in slavery by the fear of death" (2:14-15). Prayer for the dead reminds us that death is not the final word and strengthens our faith in life beyond the grave.

Praying for the departed is an *ars moriendi*—"art of dying"—exercise that prepares us to die differently than people without faith in eternal life. In the twelfth century belief in individual judgment immediately at death became dominant, with dying seen as a time of final decision for heaven or hell. In response to the widespread anxiety this caused, the Roman Catholic Church created *ars moriendi*—particular spiritual disciplines practices to prepare Christians to end life in a state of grace. This tradition blossomed in the fifteenth century as the plague ravaged Europe. Rituals used during the process of dying helped the sick reconcile with their survivors, repent of sin, and proclaim faith in Christ. Handbooks also prescribed prayers and sacraments for use at the time of death, and gave advice to the family on appropriate behavior at the bedside. The *ars moriendi* tradition, with its practices that ordered death and prepared one for it socially and spiritually, faded in the seventeenth century.[67] Prayer for the dead is, to repeat, *ars moriendi*; it makes us

---

64. Mathewes-Green, cited in Connelly, *Promise of Heaven*, 87.

65. Hugo, cited in Winter, *Living Through Loss*, 72. Lewis describes this well in *The Last Battle*—as the final catastrophe overtakes Narnia, the stable becomes a gate to eternity. Williams (*Lion's World*, 115) explains: "at first it appears that it is a doorway into torment and death: the demonic god of Calormen lives there, and will devour everything that steps through the door. But suddenly, when King Tirian has entered, it is transformed."

66. Bonhoeffer, cited in Taylor, *Dietrich Bonhoeffer*, 85 and 11 and "Stations on Way to Freedom," in *Letters and Papers*, 512-13.

67. The most famous handbook was the Latin *Ars Moriendi* and its English

ready to die in a way that expresses Christian beliefs and values. This is a practice the church desperately needs, since far too often believers deny terminal illness and thus disenfranchise dying so it is not publicly acknowledged and socially supported (but is suppressed through mutual pretense).[68] Praying for those who continue to exist right now helps us look to the future with assurance of eternal life rather than fear of extinction since, as Bruce Cockburn sings, "Joy will find a way" to turn death into resurrection.[69]

We try to conquer our fear of death by filling our lives with busyness and achievement—raising families, doing jobs, enjoying leisure—as a way of coping with anxiety and trying to feel immortal. Consider, however, one particular consequence of fear of dying—medical over-treatment at end-of-life. Research finds that as death approaches religiously devout terminally ill patients and their families are more likely than less religious individuals to want doctors to do everything possible to keep them alive. They seek aggressive, death-delaying care (such as mechanical ventilation in intensive care units) in the last week of life and do little advance care planning (such as appointing a healthcare surrogate).[70] The ways in which Christians make end-of-life decisions often contradict the gospel by showing a lack of faith in resurrection hope. But "the sacred future,"

---

translation, *The Book of the Craft of Dying*. Other manuals on preparation for death followed, such as Jeremy Taylor's *The Rule and Exercises of Holy Dying*. See Duclow, "Ars Moriendi" and Paxton, "History of Christian Death Rites." Craddock, Goldsmith and Goldsmith, *Speaking of Dying*, Moll, *Art of Dying*, and Verhey, *Christian Art of Dying* seek to recover the practice of dying well.

68. Craddock, Goldsmith, and Goldsmith, *Speaking of Dying*, demonstrate that the church does not cope well with dying. Typically, a terminal diagnosis creates denial of impending death, an inability to speak of dying, grief, and loss; instead, hope is placed in the techniques of modern medicine to beat the illness. The authors provide biblical reflection and pastoral advice, based on the Christological narrative, for care of the dying.

69. Cockburn, "Joy Will Find a Way."

70. See Brett and Jersild, "'Inappropriate' Treatment" and Phelps, "Religious Coping." Lustig ("End-of-Life Decisions") confirms that "'religious' patients often seem more intent than atheists and agnostics on receiving any and all forms of treatment to stave off imminent death.... Many religious persons insist on any and all life-sustaining treatments, even past the point of any plausible benefit." Kastenbaum ("Anxiety and Fear") notes that the relationship between death anxiety and religious belief is too complex to provide a simple pattern of findings. Death-related teachings differ, and believers may take different messages from the same basic doctrine. Historical studies and social scientific research suggest that religious faith seems to sometimes reduce and sometimes increase death anxiety.

Kenneth Vaux says, "presents us with an ethics of ... how we should die." This is how it was with my dad—his dying acted out his hope of eternal life through the risen Jesus. He knew that "all of us go down to the dust; yet even at the grave we make our song: Alleluia"—and thus did not attempt to control death once his dying was clear.[71] Belief in our resurrection destiny helps us to resist the absolutizing of physical existence and to let ourselves or a loved one go to life beyond life. Praying for the departed reminds us that until the *eschaton* human life will include sickness and death. As Bonhoeffer says:

> where death is final, fear of it combines with defiance. . . . Where, however, it is recognized that the power of death has been broken, . . . there one demands no eternities from life. . . . One doesn't cling anxiously to life. . . . One is content with measured time and does not attribute eternity to earthly things. One leaves to death the limited right that it still has. But one expects the new human being and the new world only from beyond death, from the power that has conquered death.[72]

Prayer for the dead, by teaching us fundamental truths of faith, prepares us to let death occur naturally when illness is irreversible instead of prolonging life futilely. Lewis portrays the after-death experiences of the Pevensie children and others in Narnia—they embrace Aslan, meet old friends, and enjoy happiness and peace. "You don't need to be afraid of dying if it's like it is in the Narnia stories," Richard Purtill states.[73]

Dying well requires preparation. Praying for those at rest with God reminds us that we, like them, will arrive safely at home, that the tragedy of Good Friday is followed by the triumph of Easter Sunday, that—in John Donne's words—"one short sleep past, we wake eternally."[74] Prayer for the dead, Frederick Lee says, "keeps up in us a lively sense of ... immortality" and reinforces the fact that God gives life to the dead (Rom 4:17), that Jesus is the "Resurrection and the Life" (John 11:25). It enables us to face old age, illness, and death with confidence—"in sure and certain hope of the resurrection to eternal life through Jesus Christ our

---

71. Vaux, *Death Ethics*, 167 and Episcopal Church, *Book of Common Prayer*, 499.
72. Bonhoeffer, *Ethics*, 91–92.
73. Purtill, *Tolkien*, 180. See Lewis, *Last Battle*, chapters 12–16.
74. Donne, cited in Wright, *Surprised by Hope*, 15.

Lord"—rather than fear since "Christ is risen from the dead, trampling down death by death, and giving life to those in the tomb.".[75]

Praying for the Dead Corrects Hopeless Grief

Death is a real separation—and biblical faith does not "spiritualize" the terrible reality of grief. It does not deny the raw pain of loss, the feelings of numbness, anger, and sadness; it does not expect survivors to be stoic or to "get over" their grief quickly. Resurrection hope does not remove the crushing sorrow and profound disruption of missing a loved one or provide easy answers to agonizing questions.[76] We experience both "faith's bright promise and life's dark pain," Carol Luebering writes. "If we abandon hope, we deny our faith; if we deny the pain [of loss], we refuse our own experience."[77] Having lost a brother to senseless death, my wife's family knows the heartache of grief; we also know that God is our hope and consolation.

Praying for departed loved ones can, Sidney Callahan suggests, be "a means to reconcile ourselves to their death."[78] It can help us work through the phases of grief—shock and numbness; withdrawal and confusion; disorganization and despair; reorganization of life. Praying for departed loved ones can help us accomplish the tasks of mourning—accepting the reality of the loss; experiencing and resolving painful feelings; struggling back from depression and adjusting to an environment where the deceased is missing; deciding to take up life again. Prayers for the dead can include lament in which we acknowledge sorrow and complaint. Instead of avoiding pain, pretending the loss is not real and trying to be strong, we can declare our sadness, fear, anger, doubt, and despair honestly to God. Lament is especially necessary when death is untimely or unexpected. My dad's natural death at age eighty was a homecoming, but my brother-in-law Gerry's killing at fifty-three was a tragedy—he was cut down in his prime. Even though we will be reunited with our loved ones in heaven death's sting is painful. We must not rush past grief, Allen Verhey says, "to celebrate the resurrection." Christian experience "includes

---

75. Lee, *Christian Doctrine of Prayer for Departed*, 175 and Episcopal Church, *Book of Common Prayer*, 501 and 500.

76. See, for example, Lewis, *Grief Observed*.

77. Luebering, *To Comfort All Who Mourn*, 69; sentence order changed.

78. Callahan, *With All Heart and Mind*, 189.

Holy Saturday"—we should remember "that day of anguish and sadness as readily as the day of God's triumph over death."[79] Praying for departed loved ones can give voice to pain. "While the liturgy for the dead is an Easter liturgy," the *Book of Common Prayer* states, "this joy does not make human grief unchristian. The very love we have for each other in Christ brings deep sorrow when we are parted by death. Jesus himself wept at the grave of his friend" (John 11:33–35).[80]

For Christians, Stanley Hauerwas says, "death is properly lamented, but also celebrated as new life."[81] Prayer for the dead provides comfort in our grief by reinforcing our trust that family and friends are with God, enabling us—in the words of an Episcopal prayer—"to see in death the gate of eternal life."[82] Since death is not the end of someone we love, David Winter says, "we mourn our separation from them but look ahead to a time when we shall see them again." This faith "does not eliminate our grief"; it does, however, "take away the hopelessness that would turn it into despair." He continues: "we are an Easter people" and so while death is a parting it is not finality.[83] We grieve, but not as those "who have no hope" (1 Thess 4:13). Praying for departed loved ones enables us to mourn their loss deeply but with knowledge that they have been received safely, as the Episcopal prayers put it, "into the arms of [God's] mercy, into the blessed rest of everlasting peace and into the glorious company of the saints in light."[84] It helps us say goodbye to them over the months and years with hope that we too will come to God's heavenly country and see them again. Praying for the dead allows our love to flow to them. Wright cites the story of Norman Anderson who, having lost three children in early adulthood, continued "to hold those beloved children before God

---

79. Verhey, *Christian Art of Dying*, 347–48.

80. Episcopal Church, *Book of Common Prayer*, 507.

81. Hauerwas, "Foreword," in Craddock, Goldsmith and Goldsmith, *Speaking of Dying*, xi.

82. Episcopal Church, *Book of Common Prayer*, 493.

83. Winter, *Living Through Loss*, 36 and 73. Donald Gray Barnhouse was a well-known twentieth-century preacher. Cancer killed his first wife, leaving him with three children under 12. The day of the funeral the family was driving home when a large truck passed them, casting a shadow across their car. "Tell me," Barnhouse asked his daughter, "would you rather be run over by that truck or its shadow?" "By the shadow," she replied, "it can't hurt you." Then, speaking to all his children, Barnhouse said, "your mother has not been overrun by death, but by the shadow of death. That is nothing to fear."

84. Episcopal Church, *Book of Common Prayer*, 465, slightly modified.

in prayer ... because he wanted to talk to God about them, to share ... his love for them with ... God."[85] While we cannot erase the feeling that our loved one is gone, here and now, our sense of their absence can become a sense of presence in the communion of saints. In addition, praying for the dead allows us to keep them before us as role models whose faith and virtue we should emulate: "grant that we, encouraged by the good example of your servant N., may persevere in running the race that is set before us."[86]

Individuals might pray for their dead by lighting a candle and using the burial office—adapting, for example, the ancient anthem "into paradise may the angels lead you; at your coming may the martyrs receive you, and bring you into the holy city." Grievers can use a guide such as *Devotions for Those Living with Loss* or a memoir like *Lament for a Son*—and they might use a small statue of a *pleurant* as consolation.[87] Praying for the dead also enables the church to care for the bereaved instead of ignoring their experience. Those involved in personal or congregational caregiving—friends, pastors, and counselors—can bear the griever's burden by praying with them for their loved one: "Father of all, we pray to you for [N.] we love, but see no longer; grant [him/her] your peace; let light perpetual shine upon them; and ... work in them the good purpose of your perfect will." Through such prayers, the *Book of Common Prayer* emphasizes, God will grant those who are grieving "faith and courage ... [and] strength to meet the days to come with steadfastness and patience ... and in the joyful expectation of eternal life with those they love."[88]

Grieving well requires a supportive community who walk with the bereaved through shock, deep grief, and the slow rebuilding of life.

85. Wright, *For All Saints*, 74.

86. Episcopal Church, *Book of Common Prayer*, 250. Also see the collect for All Saints Day, 245 and burial prayer, 504.

87. Ibid., 500. Miller, *Devotions* and Wolterstorff, *Lament for Son*. Sculptures of *pleurants*—"weepers"—became common in French cemeteries as expressions of late medieval devotion; they are based on real *pleurants* who roamed graveyards praying for the dead. These robed mourning figures which depict intense grief and great loss were carved into tombs in a kind of perpetual funeral procession involving weeping, praying, and singing. Physical objects like this—small *pleurants* can be ordered online—can be a focus for expressing grief. Icons can also be aids to contemplation and prayer. Reflecting on icons depicting the raising of Lazarus, the crucifixion, resurrection, and ascension open a way into praying for the dead. See Forest, *Praying with Icons*.

88. Episcopal Church, *Book of Common Prayer*, 504–5. See the entire burial office, 491–505.

The church can learn from Jewish mourning rituals.[89] Following the funeral, mourners sit one week of *shiva* during which they do nothing. The congregation visits daily and says prayers for the bereaved and the dead. Then for eleven months mourners say *kaddish*—communal prayer, including petitions for the dead—twice a day; in this spiritual support group they can voice both doubt and affirm faith. On the one year anniversary of the death—*yahrtzeit*—mourners say *kaddish* again. Beyond the year, the community continues—in four annual services for the bereaved—to commemorate the deceased. The recently departed from Christian parishes should be remembered by name in the public prayers of worship as in the ancient church—daily at first, then monthly and annually. Throughout the year congregations can hang a plaque listing the names of members who have died on a wall in the sanctuary—someone can read the names aloud during the Prayers of the People. All Saints Day is also an opportunity for the church to remember and honor members who died that year. Public prayer should combine lament which allows mourning ("I eat ashes like bread and mingle tears with my drink"—Ps 102:9) and praise which promotes hope ("death . . . will not be able to separate [our dead] from the love of God"—Rom 8:38–39). Praying for the dead can be part of healing that helps grievers acknowledge the death, integrate the loss into their experience, and begin a new life—all with hope. Such a mourning practice can help Christians grieve differently from those who do not believe in a life to come. It can help us wait with patience for the consummation of God's kingdom on the last great day.

Concluding Remarks

"Come, Holy Spirit, heavenly Dove, with all thy quickening powers; kindle a flame of sacred love in these cold hearts of ours," we sing in the hymn of Isaac Watts. "See how we trifle here below, fond of these earthly toys; our souls, how heavily they go, to reach eternal joys."[90] "Get wisdom, get understanding," Hebrew Scripture admonishes; "above all else, guard your heart, for everything you do flows from it" (Prov 4:5, 23 *NIV*). I have an electronic tuner that indicates how the pitch of my guitar compares to the pitch I want. Having determined the difference between them, I adjust the tension of the string to match the desired pitch. Spiritual prac-

---

89. See Moll, *Art of Dying*, 135–37 and Verhey, *Christian Art of Dying*, 335.
90. Watts, "Come Holy Spirit," Episcopal Church, *Hymnal*, Hymn 510.

tices are tuning devices by which we bring our beliefs, desires and actions into line with God's truth. St. Paul (2 Tim 3:16) states that God's Word is "useful for teaching, for reproof, for correction and for training in righteousness"—it straightens and realigns the distorted beliefs and desires that misshape us. Without spiritual disciplines we forget our Christian identities and become enmeshed with culture in ways that marginalize faith. Many Christians live with divided attention. We do not hear God's word because other voices compete for our attention and drown it out. Instead of keeping our ears attuned to the sound of God's voice, we become caught up in the routines and banalities of life.

Conversion is the process of being uprooted from a fabric of meaning to which we are habituated and of being re-rooted in God's truth so we live congruently with the faith we profess. "Lord! Give us weak eyes for things that do not matter and eyes full of clarity in all your truth," Søren Kierkegaard writes. Charles Taliaferro calls prayer a "meditation on values" that determines our fundamental orientation to the world. "To pray," Samuel Balentine says, "is to become a new and different self"—to be changed from the inside out. Prayer, Douglas John Hall says, "is that mode of reflection . . . through which the disciples of Jesus . . . seek to gain and regain [God's] perspective" on life.[91] Harmon Smith agrees: prayer, by saturating us in God's truth, "teaches us who . . . we are and are meant to be. Such knowledge is not something we have naturally; we have to learn it; we have to be taught it and trained in it." Through praying we are "re-minded" as God's truth "come[s] again to our minds and takes control . . . of our thoughts and passions."[92] As the *lex orandi* formula says, what we pray is what we think and love and do. Prayer for the dead, in particular, is a type of counter-speech that challenges cultural assumptions and organizes our priorities around the truth of the gospel. Praying for the dead focuses our complete attention on the values of God's kingdom and helps us ignore distractions and the voice of culture that make us deaf to God.

Prayer for the dead helps us understand the meanings surrounding dying, death, and bereavement. It corrects our general attitudes to death—foolish forgetfulness, dysfunctional fear, and hopeless grief. It gives us a glimpse of the destiny that awaits us and encourages us to live,

---

91. Kierkegaard, *Sickness Unto Death*; Taliaferro, "Prayer," 677; Balentine, *Prayer in Hebrew Bible*, 269; Hall, *When You Pray*, 59.

92. Smith, *Where Two or Three Are Gathered*, 54, 65; slightly modified. While Smith is referring to worship, his words apply to prayer as well.

THE GENERAL SPIRITUAL VALUE OF PRAYING FOR THE DEAD   183

die, and grieve with eternity in mind. In addition, each specific form of prayer—consummation, growth, purification, and salvation prayers—influences faith and practice in particular ways. I turn to them in the next chapter.

chapter 7

PARTICULAR SPIRITUAL BENEFITS OF PRAYING FOR THE DEAD

IT MIGHT SEEM THAT reading—or writing—a book on the afterlife is a waste of time since there are more important this-worldly needs to focus our efforts on. I confess to wondering this myself at times. The worry, however, assumes a false dilemma since belief in an afterlife and concern for making this world a better place for people to live in are not mutually exclusive. In fact, they are connected; as Rob Bell notes, "our eschatology shapes our ethics. Eschatology is about the last things. Ethics are about how you live. What you believe about the future shapes, informs, and determines how you live now."[1] Frank Macchia agrees: a "focus on the ultimate horizon of the Kingdom's fulfillment can have a sobering effect on our lives, directing our attention to what is most important to life as a Christian."[2] Thinking about the afterlife is a way to orient ourselves in this life.

During many of the months when I was working on this book, I was active in local politics—serving on the leadership committee and speakers bureau for a voter referendum asking property owners to approve a small tax to provide desperately-underfunded services to developmentally-disabled adults who cannot care for themselves. I was energized, not de-energized, by eschatological reflection. One evening I came home from a public presentation discouraged by the pushback our initiative was getting, frustrated at the injustice of a society that neglects the most

---

1. Bell, *Love Wins*, 46.
2. Macchia, "Pentecostal and Charismatic Theology," 287.

vulnerable. Days later Jenna gave me a poster which now hangs above my desk. It is a statement by C. S. Lewis: "If I find in myself desires which nothing in this world can satisfy, the only logical explanation is that I was made for another world."[3] Lewis means that we are made for another world *metaphysically*—for a spiritual heavenly world, not a material earthly one. Jenna assured me, however, that my discontent was a sign of being made for another world *morally*—for a righteous world of justice and peace, not a sinful and corrupt one—the world I was, in one small way, attempting to create.

In the previous chapter I argued that Christians are too often—in the words of Fred Craddock, Dale Goldsmith, and Joy Goldsmith—"victims of the wrong story," a secular worldview that shapes how we think about life, the world, and our hopes. But "the Christian story is not the same as the secular story," and when we assume a good deal of overlap between them we become victims of "secular identity theft" in which culture rewrites God's truth.[4] Unfaithful behavior results from mistaken beliefs and desires—and prayer is misbelief and misdesire therapy, a practice of perspective transformation, or renewing our hearts and minds based on God's truth, of redirecting our patterns of thinking and desiring so we "delight in the law of the Lord" and "do not follow the advice of the wicked" (Ps 1:1-2).[5] I noted in chapter six how prayer is spiritually forming, how it helps us live as faithful Christians in a secular culture—and I identified some general benefits, centered on the of meaning death, of praying for the departed. In this chapter I consider how praying for each group of the dead—the blessed, the imperfect, and the unsaved—has spiritual value by correcting particular mistakes in faith and practice.

The Spiritual Benefits of Consummation Prayer

Consummation prayer is prayer for the completion of God's kingdom—resurrection on a new earth of justice and peace. The kingdom is both present (having already been inaugurated) and future (still awaiting final completion). Consummation prayer reminds us that suffering will be transformed into joy in the life to come and that we must be working

---

3. Lewis, *Mere Christianity*, 120.
4. Craddock, Goldsmith and Goldsmith, *Speaking of Dying*, 21, 23, 26, and 29.
5 The phrase 'misbelief and misdesire therapy' is drawn from Habermas and Moreland, *Beyond Death*, 347.

toward the values of God's rule in this life, joining in God's mission to heal all creation. In the encouraging words of the African-American spiritual: "keep your lamps trimmed and burning / Christian journey soon be over / children, don't grow weary"—"for the time is drawing nigh." Charles Schulz's *Peanuts* character Sally, in jesting with her brother Charlie Brown, mispronounces the book of Revelation as "the book of Re-evaluation." Her mistake has something to teach us—eschatological consciousness, nurtured by consummation prayer, should cause us to re-examine our lives, values, and priorities so that we live more faithfully as those who carry Christ's name.[6]

Consummation Prayer Helps Us Live with Evil and Suffering

Incurable illnesses, natural disasters, and senseless crimes bring misery into our lives. In addition, faithful discipleship is costly—Jesus does not promise never-ending earthly happiness but requires taking up the cross in self-denial (Luke 9:23). Consummation prayer nurtures hope, assuring us that, while we live in a world where we experience suffering and must choose sacrifice, God can be trusted to ultimately bring good out of evil and loss.

Consummation Prayer and the Suffering That Happens to Us

This world contains horrible evils. Some are massive evils (like the Nazi Holocaust); others are personal evils (like the killing of my brother-in-law Gerry by a careless driver). Evils can be so bad, Marilyn Adams says, that they are "life-ruining"—they destroy joy and meaning and undermine faith in God's goodness and power.[7]

Consummation prayer reminds us that, while much suffering has no satisfactory answer in this life, it will be remedied in the next. "Heaven," Jerry Walls says, "is essential to make sense of . . . evils. . . . Without . . . life beyond the grave, there simply is no hope of full redemption for some evils."[8] Evils are experienced by particular persons, Adams points

---

6. Schulz, *Peanuts 2000*, 76.

7. Adams, *Horrendous Evils*, 17–18.

8. Walls, *Heaven*, 116 and 124. This discussion draws on Hasker, *Triumph of God*, chapter 8; MacDonald, *Evangelical Universalist*, 157–62; Peterson, "Eschatology and Theodicy"; Walls, *Heaven*, chapters 5 and 7; and Wright, *Evil and Justice of God*,

out—and so must be redeemed, not in the whole system of the world, but in the life of the person who suffered it. "God must guarantee each person a life that is a great good to him/her on the whole," she insists, "and one in which any participation in horrors is defeated within the context of his/her own life." "To say that horrors are defeated," Adams adds, "means that their negative value has been overcome by weaving them into a larger meaning-making framework of positive significance for the individual in question."[9] That seldom happens in this life, but in the next life—William Hasker says—"the evils . . . people have suffered . . . will be . . . engulfed in the experience of intimacy with God."[10] St. Paul asserts that "the sufferings of this present time are not worth comparing with the glory about to be revealed to us" (Rom 8:18), that our "slight momentary affliction is preparing us for an eternal weight of glory beyond all measure" (2 Cor 4:17). St. Peter (1 Pet 1:3–9) instructs Christians experiencing persecution to meditate on eternal life, refocusing their thoughts from earthly suffering to heavenly joy. Consummation prayer reminds us that suffering is not final and meaningless; in heaven's immortal gladness it is fixed and made up for.

In the consummated kingdom injustice and pain will both be ended and compensated for. First, evil will be *eliminated ontologically*. As the prophet Isaiah (25:7–8) declares, God "will swallow up death forever . . . [and] will wipe away the tears from all faces." St. John (Rev 21:4–5) reiterates this promise: God "will wipe every tear from their eyes. Death will be no more; mourning and crying and pain will be no more" when God makes all things new. Suffering will be banished when creation is put right. Second, evil will be *justified morally*. When "God's purpose of universal good is eventually attained," John Hick says, "nothing will finally have been sheerly and irredeemably evil. For everything will receive a new meaning in light of the end to which it leads. What now threatens us as final evil will prove to have been interim evil out of which good will in the end have been brought."[11] In heaven bad will be assimilated into good; God will remake our lives so they turn out happy. As Jürgen Moltmann puts it, those with "spoiled lives"—caused by serious disease or profound

---

chapter 4.

9. Adams, "Horrendous Evils," 156 and Adams, cited in Hasker, *Triumph of God*, 71.

10. Hasker, *Triumph of God*, 224. In heaven, Walls (*Heaven*, 123) says, "God [will] loosen the grip of the past on our lives and defeat its power to spoil our happiness."

11. Hick, *Evil and God of Love*, 362–64; cf. *Death and Eternal Life*, 156–66.

disability, crushing poverty, or destructive abuse—will have "the chance to become the person God meant them to be."[12] While heaven cannot change the facts of the past, it can change the value those facts have, thereby transforming them. Relationship with God is the greatest possible good; to achieve it is to be perfectly happy, despite suffering in this life. Supreme and eternal joy in God's kingdom will banish pain entirely.[13]

Consummation prayer, by reminding us that our troubles are only temporary and that there will be a final healing and restoration, creates hope and alters our view of suffering now. It teaches us to live with what Walls calls "cheerful mourning. Mourning because evil still touches our lives and tears at the fabric of what gives them meaning; cheer because of our hope that evil will be fully defeated and that even the worst tragedies can be redeemed in the end."[14]

Consummation Prayer and the Sacrifices That We Choose

Suffering is not just bad things that happen to us; it also includes self-sacrificial choices we make in order to faithfully follow Christ. Heaven, John Polkinghorne says, is "the foundation of a moral view that supports . . . the costly demands of fidelity and duty." A person's loyalty to a debilitated parent, a disappointing partner, or a disabled child creates demands and burdens. "Hope [in final consummation] can sustain the acceptance of such limitation by delivering us from the tyranny of the present, the feeling of need to grab as much as we can before all opportunity passes away forever."[15]

Jesus promises us a full and abundant life (John 10:10) and at the same time indicates that following his way involves suffering and self-denial (Matt 16:24–26). Doing the right thing sometimes requires giving up personal happiness. Suppose a man from childhood has wanted to

---

12. Moltmann, *Coming of God*, 116–17.

13. Walls, *Heaven, Hell and Purgatory*, 147–48 and Macquarrie, *Christian Hope*, 120.

14. Walls, *Heaven*, 118.

15. Polkinghorne, *God of Hope*, 48–49. Questions about the relationship between morality and personal happiness go back to Plato's *Republic*, where he argues that they are not contradictory. Immanuel Kant (*Critique of Pure Reason*, 103–13) argues that we must postulate God and immortality if happiness and virtue are to coincide in the supreme and complete good. See Walls, *Heaven*, chapter 7; *Heaven, Hell and Purgatory*, chapter 7; and Mavrodes, "Religion and Queerness of Morality."

earn a pilot license and own a small airplane—but instead gives the funds that this would have cost to a missionary hospital for treating obstetric fistulas (which make a life-changing difference to women in developing countries).[16] He faces a conflict between egoism and altruism—and chooses to follow the example of Jesus, looking out for the welfare of others rather than his own personal happiness (Phil 2:4–8), to "live in love, as Christ loved us and gave himself up for us" (Eph 5:2).[17] Whether this is a sensible or a stupid choice depends on whether there is a heaven. *If* there is no afterlife, then this life is the only one we have—and if this world is the only one there is, then the only goods that exist are this-worldly goods and the only happiness we experience is what happens in this life. If there is no heaven where sacrifices are compensated then altruism involves permanent loss. *If*—however—there is a heaven where earthly loss is rewarded, then there is no ultimate conflict between what is good for oneself and what is good for others. Because there are eternal goods that outweigh temporal goods, it is possible to sacrifice the finite goods of this life without losing the infinite goods of the next. As missionary martyr Jim Elliot famously put it, "he is no fool who gives what he cannot keep to gain that which he cannot lose."[18] This does not mean, Stephen Webb says, that heaven is "a bribe to encourage morality" or that those who sacrifice here expecting a later benefit are acting as selfish egoists, doing the right thing for the wrong reason. While there is a benefit of heavenly reward to the person who chose earthly sacrifice, that was not their motive—the reason for what they did that was altruistic. Heaven does not replace "the best intentions with mere selfishness"—Christians do not necessarily or even typically do good things in order to get into heaven or to be rewarded by God. Their concern is to make a difference in the world and to follow Christ's example.[19] It should be noted, however, that Jesus

---

16. See Singer, *Life You Can Save*, 101–3.

17. Labberton (*Dangerous Act of Worship*, 181) states that "when we choose to love in the name of Christ for the sake of justice, we allow our compassion to take us to people and to places for the sake of the other person, in advocacy for their needs, out of a compassion for their suffering, even when it means sacrifice and suffering for us."

18. Elliot, Billy Graham Center Archives.

19. Webb, *Good Eating*, 166. Psychological egoism is the theory that each person pursues only his or her own self-interest, that everyone's actions are always ultimately based on personal gain of some sort. It uses the tactic of reinterpreting motives in order to support this sweeping generalization and to explain apparently self-sacrificial actions, but only a cynic tries to imagine a self-serving motive for all altruistic behavior. Philosophers have long considered the relationship between morality and

and the apostles promise and encourage us to seek heavenly reward—for hospitality to the needy (Matt 25:37–40; Luke 14:12–14), bearing insults as Christians (Matt 5:12; Luke 6:22–23), keeping faith through trials (Jas 1:2; 1 Pet 1:6–7; Rev 2:10), generous giving (Luke 6:38; 1 Tim 6:17–19), loving enemies (Luke 6:35) and sacrificial obedience (Matt 19:29). It is not selfish for us to seek good for ourselves since we can—at the same time—seek faithful service to God and the good of our neighbor. Our own interests coincide with loving God and others.

Without consummation hope, the Roman Catholic International Theological Commission states, "it would be impossible to lead a Christian life. [There is an] intimate bond between the firm hope of future life and the possibility of responding to the demands of Christian life."[20] Heaven is the ultimate, perhaps the only, motivation for major self-sacrifice. "There is no one," Jesus says, who has given up the goods of this life "for the sake of the kingdom of God, who will not get back . . . in the age to come eternal life" (Luke 18:28–30). Even Jesus himself "for the sake of the joy that was set before him endured the cross" (Heb 12:2)—and Dietrich Bonhoeffer's belief that death is not the end but the beginning enabled his bold resistance to the evil Nazi government.

Consummation prayer, by reminding us that costly discipleship will be rewarded in the life to come, creates hope and enables lives of moral effort and personal sacrifice. Prayer for the faithful departed reminds us that we stand in the company of saints and martyrs who have gone before us on the journey of obedience to Christ. As the Episcopal prayers ask: "give us grace so to follow your blessed saints in all virtuous and godly living, that we may come to [the] ineffable joys of heaven"—"grant that we, encouraged by [their] good example . . . may persevere in running the race that is set before us, until at last we attain . . . to your eternal joy."[21]

---

personal happiness—whether they conflict or coincide with each other. It is important to distinguish between selfishness and self-interest. Selfishness is pursuing my own self-interest in a way that ignores or harms the well-being of others. I am selfish if I think only of my own good and care nothing for God and neighbor. I cannot be selfish and loving. But I can be self-interested and loving. Self-interest is looking out for my own needs and desires without harming those of others. It is obvious that concern for my own welfare is compatible with loving God and neighbor; it need not occur at their expense. For this reason, pursuing heavenly reward is not about seeking only my own good or caring only about myself without thought for others.

20. International Theological Commission, "Some Current Questions," 209.
21. Episcopal Church, *Book of Common Prayer*, 245 and 250.

Consummation Prayer Helps Us Fight against Evil and Injustice

The fact that evil is eliminated in the next life creates, it might be thought, a new problem: it undermines motivation to prevent or correct injustice in this life. The charge, Tom Wright says, is that "the present world doesn't matter so much because everything will be all right in the future one."[22] This is Karl Marx's criticism of escapist, other-worldly Christianity. Heaven—"the opium of the people"—gives the disadvantaged false consolation of relief in the next life, thereby encouraging them to be content with inhumane conditions is this life.[23] A happy afterlife is a harmful human construct that perpetuates social injustice, robbing people of political energy needed to create a good life on earth.

Bonhoeffer rejects the charge that belief in heaven is opposed to concern for earthly life. Early in his career he says, "Christ does not lead man in a religious flight from this world to other worlds beyond; rather, he gives him back to the earth as its loyal son."[24] While teaching at the underground seminary he remarks, "in following Christ [the disciple's] heavenly home has become so certain that they are truly free for life in this world."[25] From prison he writes "the Christian hope of resurrection . . . refers people to their life on earth in a wholly new way."[26] The goal of "worldly Christianity" is to bring the values of God's kingdom into public life. "The profound this-worldliness of Christianity . . . [means] living fully in the midst of life's tasks, questions, successes and failures, experiences and perplexities."[27] Bonhoeffer's own belief in final consummation enabled his involvement in the church struggle against Nazism and his political actions against the Hitler regime.

22. Wright, *Evil and Justice of God*, 145. As Bell (*Love Wins for Teens*, 76) puts it, "if you believe that when you die you go somewhere else and never again are a part of life on earth, then you won't be all that interested in partnering with God to help make the world the kind of place God intends for it to be."

23. Marx, *Early Writings*, 44. Nietzsche (*Zarathustra*, 428, 188, and 144) agrees: "we have no wish to enter the Kingdom of heaven: we have become men—so we want the earth." "Remain faithful to the earth," he says; "no longer . . . bury [your] head in the sand of heavenly things." I discuss this argument in "Bonhoeffer and False Dilemma."

24. Bonhoeffer, "Thy Kingdom Come," in Kelly and Nelson, *Testament to Freedom*, 94.

25. Bonhoeffer, *Discipleship*, 55–56.

26. Bonhoeffer, *Letters and Papers*, 447.

27. Ibid., 485. Because God and humanity have become one in the incarnation, we "can no longer see God without the world or the world without God" (*Ethics*, 58). Jesus Christ is the solution to Marx's false dilemma.

Consummation prayer corrects other-worldliness by reminding us that we will not escape from earth to be with God in heaven but will live on an earth healed of personal, social, and natural evils. While the intermediate hope is survival in a temporary place of restful happiness, the ultimate hope is the renewal of the entire cosmos, including physical resurrection and Jesus' return to an earth made new. Christian eschatology, Moltmann says, is cosmic eschatology, "for otherwise it becomes a gnostic doctrine of redemption, and is bound to teach, no longer the redemption *of* the world but a redemption *from* the world."[28] Consummation prayer prevents Christian faith from becoming world-denying. The central petitions of the Lord's Prayer—"may your title be honored, may your reign arrive, may your design be fulfilled *on earth* as in heaven"—request the coming of God's future into the present and motivates us to act toward that future now.[29]

Consummation prayer provides an "eschatological corrective" to escapism—to use Peter Kuzmic's words.[30] There are different ways of relating history and hope, present and future. *Apocalyptic eschatology*, recall from chapter 2, assumes two separate ages—the present evil age and the future good age; it looks to a time outside history when, through dramatic intervention, God will defeat evil and institute the kingdom. A totally apocalyptic, futurist eschatology of eternal life in another realm implies an ethic of world-denial. *Prophetic eschatology* looks to a time within history when God will establish peace and justice among the nations. A totally prophetic, realized eschatology strives for transformation of the world and has an ethic of world-involvement. *Inaugurated eschatology* holds that the kingdom is partly fulfilled within history and completely fulfilled beyond history. It has two stages—one present and "already," one future and "not yet." An inaugurated eschatology with its two-advent structure avoids the other-worldly detachment of a totally apocalyptic eschatology and the this-worldly utopianism of a totally prophetic eschatology.[31] It has an anticipatory ethic, the Lausanne Committee on World Evangelization says; we are to "manifest the righteousness of the Kingdom now, before it is consummated in glory."[32] Kuzmic agrees

28. Moltmann, *Coming of God*, 259 and 270, emphasis added.
29. This translation comes from Wills, *What Gospels Meant*, 87, emphasis added.
30. Kuzmic, "History and Eschatology," 154.
31. Ibid., 158.
32. Lausanne Committee, *Evangelism and Social Responsibility*, 42.

that the coming of God's rule has an "ethical summons"—"the future makes demands on our living in the present."

> Our view of the future is not only information about something we await. It is also a call to participation on the journey toward that future, and it determines the way we live in the present. Christians are called to anticipatory living that produces a proleptic lifestyle. . . . It means living anticipatorily, that is from a hope that sees that which has been inaugurated more and more realized here and now as it approaches its consummation. . . . We are called to continual realization of the eschatological values that are characteristic of the Kingdom: love, joy, life, justice, peace, freedom, brotherhood, equality, harmony, unity, etc. These future realities of heaven are to be proleptically present as they are practiced by the followers of Jesus, and they should motivate us to work toward their greater realization on earth.

We are called to responsible participation in the present kingdom, which is already here, and watchful expectation for the future kingdom, which is yet to come.[33]

The eschatological teachings of Jesus and the apostles are full of ethical content. They warn against idleness (2 Thess 3:6–14) and call us to be alert and busy in God's service (Matt 25:14–30). St. Peter (2 Pet 3:1–14), the Lausanne Committee points out, "tells us [twice] 'what sort of persons' we ought to be in this life on account of what is going to happen at the end"—and St. Paul encourages us to be "zealous for good deeds," living "lives that are self-controlled, upright and godly, while we wait for the blessed hope" of Christ's appearing (Titus 2:13–14).[34]

"To clasp hands in prayer," Karl Barth says, "is the beginning of an uprising against the disorder of the world."[35] Stanley Grenz agrees: "in prayer the Christian rebels against the *status quo*, . . . for petitionary prayer is a cry that God's Kingdom come, so that all that opposes or runs contrary to the divine will may be overturned."[36] In consummation

---

33. Kuzmic, "History and Eschatology," 157–58.

34. Lausanne Committee, *Evangelism and Social Responsibility*, 39.

35. Barth, cited in Willimon and Hauerwas, *Lord, Teach Us*, 109. The eschatology of Jesus, Lane (*Keeping Hope Alive*, 88) says, is not other-worldly and apolitical; instead, his words and deeds had a social-political dimension. "The action of God in the ministry of Jesus is affecting/subverting the social, political, economic and religious status quo by transforming the situation of those who are hungry, poor, ill and marginalized."

36. Grenz, *Prayer*, 43.

prayer we join the struggle against evil and pledge allegiance to the values and virtues of God's reign as the ultimate reality against which all other loyalties are measured. It gives us what Walter Brueggeman calls "exile consciousness"—"a deep sense of displacement" from the world's priorities and an awareness that we do not belong to mainstream society and national empire, but to God's kingdom.[37] To be a Christian is to be like Jesus; the kingdom of God was his concern, so we must develop what Dallas Willard calls "Kingdom-hearts."[38]

Consummation prayer creates an *attitude* of dissatisfaction and impatience with the present situation and a longing for God's promises to be completed. As we pray "how long?" (e.g., Ps 90:13–17) we learn to desire God's holy reign when the world is set right—the lonely befriended, the hungry fed, the sick healed, the grieving comforted, the homeless sheltered, the disabled supported, the marginalized included, the environment protected. In addition, it motivates *action* of resistance to evil—a willingness to be engaged in making God's reign real in the world now through acts of healing, reconciliation, justice, and kindness. We cannot pray "your kingdom come on earth" if we are unwilling to accept God's rule in our lives; we cannot pray "your will be done on earth" unless we are ready to give ourselves to God's service here and now. Hope means commitment to action and eschatology, John Sachs says. It "has an important ethical imperative: we must truly live what we hope for"— attempting to bring it about (as far as we are able).[39] A "focus on the ultimate horizon of the Kingdom's fulfillment," Macchia adds, "can give us an eschatological boldness to courageously resist oppressive forces in the world with full knowledge that the final triumph of God's Kingdom is only a matter of time."[40]

---

37. Bruggemann, cited in Bierma, *Bringing Heaven Down to Earth*, 172. St. Paul's "proclamation of Jesus as Son of God, Lord, and Savior directly countered Roman imperial theology," Borg and Crossan (*First Paul*, 19) emphasize. "For St. Paul, as a follower of Jesus, . . . Jesus was Lord, and the emperor was not."

38. Willard, *Divine Conspiracy*, 129.

39. Sachs, "Current Eschatology, 254. Also see Polkinghorne, *God of Hope*, 30 and 47–48. For how hope means commitment to action see Volume 1, chapter 9.

40. Macchia, "Pentecostal and Charismatic Theology," 287. Consummation prayer, Patricia Wilson-Kastner (in Migliore, *Lord's Prayer*, 117) states, "is not a cry for God to come and deliver us from the present age and whisk us off to the age to come; it is a commitment to dedicate ourselves to bringing to birth the realm of God on earth." It "does not simply gaze into the future; it presses us to live the ethics of God's realm on earth." This does not mean that we put our faith in modern science, economic

Loss of confidence in consummation—partly caused by a lack of praying for it—has two consequences, both failures of hope.[41] In the first place, eschatological forgetfulness causes resignation to a bleak future. Writing during the darkest days of the Nazi tyranny, Bonhoeffer identifies the temptation to despair: "there are people who think it frivolous and Christians who think it impious to hope for a better future on earth and to prepare for it. . . . They withdraw in resignation or pious flight from the world, from the responsibility . . . for the coming generations." He continues: "it may be that the day of judgment will dawn tomorrow; only then and no earlier will we readily lay down our work for a better future."[42] Hope is trust in a better future—and it was this that allowed Bonhoeffer to fall in love with Maria van Wedemeyer in a time of great uncertainty. As he wrote to her:

> when I . . . think about the situation of the world, the complete darkness over our personal fate and my present imprisonment, then I believe that our union can only be a sign of God's grace and kindness, which calls us to faith. . . . And I do not mean the faith which flees the world but the one that . . . loves and remains true to the world in spite of all the suffering which it contains. . . . Our marriage shall be a *yes* to God's earth; it shall strengthen our courage to act and accomplish something on the earth.[43]

His engagement was a sign of hope, an act of trust in the God who holds tomorrow.

In the second place, resignation to a bleak future causes accommodation to the present situation. Eschatological forgetfulness, Moltmann contends, "has always been the condition that makes possible the adaptation of Christianity to its environment and, as a result of this, the self-surrender of faith." When we despair that things can change we become demoralized and capitulate, we collapse into apathy. Hope, by contrast, results in motivation and resolve; we act in anticipation of what is to come. Eschatological consciousness creates a prophetic church that

---

programs and political liberation—instead, we look for the Son of Man coming on the clouds of glory.

41. For analysis of hope, see Volume 1 chapter 9.

42. Bonhoeffer, *Letters and Papers*, 51.

43. Bonhoeffer, "Letters to Fiance," in Kelly and Nelson, *Testament to Freedom*, 512.

lives toward the coming rule of God, rather than an acculturated church whose identity is incongruent with the gospel. As Moltmann says:

> those who hope in [God's future] can no longer put up with reality as it is, but begin . . . to contradict it. . . . That we do not reconcile ourselves, that there is no pleasant harmony between us and reality, is due to our unquenchable hope. . . . This hope makes the Christian Church a constant disturbance in human society. . . . It makes the Church the source of continual new impulses towards the realization of righteousness, freedom and humanity here in the light of the promised future that is to come.[44]

Since God's good future stands against present reality, hope—nurtured by consummation prayer—does not accept things as they are but motivates action to mend a broken world.

Jesus blesses those who hunger and thirst after justice (the Greek word *dikaiosunē* is better translated as "justice" rather than "righteousness"—Matt 5:4)—they burn with the desire that things be made right. Verhey comments: "justice is the food and drink of God's reign, and those who have heard the good news of that future—and long for it—will delight in any little foretaste of God's setting the world right; they will hunger for justice."[45] In order to act in line with God's coming kingdom we must know how our world is out of line with it—and this, Ronald Sider says, "requires some understanding of international economics and political structures."[46] Sin is not just personal (like lying to a friend) but systemic; we sin by participating in evil social structures (like owning stock in companies that exploit the poor and pollute the environment). We not only suffer injustice—we also perpetrate it directly by action (by buying shoes made in sweatshops or strawberries picked by migrant laborers who are not paid a living wage) and indirectly by indifference (to

---

44. Moltmann, *Theology of Hope*, 41 and 21–22.

45. Verhey, *Christian Art of Dying*, 336.

46. Sider, *Rich Christians*, 155; cf. 119. The church, Hall (*When You Pray*, 54) declares, "is full of inept and misguided lovers whose compassion and goodwill are lost because they have not been honed by discernment. We are not called by Jesus Christ to a life of romantic loving-kindness. We are instead called to a vocation of sober care, to a love that can cut through the social and moral confusion." This requires knowing facts about the contemporary world. Sin, Smith (*Imagining the Kingdom*, 140–42) agrees, is not simply the result of conscious, deliberate, individual choices but is also caused by systemic social forces that shape our beliefs and desires—thereby creating dispositions toward unjust and sinful actions. Our normal way of life, which has become habitual for us, exploits the global poor halfway around the world.

the millions who die each year of malaria or to the violence of our inner cities). In both ways we contribute to the evils of poverty and oppression. There are human beings God made, loves, and will redeem at the supply end of the goods we purchase—and so we have a responsibility to know how the production of our clothing and food, the coffee we drink and the shirts we wear, keeps millions of people poor (and to know of the alternatives: fairly-traded and sustainable products).[47] Consummation prayer critiques cultural values and calls us to be people who, in Wright's words, "live consciously out of tune with the world as it presently is and in tune with the way God intends it to be."[48] It is inherently political: it reminds us that God cares about all things, not just religious things—that material issues (how we vote and spend our money) are spiritual issues.

Contra Marx, eschatological hope, believing in final consummation, does not paralyze but mobilizes this-worldly responsibilities. "Prayer of petition," Donal Dorr asserts, "is not a distraction from political conversion but rather a powerful means of promoting it. . . . It challenges apathy and fatalism, and gives . . . a strong sense of mission."[49] At the end of history, Donald Fairbairn says, "God will not bring us up to Godself in heaven; God will bring heaven itself down to the renewed earth to complete God's redemptive work of dwelling with us. . . . From beginning to end, this world is the focus of God's activity." A reconstituted earth, not a heavenly paradise, is where God and human beings will finally dwell together. This means that "Christianity is not world-rejecting but ultimately world-affirming" and that "the believer's life in this world has direct continuity with the life we will live eternally."[50] Lewis contends that "if you read history you will find that the Christians who did the most for the present world were just those who thought most of the next. . . . It is since Christians have largely ceased to think of the other world that they have become so ineffective in this."[51] Instead of making us indifferent and

---

47. On the ethics of what we eat, for example, see my article "Good Eating." Webb (*Good Eating*, 13) suggests that we consume a "diet of hope" through eating habits that witness to God's own love for creation and that look forward to God's restoration of the world to God's original intentions.

48. Wright, *Evil and Justice of God*, 119.

49. Dorr, *Spirituality and Justice*, 254. Labberton, *Dangerous Act of Worship* and Dorr, *Spirituality and Justice* connect corporate worship and personal prayer (respectively) to the struggle for justice.

50. Fairbairn, *Life in Trinity*, 227–29. Bierma, *Bringing Heaven Down to Earth* and Cosden, *Heavenly Good of Earthly Work* make this point at length.

51. Lewis, *Mere Christianity*, 118.

resigned to suffering and injustice, consummation prayer promotes the opposite. "Hope for God's eschatological transformation of the world," Moltmann concludes, "leads to a transformative ethics" which tries to anticipate that future. It "holds instructions for resistance against the old world in anticipation of the new one. . . . Not to take things as they are but to see them as they can be in that future, and to bring about this 'can be' in the present."[52]

Consummation prayer creates the virtue of hopefulness so that we do not succumb to futility thinking or action fatigue in the face of apparently hopeless problems like world hunger and human trafficking. Wright points out that, after defending resurrection St. Paul does not say "since you have such a great hope, sit back and relax because you know God's got a great future in store for you." Instead, he concludes: "be steadfast, immovable, always excelling in the work of the Lord, because you know that . . . your labor is not in vain" (1 Cor 15:58).[53] The Second Vatican Council agrees:

> far from diminishing our concern to develop this earth, the expectation of a new earth should spur us on, for it is here that the body of a new human family grows, foreshadowing in some way the age which is to come. That is why, although we must be careful to distinguish earthly progress clearly from the increase of the Kingdom of Christ, such progress is of vital concern to the Kingdom of God, insofar as it can contribute to the better ordering of human society.[54]

---

52. Moltmann, *Ethics of Hope*, xiii, 5 and 8. Moltmann (*Theology of Hope*, 16, 324 and 335; slightly modified) says: "Christianity is eschatology, is hope, forward looking and forward moving, and therefore . . . revolutionizing and transforming the present." Christians must "regard their social roles as a new Babylonian exile. . . . Only where their resistance shows them to be . . . incapable of being assimilated . . . can they communicate . . . hope to this society"—a hope that "criticizes and transforms the present because it is open towards the universal future of the Kingdom."

53. Wright, *Surprised by Hope*, 192. "The new life of the Spirit, to which Christians are called in the present age is not a matter of sitting back and enjoying spiritual comforts in a private, relaxed, easygoing spirituality, but consists rather of the unending struggle . . . to bring God's wise, healing order into the world now" (*Evil and Justice of God*, 119).

54. Second Vatican Council, *Gaudium et Spes*, cited in Phan, "Roman Catholic Theology," 218. The Council (cited in Benedict XVI, *Fathers of Church*, 107) adds: "it is a mistake to think that, because we have here no lasting city, but seek the city which is to come, we are entitled to shirk our earthly responsibilities; this is to forget that by our faith we are bound all the more to fulfill these responsibilities."

Consummation prayer is not escapist; it turns us to the world, not from it. Instead of being safe and comfortable, it supports the dangerous act of waking up to God's purposes in the world. Prayer is not a substitute for action; instead, it is a spur to action—it brings transforming engagement with rather than complacent separation from or assimilation to the world; it calls the church to share in God's healing and saving work. Bonhoeffer points out that "our Christianity today will be confined to praying for and doing right by our fellow men."[55] Prayer and righteous action are not alternatives but complementaries. As Wright concludes: "people who believe in the resurrection, in God making a whole new world in which everything will be set right at last, are unstoppably motivated to work for that new world in the present."[56] Consummation prayer calls us to live the ethics of God's rule on earth, to promote justice in a suffering world.

The Spiritual Benefit of Growth Prayer: Countering Spiritual Laziness

Growth prayer is prayer for the blessed—that they experience ever-increasing union with God. Since God's nature is infinite and human minds are finite, there is always more of God for those in God's presence to know, love, and enjoy. "Christian life," Fairbairn says, "is the task of beginning to live now in the way we will live perfectly later."[57] As we pray growth for the blessed, we are encouraged to develop our own relationship with God now—since we, too, will be growing in that relationship forever. We must be in communion with God in this life because we will forever be in communion with God in the next.

Spiritual growth, R. Paul Stevens says, is "that process by which the ... person, in all aspects of his or her life, moves from the beginnings of life in the Spirit to full maturity."[58] Coming to know and love God is not a once-for-all event but an ongoing process. Christian Scripture

---

55. Bonhoeffer, *Letters and Papers*, 389.

56. Wright, *Surprised by Hope*, 214; cf. *After You Believe*, 96. "The promise of God's new world and of bodily resurrection," he (*Evil and Justice of God*, 119) adds, "leads not to a lack of concern with the present world but rather to a determination that the life of the future world should begin to infect the present one."

57. Fairbairn, *Life in Trinity*, 229.

58. Stevens, "Spiritual Growth," 949. This section draws on McLaren, *Finding Our Way Again*; Peace, "Spiritual Formation"; Scazzero, *Emotionally-Healthy Spirituality*; Stevens, "Spiritual Disciplines" and "Spiritual Growth."

assumes that we will make steady progress in our life with God. "We must no longer be children," St. Paul says, but "must grow up in every way into . . . Christ" (Eph 4:14–15) until we are "filled with the Spirit" (Eph 5:18) and become "mature in Christ" (Col 1:28). He is not satisfied with the stage of development he has reached but like an athlete, he says, "I press on" and "strain forward to what lies ahead" (Phil 3:12–14). The Bible offers several metaphors of growth—agricultural metaphors of seed becoming a mature plant (Matt 13:3–9; 1 Cor 3:6–7) and branches abiding in the vine (John 15:1–11); a biological metaphor of a child developing into an adult (1 Cor 3:1–2); an educational metaphor of a student maturing like the teacher (Luke 6:40); and an architectural metaphor of a building under construction (1 Pet 2:5). Kenneth Prior points out that the Greek word used most often for spiritual development is *auxanō*—a word that refers to "organic growth . . . from within as a living organism" (as plants have the principle of their growth in themselves).[59] Spiritual growth is always cooperative: human effort (planned disciplines to put on a new heart—Col 3:12–17; 2 Pet 1:5–10) and divine grace (the action of the Holy Spirit—Rom 8:10–13; Gal 5:22–26) are intertwined (Phil 2:12–13).[60] Growth prayer reminds us that since we will continually grow in knowledge and love of God in heaven, we must develop a hunger for and a deep interior life with God now.

Instead of being transformed into the likeness of Christ (2 Cor 3:18), many Christians remain spiritually immature. They are, St. Paul complains, not "spiritual people, but . . . people of the flesh, . . . infants in Christ" who are still fed "with milk" and are "not ready for solid food" (1 Cor 3:1–2 ; cf. Heb 5:12–14). We become stuck in what Peter Scazzero calls "tip-of-the-iceberg" spirituality; our spiritual development never touches what lies beneath the surface of our lives.[61] We succumb to spiritual sloth, a lack of spiritual purpose—which Henry Fairlie defines as "hatred of all spiritual things which entail effort," being complacent, indifferent, and apathetic to spiritual development.[62] A growing relationship with God requires work, but rather than being diligent in cultivating that friendship it is easy to become negligent—instead of being hot toward God, to be lukewarm (Rev 3:16). Spiritual sloth is often—para-

---

59. Prior, *Way of Holiness*, 93–94.
60. See Willard, *Divine Conspiracy*, 347.
61. Scazzero, *Emotionally-Healthy Spirituality*, chapter 1.
62. Fairlie, *Seven Deadly Sins*, 123.

doxically—the result of busyness, of the chaos and stress of our lives. We live in a blizzard of activity, Thomas Merton writes; "to surrender to too many demands, to commit oneself to too many projects . . . is to succumb to violence" that kills spiritual growth.[63] Being overworked and fatigued crowds out attention to God. The result, Maxie Dunnam and Kimberley Reisman explain, is spiritual dryness—feeling distant from God. "When we neglect prayer, worship, Bible study and other spiritual disciplines, we pay the price of shriveled and listless souls. . . . Spiritual disciplines keep the wells of refreshment and renewal full of fresh water. Spiritual laziness dries them up and leaves . . . parched and dry souls."[64] Growth prayer, by focusing our attention on communion with God, corrects these ills.

Spiritual growth is growth into the love relationship that is God. Christian life, Scazzero points out, must balance *being with* God (contemplation) and *doing for* God (action).[65] Performing lots of Christian work is not necessarily a sign of growing spirituality and can, in fact, be dangerous to spiritual health. "If we are just waking up . . . to God's passion for justice," Mark Labberton notes, "we might think the first thing to do is get as busy as we possibly can." The problem is that no matter how much we do, we "still feel like we aren't doing anything, at least compared to the scope of the need." As a result of non-stop activism we can become overwhelmed and weighed down by depression and discouragement, anxiety and frustration, or by bitterness at the indifference of other people. Because the challenges are draining, we burn out. This is why we need contemplative practices to quiet us, refocus us, renew us, refresh us. "The doing of justice," Labberton insists, "starts with rest." While the world and individuals are in deep trouble and there is much to do, praying and enjoying God's presence must also be a high priority for us. Daily and weekly Sabbath-keeping—to use Labberton's words—"say to the frantic, exhausted, distracted, fatigued people of God: please, rest."[66] Consummation prayer and growth prayer complement each other, creating an active-contemplative balance.

Growth prayer reminds us that in order to grow spiritually we must practice contemplative disciplines which enable us to slow down, to rest and recharge, to stop and breathe the air of God's presence. "Spiritual

---

63. Merton, cited in Scazzero, *Emotionally-Healthy Spirituality*, 173.
64. Dunnam and Reisman, *Workbook on Seven Deadly Sins*, 113.
65. Scazzero, *Emotionally-Healthy Spirituality*, 31–32.
66. Labberton, *Dangerous Act of Worship*, 99–100 and 95–96.

practices," Brian McLaren says, "are ways of becoming awake and staying awake to God."[67] They are channels for meeting God; they help us to be conscious and aware of God throughout the day. Through spiritual disciplines—meditating on Scripture, joining in worship, participating in community—we come to know and experience communion with God. The result is that we find extraordinary grace in ordinary life—in the laughter of a child with a dog and conversation with friends around a fireplace and wine, in the beauty of a rainbow sunset or the power of a thunderstorm, when dancing at an outdoor concert heavy with guitars, drums and vocals. Growth prayer awakens us to the fact that we live in a "God-bathed world," to use Willard's words, where "the ordinary . . . is a receptacle of the divine, a place where the life of God flows."[68]

Spiritual growth—Stevens says—has three components.[69] *Upward* growth is knowing and loving God better; it is nurtured by disciplines that enable us to center in God. Solitude is intentional isolation from other people so we can be aware of God's presence. Meditation involves slow pondering of Scripture as we reflect on its meaning for us and what God is saying to us. Contemplative prayer helps us to be still in God's presence as we empty ourselves in silence and leave our thoughts and concerns behind. We also experience Christ's sacramental presence in the Eucharist. *Inward* growth is knowing and loving ourselves better. The practice of journaling, carrying on a conversation with ourselves, helps us to sort out our thoughts and feelings; the model for this is the psalms. We can also write spiritual autobiography, putting together the trajectory of our life story with God. Confession means authentic honesty with God—perhaps a repentant reading of the Ten Commandments or Beatitudes. Imaginative reading of Scripture has us envision and experience ourselves as a participant in a biblical story. *Outward* growth is knowing and loving others better; it requires disciplines of service and intercession. The upward and inward disciplines of prayer (being in God's presence)

---

67. McLaren, *Finding Our Way Again*, 18.

68. Willard, *Divine Conspiracy*, 61 and 14. While it is good to have "holy places and things and days," Lewis (*Letters to Malcolm*, 75) says, they should not "obliterate our awareness that all ground is holy and every bush a Burning Bush." We must remain awake to the fact that "the world is crowded with God. God walks everywhere incognito." Celtic spirituality resists the dualism of matter and spirit and honors the 'thin places' where we readily sense God's presence in the created world, where the boundary between heaven and earth is thin and we are in both worlds at once.

69. Stevens, "Spiritual Growth," 949.

are meant to support the outward activities of mission (doing God's work in the world).[70]

Spiritual growth, enabled by growth prayer, requires a "rule of life"—an intentional plan for developing our spiritual lives and keeping God at the center of everything we do. To practice the presence of God we must regularly have personal devotions or use the spiritual exercises of Ignatius Loyola and must consistently meet with others to be nourished by Word and Sacrament. Spiritual growth is not a private endeavor, something to be done alone. Instead, it requires the presence and participation of others. In corporate worship all the people of God—clergy and laity alike—take part as we meet with God and each other. As together we praise God, lament the suffering of the world, and ask for grace and forgiveness we shape our religious affections and spiritual identities—developing gratitude to God, sorrow over sin, hope for justice and love for neighbor. Spiritual growth happens in a community of faithful people who build each other up in faith, hope and love—who together cultivate relationship with God.[71] We must discover the rhythms of the "daily office" (small units of time set aside for morning, midday, and evening prayer when we turn our attention to God), Sabbath (where we do nothing work-related for a twenty-four-hour period each week) and retreat (longer periods of being absent from people and things to attend to God). We may benefit from the guidance and encouragement of a spiritual director helping us discern God's presence in our lives.

Growth prayer for the departed corrects spiritual sloth by encouraging us to devote ourselves more fully to God through contemplative spiritual practice. "Diligence, discipline, fortitude, perseverance," Dunnam and Reisman say, "only these can protect us from the spiritual death sloth brings."[72] The opposite of sloth is zeal—where we actively seek God and are ambitious to know and love God with passion, joy, and wonder. The psalmist's experience of enjoyment and delight in God's presence then becomes our own: "as a deer longs for flowing streams, so my soul longs for you, O God. My soul thirsts for God" (42:1–2). The goal of spiritual growth is *theosis*—the union of our natures with the nature of God. In Bernard of Clairvaux's analogy, when an iron poker is placed in a fire its nature (which is cold and dark) begins to change as it partakes in the

---

70. Bonhoeffer (*Letters and Papers*, 366 and 373) insists that the secret disciplines of worship and prayer are necessary for effective action in a religionless world.

71. See Hotz and Matthews, *Shaping the Christian Life*.

72. Dunnam and Reisman, *Workbook on Seven Deadly Sins*, 114.

nature of fire (which is hot and light). A piece of wood catches fire when put among burning logs—and in the same way, McLaren says, if we draw near and stay close to God we will desire God more and more.[73] Spiritual life—on earth and in eternity—is a journey toward ever-increasing union with God. Growth prayer reminds us that we must practice now the relationship with God that will be our experience in eternity. As Augustine of Hippo says, "let the love of thee grow every day more and more here, that it may be full hereafter."[74] In heaven, Fairbairn notes, we "will be fully dedicated to contemplation of God and will be perfected in our communion with God"—and so we must devote ourselves "in the present to the task that will belong to us in eternity," deepening our relationship with God. Growth prayer enables spiritual growth—a deeper awareness of God's presence and grace—now. By reminding ourselves of our future life with God we learn to live our present life with God.[75]

The Spiritual Benefit of Purification Prayer: Countering Moral Indifference

Purification prayer is for the imperfect dead undergoing sanctification from sin. Heaven requires perfect holiness—and God cannot unilaterally and instantaneously give us a radically altered nature at death. Therefore, there is some kind of process after death that completes our moral transformation into the kind of persons who can enter the fellowship of the Trinity. "Christian life," to quote Fairbairn again, "is the task of beginning to live now in the way we will live perfectly later."[76] As we pray for the imperfect in purgatory we prompt ourselves to live holy lives now—since we too must have pure hearts and hands to enter God's heaven.

---

73. McLaren, *Finding Our Way Again*, 174.

74. Augustine, cited in Tutu, *African Prayer Book*, 136. John Cassian (cited in Fairbairn, *Life in Trinity*, 230) agrees: "no one will arrive at the fullness of this measure in the world to come except the person who has . . . been initiated into it in the present and who has tasted it while still living in this world . . . ; who desires only one thing, thirsts for one thing, and always directs not only every deed but even every thought to this one thing, so that he may already possess in the present what has been pledged him . . . with regard to the blessed way of life of the holy in the future—that is, that 'God may be all in all' to him."

75. Fairbairn, *Life in Trinity*, 230.

76. Ibid., 229.

Just as many Christians ignore spiritual growth, so many live by what Bonhoeffer calls "cheap grace"—forgiveness without costly discipleship. The sin of moral sloth means apathy and indifference to moral obligation. As pointed out in the last chapter, research indicates that the faith of many Christians makes little practical difference in their daily lives. When it comes to priorities, values, and moral behavior—sexual promiscuity, divorce, charitable giving, and racial prejudice—Christians are indistinguishable from secularists.[77] It is easy to think, Prior says, "that there are two standards of Christian commitment, one for [clergy and] missionaries and a lower one for ordinary Christians." But "nowhere does Scripture suggest such a double standard." Holiness is not optional or "intended [only] for the elite within the Church."[78] Bonhoeffer agrees: in church history monasticism "became a living protest against the secularization of Christianity, against the cheapening of grace. . . . Here on the boundary of the Church, was the place where the awareness that grace is costly and that grace includes discipleship was preserved." But the separation of monastic life from secular life only made matters worse by implying that there are two levels of being Christian. "Monastic life became the extraordinary achievement of individuals, to which the majority of Church members need not be obligated. The fateful limiting of the validity of Jesus' commandments to a certain group of especially qualified people led to differentiating between highest achievement and lowest performance in Christian obedience."[79] Against this, Bonhoeffer insists, *all* Christians are called to the demands of costly discipleship. Most Christians do not deliberately cultivate traits they know to be sinful; instead, we fall into bad habits due to laziness and negligence. We live like everyone else, conforming to the values of secular society rather than the counter-cultural values of God's kingdom. Another reason for low moral standards, Prior points out, "is the lack of awareness of the majesty and holiness of God and of our accountability toward God."[80] In addition, assuming instant sanctification at death may encourage moral laxity and unholy living; since God will unilaterally perfect us, we need not work at becoming good now.

---

77. See Sider, *Scandal of Evangelical Conscience*.
78. Prior, *Way of Holiness*, 12.
79. Bonhoeffer, *Discipleship*, 46–47.
80. Prior, *Way of Holiness*, 21.

Purification prayer reminds us that what happens after death should influence how we live here and now. Eschatological passages in Christian Scripture are consistently paired with an imperative to holy living; "promise and command," Moltmann observes, always go together. Law is the ethical side of promise; the eschatological question "what can I hope for?" implies the ethical question "what must I do?"[81] Jesus inaugurates his ministry by pointing out that the nearness of the kingdom has a moral implication—repent, change your behavior (Mark 1:15). Because we do not know when the Lord will come, he warns, we must always "be ready" (Matt 24:42, 44; 25:13). St. Paul tells us that because "the night is far gone, the day is near" we must "lay aside the works of darkness and put on the armor of light" (Rom 13:12). As we anticipate Christ's appearing we should "live lives that are self-controlled, upright, and godly" (Titus 2:11–14). St. Peter (2 Pet 3:11) instructs that while "we wait for new heavens and a new earth" we must lead "lives of holiness and godliness." We know that when Christ is revealed we will see him; "all who have this hope," St. John (1 John 3:2–3) says, "purify themselves." The doctrine of the second coming reminds us of "how short, precarious, temporary, and provisional a thing [life] is," Lewis comments. This realization should make us "never give all [our] heart to anything which will end when . . . life ends." Reflection on the last things through purification prayer is a way to

> train ourselves to ask more and more often how the thing which we are saying or doing (or failing to do) at each moment will look when the irresistible light streams in upon it. . . . Women sometimes have the problem of trying to judge by artificial light how a dress will look by daylight. That is very like the problem of all of us: to dress our souls not for the electric lights of the present world but for the daylight of the next.[82]

Eschatology and purgatory, kept in our minds by purification prayer, are incentives to holy living.

God's project, Wright says, is "not to snatch people away from earth to heaven but to colonize earth with the life of heaven"—and so consummation prayer and purification prayer overlap in the ethics of the kingdom. Some ways of living contradict the prayer "your kingdom come"; they keep the life of heaven out of earth and preserve the world the way

---

81. Moltmann, *Theology of Hope*, 120 and 166.
82. Lewis, *World's Last Night*, 107–13.

it is—broken and sinful—while other ways of living coincide with God's future age of peace and justice.[83] Dermot Lane agrees: Christian living points forward to the way things are in God's kingdom. It is a *prolepsis*—an anticipation in the present of the future to come, a "pre-appearance of the end, the arrival in outline of the future, . . . a preview . . . of life to come, a prototype of the future."[84] Love is the central feature of what Wright calls "Kingdom-in-advance life," and so our characters and habits of life must be formed by generous love to our neighbor—personally and politically.[85] We must be the love to each other and the world that Christ is to us—in this way we develop the virtues necessary for heaven.

Purification prayer counters sloth and encourages moral ambition. It helps us to "work out our own salvation" (Phil 2:12)—the Greek verb *katergazesthe* means to bring something to the fullness of what it is meant to be. Sanctification means replacing wrong habits of thinking, feeling, and acting with right ones, giving our thoughts and intentions to the kingdom of God.[86] Prayer for those in purgatory—to use David Crump's words—"becomes prayer for oneself . . . that God's transforming power reshape our inner and outer lives, molding us into . . . new people."[87] To pray moral purification for others we must be serious about developing moral character ourselves. The holiness we must pursue has both a negative aspect (avoiding sin—"putting off the old") and a positive aspect (doing good—"putting on the new"). Moral transformation involves both external acts and—more important—internal motivations (since we do what we do because we are what we are).

Character consists of a set of psychological dispositions—habitual ways of thinking, feeling, and acting. These ingrained tendencies, which are engraved deep in the structure of our inner lives, result in automatic behavior. Moral perfection is wholeness, an integrated character that is psychologically unified rather than fragmented. Aristotle notes that resisting desires and altering them are two different things, and that full virtue (where we do not struggle with temptation, but do right spontaneously and effortlessly) is a higher level of goodness than self-control (where

---

83. Wright, *Surprised by Hope*, 293.
84. Lane, *Keeping Hope Alive*, 123. He is paraphrasing Wolfhart Pannenberg.
85. Wright, *After You Believe*, 124.
86. Willard, *Divine Conspiracy*, 346.
87. Crump, *Knocking on Heaven's Door*, 126.

we have strong willpower and can, with effort, live by our convictions).[88] Moral change, like learning to play a musical instrument, is not a matter of deciding and trying but of training and practice. The psychological process by which character is cultivated, according to Roy Baumeister and Todd Heatherton, has three elements.[89] First, we must have clear standards (so we know right from wrong). Since beliefs guide behavior, we need strong moral convictions if we are to act as we should.[90] Second, transformation requires self-monitoring (paying attention to what we are doing). We must both be aware of our present behavior and evaluate it against our moral standards.[91] Finally, we must practice self-interruption (creating strong habits of willpower). When we notice a discrepancy between our behavior and our values, we must be able to stop what we are doing and make ourselves do what we know is right. Like fitness training or acquiring musical skill, we develop habits by repetition until they become automatic. Wright summarizes: "character is transformed by three things. First, you have to aim at the right goal. Second, you have to figure out the steps you need to take to get to that goal. Third, those steps have to become habitual, a matter of second nature."[92] Following these steps will not change long-standing habits instantly—but over time will bring small and unconscious but steady and deep moral change.

88. See Aristotle, *Nicomachean Ethics*, Book 7. Virtuous people, he says (1167b5, 144) "are in concord with themselves."

89. McLaren (*Finding Our Way*, 80) makes the trying harder versus disciplined practice distinction. Baumeister and Heatherton, "Self-Regulation Failure." Also see my articles "Becoming Good" and "Cultivating Character," as well as Snow, *Cultivating Virtue*.

90. Each morning we should renew our baptismal covenant with God by personalizing it: "I will continue in the apostles' teaching. . . . I will persevere in resisting evil. . . . I will proclaim by word and example the Good News. . . . I will seek and serve Christ in all persons, loving my neighbor as myself. . . . I will strive for justice and peace among all people and will respect the dignity of every human being." This practice places the values of God's kingdom at the forefront of our minds, making us ready to live them out in the tasks and obligations of our day. Episcopal Church, *Book of Common Prayer*, 304 and 416.

91. Praying the prayer of confession each evening can help us assess not just our external behavior (words and deeds) but our internal attitudes (thoughts, feelings, and desires)—and to evaluate both what we have done (failures of commission) and what we have left undone (failures of omission). Daily *examen* helps us know our shortcomings, analyze why we failed and strengthen our resolve to live congruently with our values. Episcopal Church, *Book of Common Prayer*, 360.

92. Wright, *After You Believe*, 29. Moral change, I repeat, is always the result of both human effort and divine grace.

Moral formation, like spiritual growth, is something that takes place in community—as Aristotle (with his emphasis on friendship) and St. Paul (think of all the 'one another' injunctions in his letters) recognized. Moral companions form us in several ways. First, they help us learn. Virtuous friends are models we can imitate; a spiritual director can mentor and guide new dispositions. Second, companions bring self-knowledge. They correct us, awakening us to the blind spots and self-deception in our characters. Third, friends hold us accountable. Honest self-disclosure and confession to someone who is trustworthy enables character change. Fourth, companions encourage and support us. They help us maintain our moral resolutions when we are discouraged or lack strength. The individual disciplines, then, must be accompanied by relationships of mutual encouragement, support, accountability and insight.

Praying for the perfect holiness of those in purgatory means praying for and working on our own sanctification now. Purification prayer should not create fear and uncertainty about salvation (since we do not make satisfaction or pay for our sins). But it does remind us that, even though we are forgiven by God, entering heaven requires being purged of all self-centeredness—and that this transformation does not take place instantaneously by God's action but is a process of gradual change in which we take part. It reinforces the fact that right relationship with God requires right relationship with others, that love of God is inseparable from love of neighbor—and that this, as we have seen, has economic and political implications. As we pray Psalm 51:10 for those in purgatory, we also pray it for ourselves here and now—"create in me a clean heart, O God, and put a new and right spirit within me." Purification prayer prompts us to dedicate ourselves to holy living, to develop the virtues of love necessary for participation in the communal life of heaven.

Spiritual growth (promoted by growth prayer) and moral holiness (promoted by purification prayer) are both necessary for following Christ. Israel, called to obey *torah* and distinguish itself as God's righteous people, failed to do so. "God's call . . . to remain separate is broken [as] their values get mixed up with those of the surrounding peoples," Labberton comments. The same is true of the church and individual Christians—we look like society around us. We let "culture, instead of God, tell us who we are and how we are to live." Rather than being mature disciples, "Christians tend to live life in terms of the culture with a splash of the gospel added to the mix." Instead of loving God first and our neighbors as ourselves, we love ourselves first. Consummation prayer, growth prayer, and purification prayer change us—they reorder our perspectives, passions, and priorities, shifting our vision and redirecting our action. They make us attentive to life as God sees it and enable us to follow Christ in daily tangible behavior and—in doing so—prepare us for eternal life with God.[93]

The Spiritual Benefits of Salvation Prayer

Salvation prayer is prayer for repentance and escape of those in hell. It assumes that both God's love and offer of salvation as well as human freedom to respond continue beyond death. Prayer for those in hell has several benefits: it corrects friend-enemy thinking and it resolves the worst aspect of the problem of evil—eternal and inescapable hell. In addition, it has a number of good pastoral and missional consequences.

Salvation Prayer Corrects Us-Them Thinking

Dual-destiny eschatology involves a future division of human beings into the saved and the unsaved. This causes us, unconsciously perhaps, to divide people in the present into those who are doomed to hell and those who will join us in heaven. "How we see humanity in this life," John Kronen and Eric Reitan say, "will inevitably be influenced by the imprint of that eternal gulf. . . . As we quietly think of us-the-saved and them-the-damned, and . . . locate human beings into one group or the other, it may be difficult to keep this ultimate in-group/out-group schism from creating its shadow divisions in this world." The doctrine of eternal hell "narrows the scope of human love and . . . compassion."[94] Moltmann shares this worry: "if the end of the world is . . . a double outcome, believers going to heaven and unbelievers to hell, then the present is inescapably dominated by . . . friend-enemy thinking." Since there is no hope for

---

93. Labberton, *Dangerous Act of Worship*, 30, 102, 189, and 63.

94. Kronen and Reitan, *God's Final Victory*, 182–83. Think of the prophet Jonah's narrow, nationalistic view of God which made it impossible for him to see the all-embracing love of God—and so he was outraged when the Ninevites repent and are forgiven. In the same way, the Pharisees were scandalized by Jesus' table fellowship—which acted out God's indiscriminate acceptance—with sinner-guests, failures and nobodies who were outside the law. The Bible, Manning (*Ragamuffin Gospel*, 39–40) says, urges us to "think big about God"—to grasp that God's compassion extends to every person without exception.

unbelievers who will eventually be punished in hell, we can treat them with contempt here and now.[95]

Believing in everlasting separation *distorts our view of other people*—turning them into unredeemable enemies who can only be condemned rather than flawed persons who can be forgiven.[96] "Too often"—Philip Gulley and James Mulholland confess—"the God of wrath was a divine pit bull to sic on our enemies. We were thankful God had loved and saved us. But we secretly delighted that God would destroy those people we disliked. . . . God was gracious to us but not to others."[97] Believing in eternal torment also *distorts our view of God*, who becomes a vindictive judge rather than a loving father. We imitate the God we believe in and act the way we think God acts—so if we believe in a God of harsh violence we will imitate that God. As Sharon Baker says, "God's fight becomes our fight. God's just anger becomes our just anger. God's violence becomes our violence." Consider the history of violence—inquisitions, crusades, persecutions, and religious wars—justified in God's name, on the assumption that God loves a favored few and hates everyone else.[98] The public Christian voices we hear today are too often judgmental, nasty,

---

95. Moltmann, *Sun of Righteousness*, 144. Kukota ("Christ, Medicine of Life," 37–38 and 56) makes the same argument: "the division of souls into the categories of 'redeemed' and 'damned' before the final judgment has drastic consequences for Christians. . . . In holding such opinions Christianity ceases to be the religion of love and openness towards . . . our fellow humans. . . . Instead of love towards one's neighbor it degenerates into counting his sins."

96. It might be thought that this objection only applies to Augustinians who affirm predestination but does not apply to non-Augustinians who do not see the fate of any living person as yet sealed and hopeless. Augustinians might reply that since we do not know who is predestined to salvation and who to damnation, we should love and respect all people. Non-Augustinians might reply that since it is possible for any person to freely receive grace in this life, we should love and respect all people. Yet given the plurality of non-Christian religions in the world, it is unlikely that many of their adherents are predestined to convert to Christianity or will do so of their own free will. And so the worry that dual-destiny eschatology motivates friend-enemy thinking is not unwarranted.

97. Gulley and Mulholland, *If Grace is True*, 65; slightly modified.

98. Baker, *Razing Hell*, 28 and 60–65. "The image of God as punishing, who demands a rightful pound of flesh in order to balance the scales of justice," she (154–55) adds, "bleeds into the structures of the world's governments, courts of law, and familial relations." We come to see using violence as positive and redemptive and to believe (as some American Christians do) that God has chosen the United States and its militaristic wars to redeem the world. Also see Evans, *Searching for Sunday*, chapter 10.

and harsh—full of condemnation verging on hatred of homosexuals or women seeking abortion, for example.

Salvation prayer *corrects our view of God* by making love the lens through which we see God. Brennan Manning says that embracing the true God means "repudiating the god of fear and wrath handed on ... by preachers, teachers and church authorities..., repudiating the strange god who sees all non-Christians as good-for-nothings, who consigns all heathen to hell."[99] It replaces belief in a violent, vengeful God who gets even with a merciful forgiving God who punishes to redeem. Where eternal hell is, as Kronen and Reitan conclude, "an impediment to compassion," salvation prayer—by reinforcing God's unlimited patience and persistent grace—motivates mercy.[100] It helps us imitate the God portrayed by Jesus—one who seeks the last sheep (Luke 15:3–7), who loves enemies and not just friends (Matt 5:43–48), who came to save and not condemn (John 3:17). Salvation prayer also *corrects our view of other people* by making love the lens through which we approach them. It reminds us that—in Bonhoeffer's words—"God loves our enemies [and] gave the beloved Son for them." It corrects "the opinion that God loves us more than God loves our enemies ... [and] that we are God's favorite children."[101] Sachs agrees: "hope for the salvation of all has an important ethical imperative." It "requires that radical love and solidarity which Christians recognize on the cross of Christ. It expresses itself in active discipleship which labors for the universal communion of love and justice which God has always intended for the world."[102] Prayer for the unsaved refutes "saved us/wicked them" thinking: all the dead without exception are loved by God—and all the living without exception are persons whom we must love here and now. Salvation prayer enables us to recognize all persons—us and them, friend and enemy—as having a mutual origin in God's love, having been imprinted with the same divine image and made for a common eternal destiny. It teaches us—in Nadia Bolz-Weber's words—to anticipate "the day in which we gather around God's throne next to all the people we never thought should be there."[103]

---

99. Manning, cited in Cockburn, *Rumors of Glory*, 315.

100. Kronen and Reitan, *God's Final Victory*, 183.

101. Bonhoeffer, "On Christ's Love and Our Enemies," in Kelly and Nelson, *Testament to Freedom*, 285–88.

102. Sachs, "Current Eschatology," 254.

103. Bolz-Weber, "Father, Can I Tell." Manning (*Ragamuffin Gospel*, 29) says, "I believe that among the countless number of people standing in front of the throne

Salvation prayer expands our love in two ways. First, because God's love has no *boundaries*, neither should ours; because it includes the unsaved ours must include sinners too. Since God will have mercy upon all people (Rom 11:32)—Moltmann says—"we must view and respect all human beings, whatever they believe or don't believe, as those on whom God has mercy. Whoever they are, God loves them, Christ has died for them" and they will eventually be with us in heaven.[104] This includes racists in South Carolina and jihadists in Afghanistan, drunk drivers who kill innocent families and pimps who force young women into prostitution. Salvation prayer develops compassion by teaching us, in Gulley's and Mulholland's words, to "recognize each other as children of a gracious God."[105] Second, since God's love has no *timelines*, neither should ours. Take an example: parents who are estranged from adult children—who want them back in their lives but only see them on rare occasions, where resentments run deep and show no signs of healing. Salvation prayer inspires us, when relationships are broken, to model our behavior after the God whose love cannot change or grow weak, but is infinitely long and patient, who always leaves the door to reconciliation open—instead of after a God who puts a time limit on repentance, gives up and closes the door to the possibility of restored relationship. Inspired by the God described in salvation prayer, we will continue to pray and persevere, even though it may take years to soften the other person's bitterness. Since God's love is steadfast and unwavering, ours must be too.

Salvation prayer teaches us to imitate God's mercy: "as God loves," Pope Francis says, "so do God's children. Just as God is merciful, so we are called to be merciful to each other."[106] Jesus taught us to pray for our

and in front of the Lamb, dressed in white robes and holding palms in their hands (Rev 7:9), I shall see the prostitute from the Kit-Kat Ranch in Carlson City, Nevada, who tearfully told me she could find no other employment to support her two year old son. I shall see the woman who had an abortion and is haunted by guilt and remorse . . . ; the businessman besieged with debt who sold his integrity in a series of desperate transactions . . . ; the sexually-abused teen molested by his father and now selling his body on the street."

104. Moltmann, *Sun of Righteousness*, 144.

105. Gulley and Mulholland, *If God is Love*, 13; cf. 54. This does not, of course, mean approving of the actions evil people do. Love, as argued in chapter 5, is compatible with—indeed demands—judgment of evil. Forgiveness does not replace, but follows, anger—which is the proper response to wrongdoing.

106. Pope Francis, "Misericordiae Vultus," in *Name of God is Mercy*, 119. Being merciful like the Father (Luke 6:36)—living "in the logic of love and selflessness" (93)—means practicing the seven corporal works of mercy (feeding the hungry, giving

enemies (Matt 5:43–48), and salvation prayer will include people who hurt us in life. This is—admittedly—extremely difficult. "I do not want to pray for my dead father-in-law—or to see him in heaven," a friend once confided to me. His wife was verbally and sexually abused by her father—and the emotional pain, spiritual wounds, and relational effects have followed her into adulthood. "The trail of damage he caused has been long and hard for both of us," my friend says; "we struggle with hatred toward him." Loving our enemies enough to pray for them is, Bonhoeffer says, the extraordinary thing about being a Christian, "the most extreme" action of love God calls us to, the time when we are most like God. "In prayer we go to our enemies, to stand at their side. We are with them, near them, for them before God." In this way we imitate "the love of Jesus Christ, who went to the cross for his enemies, and prayed on the cross for them." Praying for those who hurt us badly develops the virtue of forgiveness since "I can no longer condemn or hate [someone] for whom I pray"—Bonhoeffer points out.[107] Forgiveness is an intentional decision to overcome bitterness, surrender our desire for revenge, and rediscover the offender's humanity (reframing their behavior as motivated by their own hurts and life pressures, not by malice).[108] We can forgive our enemies, Bonhoeffer says, "by seeing [them] as they really are"—not as despicable persons but "as those for whom Christ died, whom Christ loves."[109] As my friends pray forgiveness for the father, they experience the healing of past memories; as they ask for his posthumous repentance, their hearts begin to soften. As they learn that God loves and forgives him, they, too, learn to forgive him—and as they forgive the man who hurt them in the past, they become merciful to those who hurt them in the present. The forgiveness for which they pray is not "cheap forgiveness" that excuses wrongdoing as if it does not matter. Instead, it is the costly grace of Jesus' prayer—forgive him, for he did not know what he was doing (Luke 23:34).

---

drink to the thirsty, dressing the naked, housing the homeless, visiting the sick and imprisoned, burying the dead) and the seven spiritual works of mercy (admonishing sinners, teaching the ignorant, advising those in doubt, comforting those in sorrow, bearing wrongs patiently, forgiving offenses, praying for both the living and the dead). Mercy is "a criterion for the credibility of [individual] faith" (118).

107. Bonhoeffer, *Discipleship*, 139–41 and *Life Together*, 90.

108. For literature on forgiveness see my article "Better Hearts."

109. Bonhoeffer, "On Christ's Love and Our Enemies," in Kelly and Nelson, *Testament to Freedom*, 285–88.

One more thought. Since there is no salvation without repentance and transformation, the man my friend will one day meet in heaven will no longer be the same person since—as Gulley and Mulholland say—"heaven won't be populated by the unrepentant."[110] My friend is—to paraphrase John Hick—thinking of the afterlife meeting taking place when his father-in-law is still the same cruel person who did brutal things and died without making amends. This, however, cannot happen since *that* man will have been transformed: "his perfecting will have involved his utter revulsion against his own cruelty and a deep shame and sorrow at the memory of it. . . . He will no longer be the same person; for he will have changed in character into someone who is now incapable of behaving in such a way and who is, in comparison with his former self, 'a new creature'" (2 Cor 5:17). Since heaven requires transformation as well as forgiveness, everyone in heaven will be fully sanctified—and so evildoers will not be same persons morally in heaven as the ones who did evil on earth.[111]

"God never tires of forgiving," Pope Francis says, "in ways that are new and surprising"—and posthumous forgiveness is, for many people, one of these surprising ways.[112] Salvation prayer develops a correct view of God as one who is loving through and through, a God whose grace is far and wide and deep and high enough to include us all and long enough to last through eternity (Eph 3:18–19). And it develops compassion for all people—even the most wicked, including those who trespass against us.

Salvation Prayer Answers the Intellectual Problem of Hell

Dual destiny eschatology means that the very worst evil occurs not in this life but in the next—since for unredeemed persons any temporal happiness enjoyed here will be wiped out by eternal and inescapable suffering. Only a consummation in which all people are restored to God provides a complete answer to evil—while the doctrines of exclusive salvation, closed death, and eternal hell make it far more serious. Traditional theology implies, Gregory MacDonald points out, "that very many people

---

110. Gulley and Mulholland, *If Grace is True*, 113.
111. Hick, *Death and Eternal Life*, 165. Also see Walls, *Heaven, Hell and Purgatory*, 149–53.
112. Pope Francis, "Misericordiae Vultus," in *Name of God is Mercy*, 144.

who suffer terrible injustices in this life . . . will not actually have those wrongs righted in the life to come. In fact they will find that, as far as their suffering goes, they will leap out of the frying pan into the fire. Instead of finding any compensation they will find divine condemnation."[113] If exclusive salvation and closed death are true, Rachel Held Evans bluntly observes, then "the Jews killed in the gas chambers at Auschwitz went straight to hell after their murders"—where they are further victimized by being punished for not believing in Jesus.[114] In addition, if hell is eternal then there is a final dualism of the saved and the unsaved. Some evil is not eliminated but becomes a "permanent fixture in God's [new] creation," Kronen and Reitan say. If any are forever lost then "God confronts ultimate defeat in the souls of the damned. . . . At least in some human souls, sin will prove more powerful than God."[115] Only *apokatastasis*, a universal restoration in which all things and people are gathered to God, completely resolves the problem of evil. Salvation prayer reassures us that the ultimate evil—eternal hell—will not obtain.

The problem of hell—recall—is a version of the problem of evil, a trilemma consisting of three contradictory propositions:

1. God is loving, so wants to save and enter communion with all persons.

2. God is powerful, so can save and enter communion with all persons.

3. Some persons are never saved, but remain separated from God forever.

If statement 3 is true, then either statement 1 is false (God has favorites and does not want to save everyone—God's love has boundaries and timelines) or statement 2 is false (God has weaknesses and cannot save everyone—human beings have free will, so God is unable to achieve God's purpose that all persons enjoy relationship with God). Both explanations are problematic: the first diminishes God's love and the second God's power.[116] While double-destiny eschatology compromises God's charac-

---

113. MacDonald, *Evangelical Universalist*, 157.

114. Evans, *Searching for Sunday*, 50.

115. Kronen and Reitan, *God's Final Victory*, 104 and 26. See chapter 5 footnote 150, where I argue against the view that God's purposes can be completely fulfilled even though some are eternally condemned.

116. See Gulley and Mulholland, *If Grace is True*, 91 as well as Talbott, *Inescapable Love of God*, 47–48 and "Three Pictures of God."

ter, salvation prayer corrects that damage. It reminds us that statement 1 is true—that Jesus still offers *love* to the unsaved, saying "let anyone who is thirsty come to me and... drink" (John 7:37), "come to me all you that are weary... and I will give you rest" (Matt 11:28), "listen—I am standing at the door and knocking" (Rev 3:20). And it reminds us that statement 2 is true—that God has *power* to save beyond the grave, that God is able to accomplish God's purpose in creation, that nothing, neither sociopolitical systems nor individual self-will, can frustrate God's final, unqualified victory. Salvation prayer reminds us that hell will not permanently remain alongside heaven, that creation is comic, not tragic, that God's love and power, which saves sinners after death and will completely triumph in the end, are also at work today in our broken and bleeding world.

Pastoral Benefits of Salvation Prayer

Salvation prayer has a number of pastoral benefits for those who are anxious or depressed about the eternal destiny of dead friends and family or who worry about a living loved one who has wandered from God. A friend whose adult son is indifferent to faith recently told me—"since I came to believe in salvation after death, I'm free to love and enjoy him for who he is without always worrying about his soul—fearing that he will die and go to hell forever—and always bringing up issues of God and church like I used to." Where eternal hell creates fear, salvation prayer—with its rehearsal of the truth that God saves beyond death—gives reassurance and allows her to leave her son in God's strong and loving hands, to give up her obsessive anxiety over his spiritual welfare.[117]

Another friend, a hospice nurse, struggles with the contradiction between her belief in closed death and her behavior—her inability or unwillingness to share the gospel with dying people she cares for. "I know I should," she confesses, "but I can't push people to repent and come to Jesus before they die." She is plagued by guilt since—in her mind—the unsaved are entering a hopeless eternity and she should offer them one final chance for salvation before the door of grace slams shut once and for all. Believing that the unsaved dead are not lost to God forever, being able to pray for her patients posthumously, would bring her peace of heart

---

117. This language is drawn from Callahan, *With All Heart and Mind*, 175.

and enable her to minister comfort to those in her care with less anxiety and more authenticity.[118]

Finally, consider survivors who think that a loved one died estranged from God—parents, for example, at the funeral of a child who rejected Christian faith. Bell tells of a woman, after the death of a friend, admitting he was an atheist and being told "so there's no hope then." Bell comments: "No hope? Is that the Christian message? No hope? Is that what Jesus offers the world? Is this the sacred calling of Christians—to announce that there's no hope?"[119] In the third century John Chrysostom imagines a person crying, "I am desperate because my loved one died in sin"—the assumption being that if someone dies unsaved there is no hope because salvation cannot be obtained in the next life. Chrysostom replies: if someone

> departed with sin upon him . . . , help him as far as possible . . . by prayer and supplications. . . . For not . . . in vain [do we] make mention of the departed in the . . . divine mysteries, and approach God in their behalf, beseeching the Lamb who . . . takes away the sin of the world—not in vain, but that some refreshment may thereby ensue to them. . . . Let us then give them aid and perform commemoration for them. For if the children of Job were purged by the sacrifice of their father, why do you doubt that when we too offer for the departed, some consolation arises to them? . . . Let us not then be weary in giving aid to the departed, both by offering on their behalf and obtaining prayers for them. . . . Therefore with boldness do we . . . name their names with those of martyrs, of confessors, of priests. For . . . it is possible . . . to gather pardon for them, from our prayers. . . .

---

118. My friend's dilemma is not unique to her but confronts anyone who believes in exclusive salvation and closed death. Every Christian with these convictions should, if they are logical, dedicate a great deal of time and money to evangelistic mission and personal witness—rather than spending extensive time on hobbies or significant money on luxuries like vacation homes. As Billy Graham ("Responding to God's Glory," 145) says, if we really believed in exclusive salvation we would walk across our countries on broken glass to share the gospel. No one, of course, does any such thing—but my friend, unlike most, is self-aware and honest enough to name her own hypocrisy. The same dilemma caused another friend Ron to abandon belief in exclusive salvation for a more open theology. As a hospital chaplain he found himself offering comfort to the dying rather than trying to get them to say the "sinner's prayer" in deathbed conversion.

119. Bell, *Love Wins*, 3–4.

Why therefore do you grieve? Why mourn, when it is in your power to gather so much pardon for the departed?[120]

Chrysostom also reminds his questioner that the dead do not fall into the grip of "an enemy, or one who plots against them, but into the hands of God, God who has created them, who cares for them much more than you do and knows very well what is beneficial to them."[121] The situation of the dead is not inexorably fixed after death, but can be improved. Edward Pusey encouraged salvation prayer: "instead of being haunted with the thought . . . 'was he saved?' . . . we may commend our departed ones to their Father's care, sure that . . . they are . . . still under the shadow of God's hand, longing for their consummation both of body and soul."[122] Funerals ministry often concerns those of unsettled faith and moral character, and is not conducted with integrity if clergy either assume that they are hopelessly lost or pretend that they were faithful Christians. Believing that we—clergy who conduct services and survivors who attend—can pray for the salvation of the deceased gives funerals both integrity and compassion.[123]

Missional Benefits of Salvation Prayer: How It Enhances the Church's Witness

There is one more significant benefit of salvation prayer. Many people have given up on God because they find the notion of eternal conscious torment morally revolting. Jonathan Edwards' image of an angry God too

---

120. Chrysostom, *Homily on First Corinthians*, Part 2, Homily 41.8, 592–93.

121. Chrysostom, cited in Ramelli, *Christian Doctrine of Apokatastasis*, 559, slightly modified. Cyril of Jerusalem ("Catechetical Lecture 23") says that during the Eucharist "we commemorate also those who have fallen asleep before us . . . believing that it will be a very great benefit to the souls, for whom the supplication is put up, while that holy . . . sacrifice is set forth." He defends the efficacy of prayers for the departed with an analogy suggesting judgment after death: "many say, what is a soul profited, which departs from this world either with sins, or without sins, if it be commemorated in the prayer? For if a king were to banish certain who had given him offense, and then those who belong to them should weave a crown and offer it to him on behalf of those under punishment, would he not grant a remission of their penalties? In the same way we, when we offer to God our supplications for those who have fallen asleep, though they be sinners, . . . [are] propitiating our merciful God for them as well as for ourselves." Cyril claims that prayers can benefit both the holy and the unholy.

122. Pusey, cited in Liddon, "Life of Pusey," 6.

123. See the prayers at the end of chapter 5.

often still frames the popular understanding of Christianity. "The God that holds you over the pit of hell, much as one holds a spider or some loathsome insect over the fire, abhors you and is dreadfully provoked: God's wrath towards you burns like fire; God looks upon you as worthy of nothing else, but to be cast into the fire."[124] The conventional doctrine of inescapable hell, McLaren says, creates a schizoid view of God's character. "God loves you and has a wonderful plan for your life, [but] if you don't love God back and cooperate with God's plans in exactly the prescribed way, God will torture you with unimaginable abuse, forever." More damaging than the doctrine of hell itself is the view of God from which it comes and to which it contributes.[125] It is impossible to calculate the harm that hell has done to the church's witness and to individual lives.

A colleague once explained to me why she was an atheist. Raised Roman Catholic, she was told that she was a wicked sinner and would burn in hell forever unless she did what God required of her. She could not reconcile the idea that God is love with the claim that the fate of sinners is eternal punishment. "How can God create people," she asked me, "people God supposedly loves—knowing full well that many of them will be tortured forever? Are our sins really so bad that we deserve to suffer eternally unless we are 'born again'?" She was—to use McLaren's words—"repulsed by ugly, unworthy images of a cruel, capricious, merciless, tyrannical deity." Her questions are old ones and the contradiction is easy to spot:

1. God is good, like a caring parent.
2. Caring parents do not torture their children.
3. But God will treat sinners with a cruelty that no human parent has ever been guilty of.[126]

I know my friend's questions well—since I too, left the church for a time because of them. Bertrand Russell speaks for many when explaining why he is not a Christian:

> there is one very serious defect to my mind in Christ's moral character, and that is that he believed in hell. . . . [No] person who is really profoundly humane can believe in everlasting punishment. Christ . . . as depicted in the gospels did believe

---

124. Edwards, "Sinners in Hands of Angry God," 159.
125. McLaren, *Last Word*, xix and xviii.
126. Ibid., xiii. This sentence paraphrases McLaren, *Last Word*, 105 and 140.

in everlasting punishment [Russell cites Matt 25:31–46]. . . . [But no] person with a proper degree of kindliness in his nature would have put fears and terrors of that sort into the world. . . . This doctrine, that hell-fire is a punishment for sin, is a doctrine of cruelty. It is a doctrine that put cruelty into the world and gave the world generations of cruel torture.[127]

The doctrine of hell has turned many people from Christian faith; some simply walk away from church and God, scarred perhaps—others carry deep pain and long-term depression.

The traditional doctrine of hell as eternal torment is a toxic teaching that has hurt the church's witness to the gospel. "Belief in damnation for religious disbelief," Rod Evans and Irwin Berent suggest, "has, at times, led some people to condone religious intolerance" and persecution. It has also "had the effect of frightening, and in some cases brutalizing, a large number of people."[128] The teaching of everlasting hell, Gary Amirault claims, has terrorized countless individuals across the centuries, causing psychological and spiritual damage—trauma, *angst*, and confusion—in their lives.[129] Even those who remain in the church can be harmed by thinking that they must believe in inescapable hell as part of Christian faith. "Their nagging fear that God may turn out to be less than good or kind or loving in the end," McLaren says, "makes their hearts uneasy, their worship forced and fake, and their commitment conflicted or half-hearted."[130] It also leaves their minds confused. Despite pat answers—a

127. Russell, *Why I Am Not a Christian*, 17–18.

128. Evans and Berent, *Fundamentalism*, 18 and 70. Havener ("Teaching Children Hell") contends that terrifying children by teaching them that hell and damnation are real constitutes child abuse.

129. Amirault, "Doctrine of Hell Terrorizes." His article includes many testimonies—some by people no doubt disturbed—concerning the destructive effects of the traditional doctrine. He also cites the following quote from Samuel Richardson, *The Doctrine of Eternal Hell Torments Overthrown*, edited by Thomas Whittemore and published by him in 1833. Here is what Richardson wrote in the original nearly two hundred years before 1833. "The doctrine of endless hell torments hath caused many to murder themselves, taking away their own lives . . . that they might not live to increase their sin, and increase their torments in hell." Now consider what Whittemore writes. "Here we see the same dreadful effects attended the doctrine of endless misery nearly 200 years ago which attend it now. It was then the cause of anxiety, despair, and suicide . . . as we know it has been of late years. . . . The doctrine of endless torment . . . makes men melancholy; it drives them to despair; . . . fathers and mothers . . . have murdered their children, lest they should grow up, and commit sin, and be damned. Can a doctrine which produces such dreadful consequences be the doctrine of God?"

130. McLaren, *Last Word*, xiii.

holy God cannot tolerate sin; our minds cannot understand God's ways, which are always right—it is hard to see what God's point would be in torturing people endlessly, how such a penalty (infinite punishment for finite sins) fits with any sense of justice. And then there is the question of whether anyone can joyfully love a God who will consign most of humanity to eternal torment—including all the people they know and love except for a few, maybe even their own parents, spouse, or children.[131] Can anyone truly *love* a God who would do such a thing? Fear, yes; submit, yes; hate, yes—love, no.

Salvation prayer—which teaches a God of boundless love and limitless grace—corrects the traditional understanding of hell and its destructive view of God as vengeance and hate. Churches that make salvation prayers thereby proclaim the wideness of God's love in Christ—that God's goodness and grace reach farther than we dare imagine, that because of God's unfailing love and inexhaustible patience, there is hope for all beyond hell. *That* message and *that* God will draw people to Christ, not push them away. Instead of the fear, threat, and judgment that characterize so much of the church's message, praying for those in hell tutors the church to be gracious and is a practice of grace-filled rather than fear-based Christianity. "Beliefs matter," Gulley and Mulholland write. "Beliefs are not harmless. They have the power to shape our world, for good or ill. . . . Religious beliefs are especially potent, shaping how we think of and act toward God, others and ourselves."[132] If we think God will be ungracious at the end, dividing the saved from the unsaved permanently, then we can be ungracious and judgmental now—to divorced people, gays and lesbians, Muslims and atheists. If, however, we take seriously God's unending love for all people, then we will live more loving personal lives and the church will be a more generous space—a place of healing rather than pain, of inclusion rather than exclusion. Believing in a gracious God will make us gracious Christians. How, after all, can the doctrines of hell and damnation, of a God who punishes forever with fire and brimstone, be *good* news?[133] Where traditional teaching inspires fear, a church that

---

131. This is the leading question framing McLaren's discussion of hell and damnation in *Last Word*.

132. Gulley and Mulholland, *If God is Love*, 4.

133. Recall Kenneth Kantzer's contention (cited in Talbott, *Inescapable Love*, 37) that—since most people are condemned to inescapable hell—"the biblical answer [concerning afterlife destiny] . . . is a hard and crushing word, devastating to human hope." Dixon (*Other Side of Good News*) argues that hell is the bad-news side of the

believes in a God who loves and saves beyond death and publicly prays for those in hell proclaims how compassionate Jesus is—not, as Russell thought, how cruel. This is the God that drew Frederica Mathewes-Green to faith through a statue in a church of Jesus, his hands spread open in welcome, revealing "the heart that so loved mankind."[134]

Salvation prayer can help create the kind of church Pope Francis envisions—a mercy-church, not a justice-church. While he does not mention prayer for the unsaved dead, mercy has been the cornerstone of his papacy, and he declared the year 2016 as a Jubilee of Mercy—a time in which people encounter the grace and love of God in special ways. Salvation prayer reinforces the biblical view of God: "the name of God is mercy"—so God "embraces, . . . welcomes, [and] leans down to forgive" since "the mercy of God never ends."[135] And it teaches us that mercy is "the very foundation of the Church's life." Because God loves all, the church must be "a concrete sign of the constancy of divine love that pardons and saves." It cannot—from a sense of justice—close the door on anyone, Francis asserts, but must be "an oasis of mercy" attempting "to reach all those who are looking for . . . peace and reconciliation." In the words of Pope John XXIII, the church needs "to use the medicine of mercy rather than taking up arms of severity."[136] A church that—through the practice of salvation prayer—knows God's love "doesn't reproach people for their fragility and their wounds." The church "lives an authentic life when it professes and proclaims mercy, the most amazing attribute of [God], and when it leads humanity to the font of mercy"—when it acts as a "field hospital where treatment is given above all to those who are most wounded."[137] Francis repeats: "the Church does not exist to condemn people but to bring about an encounter with the visceral love of God" for those "who are in need of . . . understanding, forgiveness and love." "The more we experience the love and infinite mercy of God"—an awareness

---

good news; since death is a fence that brings finality, hell will have permanent and unredeemable occupants.

134. Mathewes-Green, "I Didn't Mean to be Rude," 54.

135. Pope Francis, *Name of God is Mercy*, 9 and 85 and "Misericordiae Vultus," in *Name of God is Mercy*, 149.

136. Pope Francis, "Misericordiae Vultus," in *Name of God is Mercy*, 119, 133, 123, and 109.

137. Pope Francis, *Name of God is Mercy*, xi and 7-8; cf. 52. The church' "life is authentic and credible only when she becomes a convincing herald of mercy. . . . The Church is called above all to be a credible witness to mercy, professing it and living it as the core of the revelation of Jesus Christ" (149).

fostered by salvation prayer—"the more capable we are of looking upon the many 'wounded' we meet . . . with acceptance and mercy" and the more we "avoid the attitude of someone who judges and condemns from the lofty heights of their own certainty." In a mercy-church sinners "find an open door, not a closed one"—"acceptance, not judgment, prejudice or condemnation. They [are] helped, not pushed away or cast out."[138] In order to become an "effective sign" of God's love, Francis insists, we must "gaze attentively" on God's mercy. Salvation prayer—daily repeating the refrain of Psalm 136, "God's mercy endures forever"—is a way of doing this.[139] Justice-churches teach eternal, inescapable hell—and thereby turn people away from God; mercy-churches, by contrast, pray for the unsaved dead and thereby announce that the doors of grace are always open, even beyond death.

It might be objected that revising our understanding of hell is a matter of simply believing what is pleasing and comforting, as St. Paul (2 Tim 4:3-4) warns: "people will not put up with sound doctrine, but . . . will accumulate for themselves teachers to suit their own desires, and will turn away from listening to the truth and wander away to myths." This is not the case. As John Polkinghorne points out, rethinking the doctrine of hell "has come about, not through surrender to a secular sentimentality, but through the realization of its incompatibility with the mercy of a loving God, who cannot be conceived to exact infinite punishments for finite wrong."[140] Biblical revelation, not simply human reason, supports the possibility of posthumous salvation. Nor does the fact that the doctrine of hell has been misused mean that it cannot be properly used. There is a proper fear of standing before God for judgment (2 Cor 5:10) since "it is a fearful thing to fall into the hands of the living God" (Heb 10:31). We should, Jesus says, "fear him who can destroy both soul and body in hell" (Matt 10:28).

---

138. Ibid., 52-53 and 67-68, slightly modified.

139. Pope Francis, "Misericordiae Vultus," in *Name of God is Mercy*, 106. See Appendix Note 10 for excerpts from this document, the announcement of a Holy Year of Mercy.

140. Polkinghorne, *Faith of Physicist*, 170-71.

Answering Two Final Concerns

I end by considering two objections which suggest that salvation prayer has negative, not positive, spiritual value. First—to revisit a concern discussed earlier—it might be thought that praying for posthumous salvation (or for spiritual growth or character purification, for that matter) encourages moral laxity; if individuals can repent after death then there is no urgency to do so now. As Moltmann states the objection: escapism and universalism promote "light-minded recklessness that says: why should I believe and bother to lead a good and righteous life, if I and everyone else are going to be redeemed in any case?"[141] Only the threat of closed death—eternal hell with no possibility of a second chance—can motivate right believing and living now. Peter Kreeft and Ronald Tacelli agree: "if there is no hell, life's choices no longer make an infinite difference.... Drop hell, and heaven becomes a bland, automatic anything and everything for anyone and everyone."[142]

Open death, however, does not promote moral or spiritual sloth. Universalism does not claim, Kronen and Reitan note, "that one can be saved while continuing to sin," but rather "that everyone will eventually cease sinning." Posthumous salvation is not automatic; no one enters heaven unless they are perfectly holy, and so—since choices form habits, which are hard to change—we must take our moral choices seriously. The more we sin in this life the more difficult and lengthy the process of salvation after death—and so "there is excellent reason to avoid sin and seek moral sanctification" and salvation now.[143] McDonald, too, points out that "hell is something to be avoided at all costs, just as Jesus warned us. To object by saying, 'Well, if hell is not forever, it doesn't really matter if someone has a spell there,' is like suggesting that because you will recover from the long and painful illness, it isn't worth taking precautions to avoid it."[144] The church must avoid each of two mistakes. On the one hand, as discussed in the previous section, it must not teach a cruel and inescapable hell—what Wright calls "a torture chamber"—of eternal conscious torment that contradicts divine love. On the other hand, it must not deny the seriousness of judgment and the demand for moral commitment by teaching a facile and easy escapism or what Wright calls

---

141. Moltmann, *Coming of God*, 239.
142. Kreeft and Tacelli, *Handbook of Apologetics*, 283.
143. Kronen and Reitan, *God's Final Victory*, 181.
144. MacDonald, *Evangelical Universalist*, 166.

a "cheap and cheerful universalism."[145] Prayer for posthumous salvation does not undermine the moral urgency and seriousness of this life but recognizes Jesus' warning that many find the wide way to hell while few take the narrow way to heaven and his urging that we "strive to enter" the kingdom (Matt 7:13–14; Luke 13:24; cf. Ps 1).

Second, it might be thought that salvation prayer undermines motivation for evangelistic mission. If people can be saved posthumously regardless of whether they hear and believe the gospel, what was the point of my parents going to Nigeria as missionaries? Rescuing people from eternal hell, however, is not the only motivation for mission. It is—to be sure—one motive, since hell is a serious consequence to avoid and since evangelism is one means of reconciliation to God. But the assumption that salvation is only about saving souls for an otherworldly heaven is biblically shallow. The question "if eternal hell does not exist, then why should we bother to witness to others?" reveals, Baker says, "that we are more interested in obtaining fire insurance . . . than in seeing the world transformed by the power of Jesus Christ . . . that we view salvation as other-worldly rather than this-worldly."[146] The salvation Jesus brings is a new kind of life that begins now (John 10:10); it is not simply a ticket out of hell and into heaven. In Scripture the word "salvation" (Hebrew *yesha'*, Greek *sōtēria*) is a comprehensive term that refers to the mending of brokenness and is holistic, including physical and psychological healing, forgiveness of sins, restoration of relationships and liberation from social oppression.[147]

Neither escapism nor universalism undermine the motivation for missions—but they do change it. Even if all the unevangelized are saved beyond death, they miss out on the fullness of life in Christ here and now—the comfort and joy, hope, and peace that faith brings in this present life. My mother tells about a Hausa pastor who often thanked them for their work. "You have no idea what Christian faith means to us," he would say. "We used to live in fear of the spirits. We dreaded the nighttime. Now we are free."[148] The good news of salvation is not only for

---

145. Wright, *Surprised by Hope*, 175 and 180.

146. Baker, *Razing Hell*, 175–76.

147. Walters, "Salvation." Also see Sider and Parker, "How Broad Is Salvation in Scripture?"

148. She also tells of a local *emir*—a town chief—who had travelled to Mecca on *hajj*, seeking spiritual solace. Upon his return a fellow-missionary asked him: "did you find in your pilgrimage the comfort your soul needs?" After a long pause he replied sadly, "no."

the afterlife; what my parents did in Nigeria was life-changing for many people now—even if they would have been saved after death anyway. As Bell says, "the gospel isn't [only] about getting into heaven. . . . It is an invitation to enter into life with God and participate in that party, that joy, now." He goes on:

> when people say that if you take away the threat of [eternal] punishment, then no one will have any motivation to believe in Jesus, . . . they're saying something incredibly derogatory about Jesus, that the best he offers is an escape. They're revealing a seriously bankrupt, empty gospel that doesn't have much in the way of anything good, just promises that you'll avoid something bad. Jesus comes to offer us the eternal life of God now, so that we'll experience joy and peace and healing now.[149]

The fact that salvation encompasses life *before* death, not merely life *after* death, is sufficient—and deeply biblical—motivation for mission.[150] Prayer for posthumous salvation does not contradict evangelism.

Concluding Remarks

Prayer is spiritually forming. It is—to use an analogy from Todd Friesen—like the North Star giving coordinates to a sailor. By comparing their position in the ocean to that of the North Star in the sky, a navigator knows where the ship is and how to adjust its direction to get to the destination. Praying for the dead helps position us in life. "The future we pray for hangs over the present," James Smith says, giving direction and motivation for our living here and now.[151]

Prayers for the dead are forms of lament. Lament pervades covenant relationship with God, as we hear in Scripture—the weeping of Hagar, the complaints of Moses, the cry of helpless Hebrew slaves, the tears of Elijah, Job, David, and Habakkuk, Christ's cry of derelliction. Lament is not,

---

149. Bell, *Love Wins Companion*, 143 and 190. Kronen and Reitan (*God's Final Victory*, 183) agree: "there are positive life benefits (in terms of life satisfaction and resources for moral improvement) that are possible in this life if (and only if) one opens oneself up to the kind of relationship with God that . . . has been made available through Christ's life and work. Desiring that others enjoy these benefits here and now"—not just afterlife salvation—should be the focus of evangelism.

150. Wright, *Surprised by Hope*, 197. See Pinnock, *Wideness in God's Mercy*, 176–80 and Sanders, *No Other Name*, 48–50, 262–67 and 283–85.

151. Friesen, cited in Moll, *Art of Dying*, 162 and Smith, *Desiring Kingdom*, 192.

Martin Marty says, merely a "crying out" in pain, but is a "crying toward" a God who listens and cares.[152] Laments, while seemingly hopeless, Seung Yang says, "are hopeful because they are ... an expectation that [God] ... will rectify the situation."[153] Lament protests against divine indifference and is meant to mobilize God to act because of God's prior commitments and faithful character (e.g., Ps 6:4 and 35:23–24). We are what Walls calls "aching visionaries," people who are "aware of the profound difference between the state of our present world and the coming Kingdom when God's will is perfectly achieved. Our present situation is one of groaning, St. Paul says (Rom 8:19–25), as we anticipate—with all creation—the full liberation of our world from the effects of sin."[154] Prayer for the dead is lament concerning the last things. "It is not yet God's good future, still sadly not yet that future," Verhey explains. "That is why Christian hope is not inconsistent with lament." "How long, O Lord," we protest, "until you finally consummate your kingdom, until you sanctify the imperfect with hearts of love, until all persons have returned to relationship with you?" Because we are confident that God can change things, praying for the dead creates eschatological optimism, an expectant hope that overcomes eschatological pessimism, a hope—Verhey says—"that echoes to all the corners of our world's sadness, to all the niches of our own despair."[155]

Prayers for the dead are prayers of cheerful hope and expectation. Where despair brings sadness, hope creates joy—and where despair results in passive apathy, hope motivates active energy. St. Peter (1 Pet 1:13) instructs us to "set all your hope on the grace that Jesus Christ will bring you when he is revealed." Prayer for the dead is one way of doing so. The hopeful Christian

1. *desires* particular eschatological outcomes: final consummation of all things, continual growth toward God, perfectly holy character and salvation of all people;

2. *believes* confidently that these outcomes will occur, given God's promises and faithfulness; and

---

152. Marty, *Cry of Absence*, 112.

153. Yang, "Hope," 886. For literature on lament see my "Healing the Wounded Heart."

154. Walls, *Heaven*, 118.

155. Verhey, *Christian Art of Dying*, 268 and 266,

3. *incorporates* these desires and beliefs into their way of being and acting in the world now.

Prayer is one way we express hope and—Pope Benedict XVI says—"draw the future into the present, so that . . . the present is touched by the future reality."[156]

J.R.R. Tolkien's *The Lord of the Rings* trilogy traces the quest of Frodo and his companions to destroy the evil ring of power and thereby save Middle-Earth from the Dark Lord. As they approach their destination in Mordor, surrounded by danger and despair, his servant Sam asks Frodo: "I wonder what sort of a tale we've fallen into?"[157] Is it happy-ending or sad-ending? We, like Sam, ask the same question at times: what kind of story are we in? Is it a story with a happy ending, a comedy, or a sad ending, a tragedy? Prayers for the dead create particular beliefs and desires in us—and they help us incorporate those beliefs and desires into our habits of life. Praying for the departed helps us fight despair by creating an eschatology of hope: confidence in the good future God will bring—the renewal of all things (Matt 19:28; Acts 3:21)—when God "will gather up all things in [Christ], things in heaven and things on earth" (Eph 1:10)—when, in the words of Julian of Norwich, "all shall be well and all shall be well and all manner of thing shall be well."[158]

---

156. Pope Benedict XVI, *Spe Salvi*, 17. For an analysis of hope, see Volume 1, chapter 9.
157. Tolkien, *Two Towers*, 696.
158. Julian, cited in Hick, *Death and Eternal Life*, 156.

chapter 8

SAMPLE PRAYERS

JEANETTE, A FAITHFUL OLD saint and member of my parish church, died after a short illness as I was completing this chapter. A little wisp of a woman, she exuded buoyancy beyond her stature, vivacity beyond her years. I first met Jeanette when she—already elderly—was a greeter at the Walmart my disabled son and I used to frequent. On seeing us, her face would beam and she would take both of David's hands in hers, an act of genuine affection, followed by a gracious hug. David loved it. Father Don ended his email announcing her death with the traditional prayer: "May the soul of Jeanette, and the souls of all the departed, through the mercy of God, rest in peace." Amen—so it is. God, be with all who die this day; bring them to share in your heavenly city with voices of unending praise.

In the fourth century Cyril of Jerusalem reports having heard believers ask "what is a soul, leaving this world . . . , profited by being remembered in the prayer?"[1] In this book and its predecessor I have answered his question, explaining and defending the practice of *petitionary* prayer for *all* the dead. In the nineteenth century, Frederick Lee recommended petitionary prayer for all the dead without exception—"for every person . . . is our neighbor, whom by God's express commands we are enjoined to love, and for whom consequently we should continually offer up our prayers—as a primary duty of love." We should pray for *the saints* in heaven because they "will have an additional happiness bestowed upon them in the future when all the ransomed . . . are joined with them at the last"—and because "there is progress constantly going on amongst

---

1. Cyril of Jerusalem, cited in Swete, "Prayer for Departed," 510.

the departed in Christ in the region beyond the grave." We should pray for *the imperfect* in purgatory because "those who have died in the faith and fear of God must have every stain . . . removed before they are fitted for heaven." We should pray for *the unsaved* because "their eventual final state is not yet settled"—because "there are punishments inflicted after death and forgiveness of sins bestowed in the world to come." Our prayers must include "those without the pale of the visible Church, that is, for idolaters [and] unbelievers . . . , that faith may be given to" them and that they "may be freed from the error of impiety" and "receive the light of . . . truth." We pray because the state of the saved dead is not static nor the state of the unsaved irrevocable.[2] We offer this general prayer—which can be construed in terms of consummation, growth, purification, or salvation: "Father of all, we pray to you for those we love, but see no longer; grant them your peace; let light perpetual shine upon them; and in your loving wisdom and almighty power, work in them the good purpose of your perfect will; through Jesus Christ our Lord. Amen."[3]

Praying for the dead is one of the spiritual works of mercy long practiced in Christian tradition. Understanding the effectiveness of petitionary prayer—and in particular how prayer for the dead works, why they need our prayers—involves the important question of how God relates to the world. Prayer is one way in which we cooperate with God in redeeming humanity and creation. As Sidney Callahan says, "at creation God set the stage for our drama" and in consummation "has determined the finale of the script"—"God wins, we know, but *how* that victory of love will be consummated depends upon our human acts [including prayer] in this time of 'not yet.'"[4]

In the *Westminster Shorter Catechism*'s definition "prayer is the offering up of our desires unto God for things agreeable to God's will."[5] Intercessory prayer makes an *objective* difference to the departed person for whom we pray. It operates, Callahan suggests, "like a magnifying glass that can focus and intensify God's light upon a particular point" or like a magnet "that attracts God's power to a particular event" or person. The more persons who pray "the more God's light and power can be focused

---

2. Lee, *Christian Doctrine of Prayer for Departed*, 184–86; slightly modified.
3. Episcopal Church, *Book of Common Prayer*, 504.
4. Callahan, *With All Heart and Mind*, 167.
5. *Westminster Shorter Catechism*, in *Westminster Confession*, 26.

on a situation."⁶ In praying for the dead we breathe God's love and power onto them. Consummation prayer concerns all the departed and asks for completion of God's plan, their resurrection in a new heaven and earth. Growth prayer concerns the blessed in heaven and asks for their increasing participation in God's life. Purification prayer concerns the imperfect in purgatory and asks for their moral transformation in love. Salvation prayer concerns the unsaved in hell and asks for their restored relationship with God. These are all "things agreeable to God's will."

Intercessory prayer also makes a *subjective* difference in the person who prays. Psychologically, it creates what Callahan calls "habits of attention [right belief] and attachment [right desire]" that transform our thoughts, feelings, and behavior toward God and the pursuit of God's kingdom. Through praying for the dead we find ourselves reassured of God's care for us—"the truth gradually sinks in: . . . God really does love us dearly." This realization raises our sense of self-worth. Prayer also moves us out of ourselves. As we become more aware that God loves each person, we are able to love them better as "God's love for us overflows in love for others." To pray for the dead, and especially dead enemies, is to recognize them as fellow persons created and loved by God, co-members in the human community. It is to "enlarge our narrow perspective and break out of the egocentric point of view."⁷

There are two contexts of prayer for the departed: it should occur in the public worship of the whole church and as part of personal daily devotion. We need both kinds of prayer: corporate prayer in the collective community of the church's liturgy and individual prayer in the privacy of our relationship with God. Most public rituals can be used when praying alone. Numerous petitions are found throughout the two volumes of this work, and this final chapter contains a collection of prayers. I have modeled these prayers after the collects used in the worship of liturgical churches. Collects are prayers that gather up and express the petitions of the church or the individual. Collects have a specific structure:

1. address to God;
2. description of God—of the divine attributes that encourage the prayer;
3. petition—the request itself;

---

6. Callahan, *With All Heart and Mind*, 185.
7. Ibid., 170 and 175.

4. reason for or desired outcome of prayer; and

5. ending—leaving the results in God's good hands.

Consider, for example, this Episcopal Church burial prayer: "[1] O God, [2] whose mercies cannot be numbered: [3] accept our prayers on behalf of your servant N. [4] and grant him/her an entrance into the land of light and joy, in the fellowship of your saints; [5] through Jesus Christ our Lord, who lives and reigns with you and the Holy Spirit, one God, now and forever. Amen." Not all the sample prayers have this structure, but many do.[8] Spontaneous unwritten prayers can also be made from our hearts in our own words.

Consummation Prayers

Loving God, in your infinite mercy bring N., together with the whole church, living and departed in the Lord Jesus, to a joyful resurrection and the fulfillment of your eternal purpose. Unite us together again to rejoice in your kingdom and sing your praise forever and ever. In the name of the One who has come and is coming again. Amen.

Faithful God, we give thanks for N. and for all who have passed beyond trouble and darkness and are now at peace. Accomplish what remains of his/her redemption—perfect consummation of bliss in the kingdom of heaven for ever. We wait for you, Lord, in your word we hope—in your coming reign of justice, peace, and love we are confident. Amen.

May it please you, Eternal God, to hasten your kingdom—that we, with all those departed in your love, may know your everlasting glory, in a place of refreshment from which all sickness, sighing, and sorrow have fled away. Through Christ—who lives and reigns and is to come. Amen.

God of history, finish your new creation—redeeming the world from sin and death and into the flourishing of righteousness and

---

8. Episcopal Church, *Book of Common Prayer*, 493. I have drawn on the *Book of Common Prayer* and on prayers and wording found on various Roman Catholic and Eastern Orthodox websites—as well as from Piguet, *100 Prayers* and Sheppy, *In Sure and Certain Hope*.

life. Restore all things and bring the feast of eternal joy to N. and all your people. Keep us sure-footed on the path to your holy reign, that we follow the way of holiness and love. *Maranatha*—come quickly Lord Jesus. Amen.

Consummating God, increase your dominion until the earth is filled with the knowledge of your love as the waters cover the sea. Give N. the crown of life in the day of resurrection—and bring joy to him/her and the whole world. Raise up things which were cast down, make new things which have grown old, bring all things to their perfection by him through whom they were made—your Son, Jesus Christ our Lord. Amen.[9]

Lord Jesus Christ, we hunger in the darkness for your light. Give us the great hope that the future is yours, that time cannot hide you from us forever, that at the end you who came will come back in power and glory to work joy in us, and in N. and in your whole church. Lord Jesus, come quickly to your world. Amen.[10]

God, we thank you for N. who has entered into your joy. Bring your heavenly kingdom quickly, and may we share with him/her in the victory of your Son's resurrection, in your eternal light that knows no evening. We trust in your power to restore the brokenness of this world and to lead us to everlasting peace. Faithful God, keep your promise. We keep our hope fixed on you. Amen.

Astonishing God, you give us a vision of the heavenly city, the New Jerusalem, your home among human beings on earth. Bring your world made new in Christ quickly, we ask—and may N. and all of us share in its joys with voices of unending praise. Lord Jesus, come and renew the face of the earth. Amen.

God of promise, you have a plan to reform the world into your perfect kingdom. Lord Jesus, return quickly—sweep away evil and reunite us with all our brothers and sisters [with N.] who now rest in your embrace. Spirit of God, send forth your light—renew the face of the earth and lift all hearts to your praise. God of promise, in you is the hope of the world. Amen.

---

9. Based on the Solemn Collects for Good Friday, Episcopal Church, *Book of Common Prayer*, 280.

10. Based on Buechner, *Hungering Dark*, 125.

Growth Prayers

Good and gracious God: we rejoice with the church triumphant and pray for loved ones who have entered life eternal and now rest in the love of the Father, the peace of the Son, and the joy of the Holy Spirit. We ask that in your presence N. will grow in your love, be refreshed with your peace and be filled with your joy, until he/she sees you as you are. Amen.[11]

Eternal rest grant unto N., O Lord. May perpetual light shine upon him/her. May he/she rest in peace. Receive him/her more and more into your joyful service, and graciously bestow upon him/her your promised blessing. Let his/her love for you grow more and more, that his/her joy may be full. Through Christ our Lord. Amen.

Hear our prayers, O Lord. We rejoice with our brother/sister N. who now experiences the glorious liberty of the children of God. Grant to him/her those things which eye has not seen, nor ear heard, nor the human heart imagined. Feed him/her at the table of eternal life where the voice of those who keep high festival never ceases, and where endless is the sweetness of those who behold the beauty of your countenance. May he/she grow in deeper reverence and love, for you are the true happiness of those who know you. Amen.

Infinite God, grant that, increasing in knowledge and love of you and the whole communion of saints, N. may go from strength to strength in the life of perfect service in your heavenly kingdom. Multiply to him/her the blessings of your love. Fill him/her with your joy and presence—and sustain him/her in the green pasture, by the water of rest in the *paradise* of joy. Through Christ. Amen.

Loving God, we pray that, having opened to N. the gates of larger life, you will receive him/her more and more into your joyful service. Grant him/her whatever is best in his/her present state—that his/her life may unfold in your sight. May he/she find sweet enjoyment in the spacious fields of eternity, in the ample house of your great love. Blessed Lord, hear us. Amen.[12]

---

11. Based on Catechism, Episcopal Church, *Book of Common Prayer*, 862.
12. Based on Archbishop's Commission, *Prayer and Departed*, 91.

God of heavenly joy: we thank you that N. is in your presence where there is fullness of joy and pleasure forevermore. We ask that he/she be transformed from one degree of glory to another, being drawn more and more into your unending life and finding increasing joy in the glory that is yours from all eternity. Lord, fill them with your love. Amen.

God of growth and change, draw N. and all who rest in your presence into fuller knowledge of your love and the splendor of your presence. For this we give thanks and bless your name. Amen.

God who says "Come to the table I have set before you"—we pray for friends and loved ones, especially N., who have passed into your presence in hope of resurrection. Feed them with your life. Nourish them in the light of your love and in the communion of saints now at rest. Their spirits long for you. Quench their thirst and refresh their hearts. Fill them to overflowing with your joy and peace. Amen.[13]

Healing God, we pray for N. who was disabled in this life. By your grace remove his/her impairments—make the eyes of the blind see, the ears of the deaf hear, the lame leap like deer, the tongues of the speechless sing for joy, and the minds of the slow know and understand. We ask for his/her wholeness as we pray to you, O Lord. Amen.

Purification Prayers

God of grace, set the hearts of your imperfect people now departed on fire with love for you. Remove their self-centeredness. Transform them so their desires perfectly align with yours—so they are centered in love alone. God, in your loving kindness, hear our prayer. Amen.

Gracious God, grant to the departed purification from all their sins, that they may obtain that holiness which fits them for heaven. In your great mercy purify N. from every sin. Heal and restore him/her that he/she may love you without hindrance.

---

13. Based on Piguet, *100 Prayers*, 211.

Lord, show him/her your way and teach him/her your paths. Amen.

We pray, Lord God, for our brothers and sisters who have passed through the shadow of death, that you will cleanse their every sin and give them their lot in the land of the blessed. Purify them by the fire of your love and establish them in the courts of your saints. Wipe away the stain of sin that clings to them and bring them to your kingdom of light and life, to the *paschal* fullness of your table. We ask this Lord, for your mercy is great. Amen.

Lord Jesus, in your merciful kindness and by the power of your holy cross, grant those who need purification a speedy entry into the *Sabbath* rest of heaven. Make them ready for the sight of your glory. Lord, fill them with your love. Amen.[14]

Purifying God, sever your selfish children from themselves that they may be grateful to you; let them die to themselves that they may live in you; make them wither to themselves that they may blossom in you; empty them of themselves that they may abound in you; make them nothing to themselves that they may be all to you. Amen.[15]

Holy God, may N., who died sinful, complete the process of sanctification in your perfect presence. May the selfishness which remains in his/her character be purified until he/she is perfected in the ability to love. God, do good work within him/her—that he/she soon come to complete union with you in the fullness of heaven. Lord, in your mercy, hear our prayer. Amen.

Sanctifying God, make N. holy and blameless—purify him/her entirely with your gift of life and love eternal. Give him/her a broken and contrite heart. Purge him/her and he/she shall be clean; wash him/her, and he/she shall be whiter than snow. Create in him/her a clean heart and put a new and right spirit within him/her. For your glory, we ask. Amen.[16]

Most loving Father, we pray that in your presence N. grows in love until it permeates all layers of his/her personality and he/

---

14. Based on Saward, *Sweet and Blessed Country*, 112.
15. Based on Erasmus of Rotterdam, cited in Bakken, *Journey into God*, 81.
16. Based on 1 Thess 5:23 and Psalm 51.

she sees you as you are. Draw N.'s whole self into your love—let it seize his/her entire being and possess him/her completely until he/she is transformed from love of self to love of you. Loving God, hear our prayer. Amen.[17]

Blessed Savior, purify N. until they love you alone, follow you alone, seek you alone, serve you alone. Convert them wholly to yourself—let nothing prevent this. Amen.[18]

God, stir up your power and come to N. Because he/she is sorely hindered by his/her sins, let your bountiful grace and mercy speedily help and deliver him/her—so he/she enters quickly into the fullness of heaven. Through Jesus Christ. Amen.[19]

O God, creator and redeemer of all the faithful, look down upon the departed who yet need perfection. Grant to them, your children, full sanctification from all their sins. Cleanse them and fulfill their desire to be behold you face to face in your glory. Amen.

Holy God, accept all that was good in N—and cleanse him/her from all that was wrong. Draw him/her into the likeness of your Son, that he/she may grow in peace with you and in love for others. Make his/her heart firm, that he/she may enter your eternal dwelling. Amen.

Jesus, healer and reconciler, touch N. and make him/her whole. Break the sinful habits that control him/her so he/she thinks new thoughts and becomes the person you meant him/her to be. Immerse him/her in your presence and peace. Hear us, Lord, for your mercy is great. Amen.

Blessed are you, compassionate God. Radiate your love into the lives of your departed children that remain self-centered. Change them and turn them around so they love you with gladness and singleness of heart. Bring them to a new way of being. We pray in confidence that you do as we ask. Amen.

---

17. Based on Anselm of Canterbury, cited in Doctrine Commission, *Mystery of Salvation*, 108.

18. Based on Tutu, *African Prayer Book*, 137.

19. Based on Episcopal Church, *Book of Common Prayer*, 212.

Lord God, N.'s life was full of mistakes and failures, sin and selfishness. Renew and recreate his/her heart. Send your Spirit to break the chains that bind him/her. Cleanse him/her of all that keeps him/her from fully sharing your presence. Blessed Lord, set your people free. Amen.

Loving Shepherd of Souls—open the hearts of your imperfect people now gone from this world to be transformed to love you perfectly. Soften their stony hearts and free their selfish minds that they may truly love you. Bring them into the fullness of heaven, that in your presence they may rejoice in peace. Amen.

Jesus, gentle shepherd—lead N. out of his/her blindness and weakness. Set him/her on the path of holiness and wholeness. Conform him/her to your image as you cleanse his/her heart and mind. Make your love the reality of his/her life—that he/she may love you fully. Re-creating God, answer our prayer. Amen.

Salvation Prayers

God of unending grace, who is ever merciful and bountiful in love—look down upon those separated from you. Call all the departed, even those who do not know you, to the banquet of your love. Help them open the door to Jesus who knocks—and receive them into eternal happiness. Lord, in your mercy, hear our prayer. Amen.

Most gentle Jesus, full of love for the souls in hell, have mercy on them. Do not be severe in your judgment but send your angels to bring them to a place of refreshment, light, and peace. Lead N. home to you, that he/she may rest where pain and sorrow are no more. Thanks be to you, O Lord. Amen.

Merciful God, whose loving heart is always burdened with the sorrows of others, look down with pity on our loved one, N. Be gracious to him/her. Temper your justice with mercy and open the gates of heaven for him/her—that he/she may pass from death to life everlasting. We ask this through the One who came to love, heal, and forgive each of us. Amen.

Most compassionate Jesus, have mercy on those in hell, for whose redemption you took upon yourself human nature and died an evil death. Look with pity on their tears and release them from the pain due their sins. Refresh and revive their souls, stretch out your strong arm and lead them to the joys of heaven. For your tender mercy's sake. Amen.

Saving God, we commend N. to your eternal love. Deliver him/her from sin and stubbornness. Do not be exceedingly angry, O Lord, and do not remember his/her iniquity forever. Remember that he/she is your creation and the work of your hand. Merciful God, hear me/us. Amen.[20]

Lord God, bless with the gift of life eternal our friends and loved ones and all who did not love you in this life. We place them in the strong hands of your love. You did not create them to be prisoners in hell, but to find rest and true happiness in you. Remember them when you come into your kingdom. Saving God, hear our prayer. Amen.

Merciful God, creator of all the peoples of the earth and lover of souls; have compassion on all who do not know you as you are revealed in your Son Jesus Christ. Let your gospel come with grace and power to those/to N. who did not hear it in this life. Turn the hearts of those/N. who resist/resists it and bring home to your fold those/N. who in this life went astray—that there may be one flock under one Shepherd. Amen.[21]

Gracious God, we pray for all/N. who in this life did not receive the gospel of Christ; for those/N. who never heard the word of salvation; for those/N. who lost their/his/her faith; for those/N. hardened by sin and indifference; for the contemptuous and those who were enemies of the cross of Christ and persecutors of his disciples—that you will open their hearts to the truth and lead them to repentance and faith. Hear me/us, O God, in your mercy. Amen.[22]

---

20. Based on Isa 64:8–9.

21. Based on the Solemn Collects for Good Friday, Episcopal Church, *Book of Common Prayer*, 279.

22. Ibid, 279.

Loving God, your grace can steal its way into hearts and begin to spread itself out there more and more. We ask this for N.—that as your love occupies him/her, he/she will not remain closed to it. We ask that your grace win ground from the things that fill N.'s soul, repelling the effects of sin. Draw him/her into your love and lead him/her into *paradise*. Lord have mercy. Christ have mercy. Lord have mercy. Amen.[23]

Eternal God, salvation belongs to you, who hold the keys of heaven and hell. Keep N. in your eternal care. Call him/her to new life in you—and bring him/her to the feast of your new creation. Hasten, O Christ, that day when every heart will know and love you. In you is strength and salvation, and to you be glory and praise forever. Amen.

Stir up your power, O Lord, and with great might come to those separated from you. Because they are sorely hindered by their sins, let your bountiful grace and mercy speedily help and deliver them. Lord of light and love, save your erring children. Amen.[24]

Caring God, we bring N.—our departed loved one—before you. He/she was broken and defeated in life. In your mercy, Lord, draw him/her to yourself. Work in him/her the good purpose of your will, that he/she may share in the glory which is everlasting. With hope we pray. Amen.[25]

Lord, catch N. up in your eternal love. Show him/her your mercy and clothe him/her with life everlasting. Do not leave him/her under the power of sin and do not forget him/her—but gather him/her into the company of those who praise your name forever. In your mercy grant him/her safe lodging, a holy rest, and peace in a heavenly home at the last. Amen.

Almighty God, who is always ready to forgive, and to whom no prayer is made without hope of mercy. Open wide a heavenly home for N.; make safe the way that leads on high and close the path to misery. Help us to believe that he/she has been taken

---

23. Based on Balthasar, *Dare We Hope?* 219–20.

24. Based on the Collect for the Third Sunday of Advent, Episcopal Church, *Book of Common Prayer*, 212.

25. Based on Colquhoun, *Parish Prayers*, 57.

into the safe keeping of your eternal love and unfailing compassion. Amen.[26]

Holy and loving Father, who graciously shows mercy to your children though they rebel against you. Remember N. according to the favor that you have to all people. Pity his/her ignorance, his/her foolishness, his/her weakness. Deliver him/her from his/her distress. Grant unto him/her the forgiveness of all his/her sins and a place in your kingdom. Amen.[27]

Loving Lord, you seek us, you desire to deliver us from trouble, you set out to rescue us from oppression. Come to N. now and bring him/her home through your saving and healing power. Lord of light and love, hear our prayers, and save all the dead. Amen.

Look favorably, gracious God, upon those who scarcely knew your grace. Grant mercy to those who have departed this life in ignorance or defiance of you. We plead for them in the spirit of him who prayed, "Father, forgive them, for they know not what they do." Lord, in your mercy hear our prayer. Amen.[28]

We place N., O Lord, in your merciful hands. His/her life was filled with sin and struggle, but only you perceive what mustard seed of faith was hidden in his/her heart. We commend N. to your merciful care, knowing that you will do right. Amen.[29]

Gracious God, we commit those who are dear to us to your never-failing love. Fulfill in them your purpose that reaches beyond time and death. Give them entrance into the land of light and joy, into the fellowship of your saints. Hear us Lord. Amen.

O God of infinite mercy and justice, who has made man in thine own image, and hatest nothing that thou hast made, we rejoice in thy love for all creation and commend all men to thee, that in them thy will be done. Amen.[30]

---

26. Based on ibid., 245 and on the advent hymn "O Come, O Come Immanuel."
27. Based on ibid., 245 and 253.
28. Based on United Methodist Church, *Service of Death and Resurrection*, 83.
29. Based on Vander Zee, *In Life and Death*, 203–4.
30. Based on Archbishop's Commission, *Prayer and Departed*, 55.

O Christ our God, who has descended into hell and shattered the eternal bars, revealing the way of ascent for those who dwell in that lower world. Accept our prayers on behalf of those held fast in hell, and send down on them relaxation of their torments and consolation. Do not abandon into the abyss the souls of those who were infected by the plague of the soul-tainting world. Deliver them from fire eternal that they may sing praises unto you forever. For your tender mercies' sake, set them free. Amen.[31]

Ever-merciful God, Christ who died for all, Renewing Spirit—do not reject those who rejected you or died without hearing your gospel. Do not let your eternal love draw back before them. Can a woman forget the infant at her breast or a mother the child of her womb? Even if these should forget, merciful God, you will not forget these; you have inscribed them on your hands. Bring them to repentance and salvation—open to them the gates of your kingdom. Amen.[32]

God who seeks and saves the lost, find and save N.—who died and did not know you. Even when there are ninety-nine, without N., you are not satisfied and we are not whole. Break down N.'s defenses. Chase away his/her blindness. Touch him/her, so he/she desire your presence. We know that you are doing better things for him/her than we can either desire or pray for. Amen.[33]

Lord Jesus, you stretched out your arms on the hard wood of the cross that everyone might come within the reach of your saving embrace. Bring N., who did not know you, to love you and rest in your dwelling place. Let the light of your perpetual grace shine upon him/her. Christ, Mediator and Redeemer, have mercy. Amen.

Holy God, holy and mighty, holy and merciful Savior—we pray for those who did not know you in life. While you are justly angry at their sins, do not turn away from them or deliver them into the bitterness of eternal death. Spare them, O Lord—do not shut your ears to our prayer. Amen.[34]

---

31. Based on Ware, "One Body in Christ," 189–90.

32. Based on Helmut Thielecke, cited in Balthasar, *Dare We Hope?* 36, Tutu, *African Prayer Book*, 100 and Isa 49:14–16.

33. Based on Tutu, *African Prayer Book*, 113 and 135.

34. Episcopal Church, *Book of Common Prayer*, 492.

Lamb of God, out of love for N. you suffered and died that he/she might live forever with you. Help him/her to know and respond to your healing grace. Give him/her power to turn to you, not to be paralyzed by pride or crippled by sin. Show him/her the path of life and accept him/her as your child. And give us grace to believe that he/she has not wandered so far that you cannot save. Amen.

God of all ages, you are Lord of both the living and the dead. Your love for all spans life and reaches into death. In your Son, Jesus Christ, you offer all the gift of salvation. Shower your love upon N. Send your light into the darkest recesses of his/her heart, and show him/her the way home. Arise, God of love, come to his/her aid. Amen.[35]

Blessed are you, Good and Faithful Shepherd. Bring your healing love to all the dead separated from you. Bring them to repent and fulfill your promise to reconcile all people to yourself. Bring them—including N.—to the feast of love in your kingdom. Lord, in your mercy, hear our prayer. Amen.

Jesus, your saving suffering on the cross flows out over the ages, over all nations and people, over all creation, over all time. Overshadow N. with your love. Convert his/her restless spirit and hungry soul, that all may know your welcome to sit down at table. Lord, come to their help. Amen.

Compassionate God—you love N., but because of his/her hurts and challenges in life he/she refused to or could not love you in return. Do not let go of him/her but claim him/her as your own. Draw him/her into your forgiveness, into your reconciling love and eternal joy. In the name of Christ your Son the Savior. Amen.

God of endless love and infinite mercy—wash those who do not know you clean from their sins. Open their minds to understand your grace, that they may share in the forgiveness you offer. Welcome and enfold them in your great love. Lord of compassion, deliver them from suffering. Amen.

Lord Jesus, you welcomed the stranger, the despised, the foreigner, the sinner into your compassionate and healing love.

---

35. Wording in this and the remaining prayers draws from Piguet, *100 Prayers*.

Have mercy on N. Give forgiveness instead of punishment. We entrust him/her to your great mercy. Amen.

God who loved N. into being—beckon him/her into your life. Draw him/her to your welcoming arms. Enlighten his/her heart and mind to know and love you. Free him/her from his/her sins and reconcile him/her to you, the Father of all. We ask this in sure and certain hope. Amen.

Jesus, Son of David, have pity on all who died without knowing or loving you. You are the light that heals all blindness. You are the love that feeds all longing. You are the grace that enables hearts to repent and love you. Jesus, Son of David, have mercy. Amen.

God of free forgiveness and unconditional love—in the face of continued human sin your relentless response has always been the same. Time and time again you have forgiven your sinful children. Even when your love is refused you do not cease to love. Radiate that grace and mercy into N.'s heart. Lift him/her from darkness, from weakness and foolishness—and awaken him/her to your love. Lord, in your mercy hear our prayer and come to his/her help. Amen.

At the memorial service for the victims of the 9/11 attacks led by President George W. Bush at the Episcopal National Cathedral in Washington D.C. on September 14, 2001, his remarks began with "We come before God to pray for the missing and the dead, and for those who loved them" and ended with this petition, "May God bless the souls of the departed."[36] This—perhaps—is the most general and basic prayer for the dead: may God bless them—all of them, workers at desks, passengers on airplanes and brave first responders, but also the hijackers who acted with stealth and deceit and murder. May God bless the faithful with increasing participation in God's life; may God bless the imperfect with moral transformation into characters of holy love; may God bless the unsaved with repentance and restored relationship with God. Amen.

---

36. Bush, "Remarks." The President, I am sure, did not mean to include the perpetrators in his prayer—only the victims. His language, however, is inclusive and I find even the attackers included.

Appendix

Additional Notes

1. Prayer for the Dead and Temporary Non-Existence

THERE IS NOTHING INCOHERENT about intermittent existence since identity can cross time gaps, periods of non-existence. Extinction-recreation appears to rule out prayer for the dead (which disallows non-existence, a gap in time between death and resurrection). It may, however, be possible for those who believe in extinction-resurrection to pray for the dead. Jerry Walls suggests that temporary non-existence is not logically incompatible with purgatory—and, by extension, prayer for the dead. Trenton Merricks attempts to square the practice of prayer *to* the saints (and, by implication, prayer *for* the dead) with denial of a conscious intermediate state.[1]

In the extinction-recreation scenario we pray for individuals who, by definition, do not exist now. *Consummation prayers* can be effective in bringing resurrection to pass more quickly for those now non-existent persons. *Growth, purification,* and *salvation prayers* take effect after the dead return to consciousness at the last day (such prayers are actually for post-resurrection not pre-resurrection persons). It is logically possible that prayers for the dead which I make now will not reap results until after final consummation. I may make salvation prayers now for a dead friend who—because he is non-existent now—will not repent until after final consummation has taken place. This assumes, of course, that

1. Walls, *Purgatory*, 191 and Merricks, "Resurrection of Body," in *OHPT*, 485–86.

salvation can occur after final judgment. The same may be true of sanctification prayers. God could, as it were, store up our prayers for the dead and answer them after final consummation. This assumes that transformation beyond the start of new creation is possible—a notion that is not obviously unbiblical since Revelation 21–22 seems to suggest purification and salvation of those those in the 'lake of fire' after the kingdom is completed. Perhaps prayers made now speed up sanctification of those in purgatory and deliverance of those in hell after judgment day.[2]

At the very minimum, prayer for the dead requires that the individuals prayed for be conscious *at some point* after death, not that they be conscious *immediately* at death. As long as they eventually become conscious, prayers for them can make sense since they will exist again to enjoy the fruits of our prayers. My prayers may be effective after final consummation *even if* the dead are conscious now. Suppose that I pray for a loved one who died yesterday but final consummation happens today—before sufficient time has elapsed for them to become perfectly holy or repent from sin. Their purification or salvation will occur after final consummation, with my prayers offered *now* being effective *then*.[3]

An extinction-recreation view of the afterlife and prayer for the dead is possible. But since non-existence during the intermediate state conflicts with Scripture, it is not a feasible afterlife scenario.

2. The Nature of Perfect Holiness

Holiness is conformity to the nature of God. Being holy means practical righteousness (Isa 5:8–23; 33:14–15; Luke 1:75).

In Hebrew Scripture the term *qādosh* (translated as "holy" or "holiness") means "set apart"—separated, dedicated, consecrated. The covenant required Israel to be "a people holy to the Lord" (Deut 26:19)—and Hebrew holiness, Jacob Milgrom says, "embraces positive ethical standards that are illustrative of God's nature: as God relates to . . . creation, so should Israel relate to each other."[4] The great commandments of the Mosaic law are to "love the Lord your God" (Deut 6:5; 11:2) and to "love your neighbor as yourself" (Lev 19:18). The humanitarian deeds

---

2 See MacDonald, *Evangelical Universalist*, 114–32.

3. Thanks to my colleague Timothy Linehan and editor Robin Parry for pressing me on this point.

4. Milgrom, "Holy," 852. Also see Kornfeld and Ringgren, "Qds."

mentioned in the Holiness Code, Milgrom notes, "emphasize the divine attribute of compassion, essential to God's holy nature."[5] The prophets insist that knowing God cannot be separated from acts of compassion toward the neighbor—"what does the Lord require of you but to do justice and to love kindness" (Mic 6:8; cf. Isa 1:10–17; 58:3–7; Jer 22:13–19; Amos 5:21–24).

In Christian Scripture the main significance of holiness is moral. The Greek word *hagios* means "pure" and refers, Andy Johnson says, "to the pattern of activity embodied by [Jesus Christ] who effects the saving, reconciling purposes of the Triune God."[6] In the Sermon on the Mount (Matt 5:43–48), Sharon Baker points out, Jesus' "exhortation to be holy as God is holy falls in the context of loving others. To love as God loves is to be holy as God is holy."[7] Jesus taught the double-love command: "love the Lord your God . . . and your neighbor as yourself" (Luke 10:25–28). "On these two commandments," he says, "hang all the law and the prophets" (Matt 22:34–40; cf. John 15:12). To be impure is to fail to act in ways that reflect God's compassion—"neglecting justice and the love of God" (Luke 11:37–42). On the night he was betrayed, Jesus gave a "new commandment, that you love one another"—as shown in his example of servanthood, washing the disciples' feet (John 13:1–17, 34; 15:9–17). In St. Paul's letters love is the essence of holiness: "the whole law is summed up in a single commandment, 'You shall love your neighbor as yourself'" (Gal 5:6; cf. Rom 13:8–10; Gal 5:22; Eph 1:4; Col 3:14). If a person does "not have love" then they are "nothing" since among virtues "the greatest . . . is love" (1 Cor 13:1–3, 13). Love means imitating Jesus' self-emptying *kenosis* that does "nothing from selfish ambition . . . , but . . . regards others as better than yourselves," that "looks not to your own interests, but to the interests of others" (Phil 2:3–8). St. James (2:8) defines "the royal law according to the scripture [as] 'You shall love your neighbor as yourself.'" The letters of St. John also indicate that "those who love God must love their brothers and sisters also" (1 John 4:20–21; cf. 3:11–18). Holiness means love of God and neighbor. The apostles consistently call believers to holiness: "let us cleanse ourselves from every defilement of body and of spirit, making holiness perfect" (2 Cor 7:1) and "clothe yourselves with the new self, created according to the likeness of God in true righteousness

---

5. Ibid., 856.

6. Johnson, "Holy," 846–47. Also see Borg, *Meeting Jesus Again*, chapter 3 and Procksch and Kuhn, "Hagios."

7. Baker, *Razing Hell*, 77.

and holiness" (Eph 4:24). Perfect holiness is eliminating all sin—internal attitudes and external actions—from the totality of one's life; it is being transformed to the full measure of Christ (Eph 4:13) and changed into God's likeness (2 Cor 3:18).

Perfect holiness means to "love . . . with *all* your heart, and with *all* your soul, and with *all* your strength and with *all* your mind" (Deut 6:5; Luke 10:27). We must be perfect in love as God is perfect in love. An Evangelical–Roman Catholic ecumenical document states that we are called "to live according to the law of love in obedience to Jesus Christ as Lord. Scripture calls this the life of holiness or sanctification."[8] Love must be integrated into our characters so that it permeates the entirety of who we are. Those who are pure in heart, Dietrich Bonhoeffer remarks, "have completely given their hearts to Jesus, so that he alone rules in them. . . . A pure heart . . . belongs entirely and undivided to Christ."[9] A morally perfect person, the Greek philosophers emphasize, has a character that is integrated and whole. Plato divides the *psyche* into three aspects—appetitive (desires that demand gratification), reflective (reason that knows what is best to do), and executive (spirit that moves us to act). This division of elements causes inner conflict—the "civil war between the three parts" that is described so well by St. Paul (Rom 7:15–25). A morally imperfect person has a character that is fragmented, where the elements of personality oppose each other. A morally perfect person, by contrast, has a character that is psychologically unified, an integrated character in which each part of the *psyche* performs its proper task, when reason, assisted by spirit, rules the desires. Such a person, Plato says, "harmonizes the three parts . . . and . . . from a plurality becomes a unity."[10] Aristotle says that there is a difference between doing the right kind of action and being the right kind of person. Someone may *act* kindly, politely, or patiently without it being a part of them—but when someone *is* kind, polite, or patient those traits constitute their identity. Aristotle identifies two types of good character. The self-controlled person has faulty beliefs and bad desires, but because they have strong willpower can live by their moral convictions, resist their impulses, and do what is right. Such a person is half good—they are divided and conflicted since what they want to do and what they know they should do pull in opposite

---

8. Evangelical-Roman Catholic ecumenical statement, cited in Walls, "Purgatory for Everyone," 2.

9. Bonhoeffer, *Discipleship*, 107.

10. Plato, *Republic* 444b, 108, and 443d–e, 107.

directions. The temperate person, by contrast, has no false beliefs or bad desires to control—and so they do not struggle with temptation. Doing right is automatic—and they do so gladly, because they want to. "No one would call a person just," Aristotle says, "if he did not enjoy doing just actions, or generous if he did not enjoy generous actions." Having eliminated bad from their character, such a person is completely good.[11] The perfectly holy, in the Episcopal Church Prayer of Confession, "delight in God's will and walk in God's ways"—or as the Prayer after Communion says, "love and serve God with gladness and singleness of heart." The Collect of Purity asks God to "cleanse the thoughts of our hearts . . . that we may perfectly love you," and the Collect of Lent 5 asks that God enable us to love—not just do—what God commands.[12] Moral perfection requires having *both* the right external actions (what we do) *and* the right internal attitudes (how we feel when we act).

Harry Frankfurt defines a self as a hierarchy of desires and distinguishes first-order from second-order desires. A *first order desire* is a basic desire—a desire to drink alcohol, for example. A *second order desire* is a desire about a first order desire—a desire to have or not have a particular desire (I can desire that I not desire to drink alcohol). A second-order desire can go unfulfilled due to uncontrolled first-order desires; the alcoholic drinks even though he would like to stop. In an integrated self first-order desires are ordered in response to second-order desires. An integrated person wholeheartedly identifies with his beliefs and desires—they constitute who he is and who he wants to be. They are ones he welcomes; those he does not want have been removed. A disintegrated person experiences conflict between their first-order and second-order desires. They are a divided self, having dispositions they do not want to have. An unwilling addict, for example, is deeply conflicted.[13] A wholly good person, to repeat, has right beliefs and a good will, with no conflicting desires.

The master virtue of perfect love is composed of two types of virtues: substantive and enabling. "Virtues like honesty, compassion, justice, generosity, promise-keeping, and kindness [are] substantive," Robert C. Roberts says, "because they are . . . the substance of the ethical patterns

---

11. Aristotle, *Nicomachean Ethics* 1099a20, 11; also 1105a30, 22.

12. Episcopal Church, *Book of Common Prayer*, 360, 365, 355, and 219.

13. See Buckareff and Plug, "Value, Finality and Frustration," Swinburne, *Evolution of Soul*, chapter 14 and Walls, *Haven*, 56. They are summarizing Frankfurt, "Freedom of Will."

of behavior and judgment and emotion." Enabling virtues, by contrast, are "capacities for resisting adverse inclinations"—such as "controlling one's emotions, resisting temptation, persevering in the face of discouragement." Willpower virtues lack moral substance; instead, they are skills of self-management that enable us to regulate inclinations like fear or despair, which make moral action difficult. Roberts concludes: "the relation . . . between the virtues of willpower and the substantive virtues is mutual need: neither kind can exist as moral virtues without the other kind. Without the virtues of willpower, the moral motives would too often be sabotaged by counter-moral impulses. . . . On the other hand, the character of a person who had only the virtues of willpower would be empty of moral content."[14] To be perfect lovers we need both the great virtues of justice and compassion (being motivated by another person's needs) and the little virtues of self-control (which are necessary to live out the great virtues).

Holiness also means refusing to separate our daily decisions from our Christian convictions. Bonhoeffer rejects compartmentalizing life into spiritual and secular as a form of "cheap grace"—forgiveness of sins "without discipleship"—in which faith becomes intellectual assent and Christian lifestyle indistinguishable from the rest of the world. "Cheap grace means justification of sin but not of the sinner. Because grace alone does everything, everything can stay in its old ways. . . . The Christian should live the same way the world does . . . and not venture to live a different life under grace from that under sin. . . . The Christian need not follow Christ, since the Christian is comforted by grace. That is cheap grace"—when there is "no difference between Christian life and worldly life."[15] Or as Bonhoeffer put it elsewhere:

> Christ has, in effect, been eliminated from our lives. Christ has become a matter of the church, not a matter of life. Religion plays for the *psyche* of the twentieth century the role of the so-called Sunday room into which one gladly withdraws for a couple of hours but only to get back to one's place of work immediately afterwards. However, Christ did not go to the cross to ornament and embellish our life. If we wish to have him, then he demands the right to say something decisive about our entire life. We do not understand him if we arrange for him only a small compartment in our life. Rather, we understand our spiritual life only if

---

14. Roberts, "Willpower and the Virtues," 123, 122, and 127.
15. Bonhoeffer, *Discipleship*, 43–45.

we take Christ seriously in the demand he makes on us by his question: will you follow me wholeheartedly or not at all? The religion of Christ is not a tidbit after one's bread; on the contrary, it is bread or it is nothing.[16]

Bonhoeffer notes—however—that Jesus demands a change of life. The call "follow me" (Mark 2:14) means that we must "step out of our previous existence.... Former things are left behind; they are completely given up.... Staying in the old situation and following Christ mutually exclude each other." Discipleship "is a commitment solely to the person of Jesus Christ." The heart of a disciple is not "attracted by the goods of the world, or even by Christ *and* the goods of the world'—instead, "it stands by Christ alone." Baptism, Bonhoeffer adds, is a break with the world: "those who are baptized no longer belong to the world.... They belong to Christ alone, and relate to the world only through Christ."[17] Because the gospel is comprehensive, affecting every aspect of life, "costly discipleship" does not privatize faith by restricting it to personal piety. Living *holy* is living *wholly* as a Christian—with Christian convictions integrated into all of life. As the Christian Reformed Church doctrinal statement puts it: "the rule of Jesus Christ covers the whole world. To follow this Lord is to serve God everywhere, without fitting in, as light in the darkness, as salt in a spoiling world [Matt 5:13-16]."[18]

3. The Decline of Hell

David Powys argues that belief in eternal hell was the logical result of combining two ideas: 1. the natural immortality thesis (at death no one ceases to exist, but all persons survive eternally) and 2. the retributive punishment thesis (at death the wicked are assigned to irreversible torment).[19]

Annihilationists rejected 1. In the nineteenth century, Richard Wright advocated a materialist anthropology in which any future life depends completely on "the pure goodness and sovereign will of God" rather than human nature. Edward White defended the biblical view of

---

16. Bonhoeffer, "Jesus Christ and the Essence of Christianity," in Kelly and Nelson, *Testament to Freedom*, 53.

17. Bonhoeffer, *Discipleship*, 58-59, 62, 161-62, 208; slightly modified.

18. Christian Reformed Church, "Our World Belongs to God," 45, 1033.

19. Powys, *Hell*, 18; cf. "Nineteenth and Twentieth Century Debates."

human beings as ensouled bodies rather than embodied souls. He suggests that "immortality is the particular privilege of the regenerate."[20] William Temple says that "if [theologians] had not imported the Greek and unbiblical notion of the natural indestructibility of the individual soul, and then read the New Testament with that already in their heads, they would have drawn from it a belief, not in everlasting torment, but in annihilation."[21]

Escapists and universalists denied 2. In the nineteenth century Frederick Maurice, Frederick Farrar, and Edward Plumptre affirmed "extended probation," with many being saved after death. Maurice argued that exegetically "eternal" life and punishment are existential and qualitative, rather than temporal and quantitative concepts, that posthumous repentance is possible, but that we cannot know if all will be saved.[22] Farrar, in a set of sermons titled "Eternal Hope," denied both eternal punishment and closed death. "God's mercy may extend beyond the grave," he insisted, and this means that the fate of the unrighteous is reversible rather than final: human "destiny stops not at the grave and . . . many who know not Christ here will know Him there."[23] William Alger, Samuel Cox, and others went further, defending not just posthumous, but universal, salvation. Alger claimed that an unchangeable punitive fate is "incompatible with any worthy idea of the character of God." Cox opposed the dogmas that "there is no probation beyond the grave, that when men leave this world their fate is fixed beyond all hope of change; that if, when they die, they have not repented of their sins, so far from finding a place of repentance open to them in the life to come, they will be condemned to an eternal torment or . . . to a destructive torment which will annihilate them."[24] John Henry Newman and Edward Pusey, while embracing escapism, rejected universalism—arguing that eternal punishment is a correlate of free will.

Three factors, Geoffrey Rowell says, supported open death.[25] First, the intellectual climate, particularly science, included evolutionary concepts where human destiny came to be conceived as unending progress

---

20. Wright and White, cited in Rowell, *Hell and Victorians*, 41 and 188.
21. Temple, *Christian Faith*, 87.
22. Maurice, cited in Rowell, *Hell and Victorians*, 83.
23. Farrar, cited in Rowell, *Hell and Victorians*, ix and Powys, *Hell*, 36.
24. Alger and Cox, cited in Powys, *Hell*, 36 and 56.
25. Rowell, *Hell and Victorians*, 14–16, 190, and 216.

rather than a fixed and unalterable state entered at death. Second, the utilitarian penal reform movement insisted that punishment not simply give offenders their just deserts but have beneficial consequences. Where retributive punishment supports closed death, remedial punishment—aimed at the sinner's good—suggests that posthumous salvation is available. Third, the reaction against eternal hell "was helped . . . by the missionary movement. Large numbers of Christians became aware of the immense numbers [of people] destined for hell" if traditional doctrines were correct. John Casey suggests that "a gradual strengthening of humane sentiment . . . eventually undermined belief in hell"—which came to be seen as both unjust (if it is meant to punish rather than torment then it will not go on forever) and unkind (since no loving person can endure seeing others suffer). Humanistic "moral sense and spiritual intuition"—Powys says—upset "religious orthodoxy."[26]

4. Permanently Open Death

Gordon Knight defends permanently open death.[27] Since human beings have libertarian free will, what they choose is up to them and not determined by God. Until the person chooses it is not settled which way they will choose; thus God cannot infallibly know in advance what the person will do. Imagine that Carlos dies at time 1 before being saved. Because God cannot know what he would have chosen in the future, God cannot know whether, had Carlos lived beyond time 1, he would have been saved. If death is closed then, for all God knows, God gives up on him at earthly time 1 when he would have been saved at a later earthly time 2. This same logic requires God to keep death open permanently—because God loves the unsaved person and because God cannot know whether they will repent in the future if given further opportunities, God will not put a time limit on salvation. There is not simply *a* chance of salvation after death, but *endless* chances. Perhaps some people, like Mahatma Gandhi, will need only one post-mortem opportunity—those whose moral wills are attuned to Christ's spirit and teachings will immediately recognize the truth that they desired him all along. For righteous non-Christians, Jerry Walls says, open death means "a time to adjust one's mental life to one's

---

26. Casey, *Afterlives*, 193 and 216–18 and Powys, *Hell*, 18. On nineteenth-century views of "future probation" see McDannell and Lang, *Heaven*, 283–84 and 390.

27. Knight, "Universalism for Open Theists."

moral intentions and aspirations." Others, like Adolf Hitler, whose lives were deeply resistant to God, may require many chances; repentance will take a long time because their moral characters need complete transformation.[28] In either case, the offer of salvation is not withdrawn at death and continues even after repeated rejection. John Kronen and Eric Reitan make a similar "infinite opportunity argument"—God leaves the choice of communion with God an "open choice" such that every person is free to choose it at any time.[29] Marilyn Adams says that "if God's primary purpose in creating us is that we should become the sort of persons who can and do enter into loving personal relationships with God . . . , and if God's love never ends, [then] it would seem that God would never give up on any one of us or despair of our eventual cooperation." C. S. Lewis believes that "if a million chances were likely to do good, they would be given"—he is skeptical they are, I am not.[30]

5. Justice and Love

It seems that there are two images of God in the Bible—an angry God of retributive violence and a compassionate God of forgiving love. This suggests to some that divine justice and divine love are opposed—but this is not true. Sharon Baker argues that—first—the Hebrew texts arose in a culture of retribution and retaliation; these cultural perspectives were projected onto the divine, creating an image of a vengeful God behaving as a tribal warrior that became assimilated into Hebrew Scripture. Second, we all use some beliefs as control beliefs through which we interpret other verses. The control belief, the lens through which we must interpret the biblical "texts of terror" is the revelation of God in Jesus as a peaceful, compassionate, and merciful God who offers unconditional forgiveness. Jesus came to save, not condemn, to love enemies, not just friends, to weep over Jerusalem and seek the last missing sheep. Baker points out that in the Nazareth manifesto (Luke 4:16–20) Jesus omits a key line— "the day of vengeance"—from the reading of Isaiah 61.[31]

---

28. Walls, *Purgatory*, 138.

29. Kronen and Reitan, *God's Final Victory*, 160.

30. Adams, "Divine Justice, Divine Love and Life to Come," 20 and Lewis, *Problem of Pain*, 112.

31. Baker, *Razing Hell*, chapter 5.

Stephen Travis argues that "God's wrath must be understood in relation to God's love. Wrath is not a permanent attribute of God. For whereas love and holiness are part of God's essential nature, wrath is contingent upon human sin; if there were no sin, there would be no wrath."[32] Anthony Thiselton agrees: "whereas love is a permanent quality and characterizes God, wrath does not last eternally." God's anger is motivated by love; indeed, the opposite of love is not anger, but indifference. Sinners are punished because they are loved—and hell is part of God's love.[33] Gary Herion observes that "despite its tragic necessity, . . . anger is not depicted as an emotion God delights in; instead, it grieves God to be angry (Lam 3:33) and God would prefer to avoid it altogether (Isa 27:2–3; Hos 11:9)."[34]

C. S. Lewis distinguishes tolerant kindness and tough love. Kindness is shallow; its goal is to make people content. Love, by contrast, is demanding; it looks out for the person's best interest—a professor or sports coach is willing to cause hurt in order to improve a student's or athlete's abilities. Their tough love expresses care and concern. Kindness, because it is indifferent and does not care whether the other flourishes or fails, is incompatible with anger, judgment, and punishment. Love, however, is not—in fact, it demands them. God's love, as true love, is more than mere kindness.[35] Thomas Talbott agrees: "there is nothing sentimental about the kind of . . . love we are talking about here. A father who does nothing when his teen-aged son is caught swindling old ladies might be indifferent, but not truly loving." Similarly, "God's love . . . in no way precludes our experiencing that love as punishment, or as harsh judgment or even as divine wrath." And so "God's strategy for accomplishing [salvation] is two-fold:" to those who repent, there is forgiveness—while "for those who refuse . . . God has an alternative strategy: . . . they will experience God's love as . . . wrath, as punishment, and, in the end, as a means of correction."[36]

Afterlife punishment is aimed at the sinner's good—their repentance and salvation. "By punishing those who deserve punishment," Origen of Alexandria asks, "does not God punish them with a view to their

---

32. Travis, "Wrath of God," 997.
33. Thiselton, *Life After Death*, 159.
34. Herion, "Wrath of God," 995.
35. Lewis, *Problem of Pain*, 28–29.
36. Talbott, *Inescapable Love*, 106.

own good?" The ancient Greeks drew a distinction between retributive punishment (*timoria*) and corrective punishment (*kolasis*)—and Christian Scripture commonly uses the latter to refer to divine punishment.[37] Gregory of Nazianzus argues that punishment "is applied [by God] out of love for human beings, and in a way that is worthy of the One who punishes." Eternal damnation is not worthy of God; only if punishment has a positive, constructive purpose is it compatible with a God who loves sinners and seeks their good—only then are justice and love compatible. Because punishment has a corrective aim, it is necessarily of limited duration. Early theologians used two metaphors for loving punishment: in the medical analogy *Christus Medicus* is a physician who heals the soul, and in the pedagogical analogy God is a teacher who instructs and illumines the soul. Clement of Alexandria hopes that even heretics will be saved. Length of time in hell depends on the seriousness of sin and the degree of remorse—and otherworldly punishment may be terrible and long.[38] "God's judgments have a loving and constructive purpose," Clark Pinnock and Robert Brow assert. "God's wrath falls upon men and women in order to warn, correct, and teach them."[39] Where remedial punishment is meant to produce repentance, retributive punishment—especially if death is closed and hell endless—is both pointless (it does nothing for sinners since escape is not possible) and at some point undeserved (since the temporary sins of this life cannot merit eternal punishment). For what possible purpose would God punish human beings retributively forever?

Corrective punishment, the ancient theologians hold, restores sinners to health and wholeness by doing two things—illuminating the mind (creating true thoughts) and purifying the will (creating good desires). Sin, recall, is caused by both intellect and appetites—ignorance of the mind (deception and mistaken judgment) and enslavement of the will (immersion in passion). The mind is blinded by sin and needs illumination from deception; punishment instructs the sinner in knowledge of God. The will is enslaved by sin and needs freedom from passions; punishment frees the sinner for love of God.[40]

---

37. As mentioned in chapter 5 footnote 78, the meaning of the word *kolasis* seems to have broadened over the centuries before the Christian Scriptures were written.

38. Origen, Gregory, and Clement, cited in Ramelli, *Christian Doctrine of Apokatastasis*, 184, 451, and 96 respectively. Also see pages 127 and 434.

39. Pinnock and Brow, *Unbounded Love*, 71.

40. See Ramelli, *Christian Doctrine of Apokatastasis*, 340, 428, and 472.

Biblical interpreters, Christopher Marshall says, have "brought to the text an essential Western concept of retributive justice, which is largely based on metaphysical law, rather than a Hebraic concept of covenant justice based on relationship." And so, he concludes, "it is debatable whether retribution . . . is as foundational to biblical conceptions of . . . justice as is sometimes claimed."[41] Jürgen Moltmann observes that "if we compare the ideas of justice in Babylon and Egypt, we find on the one hand the concept of a justice which puts things right, which saves and heals, and on the other hand a justice which assesses and requites." Where Hebrew Scripture was influenced by Babylonian concepts of restorative justice, Christian tradition adopted Egyptian representations of retributive judgment. "A victim-orientated expectation of saving justice was turned into a perpetrator-orientated moral judgment based on the justice whose purpose is retribution."[42] Judgment is how God delivers creation from evil—both evils suffered by victims and evils committed by perpetrators. The goal of judgment is restorative for all—it is not restorative for victims and retributive for perpetrators. The two cries for justice differ, Moltmann says. The cry of victims requires vindication (liberation from the violence and oppression that violates their rights) and the cry of perpetrators requires transformation (from the "insane blindness and compulsive acts" that enslave them). "On the side of the victims God's righteousness is a righteousness that brings about justice, and . . . on the side of the offenders a righteousness that sets them on the right path."[43] Moltmann adds: "when the victims are raised up and the perpetrators are put right, the purpose is not the great reckoning, with reward and punishment; the intention is to bring about the victory of the creative divine righteousness. . . . This victory . . . does not lead to the separation of human beings into the saved and the damned . . . ; its purpose is to lead to God's great day of reconciliation." This is a judgment that, while not condoning evil, offers hope.[44]

The purpose of divine punishment—whether it is healing punishment meant to do the sinner good or vengeful punishment meant to give the sinner their just deserts—divided the church fathers. Clement of Alexandria insisted that they are remedial: "God does not exact vengeance

---

41. Marshall, *Beyond Retribution*, 47 and 120.
42. Moltmann, *Sun of Righteousness*, 130–31 and 135.
43. Moltmann, *In the End*, 56.
44. Moltmann, *Sun of Righteousness*, 137.

(for vengeance is retribution for evil), but rather God punishes for the good ... of those who are being punished." Divine punishment is "saving and disciplinary, leading to conversion."[45] Origen of Alexandria agrees: "all the torments of a good God are designed for the benefit of those who endure them." Punishment is a "school of souls" to correct and reform sinners—pedagogical and curative—and therefore temporary. Gregory of Nyssa also believed that all punishment is corrective and educative, not vindictive; so did Isaac the Syrian.[46] John Chrysostom, by contrast, rejected the idea that eschatological punishment is medicinal: the punishments of this life "are for our correction, but later they will be for vindication."[47] Augustine of Hippo also thought that punishment of the wicked after death is wholly vindictive and imposed "in retribution for sin." Only punishment in this life is remedial: we "should not imagine that any pains will be purificatory, except those that precede that ultimate and terrible judgment." The purpose of eschatological punishment is to pay sinners back for their wrongdoing.[48]

6. Tame Versus Terrible Hell

Thomas Talbott claims that it is those who believe in eternal hell, not escapists, who must minimize biblical depictions of hell's horror. Hell is either 1. inescapable but tame or 2. escapable but severe. A hell of *eternal* and *terrible* suffering is morally indefensible because it violates the proportionality requirement—that punishment fit the crime. No temporal sin can merit eternal and terrible punishment—so the only option for closed death theology is to affirm an eternal but tame hell. "We can appreciate," Talbott says, why those who reject escapism "might want to water down the [biblical] picture of hell as a place of unbearable suffering; an eternity of such suffering would be . . . utterly pointless, and a god who would actually inflict such suffering forever would be unspeakably barbaric."[49] Raymond VanArragon defends a tame hell as the only scenario in which people can freely reject God forever—since if

---

45. Clement, *Stromata* 7.16.102.5 and 6.6, 490.

46. Origen, cited in Daley, *Hope of Early Church*, 57. On Gregory see Daley, *Hope of Early Church*, 86. On Isaac the Syrian see Alfeyev, "Eschatology," 116–17.

47. Chrysostom, cited in Daley, *Hope of Early Church*, 108.

48. Augustine, *City of God*, Book 21.13 and 16, 990 and 994.

49. Talbott, *Inescapable Love*, 197.

hell resembles a torture chamber then sinners would be forced by sheer pain to repent. A tame hell preserves freedom, but may not actually turn sinners to God—whereas Talbott's harsh hell will cause all the unsaved, eventually, to repent but may compromise their freedom in doing so.[50] Andrei Buckareff and Allen Plug also defend a tame hell. While hell is bad in some respects compared to heaven, "being in hell affords some well-being to agents who . . . reside there."[51] Jerry Walls suggests that the unsaved experience a kind of illusory happiness: "those in hell may be almost happy. . . . They do not, of course, experience . . . genuine happiness. But perhaps they experience a certain perverse sense of satisfaction, a distorted sort of pleasure."[52] Eleonore Stump also argues that because God can do nothing to induce the unsaved to freely repent, God makes them as comfortable as possible in the hell they have chosen.[53] Even conservative scholars like Gary Habermas and James Moreland say that hell is not a place "where God actively tortures people forever and ever;" instead, banishment from heaven is a state with a "low quality of life."[54]

Where supporters of eternal hell must water down its terrors, those who affirm open death can accept at face value the seriousness of the biblical images and language of wrath, judgment, and hell. Gregory MacDonald states that those who affirm open death "have a lot to say about God's justice and God's punishment. They believe in the severity of God, and . . . do not shrink from warning of the wrath to come." This is not the "cheep and cheerful" posthumous or universal salvation condemned by Tom Wright—where all the dead, no matter their moral or spiritual condition, go straight to heaven. Nor is it the domesticated, even pleasant, hell that separatists offer.[55]

50. VanArragon, "Is It Possible to Freely Reject God Forever?"
51. Buckareff and Plug, "Value, Finality and Frustration," 83.
52. Walls, *Hell*, 126.
53. Stump, "Dante's Hell."
54. Habermas and Moreland, *Beyond Death*, 303 and 308.
55. MacDonald, *Evangelical Universalist*, 164; slightly modified and Wright, *Surprised by Hope*, 180.

7. Metaphysical Arguments for Why Human Freedom Ends at Death

Two metaphysical arguments are given for why human freedom does not continue in hell. The *timeless eternity argument* states that since the afterlife is an eternal timeless moment, a static condition without change, freedom to repent ends at death. Giacomo Biffi claims that the will of the unsaved becomes immutable because "in the state that awaits us after death . . . beyond time, humans do not experience succession and therefore are incapable of changing."[56] The problem with this argument is that, given its controversial metaphysical assumption, it will only convince those who believe in timeless eternity. If—as argued in Volume 1, chapter 7—the afterlife is dynamic and has a developing history then post-mortem repentance may be possible.

The *disembodied existence argument* claims that because we survive death as souls separated from bodies, we are no longer able to change our wills. Fundamental inclinations can only be changed when the soul is connected to a body, and so we cannot repent after death. Brian Daley describes John Chrysostom's view: "once the soul is separated from the body, we are no longer 'masters of our own conversion' because we lack the freedom to change our fundamental orientation."[57] Thomas Aquinas believed that the human person is neither body or soul alone, but a soul-body composite in which each part needs the other for mutual completion. Without an essential aspect of human nature the unsaved cannot change their disordered wills. "A disposition of the soul is changed incidentally with some change in the body, for, since it is at the service of the soul for its very own operation, the body was given to the soul . . . with this in view: that the soul existing within the body be . . . , as it were, moved toward its perfection."[58] A disembodied soul, John Lamont explains, has no emotions; it cannot, therefore, be attracted to or repelled by—and so cannot choose—a new ultimate end. "There is nothing left to the disembodied soul . . . that can influence [the person] to change [their] existing state of will. . . . What is left of the person who is damned is . . . an entity whose entire volitional activity is directed toward the evil

---

56. Biffi, cited in O'Callaghan, *Christ Our Hope*, 207. Also see Walls, *Purgatory*, 143.

57. Daley, *Hope of Early Church*, 108.

58. Aquinas, cited in Seymour, *Theodicy of Hell*, 168. Also see Potts, "Aquinas, Hell and the Resurrection of the Damned."

end that was its ultimate goal during life." Without a body, the soul cannot change its fundamental orientation towards or away from God—and so free choice ends at death.[59]

If true, this argument would only apply to the intermediate state, leaving open the possibility of moral change after re-embodiment at resurrection. This argument also involves metaphysical assumptions that are subject to dispute and so only has force for those who accept a dualist anthropology and a disembodied afterlife. If—as argued in Volume 1, chapter 6—the state of the dead is embodied then post-mortem salvation may be possible. Materialists claim that a body is necessary for moral change. We are holistic beings; both sinfulness and goodness involve a composite of body and mind, and moral change involves transformation of psychological attitudes and physical behaviors. Virtues such as repentance and regret require right feelings, not just right actions—and physical sensation, bodily reaction, is a necessary element of emotional response.

8. Molinism and the Problem of Hell

The Reformation-era Spanish Jesuit Luis de Molina offered an ingenious solution to the problem of freedom and foreknowledge.[60] He wished to reconcile libertarian freedom (in which if a person A is free with respect to an action X then A has the alternatives of either doing X or not doing X) and a strong view of providence (in which God foreknows, indeed controls, everything that happens in the world). Molina attempted to do this by using the idea of a "counterfactual of freedom"—a statement of this sort: if person A were placed in circumstance C, then A would freely do action X (for example, if it is cloudy next Sunday, then I would freely go to church).

According to Molina there are three kinds of knowledge that God has—and these three "moments" occur in lexically-ordered succession.

1. In the first moment, God has *natural knowledge*. God knows all possibilities. As William Lane Craig says, "God knows all the possible individuals God could create, all the possible circumstances God

---

59. Lamont, "Justice and Goodness of Hell," 168–69.

60. See Craig, *Only Wise God* and "Middle Knowledge"; Flint, *Divine Providence* and "Two Accounts of Providence."

could place them in, all their possible actions and reactions."⁶¹ God knows all logically possible states of affairs and combinations of choices and events—including what every free person could do in any set of circumstances. For example, God knows everything that I could possibly do next Sunday. This knowledge is "natural" because its content does not depend on God's will and is essential to God.

2. In the second moment, God has *middle knowledge*. God knows all counterfactuals of freedom—what every person would freely do in every situation they could be in. As Craig says, "God knows what every possible creature would do (not just could do) in any possible set of circumstances."⁶² God knows that person A would do action X if placed in circumstance C1, action Y if placed in circumstance C2, and action Z if placed in circumstance C3. By natural knowledge God knows what I *could do* next Sunday; by middle knowledge God knows what I *would do* next Sunday depending on whether I am in circumstance C1 (it is rainy and I freely choose to sleep in), C2 (it is sunny and I freely choose to go on a motorcycle ride), or C3 (it is cloudy and I freely choose to go to church). God does not determine what free persons will do in various circumstances, and thus the content of counterfactuals of freedom is not under God's control; it is not up to God, but up to me, what I do in each situation. If in circumstance C1 I would freely choose to sleep in next Sunday, then God cannot bring it about that I would freely choose to go to church. God cannot create a world where it is rainy next Sunday *and* where I freely attend worship. This knowledge is "middle" knowledge because it stands between God's natural knowledge and God's free knowledge.

In between middle knowledge and free knowledge comes God's decision to create a particular world. By natural knowledge God knows all logically possible worlds; by middle knowledge God knows the subset of possible worlds that are feasible for God to actually create. Human choices limit the possible worlds that God can make. Knowing all feasible worlds through middle knowledge, God deliberates and—using the knowledge of counterfactuals—picks one to create.

3. In the third moment, God has *free knowledge*. Having decided which world to create God knows all the details of that world. Specifically,

61. Craig, *Only Wise God*, 129.
62. Ibid., 130.

God has absolute foreknowledge of the future free choices of human beings in that world. This foreknowledge flows logically from middle knowledge and the decision to create a certain world. This knowledge is "free" knowledge because it depends on God's free decision about which world to make.

In summary, God knows how people would freely act in any situation. God knows that person A will freely choose to do action X if placed in circumstance C_1 and will freely choose to do action Y if placed in circumstance C_2—so when God creates C_1 God knows that A will do X, and yet A does X freely. Counterfactuals of freedom limit which worlds God can create—but once God makes a world God knows exactly how every free person will actually choose in that world. In this way Molinism reconciles genuine freedom, absolute foreknowledge and a strong notion of providence.

It should be apparent how Molinism applies to the problem of hell—both to those who die unsaved and those who never had a chance to hear of Christ.[63] God knows every possible person and every possible response they would make to the gospel in every possible circumstance—if and when they would freely accept or reject Christ. These counterfactuals of freedom may be such that God cannot create a world in which everyone is saved. Stephen Kershnar points out two possibilities.[64] Some individuals might suffer what Craig calls *transworld damnation*, being lost in every world that is feasible for God to make (since there is no situation in which they would freely accept Christ). Because God cannot guarantee that a free person will accept salvation, there may be some people—perhaps many—who would not freely turn to God under *any* circumstance but who remain unsaved in all possible worlds. This, Craig claims, solves the problem of those who never hear the gospel: for anyone who dies without hearing of Christ there are *no* situations in which they would have believed had they heard. Through middle knowledge God sees whether such a person would have responded had they been evangelized—and creates a world in which those who never hear of Christ

---

63. See Craig, "No Other Name" and Habermas and Moreland, *Beyond Death*, 309–19. Craig applies Plantinga's use of Molinism in the free will defense of evil (*Nature of Necessity*, 164–95 and *God, Freedom and Evil*, Part 1) to the problem of hell. His notion of transworld damnation is modeled after the notion of transworld depravity—the notion that some persons would sin in any circumstances in which they were created.

64. Kershnar, "Hell and Punishment," 123.

are all persons who not have been receptive *even if* they had heard. Gary Habermas and James Moreland state that perhaps "in unevangelized areas there will be no one who will go to hell who would have accepted the gospel if someone had taken it to them."[65]

Alternatively, some individuals might suffer *contingent damnation*, where who is lost and who is saved varies between possible worlds, where some who reject Christ would, in other situations, have accepted the gospel. There may be no world God could have created in which *all* persons freely accept Christ—and so God faces the choice of either making a world in which some people are damned or not making any world at all. Gregory MacDonald explains: "there may be no world in which some people [John Smith, for example] freely choose salvation without others [Julie Smith, perhaps] freely rejecting it"—in which case God makes a world in which some people freely reject Christ but the number of those who freely receive him is maximized.[66] As Habermas and Moreland put it: "consider two worlds, W1 and W2. In W1, suppose 50 million are saved and 5 million are lost, while in W2, 5 million are saved and none are lost. It is not clear that W2 is morally preferable to W1 . . . . It may be worth having more people go to heaven to allow more to go to hell." To summarize: while there are logically possible worlds in which everyone is both free and accepts the gospel, such worlds may not be feasible for God to create—since in every feasible world some persons will never convert to Christ. Given human freedom, God may not be able to make a world where all people are saved.

Numerous scholars find the Molinist explanation of damnation lacking. I leave aside philosophical concerns about its account of divine omniscience and providence, emphasizing instead its moral problems. John Kronen and Eric Reitan reject the assumption that human freedom means that some persons would finally and irrevocably reject God in any world that God could create. While possible, it is unlikely that all who do not hear the gospel—for example—would, in any possible circumstance, have rejected Christianity.[67] MacDonald concurs: "there is a plausibility problem with the notion of *transworld damnation* . . . . To seriously believe, or even think plausible, the suggestion that someone who never heard the gospel before they died would never have freely responded to

---

65. Habermas and Moreland, *Beyond Death*, 317 and 318.
66. MacDonald, *Evangelical Universalist*, 182.
67. Kronen and Reitan, *God's Final Victory*, 194 n18 and 212 n13.

it in any circumstances God could have actualized" seems very hard to accept.[68] Indeed, as Charles Seymour points out, Jesus himself suggests a counterfactual of freedom: *if* the deeds of power done in Chorazin, Bethsaida, and Capernaum had been done in Tyre, Sidon, and Sodom *then* the inhabitants of those cities would have freely repented and been saved (Matt 11:20-24). This suggests that "not all who are damned in our world choose damnation in any world in which they existed. And so not all who are damned are transworldly damned." It is very possible, for example, that had Mahatma Gandhi been born in different circumstances, he would have been a Christian—and it is hard to believe that none of those people in areas untouched by the gospel would have accepted Christ had they been raised in pious Christian homes. But if this is true, then not all who reject Christ suffer from transworld damnation.[69] Gordon Knight, too, objects that Craig's theory "is hardly plausible as a blanket explanation for every case of a person who" is damned— for "the vast majority of those who Craig believes to be transworldly damned have, historically, had little contact with those who hear the gospel and have the opportunity to accept or reject it." And if transworld damnation was true, then "merely in the act of creation God is guaranteeing that for many of God's creatures an eternal life that is much worse than not having existed at all."[70] Jerry Walls is another who rejects the idea that God has arranged things so that those who never hear the gospel are all persons who would not have accepted it if they had heard. Craig thinks it not only possibly true but probably true that God sends the gospel to all those who God knows will respond if they hear it, and so no one who would respond if they heard it will be lost. Walls, however, finds this implausible: "it is exceedingly hard to entertain seriously the notion that all the persons who lived and died in countries the gospel did not reach for centuries would have rejected it if they had heard it." It is also hard to believe that someone who dies prematurely without believing would, in all possible futures, have remained unsaved. Walls imagines two young people—call them Ken and Barbie—both raised in Christian homes, who reject God. They are in a car crash where Ken is killed but Barbie lives and is eventually converted. Now suppose God knows *via* middle knowledge that Ken, now in hell, would also have been converted had he lived to a normal age

---

68. MacDonald, *Evangelical Universalist*, 180–81; emphasis added.
69. Seymour, *Theodicy of Hell*, 105 and 114.
70. Knight, "Molinism and Hell," quotes at random from 109–14.

before dying. In this story Ken's damnation and Barbie's salvation depend on fortuitous circumstances since—like Tyre and Sidon—Ken would have been saved had he lived longer. But a God who does all God can to save persons will not let some be damned through unfavorable factors that disadvantage them (since Ken would have accepted Christ had he had the opportunity Barbie had).[71]

Then there is the notion of *contingent damnation*: every world that God could create is one in which some persons forever reject God—and so God can only create a world with an optimal ratio of the blessed in heaven to the damned in hell. This, too, is problematic. Craig thinks Scripture teaches that the vast majority of persons in the world will be lost forever—and MacDonald protests that it is extremely implausible that "this grisly lack of balance" between saved and lost is the best that God can achieve. That there is no better ratio seems very hard to believe (like thinking a world with 100 really happy children and 1,000 really miserable children is the best feasible world).[72] Knight calls Craig's solution "the cannon fodder view of the unredeemed" in which God sacrifices the interests of the damned to the interests of the saved. "A deity who intentionally creates persons who God knows will suffer eternally in hell . . . is like a general who sends out many of his troops as cannon fodder, as sacrificial casualties in the name of ultimate victory over the enemy." Despite fine-tuning the world to ensure the best balance of saved to lost, God, in making persons God knows will never accept Christ, shares responsibility for their suffering in hell. Worse yet, "God creates some persons who will be damned solely in order to allow that other people will be saved." This violates the duty, declared by Immanuel Kant, not to use other people simply as a means to an end. And "such a view is hardly one befitting the God of overflowing love and perfect goodness." It conflicts with God's character as one who cares, individually, about each person God creates—since "to love is to value an individual for their own sake, to wish for the good of that individual." No decent parent, Knight argues, would conceive a child so that its organs could be used to save

---

71. Walls, *Hell*, 97 and 86–87. This also rebuts Habermas and Moreland's (*Beyond Death*, 301) claim that "if God permits a person to die and go to hell, it seems reasonable to think that God no longer believes that this person is saveable." If "all a person needed was more time to make a decision, God would see to it that the individual got the extra time. No one will go to hell who would have gone to heaven if he had needed one more chance."

72. MacDonald, *Evangelical Universalist*, 182.

the lives of others. This utilitarian approach to human persons, where some are sacrificed for the greater good, is morally unacceptable; this is because the unsaved have value for their own sake, not merely as instruments to be used for ulterior ends. As a general claim about the relationship between the saved and the lost, Knight says, we must conclude that Craig's claims are totally implausible.[73] MacDonald, too, emphasizes that for Molinist defenses of eternal hell everything hinges on the plausibility of the notion that a free agent could choose forever and in every possible situation to reject God. But if—as argued in chapter 5—"free will requires 1. a certain amount of rationality and 2. an adequate appreciation of the facts relevant to the choice in question, then a fully-informed, free decision to reject God is an incoherent notion." If after death "God brings people to a point where they appreciate the consequences of their decision to . . . reject salvation," then "there is no possible world in which any people choose to reject God forever."[74] And so the Molinist case for permanent damnation collapses. Seymour makes a similar argument.

> It is harder to be transworldly damned on liberal than on conservative views. To be transworldly damned on conservative views, it need only be the case that there are no feasible worlds in which one is free and chooses salvation *before death*. But to be transworldly damned on the liberal view is more difficult; one needs to be so impenitent that there are no feasible worlds in which one freely accepts salvation, even if the choice is repeatedly offered *after death* into eternity.[75]

Molinism is better, perhaps, than Augustinianism's double predestination—and it has advantages over views that deny middle knowledge, in which (as Walls points out), God is a gambler willing to risk the eternal fate of millions of people in the hope of having some freely decide to accept salvation.[76] That said, Molinism's solution to the problem of hell is not—all things considered—plausible.

---

73. Knight, "Molinism and Hell," quotes at random from 109–14.

74. MacDonald, *Evangelical Universalist*, 182.

75. Seymour, *Theodicy of Hell*, 118; emphasis added. I prefer the terms "escapist" and "non-escapist" rather than "liberal" and "conservative."

76. Walls, *Hell*, 50–52. Also see "Is Molinism as Bad as Calvinism?"—to which Walls answers with a very qualified no.

9. Universal Salvation Explained

The question of whether all are saved involves reconciling two truths: divine love (which suggests universal salvation) and human freedom (which suggests eternal hell). Universal salvation is, however, compatible with free will. Separatists assume that the only way God can save all is by coercion. This assumption is false: God can save all by persuasion. God's love does not compel or override freedom but elicits a free response. This is especially true, John Hick says, if we assume that "the divine Therapist has perfect knowledge of each human heart, is infinitely wise in the healing of its ills, has unbounded love for the patient and unlimited time to devote to him."[77] John Kronen and Eric Reitan agree: "that someone created in the divine image, and hence naturally ordered towards the good, should eternally reject God, the perfect good, [is] *prima facie* unlikely, especially if God has not given up on the creature and continues unremittingly to seek the creature's repentance."[78]

Thomas Talbott explains why no one will refuse God forever.

> If God is the ultimate source of human happiness and separation from God can bring only greater and greater misery into one's life, ... then why should anyone want to reject God? Well, the person might be ignorant of certain facts about God, or mired in self-deception or (perhaps as a consequence of previous bad choices) in bondage to unhealthy desires; any one of these conditions might provide them with a motive for rejecting God. Under such conditions as these, however, it would always remain open to God to remove their ignorance, or to shatter their illusions, or to free them from their bondage to desire; far from interfering with the person's freedom of choice, such actions would ... restore true freedom of choice.[79]

Or as he puts it elsewhere:

> what might qualify as a motive for someone's making a fully informed decision to reject God? Once one has learned, perhaps through bitter experience, that evil is always destructive, always contrary to one's own interest ... , and once one sees clearly that God is the ultimate source of human happiness and that rebellion can bring only greater and greater misery into one's

---

77. Hick, *Death and Eternal Life*, 345.
78. Kronen and Reitan, *God's Final Victory*, 217 and 160.
79. Talbott, "Providence, Freedom and Human Destiny," 228, slightly modified.

own life . . . , an intelligent motive for such rebellion no longer seems even possible.[80]

Talbott adds: once we are free of salvation inhibitors, "once all ignorance and deception and bondage to desire is removed, so that a person is truly 'free' to choose, there can no longer be any motive for choosing eternal misery for oneself."[81]

Jerry Walls critiques Talbott's argument.[82] Since human beings are free, God cannot guarantee that they will choose salvation—and if they do not, will respect their choice to refuse. Because God values human freedom and because of the voluntary nature of love, God will not force salvation on sinners. As C.S. Lewis writes:

> if the happiness of a creature lies in (free) self-surrender, no one can make that surrender but himself . . . . I would pay any price to be able to say truthfully, "All will be saved." But my reason retorts, "Without their will, or with it?" If I say, "Without their will," I at once perceive a contradiction; how can the . . . voluntary act of self-surrender be involuntary? If I say, "With their will," my reason replies, "How if they will not give in?"[83]

God cannot do things that are meaningless and self-contradictory, such as making free persons choose good. Despite appearances however, Walls, the hopeful universalist, and Talbott, the convinced universalist, share much more than separates them. Both believe that God continues to love the unsaved dead, that death is open and that many are saved after death—and Walls, a separatist, concedes that eternally free choice against God is puzzling.[84]

No one can freely choose against God forever. But suppose that they could. In that case God would not permit it. A loving God would not let anyone destroy themselves but would intervene to prevent the severe irreparable harm of eternal damnation. Freedom is not the highest value and the duty to respect autonomy is not absolute—it can be overridden

---

80. Talbott, *Inescapable Love*, 186.

81. Talbott, "Everlasting Punishment," 37. The sinner can then say "I was blind but now I see—I was bound but now I'm free."

82. See Walls, "Eternal Hell and Christian Concept of God"; "Heaven and Hell" (both articles); *Hell*, chapter 5; *Heaven, Hell and Purgatory*, 78–82. For an exchange on these matters see articles by Walls and Talbott in *Religious Studies* 40 (2004) 203–27.

83. Lewis, *Problem of Pain*, 106–7.

84. Walls, *Heaven, Hell and Purgatory*, 86.

by considerations of human welfare (as in suicide prevention). As Gregory MacDonald says, "if a person's choices are . . . self-destructive and irrational . . . , we would generally see no problem in restricting his or her freedoms and making some decisions for the person's own good."[85] Kronen and Reitan note that parents can override the freedom of their children concerning serious choices about health or safety.

> There is reason to think that when it comes to our ultimate destinies we are like infants, and therefore God legitimately reserves this kind of parental veto power should we make poor use of our nascent capacity for choice. . . . Given our broken state we are no more competent to be entrusted with our eternal destinies than a toddler is to be entrusted with life-and-death decisions. On the matter of our eternal destiny we are as infants—and just as parents retain veto power when it comes to the more serious choices children make, God might retain such power when it comes to our eternal fate.

If so, then God might exercise efficacious grace that overrides freedom.[86] Clyde Ragland agrees: if they conflict, God prioritizes someone's objective good over their subjective preferences—since their real good is more important than their distorted apparent good. Because hell is a horrendous evil, it would be unloving for God to defer to the sinner's subjective preference for hell. While freedom has some value, union with God has more.[87]

10. Pope Francis' Teaching on Mercy

Pope Francis' declaration of a Holy Year of Mercy in 2016 included several themes, which I have excerpted verbatim and at length from *Misericordiae Vultus*.[88] In it he challenges the church to exemplify the compassionate God of the Bible.

---

85. MacDonald, *Evangelical Universalist*, 29.
86. Kronen and Reitan, *God's Final Victory*, 148.
87. Ragland, "Love and Damnation," 215–18.
88. Pope Francis, "Misericordiae Vultus," in *Name of God is Mercy*; also found online: im.va.

God's Mercy

We need constantly to contemplate the mystery of mercy. . . . Mercy: the word reveals the very mystery of the Most Holy Trinity. . . . Mercy: the bridge that connects God and man, opening our hearts to the hope of being loved forever despite our sinfulness. . . . When faced with the gravity of sin, God responds with the fullness of mercy. Mercy will always be greater than any sin, and no one can place limits on the love of God who is ever ready to forgive .

The mercy of God is not an abstract idea, but a concrete reality with which God reveals God's love as of that of a father or a mother, moved to the very depths out of love for their child. It is hardly an exaggeration to say that this is a "visceral" love. It gushes forth from the depths naturally, full of tenderness and compassion . . . and mercy.

"For his mercy endures forever." This is the refrain that repeats after each verse in Psalm 136 as it narrates the history of God's revelation.

Everything in God speaks of mercy. Nothing in God is devoid of compassion.

In the parables devoted to mercy, Jesus reveals the nature of God as that of a Father who never gives up until he has forgiven the wrong and overcome rejection with compassion and mercy. We know these parables well, three in particular: the lost sheep, the lost coin, and the father with two sons (Luke 15:1–32). In these parables, God is always presented as full of joy, especially when God pardons. In them we find the core of the gospel and of our faith, because mercy is presented as a force that overcomes everything.[89]

---

89. In reflecting on the parables in Luke 15:1–32, Barron ("Coin, Sheep, Son") says that the heart of the gospel is that God searches for us in a passionate, unrelenting way. No rational shepherd would put 99 sheep in danger to search for one who has wandered away—yet God frets over one lost person. No sensible woman would turn her house upside down to find a nickel—yet God diligently searches for the least significant among us. No self-respecting father who has been grievously insulted by his son would wait and welcome him back with open arms—yet God does just that with sinners who have consciously rebelled against God. Jesus' audience was meant to feel the craziness of the shepherd, the woman and the father. As Catherine of Sienna puts it, God is *pazzo d'amore*—"crazy in love" with us.

Justice and Mercy

"Patient and merciful." These words often go together in the Old Testament to describe God's nature. God's being merciful is concretely demonstrated in God's many actions throughout the history of salvation where God's goodness prevails over punishment and destruction.

It would not be out of place at this point to recall the relationship between justice and mercy. These are not two contradictory realities, but two dimensions of a single reality that unfolds progressively until it culminates in the fullness of love.

Mercy is not opposed to justice but rather expresses God's way of reaching out to the sinner, offering them a new chance to . . . convert, and believe. The experience of the prophet Hosea can help us see the way in which mercy surpasses justice. The era in which the prophet lived was one of the most dramatic in the history of the Jewish people. The kingdom was tottering on the edge of destruction; the people had not remained faithful to the covenant; they had wandered from God and lost the faith of their forefathers. According to human logic, it seems reasonable for God to think of rejecting an unfaithful people; they had not observed their pact with God and therefore deserved just punishment: in other words, exile. The prophet's words attest to this: "they shall not return to the land of Egypt, and Assyria shall be their king, because they have refused to return to me" (Hos 11:5). And yet, after this invocation of justice, the prophet radically changes his speech and reveals the true face of God: "how can I give you up, O Ephraim! How can I hand you over, O Israel! How can I make you like Admah! How can I treat you like Zeboiim! My heart recoils within me, my compassion grows warm and tender. I will not execute my fierce anger, I will not again destroy Ephraim; for I am God and not man, the Holy One in your midst, and I will not come to destroy" (11:8–9). Saint Augustine, almost as if he were commenting on these words of the prophet, says: "It is easier for God to hold back anger than mercy." And so it is. God's anger lasts but a moment, God's mercy forever.

If God limited Godself to only justice, God would cease to be God, and would instead be like human beings who ask merely that the law be respected. But mere justice is not enough. . . . God goes beyond justice with . . . mercy and forgiveness. Yet this does not mean that justice should be devalued or rendered superfluous. On the contrary: anyone who makes a mistake must pay the price. However, this is just the beginning of conversion, not its end, because one begins to feel the tenderness and mercy of God. God does not deny justice. God rather envelopes it and surpasses it with an even greater event in which we experience love as the foundation of true justice.

Merciful Christians

We are called to gaze . . . attentively on mercy so that we may become a more effective sign of the Father's action in our lives.

We recall the poignant words of Pope John XXIII: the Church needs "to use the medicine of mercy rather than taking up arms of severity."

The Church [must] be a living sign of the Father's love in the world . . . .

How much I desire that the [Church] will be steeped in mercy, so that we can go out to every man and woman, bringing the goodness and tenderness of God! May the balm of mercy reach everyone, both believers and those far away . . . .

"Should not you have had mercy on your fellow servant, as I had mercy on you?" (Matt 18:33). . . . This parable contains a profound teaching for all of us. Jesus affirms that mercy is not only an action of the Father, it becomes a criterion for ascertaining who his true children are. In short, we are called to show mercy because mercy has first been shown to us.

The mercy of God is God's loving concern for each one of us. God . . . desires our wellbeing and . . . wants to see us happy, full of joy, and peaceful. This is the path which the merciful love of Christians must also travel. As the Father loves, so do his children. Just as God is merciful, so we are called to be merciful to each other.

We want to live . . . in light of the Lord's words: . . . "be merciful just as your Father is merciful" (Luke 6:36).

A Church of Mercy

Mercy is the very foundation of the Church's life. All of her pastoral activity should be caught up in the tenderness she makes present . . . ; nothing in her preaching and in her witness to the world can be lacking in mercy. The Church's very credibility is seen in how she shows merciful and compassionate love.... Perhaps we have long since forgotten how to show and live the way of mercy. The temptation ... to focus exclusively on justice made us forget that this is only the first, albeit necessary and indispensable step. But the Church needs to go beyond and strive for a higher and more important goal.

Let us listen to [Pope John Paul II's] words ...: "the Church lives an authentic life when she professes and proclaims mercy—the most stupendous attribute of the Creator and of the Redeemer—and when she brings people close to the sources of the Savior's mercy, of which she is the trustee and dispenser."

The Church is commissioned to announce the mercy of God, the beating heart of the gospel.... The [Church] must pattern her behavior after the Son of God who went out to everyone without exception. In the present day ... the theme of mercy needs to be proposed again and again with new enthusiasm and renewed pastoral action. It is absolutely essential for the Church and for the credibility of her message that she herself live and testify to mercy. Her language and her gestures must transmit mercy, so as to touch the hearts of all people and inspire them once more to find the road that leads to the Father....

Wherever the Church is present, the mercy of the Father must be evident. In our parishes, communities, associations, and movements, in a word, wherever there are Christians, everyone should find an oasis of mercy....

I present, therefore, this Extraordinary Jubilee Year dedicated to living out in our daily lives the mercy which the Father constantly extends to all of us. In this Jubilee Year, let us allow God to surprise us. God never tires of casting open the doors of God's heart and of repeating that God loves us and wants to share God's love with us. The Church feels the urgent need to proclaim God's mercy. Her life is authentic and credible only when she becomes a convincing herald of mercy. She knows that her primary task ... is to introduce everyone to the great mystery of God's mercy.... The Church is called above all to be a credible witness to mercy, professing it and living it as the core of the revelation of Jesus Christ. From the heart of the Trinity, from the depths of the mystery of God, the great river of mercy wells up and overflows unceasingly. It is a spring that will never run dry, no matter how many people draw from it. Every time someone is in need, he or she can approach it, because the mercy of God never ends.

In this Jubilee Year, may the Church echo the word of God that resounds strong and clear as a message and a sign of pardon, strength, aid and love. May she never tire of extending mercy, and be ever patient in offering compassion and comfort. May the Church become the voice of every man and woman, and repeat confidently without end: "Be mindful of your mercy, O Lord, and your steadfast love, for they have been from of old" (Ps 25:6).

ABBREVIATIONS

ABD   *Anchor Bible Dictionary.* Edited by David Freedman. 6 Volumes. New York: Doubleday, 1992.

ANF   *Ante-Nicene Fathers.* Edited by Alexander Roberts and James Donaldson. 10 Volumes. Peabody, MA: Hendrickson, 2004.

CD   *Contemporary Debates in Philosophy of Religion.* Edited by Michael Peterson and Raymond VanArragon. Oxford: Blackwell, 2004.

NIDB   *New Interpreters Dictionary of the Bible.* Edited by Katharine Doob Sakenfeld. 5 Volumes. Nashville: Abingdon, 2009.

NPNF   *Nicene and Post-Nicene Fathers.* First Series. 14 Volumes. Edited by Philip Schaff. Peabody, MA: Hendrickson, 2004.

NPNF   *Nicene and Post-Nicene Fathers.* Second Series. 14 Volumes. Edited by Philip Schaff and Henry Wace. Peabody, MA: Hendrickson, 2004.

OHE   *The Oxford Handbook of Eschatology.* Edited by Jerry Walls. Oxford: Oxford University Press, 2008.

OHPT   *The Oxford Handbook of Philosophical Theology.* Edited by Thomas Flint and Michael Rea. Oxford: Oxford University Press, 2009.

PH   *The Problem of Hell: A Philosophical Anthology.* Edited by Joel Buenting. Farnham, UK: Ashgate, 2010.

RCPR	*The Routledge Companion to Philosophy of Religion.* Edited by Chad Meister and Paul Copan. 2nd ed. London: Routledge, 2013.
TDNT	*Theological Dictionary of the New Testament.* Edited by Gerhard Kittel and Gerhard Friedrich. 10 Volumes. Grand Rapids: Eerdmans, 1984.
TDOT	*Theological Dictionary of the Old Testament.* Edited by Johannes Botterweck, Helmer Ringgren, and Heinz-Josef Fabry. 15 Volumes. Grand Rapids: Eerdmans, 2003.

BIBLIOGRAPHY

Adams, Marilyn. "Divine Justice, Divine Love and Life to Come." *Crux* 13 (1976–77) 12–28.
———. *Horrendous Evils and the Goodness of God*. Ithaca, NY: Cornell University Press, 1999.
———. "The Problem of Hell: A Problem for Christians." In *Reasoned Faith*, edited by Eleonore Stump, 301–27. Ithaca, NY: Cornell University Press, 1993.
Alcorn, Randy. *Heaven*. Carol Stream, IL: Tyndale House, 2004.
———. *Heaven Workbook*. Nashville: Lifeway, 2006.
Alexander, Eben. *Proof of Heaven: A Neurosurgeon's Journey into the Afterlife*. New York: Simon and Schuster, 2012.
Alfeyev, Hilarion. *Christ the Conqueror of Hell: The Descent into Hades from an Orthodox Perspective*. Crestwood, NY: St. Vladimir's Seminary Press, 2009.
———. "Eschatology." In *The Cambridge Companion to Orthodox Christian Theology*, edited by Mary Cunningham and Elizabeth Theokritoff, 107–20. Cambridge: Cambridge University Press, 2008.
Allison, Dale. "Day of the Lord." In *NIDB* 2: 46–47.
———. "Eschatology of the New Testament." In *NIDB* 2: 294–99.
Amirault, Gary. "The Doctrine of Hell Terrorizes." Online: tentmaker.org.
Aquinas, Thomas. *Summa Contra Gentiles*. Online: dhspriory.org.
———. *Summa Theologiae*. Blackfriars Edition. New York: McGraw-Hill, 1964.
———. *Summa Theologica*. 2nd rev. ed. Vol. 3. New York: Benzinger Brothers, 1948.
Archbishops' Commission on Christian Doctrine. *Prayer and the Departed*. London: SPCK, 1971.
Aristotle. *Metaphysics*. Grinell, IA: Peripatetic, 1979.
———. *Nicomachean Ethics*. Indianapolis: Hackett, 1999.
Arnold, Bill. "Old Testament Eschatology and the Rise of Apocalypticism." In *OHE*: 23–39.
Atwell, Robert. "Aspects in St. Augustine of Hippo's Thought and Spirituality concerning the State of the Faithful Departed, 354–430." In *The End of Strife*, edited by David Loades, 3–13. Edinburgh: T. & T. Clark, 1984.
———. "From Augustine to Gregory the Great: an Evaluation of the Emergence of the Doctrine of Purgatory." *Journal of Ecclesiastical History* 38 (1987) 173–86.
Augsburg Confession. Online: bookofconcord.org
Augustine of Hippo. *City of God*. Harmondsworth, UK: Penguin, 1972.

———. *Confessions*. Oxford: Oxford University Press, 1991.
———. *Enchiridion*. In *NPNF*, First Series 3: 237–81.
———. *On Christian Doctrine*. In *NPNF*, First Series 2: 519–97.
Baggini, Julian. *The Pig That Wants to be Eaten*. New York: Plume, 2005.
———. *The Virtues of the Table*. London: Granta, 2014.
Baker, Sharon. *Razing Hell*. Louisville, KY: Westminster John Knox, 2010.
Bakken, Kenneth. *Journey into God*. Minneapolis: Augsburg-Fortress, 2000.
Balentine, Samuel. *Prayer in the Hebrew Bible*. Minneapolis: Fortress, 1993.
Balthasar, Hans Urs von. *Dare We Hope That All Men Be Saved?* San Fransisco: Ignatius, 1988.
Barnard, Justin. "Purgatory and the Dilemma of Sanctification." *Faith and Philosophy* 24 (2007) 311–30.
Barnhouse, Donald Gray. Online: bible.org.
Barron, Robert. "A Coin, A Sheep, A Son." Homily for September 11, 2015. Online: wordonfire.org.
———. "Daniel and the New Kingdom." Homily for November 15, 2015. Online: wordonfire.org.
———. "*Hesed* All the Way Through." Homily for March 15, 2015. Online: wordonfire.org.
———. "*Vitae Spiritualis Ianua*." Homily for January 10, 2016. Online: wordonfire.org.
———. "What Does it Mean to Say That Christ is King?" Homily for November 22, 2015. Online: wordonfire.org.
Bartelmus, G. "Samayim." In *TDOT* 15: 204–36.
Bauckham, Richard. "Eschatology." In *Oxford Companion to Christian Thought*, edited by Adrian Hastings, 206–9. Oxford: Oxford University Press, 2000.
———. "Universalism: A Historical Survey." *Themelios* 4 (1978) 47–54.
Baumeister, Roy, and Todd Heatherton. "Self-Regulation Failure: An Overview." *Psychological Inquiry* 7 (1996) 1–15.
Bell, Rob. *Love Wins: A Book about Heaven, Hell and the Fate of Every Person Who Ever Lived*. New York: Harper Collins, 2011.
———. *The Love Wins Companion*. New York: Harper Collins, 2012.
———. *Love Wins for Teens*. New York: Harper Collins, 2013.
Benzoni, Francisco. "An Augustinian Understanding of Love in an Ecological Context." *Quodlibet Journal* 6 (2004). Online: quodlibet.net.
Bierma, Nathan. *Bringing Heaven Down to Earth*. Phillipsburg, PA: P. & R., 2005.
Bloesch, Donald. *Essentials of Evangelical Theology*. Vol. 2. New York: Harper and Row, 1978.
———. *The Last Things: Resurrection, Judgment, Glory*. Downers Grove, IL: IVP, 2004.
Bolz-Weber, Nadia. "Father, Can I Tell Your Congregation How Resurrection Really Feels." Online: patheos.com.
Bonda, Jan. *The One Purpose of God: An Answer to the Doctrine of Eternal Punishment*. Grand Rapids: Eerdmans, 1998.
Bonhoeffer, Dietrich. *Christmas Sermons*. Grand Rapids: Zondervan, 2005.
———. *Discipleship*. Minneapolis: Fortress, 2003.
———. *Ethics*. Minneapolis: Fortress, 2009.
———. *Letters and Papers from Prison*. Minneapolis: Fortress, 2010.
Borg, Marcus. *The Heart of Christianity*. San Francisco: Harper San Francisco, 2003.

———. *Meeting Jesus Again for the First Time*. San Francisco: Harper San Francisco, 1994.
Borg, Marcus, and John Dominic Crossan. *The First Paul*. New York: Harper One, 2009.
Boudreaux, Florentin. *The Happiness of Heaven*. Baltimore: Murphy, 1871. Online: gutenberg.org.
Bratt, James, ed. *Abraham Kuyper: A Centennial Reader*. Grand Rapids: Eerdmans, 1998.
Brett, Alan, and Paul Jersild. "'Inappropriate' Treatment Near the End of Life." *Archives of Internal Medicine* 163 (2003) 1645–49.
Brown, Christopher. "Friendship in Heaven: Aquinas on Supremely Perfect Happiness and the Communion of Saints." In *Metaphysics and God: Essays in Honor of Eleonore Stump*, edited by Kevin Timpe, 225–48. New York: Routledge, 2009.
———. "Making the Best Even Better: Modifying Pawl and Timpe's Solution to the Problem of Heavenly Freedom." *Faith and Philosophy* 32 (2015) 63–80.
Brown, David. "No Heaven without Purgatory." *Religious Studies* 21 (1985) 447–56.
Brown, Peter. *The Ransom of the Soul: Afterlife and Wealth in Early Western Christianity*. Cambridge: Harvard University Press, 2015.
Brueggemann, Walter. *Biblical Perspectives on Evangelism*. Nashville: Abingdon, 1993.
———. *The Collected Sermons of Walter Brueggemann*. Louisville, KY: Westminster John Knox, 2011.
———. *The Covenanted Self*. Minneapolis: Fortress, 1999.
———. "Preaching as Reimagination." *Theology Today* 52 (1995) 313–29.
———. *The Prophetic Imagination*. 2nd ed. Minneapolis: Fortress, 2001.
Buckareff, Andrei, and Allen Plug. "Escaping Hell: Divine Motivation and the Problem of Hell." *Religious Studies* 41 (2005) 39–54.
———. "Value, Finality and Frustration: Problems for Escapists?" In *PH*: 77–90.
Buechner, Frederick. *The Hungering Dark*. San Francisco: Harper Collins, 1969.
Bullard, Roger. *Messiah: The Gospel according to Handel's Oratorio*. Grand Rapids: Eerdmans, 1993.
Bush, George. "Remarks at the National Day of Prayer & Remembrance Service." Online: freerepublic.com.
Burpo, Todd, and Lynn Vincent. *Heaven Is For Real: A Little Boy's Astounding Story of His Trip to Heaven and Back*. Nashville: Thomas Nelson, 2010.
Cain, James. "Why I am Unconvinced by Arguments against the Existence of Hell." In *PH*: 133–44.
Callahan, Sidney. *With All Our Heart and Mind: The Spiritual Works of Mercy in a Psychological Age*. New York: Crossroad, 1989.
Calquhoun, Frank. *Parish Prayers*. London: Hodder and Stoughton, 2967.
Calvin, John. *Institutes of the Christian Religion*. Philadelphia: Westminster, 1960.
Casey, John. *Afterlives: A Guide to Heaven, Hell and Purgatory*. Oxford: Oxford University Press, 2009.
Catherine of Genoa. *Treatise on Purgatory*. Online: catholictreasury.info.
Chapman, David. "Rest and Light Perpetual: Prayer for the Departed in the Communion of Saints." *One in Christ* 34 (1998) 39–49.
Charlesworth, James. "Paradise." In *ABD* 5: 154–55.
———. "Paradise." In *NIDB* 4: 377–78.
Christensen, Michael, and Jeffrey Wittung, eds. *Partakers of the Divine Nature*. Grand Rapids: Baker Academic, 2007.

Christensen, Michael. "John Wesley: Christian Perfection as Faith Filled with the Energy of Love." In *Partakers of the Divine Nature*, edited by Michael Christensen and Jeffrey Wittung, 219–29. Grand Rapids: Baker Academic, 2007.

Christian Reformed Church. "Our World Belongs to God." In *Psalter Hymnal*. Grand Rapids: CRC, 1988.

Chrysostom, John. *The Homily of St. John Chrysostom on the First Epistle of Paul the Apostle to the Corinthians*. Oxford: Parker, 1939.

Church of England. *Common Worship*. Online: churchofengland.org.

———. *Homily on Prayer*. Online: anglicanlibrary.org.

Ciurria, Michelle. "Moral Responsibility Ain't Just in the Head." *Journal of the American Philosophical Association* 1 (2015) 601–16.

Clement of Alexandria. *Stromata*. In *ANF* 2: 299–568.

Clendenin, Daniel. *Eastern Orthodox Christianity: A Western Perspective*. 2nd ed. Grand Rapids: Baker Academic, 2003.

Cockburn, Bruce. "Festival of Friends." *In the Falling Dark*. True North Productions, 1976.

———. "Joy Will Find a Way (A Song about Dying)." *Joy Will Find a Way*. True North Productions, 1975.

———. *Rumors of Glory: A Memoir*. Toronto, ON: Harper Collins, 2014.

Colquhoun, Frank. *Parish Prayers*. London: Hodder and Stoughton, 1967.

Connelly, Douglas. *The Promise of Heaven*. Downers Grove, IL: IVP, 2000.

Cooper, John. *Body, Soul and Life Everlasting: Biblical Anthropology and the Monism-Dualism Debate*. Grand Rapids: Eerdmans, 1989.

Cosden, Darrell. *The Heavenly Good of Earthly Work*. Peabody, MA: Hendrickson, 2006.

Council of Trent. Online: americancatholictruthsociety.com.

Craddock, Fred, Dale Goldsmith, and Joy Goldsmith. *Speaking of Dying: Recovering the Church's Voice in the Face of Death*. Grand Rapids: Brazos, 2012.

Craig, William Lane. "Middle Knowledge: A Calvinist—Arminian Rapprochement?" In *The Grace of God, The Will of Man*, edited by Clark Pinnock, 141–64. Grand Rapids: Zondervan, 1989.

———. "No Other Name: A Middle Knowledge Perspective on the Exclusivity of Salvation through Christ." *Faith and Philosophy* 6 (1989) 297–308.

———. *Only Wise God*. Grand Rapids: Baker, 1987.

———. "Talbott's Universalism." *Religious Studies* 26 (1991) 297–308.

Crump, David. *Knocking on Heaven's Door*. Grand Rapids: Baker, 2006.

Cullmann, Oscar. *Christ and Time: The Primitive Christian Conception of Time and History*. Rev. ed. Philadelphia: Westminster, 1964.

Currie, David. *Born Fundamentalist—Born Again Catholic*. San Francisco: Ignatius, 1996.

Cyril of Jerusalem. "Catechetical Lecture 23, 'On the Mysteries: On the Sacred Liturgy and Communion.'" Book 5. 9–10. In *NPNF*, Second Series 7: 153–57.

Dalai Lama and Daniel Groleman. *Disturbing Emotions: How Can We Overcome Them?* New York: Bantam, 2003.

Daley, Brian. *The Hope of the Early Church*. Cambridge: Cambridge University Press, 1991.

———. "Old Books and Contemporary Faith." In *Ancient Faith for the Church's Future*, edited by Mark Husbands and Jeffrey Greenman, 53–68. Downers Grove, IL: IVP, 2008.
Dante Alighieri. *The Divine Comedy*. In *The Portable Dante*, edited by Mark Musa. New York: Penguin, 1995.
Date, Christopher, Gregory Stump, and Joshua Anderson, eds. *Rethinking Hell: Readings in Evangelical Conditionalism*. Eugene, OR: Cascade, 2014.
Davis, Stephen. "Hell, Wrath and the Grace of God." In *PH*: 91–102.
———. *Risen Indeed: Making Sense of the Resurrection*. Grand Rapids: Eerdmans, 1993.
———. "Universalism, Hell and the Fate of the Ignorant." *Modern Theology* 6 (1990) 173–86.
Day, J. P. *Hope: A Philosophical Inquiry*. Helsinki: Philosophy Society of Finland, 1991.
Defense of Augsburg Confession. Online: bookofconcord.org.
Dixon, Larry. *The Other Side of the Good News*. Wheaton, IL: Victor, 1992.
Doctrine Commission of the General Synod of the Church of England. *The Mystery of Salvation*. London: Church House, 1995.
Dorr, Donal. *Spirituality and Justice*. Maryknoll, NY: Orbis, 1984.
Duclow, Donald. "Ars Moriendi." In *The Encyclopedia of Death and Dying*, edited by Robert Kastenbaum. Online: deathreference.com.
———. "Memento Mori." In *The Encyclopedia of Death and Dying*, edited by Robert Kastenbaum. Online: deathreference.com.
Dunnam, Maxie, and Kimberley Reisman. *The Workbook on the Seven Deadly Sins*. Nashville: Upper Room, 1997.
Edwards, David, and John Stott. *Essentials*. London: Hodder and Stoughton, 1988.
Edwards, Jonathan. "Sinners in the Hands of an Angry God." In *Jonathan Edwards: Basic Writings*, edited by Ola Winslow, 150–167. New York: New American Library, 1966.
Elliott, Jim. Billy Graham Center Archives. Online: wheaton.edu.
Eno, Robert. "The Fathers and the Cleansing Fire." *Irish Theological Quarterly* 53 (1987) 184–202.
Episcopal Church. *Book of Common Prayer*. New York: Seabury, 1979.
———. "The Episcopal Faith." Online: episcopalchicago.org.
———. *The Hymnal 1982*. New York: Church Publishing, 1982.
Evans, Rachel Held. *Searching for Sunday*. Nashville: Thomas Nelson, 2015.
Evans, Rod, and Irwin Berent. *Fundamentalism: Hazards and Heartbreaks*. La Salle, IL: Open Court, 1988.
Fackre, Dorothy and Gabriel. *Christian Basics: A Primer for Pilgrims*. Grand Rapids: Eerdmans, 1991.
Fairlie, Henry. *The Seven Deadly Sins Today*. Notre Dame, IN: University of Notre Dame Press, 1979.
Fairbairn, Donald. *Life in the Trinity*. Downers Grove, IL: IVP, 2009.
Fatima Prayer. Online: ourcatholicprayers.com.
Fensham, Frank. "Crime and Punishment." In *The New Bible Dictionary*, edited by J. D. Douglas, 275–78. Grand Rapids: Eerdmans, 1962.
Ferguson, Everett. "God's Infinity and Man's Mutability: Perpetual Progress according to Gregory of Nyssa." *Greek Orthodox Theological Review* 18 (1973) 59–78.
Fischer, John Martin. "Why Immortality is Not So Bad." *International Journal of Philosophical Studies* 2 (1994) 262–67.

Flint, Thomas. *Divine Providence: The Molinist Account*. Ithaca, NY: Cornell University Press, 1998.

———. "Two Accounts of Providence." In *Divine and Human Action*, edited by Thomas Morris, 147–81. Ithaca, NY: Cornell University Press, 1988.

Florovsky, George. *Creation and Redemption*. Vol. 3. Belmont, WA: Nordland, 1976.

Ford, David. "Prayer and the Departed Saints." Online: protomartyr.org.

Forest, Jim. *Praying with Icons*. Maryknoll, NY: Orbis, 1997.

Formula of Concord. Online: bookofconcord.org.

Fourth Lateran Council. Online: fordham.edu.

France, R. T. *The Gospel of Matthew*. Grand Rapids: Eerdmans, 2007.

Frankfurt, Harry. "Freedom of the Will and the Concept of a Person." *Journal of Philosophy* 68 (1971) 5–20.

Fudge, Edward. *The Fire that Consumes*. Houston: Providential, 1982.

Fulghum, Robert. *It Was On Fire When I Lay Down On It*. New York: Ivy, 1989.

Geach, Peter. *The Virtues*. Cambridge: Cambridge University Press, 1977.

Gilligan, Carol. *In a Different Voice*. Cambridge: Harvard University Press, 1982.

Gould, James B. "Becoming Good: The Role of Spiritual Practice." *Philosophical Practice* 1 (2005) 135–47.

———. "Better Hearts: Teaching Applied Virtue Ethics." *Teaching Philosophy* 25 (2002) 4–25.

———. "Bonhoeffer and the False Dilemma of German Atheism." *Toronto Journal of Theology* 14 (1998) 61–81.

———. "Broad Inclusive Salvation: The Logic of 'Anonymous Christianity.'" *Philosophy and Theology* 20 (2008) 175–98.

———. "Cultivating Character: Hume's Techniques for Self-improvement." *Philosophical Practice* 6 (2011) 832–43.

———. "Good Eating: Food as a Single-topic Ethics Course." *Teaching Ethics* 14 (2014) 149–74.

———. "Healing the Wounded Heart through Ritual and Liturgy." In *The Long Journey Home: Understanding and Ministering to the Sexually Abused*, edited by Andrew Schmutzer, 293–313. Eugene, OR: Wipf and Stock. 2011.

———. "Make Today Count: Motorcycling as *memento mori*." *International Journal of Motorcycle Studies* 9 (2013). Online: ijms.org.

Graham, Billy. "Responding to God's Glory." In *Declare His Glory among the Nations*, edited by David Howard, 141–54. Downers Grove, IL: IVP, 1977.

Green, Melody. "There is a Redeemer." In *Sing: A New Creation*. Grand Rapids: CRC, 2001.

Gregory of Nyssa. *Commentary on Song of Songs*. Brookline, MA: Hellenic College Press, 1987.

———. *The Life of Moses*. New York: Paulist, 1978.

———. *The Soul and the Resurrection*. Crestwood, NY: St. Vladimir's Seminary Press, 1993.

Gregory the Great. *Dialogues*. New York: Fathers of the Church, 1959.

Grenz, Stanley. *Prayer: The Cry for the Kingdom*. Peabody, MA: Hendrickson, 1988.

Griffiths, Paul. "Purgatory." In *OHE*: 427–45.

Gulley, Philip, and James Mulholland. *If God Is Love: Recovering Grace in an Ungracious World*. San Francisco: Harper, 2004.

———. *If Grace Is True: Why God Will Save Every Person*. San Francisco: Harper, 2003.

Guroian, Vigen. *Incarnate Love: Essays in Orthodox Ethics*. Notre Dame, IN: Notre Dame University Press, 1987.
Habermas, Gary, and J. P. Moreland. *Beyond Death: Exploring the Evidence for Immortality*. Wheaton, IL: Crossway, 1998.
Hadot, Pierre. *Philosophy as a Way of Life: Spiritual Exercises from Socrates to Foucault*. Oxford: Blackwell, 1995.
Hall, Douglas John. *When You Pray*. Valley Forge, PA: Judson, 1987.
Hardy, Edward. "The Blessed Dead in Anglican Piety." *Sobornost* 3 (1981) 160–78.
Hasker, William. *The Triumph of God over Evil: Theodicy for a World of Suffering*. Downers Grove, IL: IVP, 2008.
Havener, Timothy. "Teaching Children Hell is Child Abuse." Online: youtube.com.
Hawkins, Peter. *Undiscovered Country: Imagining the World to Come*. New York: Seabury, 2009.
Hayes, Zachary. "The Purgatorial View." In *Four Views on Hell*, edited by William Crockett, 91–118. Grand Rapids: Zondervan, 1992.
Hebblethwaite, Brian. *The Christian Hope*. Rev. ed. Oxford: Oxford University Press, 2010.
Heidegger, Martin. *Being and Time*. New York: Harper & Row, 1962.
Heidelberg Catechism. Online: crcna.org.
Herion, Gary. "Wrath of God, OT." In *ABD* 6: 989–96.
Hershenov, David. "The Metaphysical Problem of Intermittent Existence and the Possibility of Resurrection." *Faith and Philosophy* 20 (2003) 24–36.
Hick, John. *The Center of Christianity*. San Francisco: Harper and Row, 1978.
———. *Death and Eternal Life*. Louisville, KY: Westminster John Knox, 1994.
———. *Evil and the God of Love*. Rev. ed. New York: Harper and Row, 1978.
Hiers, Richard. "Day of the Lord." In *ABD* 2: 82–83.
Hoekema, Anthony. *The Bible and the Future*. Grand Rapids: Eerdmans, 1979.
Hotz, Kendra, and Matthew Matthews. *Shaping the Christian Life*. Louisville, KY: Westminster John Knox, 2006.
International Theological Commission. "Some Current Questions in Eschatology." *Irish Theological Quarterly* 58 (1992) 209–43.
Johnson, Andy. "Holy, Holiness, NT." In *NIDB* 2: 846–50.
Johnson, Thomas. "A Wideness in God's Mercy: Universalism in the Bible." In *Universal Salvation? The Current Debate*, edited by Robin Parry and Christopher Partridge, 77–102. Grand Rapids: Eerdmans, 2003.
Judisch, Neal. "Sanctification, Satisfaction, and Purpose of Purgatory." *Faith and Philosophy* 26 (2009) 167–85.
Kagan, Shelly. *Death*. New Haven: Yale University Press, 2012.
Kant, Immanuel. *Critique of Pure Reason* (excerpts). In *Happiness: Classic and Contemporary Readings in Philosophy*, edited by Steven Cahn and Christine Vitrano, 113–14. Oxford: Oxford University Press, 2008.
Kastenbaum, Robert. "Anxiety and Fear." In *The Encyclopedia of Death and Dying*, edited by Robert Kastenbaum. Online: deathreference.com.
Kelly, Geffrey and Burton Nelson, eds. *A Testament to Freedom: The Essential Writings of Dietrich Bonhoeffer*. San Francisco: Harper, 1990.
Kelsey, Morton. *Healing and Christianity*. Minneapolis: Augsburg, 1995.
Kempis, Thomas. *The Imitation of Christ*. Garden City, NY: Image, 1955.
Kerr, Hugh, ed. *A Compend of Luther's Theology*. Philadelphia: Westminster, 1966.

Kershnar, Stephen. "Hell and Punishment." In *PH*: 115–32.
Kierkegaard, Søren. *The Sickness unto Death*. Princeton: Princeton University Press. 1983.
Kimel, Aidan. "*Apocatastasis*: The Heresy that Never Was." Online: afkimel.wordpress.com.
Knight, Gordon. "Molinism and Hell." In *PH*: 103–14.
———. "Universalism for Open Theists." *Religious Studies* 42 (2006) 213–23.
Kornfeld, W., and Helmer Ringgren. "Qds." In *TDOT* 12: 521–45.
Kreeft, Peter and Tacelli, Ronald. *Handbook of Christian Apologetics*. Downers Grove, IL: IVP, 1994.
Kronen, John, and Eric Reitan. *God's Final Victory: A Comparative Philosophical Case for Universalism*. New York: Continuum, 2011.
Kukota, Irina. "Christ, the Medicine of Life: The Syriac Fathers on the Lord's Descent into Hell." *Road to Emmaus* 6 (2005) 17–56.
Kuzmic, Peter. "History and Eschatology: Evangelical Views." In *In Word and Deed: Evangelism and Social Responsibility*, edited by Bruce Nichols, 135–64. Grand Rapids: Eerdmans, 1985.
Kvanvig, Jonathan. "Hell." In *OHE*: 413–26.
———. *The Problem of Hell*. New York: Oxford University Press, 1993.
La Due, William. *The Trinity Guide to Eschatology*. New York: Continuum, 2004.
Labberton, Mark. *The Dangerous Act of Worship*. Downers Grove, IL: IVP, 2007.
Lamont, John. "The Justice and Goodness of Hell." *Faith and Philosophy* 28 (2011) 152–73.
Lammott, Anne. *Grace (Eventually): Thoughts on Faith*. New York: Riverhead, 2007.
———. *Help, Thanks, Wow: The Three Essential Prayers*. New York: Riverhead, 2012.
Lane, Dermot. *Keeping Hope Alive*. Mahwah, NJ: Paulist, 1996.
Larchet, Jean-Claude. *Life After Death According to the Orthodox Tradition*. Rollinsford, NH: Orthodox Research Institute, 2012.
Lausanne Committee for World Evangelization. *Evangelism and Social Responsibility*. World Evangelical Fellowship, 1982.
Le Goff, Jacques. *The Birth of Purgatory*. Chicago: University of Chicago Press, 1984.
Lee, Frederick. *The Christian Doctrine of Prayer for the Departed*. London: Daldy, Isbister and Co., 1875.
Lewis, C.S. *The Great Divorce*. New York: Macmillan, 1946.
———. *A Grief Observed*. New York: Bantam, 1961.
———. *The Last Battle*. New York: Scholastic, 1956.
———. *Letters to Malcolm*. San Diego: Harcourt, 1963.
———. *Mere Christianity*. New York: Macmillan, 1952.
———. *Prince Caspian*. New York: Scholastic, 1951.
———. *The Problem of Pain*. London: Fontana, 1940.
———. *Reflections on the Psalms*. New York: Harcourt, Brace and World, 1958.
———. *The Screwtape Letters*. New York: Macmillan, 1961.
———. *The Voyage of the Dawn Treader*. New York: Scholastic, 1952.
———. *The World's Last Night*. New York: Harcourt, 1952.
Liddon, Henry. "Life of Edward Bouverie Pusey." Online: anglicanhistory.org.
Louth, Andrew. "Eastern Orthodox Eschatology." In *OHE*: 233–47.
———. *Introducing Eastern Orthodox Theology*. Downers Grove, IL: IVP, 2013.

Luebering, Carol. *To Comfort All Who Mourn: A Parish Handbook for Ministry to the Grieving*. Cincinnati: St. Anthony Messenger, 1980.
Lustig, Andrew. "End-of-Life Decisions: Does Faith Make a Difference?" *Commonweal*. May 23, 2003. Online: findarticles.com.
Luther, Martin. *Large Catechism*. Online: bookofconcord.org.
———. *Smalcald Articles*. Online: bookofconcord.org.
MacDonald, Gregory. *The Evangelical Universalist*. 1st ed. Eugene, OR: Cascade Books, 2006.
Macchia, Frank. "Pentecostal and Charismatic Theology." In *OHE*: 280–94.
Macquarrie, John. *Christian Hope*. New York: Seabury, 1978.
Malarkey, Kevin and Alex. *The Boy Who Came Back from Heaven*. Wheaton, IL: Tyndale House, 2010.
Manning, Brennan. *The Ragamuffin Gospel*. Sisters, OR: Multnomah Books, 1980.
Marshall, Christopher. *Beyond Retribution: A New Testament View of Justice, Crime and Punishment*. Grand Rapids: Eerdmans, 2001.
Marshall, Peter. *Belief and the Dead in Reformation England*. Oxford: Oxford University Press, 2002.
Marty, Martin. *Cry of Absence*. San Francisco: Harper, 1983.
Marx, Karl. *Early Writings*. New York: McGraw-Hill, 1964.
Mathewes-Green, Frederica. "I Didn't Mean to be Rude." *Christianity Today*, May 18, 1998.
Maurice, Frederick. "The Word 'Eternal' and the Punishment of the Wicked." Online: anglicanhistory.org.
Mavrodes, George. "Religion and the Queerness of Morality." In *Rationality, Religious Belief and Moral Commitment*, edited by Robert Audi and William Wainwright, 213–26. Ithaca, NY: Cornell University Press, 1986.
McDannell, Colleen, and Bernhard Lang. *Heaven: A History*. 2nd ed. New Haven: Yale University Press, 2001.
McGrath, Alister. *A Brief History of Heaven*. Oxford: Blackwell, 2003.
McLaren, Brian. *Finding Our Way Again: The Return of the Ancient Practices*. Nashville: Thomas Nelson, 2008.
———. *The Last Word and the Word after That*. San Francisco: Jossey-Bass, 2005.
McMahan, Jeff. "Radical Cognitive Limitation." In *Disability and Disadvantage*, edited by Kimberley Brownlee and Adam Cureton, 240–59. Oxford: Oxford University Press, 2009.
Mealy, J. Webb. *The End of the Unrepentant: A Study of the Biblical Themes of Fire and Being Consumed*. Eugene, OR: Wipf and Stock, 2012.
Merricks, Trenton. "The Resurrection of the Body." In *OHPT*: 476–90.
Meyendorff, John. *Byzantine Theology: Historical Trends and Doctrinal Themes*. New York: Fordham University Press, 1974.
Migliore, Daniel, ed. *The Lord's Prayer*. Grand Rapids: Eerdmans, 1993.
Milgrom, Jacob. "Holy, Holiness, OT." In *NIDB* 2: 850–58.
Miller, Lisa. *Heaven*. New York: Harper Collins, 2010.
Miller, Mary. *Devotions for Those Living with Loss*. Chicago: Covenant, 1991.
Moll, Rob. *The Art of Dying*. Downers Grove, IL: IVP, 2010.
Moltmann, Jürgen. *The Coming of God: Christian Eschatology*. Minneapolis: Fortress Press, 1996.
———. *Ethics of Hope*. Minneapolis: Fortress, 2012.

———. *In the End—In the Beginning*. London: SCM, 2004.
———. "Is There Life After Death?" In *The End of the World and the Ends of God*, edited by John Polkinghorne and Michael Welker, 238–55. Harrisburg: Trinity Press International, 2000.
———. *Sun of Righteousness Arise! God's Future for Humanity and the Earth*. London: SCM, 2010.
———. *Theology of Hope*. New York: Harper & Row, 1967.
Mouw, Richard. *Distorted Truth*. San Francisco: Harper and Row, 1989.
———. *Uncommon Decency*. Downers Grove, IL: IVP, 1992.
———. *When the Kings Come Marching In*. Grand Rapids: Eerdmans, 1983.
Mulholland, M. Robert. *Invitation to a Journey: A Roadmap for Spiritual Formation*. Downers Grove, IL: IVP, 1993.
Murray, Michael. "Heaven and Hell." In *Reason for the Hope Within*, edited by Michael Murray, 287–317. Grand Rapids: Eerdmans, 1999.
———. "Three Versions of Universalism." *Faith and Philosophy* 16 (1999) 55–68.
Nation, Mark, Anthony Siegrist, and Daniel Umbel. *Bonhoeffer the Assassin?* Grand Rapids: Baker, 2013.
Neuhaus, Richard. *Death on a Friday Afternoon*. New York: Basic, 2000.
Newman, John Henry. "Tract 72: Archbishop Ussher on Prayers for the Dead." Online: anglicanhistory.org.
Nichols, Terence. *Death and Afterlife: A Theological Introduction*. Grand Rapids: Brazos, 2010.
Nietzsche, Friedrich. *Thus Spake Zarathustra*. In *The Portable Nietzsche*, edited by Walter Kaufmann. New York: Viking, 1954.
Nussbaum, Martha. "Transitional Anger." *Journal of the American Philosophical Association* 1 (2015) 41–56.
O'Callaghan, Paul. *Christ Our Hope: An Introduction to Eschatology*. Washington, DC: Catholic University of America Press, 2011.
O'Keefe, Mark. *Becoming Good, Becoming Holy*. Mahwah, NJ: Paulist, 1995.
Ochs, Peter. "Morning Prayer as Redemptive Thinking." In *Liturgy, Time and the Politics of Redemption*, edited by Randi Rashkover and C. C. Pecknold, 50–87. Grand Rapids: Eerdmans, 2006.
Oden, Thomas. *Life in the Spirit*. Vol. 3, *Systematic Theology*. San Francisco: Harper San Francisco, 1992.
Oepke, Albrecht. "Parousia." In *TDNT* 5: 858–71.
Olson, Roger. "Is There a Protestant Purgatory?" Online: patheos.com.
Ombres, Robert. *Theology of Purgatory*. Dublin: Mercier, 1978.
Origen of Alexandria. *De Principiis*. In *ANF* 4: 238–382.
Pascal, Blaise. *Pensees*. New York: Harper & Row, 1962.
Pawl, Timothy, and Kevin Timpe. "Incompatiblism, Sin and Free Will in Heaven." *Faith and Philosophy* 26 (2009) 398–419.
Paxton, Frederick. "History of Christian Death Rites." In *The Encyclopedia of Death and Dying*, edited by Robert Kastenbaum. Online: deathreference.com.
Payne, David. "2 Peter." In *The International Bible Commentary*, edited by F. F. Bruce, 1564–70. Grand Rapids: Zondervan, 1979.
Peace, Richard. "Spiritual Formation." In *The Complete Book of Everyday Christianity*, edited by Robert Banks and R. Paul Stevens, 938–43. Downers Grove, IL: IVP, 1997.

Perry, John. *A Dialogue on Personal Identity and Immortality*. Indianapolis: Hackett, 1978.
Peterson, Michael. "Eschatology and Theodicy." In *OHE*: 518–33.
Phan, Peter. "Roman Catholic Theology." In *OHE*: 215–32.
Phelps, Andrea, et al. "Religious Coping and Use of Intensive Life-Prolonging Care Near Death in Patients with Advanced Cancer." *Journal of American Medical Association* 301 (2009) 1140–47.
Pieper, Josef. *On Hope*. San Francisco: Ignatius, 1986.
Piguet, Leo, ed. *100 Prayers for Celebrating the Liturgical Seasons*. Notre Dame, IN: Ave Maria, 1982.
Pinnock, Clark. "Annihilationism." In *OHE*: 462–75.
———. "The Conditional View." In *Four Views of Hell*, edited by William Crockett, 135–66. Grand Rapids: Zondervan, 1992.
———. "The Destruction of the Finally Impenitent." *Criswell Theological Review* 4 (1990) 243–59.
———. "Response to Zachary Hayes." In *Four Views of Hell*, edited by William Crockett, 127–31. Grand Rapids: Zondervan, 1992.
———. *A Wideness in God's Mercy*. Grand Rapids: Zondervan, 1992.
Pinnock, Clark, and Robert Brow. *Unbounded Love*. Downers Grove, IL: IVP, 1994.
Piper, Don. *Ninety Minutes in Heaven*. Grand Rapids: Baker/Revell, 2004.
Plantinga, Alvin. *God, Freedom and Evil*. Grand Rapids: Eerdmans, 1974.
———. *The Nature of Necessity*. Oxford: Clarendon, 1974.
Plato. *Protagoras*. In *The Dialogues of Plato*, edited by Benjamin Jowett. Vol. 1. Oxford: Clarendon, 1964.
———. *Republic*. Indianapolis: Hackett, 1992.
Polkinghorne, John. "Eschatology: Some Questions and Some Insights from Science." In *The End of the World and the Ends of God*, edited by John Polkinghorne and Michael Welker, 29–41. Harrisburg, PA: Trinity, 2000.
———. *The Faith of a Physicist*. Princeton: Princeton University Press, 1994.
———. *The God of Hope and the End of the World*. New Haven: Yale, 2002.
Polkinghorne, John, and Michael Welker. "Introduction." In *The End of the World and the Ends of God*, edited by John Polkinghorne and Michael Welker, 1–16. Harrisburg, PA: Trinity, 2000.
Pope Benedict XVI. Encyclical Letter *Spe Salvi*. 2007. Online: vatican.va.
———. *The Fathers of the Church*. Grand Rapids: Eerdmans, 2009.
Pope Francis. *The Name of God is Mercy*. New York: Random House, 2016.
Potts, Michael. "Aquinas, Hell and the Resurrection of the Damned." *Faith and Philosophy* 15 (1998) 341–51.
Powys, David. *Hell: A Hard Look at a Hard Question*. Paternoster Biblical Monographs. Carlisle, UK: Paternoster, 1997.
———. "The Nineteenth and Twentieth Century Debates about Hell and Universalism." In *Universalism and the Doctrine of Hell*, edited by Nigel Cameron, 93–138. Carlisle, UK: Paternoster, 1992.
Prior, Kenneth. *The Way of Holiness: A Study in Christian Growth*. Downers Grove, IL: IVP, 1982.
Procksch, Otto, and Karl Kuhn. "Hagios." In *TDNT* 1: 88–110.
Punt, Neal. *So Also in Christ: Reviewing the Plan of Salvation*. Allendale, MI: Northland, 2002.

Purtill, Richard. *J. R. R. Tolkien: Myth, Morality and Religion*. San Francisco: Harper and Row, 1984.
Ragland, C. P. "Love and Damnation." In *Metaphysics and God: Essays in Honor of Eleonore Stump*, edited by Kevin Timpe, 206–24. New York: Routledge, 2009.
Rahner, Karl. *Foundations of Christian Faith*. New York: Crossroad, 1982.
———. *Theological Investigations*. Vol. 6. London: Darton, Longman and Todd, 1966.
———. *Theological Investigations*. Vol. 17. London: Darton, Longman and Todd, 1981.
———. *Theological Investigations*. Vol. 19. London: Darton, Longman and Todd, 1983.
Ramelli, Ilaria. *The Christian Doctrine of Apokatastasis*. Leiden: Brill, 2013.
Ramelli, Ilaria, and David Konstan. *Terms for Eternity*. Piscataway, NJ: Gorgias, 2007.
Ratzinger, Joseph. *Eschatology: Death and Eternal Life*. Washington, DC: Catholic University of America Press, 1988.
Reddish, Mitchell. "Heaven." In *ABD* 3: 90–91.
Roberts, Arthur. *Exploring Heaven*. San Francisco: Harper, 2003.
Roberts, Robert. "Willpower and the Virtues." In *The Virtues: Contemporary Essays on Moral Character*, edited by Robert Kruschwitz and Robert Roberts, 121–36. Belmont, CA: Wadsworth, 1987.
Robinson, John A. T. *In the End God*. 2nd ed. New York: Harper and Row, 1968.
Roman Catholic Church. *Catechism of the Catholic Church*. Ligouri, MO: Ligouri, 1994.
Rowell, Geoffrey. *Hell and the Victorians*. Oxford: Clarendon, 1974.
———. *The Liturgy of Christian Burial: An Introductory Survey of the Historical Development of Christian Burial Rites*. London: SPCK, 1977.
Rowland, Christopher. "The Eschatology of the New Testament Church." In *OHE*: 56–72.
———. "Parousia." In *ABD* 5: 166–70.
———. "Parousia." In *NIDB* 4: 384–85.
Russell, Bertrand. *Why I Am Not a Christian and Other Essays on Religion and Related Subjects*. New York: Simon and Schuster, 1957.
Russell, Jeffrey Burton. *A History of Heaven: The Singing Silence*. Princeton: Princeton University Press, 1997.
———. *Paradise Mislaid: How We Lost Heaven and How We Can Regain It*. Oxford: Oxford University Press, 2006.
Sachs, John. "Current Eschatology: Universal Salvation and the Problem of Hell." *Theological Studies* 52 (1991) 227–54.
Saliers, Don. "Liturgy and Ethics: Some New Beginnings." *Journal of Religious Ethics* 7 (1979) 173–89.
Sanders, John. *No Other Name: An Investigation into the Destiny of the Unevangelized*. Grand Rapids: Eerdmans, 1992.
Sasse, Hermann. "Aion, Aionios." In *TDNT* 1: 197–209.
Saward, John. *Sweet and Blessed Country: The Christian Hope for Heaven*. Oxford: Oxford University Press, 2005.
Scazzero, Peter. *Emotionally-Healthy Spirituality*. Nashville: Integrity, 2006.
Schneider, Johannes. "Kolazo, Kolasis." In *TDNT* 3: 814–17.
Schulz, Charles. *Peanuts 2000*. New York: Ballantine, 2000.
Second Helvetic Confession. Online: ccel.org.
Second Vatican Council. *Lumen Gentium*. Online: cin.org.
Sells, Michael. *Approaching the Qur'an*. Ashland, OR: White Cloud, 1999.
Seneca the Younger. *On the Shortness of Life*. London: Penguin, 2005.

Seraphim Rose. *The Soul After Death*. Platina, CA: Saint Herman of Alaska Brotherhood, 1993.
Seymour, Charles. *A Theodicy of Hell*. Dordrect: Kluwer, 2000.
Sheppy, Paul. *In Sure and Certain Hope: Liturgies, Prayers and Readings for Funerals and Memorials*. Nashville: Abingdon, 2003.
Sherman, Nancy. "The Habituation of Character." In *Aristotle's Ethics: Critical Essays*, edited by Nancy Sherman, 231–60. Lanham, MD: Rowman and Littlefield, 1999.
Sickler, Bradley. "Infernal Voluntarism and 'The Courtesy of Deep Heaven.'" In *PH*: 163–78.
Sider, Ronald. *Rich Christians in an Age of Hunger*. Downers Grove, IL: IVP, 1977.
———. *The Scandal of the Evangelical Conscience*. Grand Rapids: Baker, 2004.
Sider, Ronald, and James Parker. "How Broad is Salvation in Scripture?" In *In Word and Deed: Evangelism and Social Responsibility*, edited by Bruce Nichols, 85–108. Grand Rapids: Eerdmans, 1985.
Sider, Theodore. "Hell and Vagueness." *Faith and Philosophy* 19 (2002) 58–68.
Singer, Peter. *The Life You Can Save*. New York: Random House, 2010.
Smith, Harmon. *Where Two or Three Are Gathered: Liturgy and the Moral Life*. Cleveland, OH: Pilgrim, 1995.
Smith, James. *Desiring the Kingdom: Worship, Worldview and Cultural Formation*. Grand Rapids: Baker Academic, 2009.
———. *Imagining the Kingdom: How Worship Works*. Grand Rapids: Baker Academic, 2013.
Snow, Nancy, ed. *Cultivating Virtue: Perspectives from Philosophy, Theology and Psychology*. Oxford: Oxford University Press, 2014.
Stassen, Glen, and David Gushee. *Kingdom Ethics*. Downers Grove, IL: IVP, 2003.
Stauffer, Ethelbert. "Agape." In *TDNT* 1: 21–55.
Stevens, R. Paul. "Spiritual Disciplines." In *The Complete Book of Everyday Christianity*, edited by Robert Banks and R. Paul Stevens, 932–38. Downers Grove, IL: IVP, 1997.
———. "Spiritual Growth." In *The Complete Book of Everyday Christianity*, edited by Robert Banks and R. Paul Stevens, 949–53. Downers Grove, IL: IVP, 1997.
Stump, Eleonore. "Dante's Hell, Aquinas' Moral Theory and the Love of God." *Canadian Journal of Philosophy* 16 (1986) 181–98.
Swete, H. B. "Prayer for the Departed in the First Four Centuries." *The Journal of Theological Studies* 18 (1907) 500–514.
Swinburne, Richard. *The Evolution of the Soul*. Oxford: Clarendon, 1986.
———. *Providence and the Problem of Evil*. Oxford: Clarendon, 1998.
———. "A Theodicy of Heaven and Hell." In *The Existence and Nature of God*, edited by Alfred Freddoso, 37–54. Notre Dame, IN: University of Notre Dame Press, 1983.
Talbott, Thomas. "Christ Victorious." In *Universal Salvation? The Current Debate*, edited by Robin Parry and Christopher Partridge, 15–31. Grand Rapids: Eerdmans, 2003.
———. "The Doctrine of Everlasting Punishment." *Faith and Philosophy* 7 (1990) 19–43.
———. "Heaven and Hell in Christian Thought." *Stanford Encyclopedia of Philosophy*. Online: plato.stanford.edu
———. *The Inescapable Love of God*. 1st ed. Boca Raton, FL: Universal, 1999.
———. "No Hell." In *CD*: 278–87, 288–89.

———. "A Pauline Interpretation of Divine Judgment." In *Universal Salvation? The Current Debate*, edited by Robin Parry and Christopher Partridge, 32–52. Grand Rapids: Eerdmans, 2003.

———. "Providence, Freedom and Human Destiny." *Religious Studies* 26 (1990) 227–45.

———. "Three Pictures of God in Western Theology." *Faith and Philosophy* 12 (1995) 79–94.

———. "Universalism and the Greater Good: Reply to Gordon Knight." *Faith and Philosophy* 16 (1999) 102–5.

———. "Universalism." In *OHE*: 446–61.

Taliaferro, Charles. *Contemporary Philosophy of Religion*. Oxford: Blackwell, 1998.

———. "Prayer." In *RCPR*: 677–85.

Tasker, R. V. G. *The Gospel according to St. Matthew*. Grand Rapids: Eerdmans, 1961.

———. "Wrath." In *The New Bible Dictionary*, edited by J. D. Douglas, 1341. Grand Rapids: Eerdmans, 1962.

Taylor, Aileen. *Dietrich Bonhoeffer*. Springfield, IL: Templegate, 1992.

Taylor, Barbara Brown. *Gospel Medicine*. Lanham, MD: Cowley/Rowman & Littlefield, 1995.

Temple, William. *Christian Faith and Life*. London: SCM, 1963.

Thiselton, Anthony. "Can Hermeneutics Ease the Deadlock?" In *The Way Forward? Christian Voices on Homosexuality and the Church* 2nd ed, edited by Timothy Bradshaw, 145–96. Grand Rapids: Eerdmans, 2004.

———. *Life After Death*. Grand Rapids: Eerdmans, 2012.

Thomas, Owen. *Introduction to Theology*. Cambridge: Greeno, Hadden and Co., 1973.

Tiessen, Terrance. *Providence and Prayer: How Does God Work in the World?* Downers Grove, IL: IVP, 2000.

Tolkien, J.R.R. *The Two Towers*. Boston: Houghton-Mifflin, 1954.

Tolstoy, Leo. *The Death of Ivan Ilyich*. New York: Bantam, 1981.

Traub, Helmut. "Ouranos." In *TDNT* 5: 497–543.

Travis, Stephen. *Christ and the Judgment of God*. 2nd ed. Milton Keynes: Paternoster, 2008.

———. "Wrath of God, NT." In *ABD* 6: 996–98.

Trumbower, Jeffrey. *Rescue for the Dead: The Posthumous Salvation of Non-Christians in Early Christianity*. Oxford: Oxford University Press, 2001.

Tutu, Desmond. *An African Prayer Book*. New York: Doubleday, 1995.

U.S. Lutheran-Catholic Dialogue. *The Hope of Eternal Life*. Edited by Lowell Almen and Richard Sklba. Minneapolis: Lutheran University Press, 2011.

United Methodist Church. *A Service of Death and Resurrection: The Ministry of the Church at Death*. Supplemental Worship Resources 7. Nashville: Abingdon, 1979.

VanArragon, Raymond. "Is It Possible to Freely Reject God Forever?" In *PH*: 29–44.

Van Tholen, James. *Where All Hope Lies*. Grand Rapids: Eerdmans, 2003.

Vander Laan, David. "The Sanctification Argument for Purgatory." *Faith and Philosophy* 24 (2007) 331–39.

Vander Zee, Leonard. *In Life and In Death: A Pastoral Guide for Funerals*. Grand Rapids: CRC, 1992.

Vassiliadis, Nikolaos. *The Mystery of Death*. Athens: Orthodox Brotherhood of Theologians, 1997.

Vaux, Kenneth. *Death Ethics*. Philadelphia: Trinity, 1992.

Verhey, Allen. *The Christian Art of Dying*. Grand Rapids: Eerdmans. 2011.
Wainwright, Geoffrey. "The Saints and the Departed: Confessional Controversy and Ecumenical Convergence." *Studia Liturgia* 34 (2004) 65–91.
Walker, Daniel. *The Decline of Hell: Seventeenth-Century Discussions of Eternal Torment*. Chicago: University of Chicago Press, 1964.
Wallis, Gerhard. "Ahabh." In *TDOT* 1: 99–118.
Walls, Jerry L. "Eternal Hell and the Christian Concept of God." In *CD*: 268–78, 287–88.
———. *Heaven: The Logic of Eternal Joy*. Oxford: Oxford University Press, 2002.
———. "Heaven." In *OHE*: 399–412.
———. "Heaven and Hell. In *RCPR*: 645–54.
———. "Heaven and Hell." In *OHPT*: 491–511.
———. *Heaven, Hell and Purgatory*. Grand Rapids: Brazos, 2015.
———. *Hell: The Logic of Damnation*. Notre Dame: University of Notre Dame Press, 1992.
———. "Is Molinism as Bad as Calvinism?" *Faith and Philosophy* 7 (1990) 85–98.
———. *Purgatory: The Logic of Total Transformation*. Oxford: Oxford University Press, 2012.
———. "Purgatory for Everyone." *First Things* (April 2002). Online: firstthings.com.
Walters, G. "Salvation." In *The New Bible Dictionary*, edited by J. D. Douglas, 1126–30. Grand Rapids: Eerdmans, 1962.
Ware, Timothy. "'One Body in Christ:' Death and the Communion of Saints." *Sobornost* 3 (1981) 179–91.
Washburn, Phil. *Philosophical Dilemmas*. 3rd ed. Oxford: Oxford University Press, 2008.
Webb, Stephen. *Good Eating*. Grand Rapids: Brazos, 2001.
Wenham, John. "The Case for Conditionalism." In *Universalism and the Doctrine of Hell*, edited by Nigel Cameron, 161–90. Carlisle, UK: Paternoster, 1992.
Westminster Confession of Faith. Atlanta: Presbyterian Church in America, 1986.
Willard, Dallas. *The Divine Conspiracy*. San Francisco: Harper San Francisco, 1998.
———. *Renovation of the Heart*. Colorado Springs: NavPress, 2002.
———. *The Spirit of the Disciplines*. New York: Harper Collins, 1988.
Williams, Bernard. "The Makroupolos Case: Reflections on the Tedium of Immortality." In *The Metaphysics of Death*, edited by John Martin Fischer, 71–92. Stanford: Stanford University Press, 1993.
Williams, Rowan. *The Lion's World: A Journey into the Heart of Narnia*. Oxford: Oxford University Press, 2012.
Willimon, William. *Who Will Be Saved?* Nashville: Abingdon, 2008.
Willimon William, and Stanley Hauerwas. *Lord, Teach Us: The Lord's Prayer and the Christian Life*. Nashville: Abingdon, 1996.
Wills, Gary. *What the Gospels Meant*. New York: Viking Penguin, 2008.
Wink, Walter. *Engaging the Powers*. Minneapolis: Fortress, 1992.
Winter, David. *Living through Loss: God's Help in Bereavement*. Wheaton, IL: Shaw, 1986.
Wolterstorff, Nicholas. *Lament for a Son*. Grand Rapids: Eerdmans, 1987.
Wright, J. Edward. "Heaven." In *NIDB* 2: 766–67.
Wright, N. T. *After You Believe: Why Christian Character Matters*. New York: Harper One, 2010.
———. *Evil and the Justice of God*. Downers Grove, IL: IVP, 2006.

———. *Following Jesus*. Grand Rapids: Eerdmans, 1995.
———. *For All the Saints: Remembering the Christian Departed*. New York: Morehouse, 2003.
———. *How God Became King*. New York: Harper One, 2012.
———. *The Last Word*. New York: HarperCollins, 2005.
———. *The Lord and His Prayer*. Grand Rapids: Eerdmans, 1996.
———. *The Resurrection of the Son of God*. London: SPCK, 2003.
———. *Simply Jesus*. New York: Harper One, 2011.
———. *Surprised by Hope: Rethinking Heaven, the Resurrection and the Mission of the Church*. New York: Harper Collins, 2008.
Yancey, Philip. *Prayer: Does It Make Any Difference?* Grand Rapids: Zondervan, 2006.
Yang, Seung. "Hope." In *NIDB* 2: 885–89.
Yong, Amos. *The Bible, Disability and the Church*. Grand Rapids: Eerdmans, 2011.
———. *Theology and Down Syndrome*. Waco, TX: Baylor University Press, 2007.
Zagzebski, Linda. "Heaven." In *Routledge Encyclopedia of Philosophy*, edited by Edward Craig. London: Routledge, 1998. Online: routledge.com.
Zimmerman, Dean. "Christians Should Affirm Mind-Body Dualism." In *CD*: 315–27, 338–41.
Zobel, Hans-Jurgen. "Hesed." In *TDOT* 5: 44–64.

Names Index

Acts of Paul and Thecla, 113n23
Adams, Marilyn, 98n80, 119n44, 136–37, 146, 153n162, 186–87, 256
Addison, Joseph, 57
Alcorn, Randy, 24n9, 25, 29, 38–39, 40n68, 71
Alexander, Eben, 31n35
Alfeyev, Hilarion, 2, 107, 117, 131n79, 156, 157n185
Alger, William, 254
Alhonsaari, Antti, 169
Allison, Dale, 31n38, 42n75
Ambrose of Milan, 156
Amirault, Gary, 221
Anderson, Norman, 179–80
Angela of Foligno, 56
Anselm of Canterbury, 2, 103, 238n17
Apostles' Creed, 26, 116n33
Aquinas, Thomas, 27n18, 29–30, 41–42, 52–54, 56n27, 60–61, 63n67, 83, 86n42 87n45, 96, 108, 118, 262
Archbishop's Commission, 45, 60–61, 154, 235n12, 242n30
Arnold, Bill, 32n39
Aristotle, 36, 53, 95, 137, 162n13, 166n29, 207–9, 250–51
Athanasian Creed, 112n21, 116n33
Atwell, Robert, 77n12, 78n13
Augsburg Confession, 27, 112n21
Augustine of Hippo, 29–30, 53, 62–63, 66, 76n9, 77, 96n72, 97, 114, 116n32, 137, 162–63, 204, 260

Baggini, Julian, 6–7, 98n80, 170
Baker, Sharon, 211, 226, 249, 256
Balentine, Samuel, 182
Balthasar, Hans Urs von, 100, 116n30, 145n135, 148n144, 156n175, 241n23
Barclay, William, 130, 150–51
Bardaisan, 114n25
Barnard, Justin, 82, 85n40, 90n54, 98n80
Barnhouse, Donald Gray, 179n83
Barron, Robert, 43n81, 44, 129n75, 158n1, 273n89
Bartelmus, G., 26n16
Barth, Karl, 30, 116n30, 155–56, 193
Bauckham, Richard, 29, 116
Baumeister, Roy, 93n62, 208
Baxter, Richard, 30n33, 40n66, 63n66
Bell, Rob, 124, 128, 147, 151, 184, 191n22, 218, 227
Benzoni, Francisco, 163n15
Berent, Irwin, 221
Berkhof, Hendrikus, 51, 59
Bernard of Clairvaux, 27n18, 55–56, 203–204
Bierma, Nathan, 197n50
Biffi, Giacomo, 262
Bloesch, Donald, 40n68, 76n8, 81, 89n51, 91n58, 124–25, 154
Bolz-Weber, Nadia, 212
Bonaventure, 30
Bonda, Jan, 110n13, 132, 149n146

297

Bonhoeffer, Dietrich, 20n1, 165–66, 175, 177, 190–91, 195, 199, 203n70, 205, 212, 214, 250, 252–53
Borg, Marcus, 31, 33n42, 65, 100n85, 194n37, 249n6
Boros, Ladislaus, 91n59, 134, 141n118, 141n119
Bosch, Hieronymus, 106
Boudreaux, Florentin, 55, 60n51, 62–63
Brett, Alan, 176n70
Brow, Robert, 106, 258
Brown, Christopher, 60, 96n70
Brown, David, 51–52,, 94n66, 96
Brown, Peter, 24n9, 76n9, 165n20
Brueggemann, Walter, 105n2, 164–65, 169, 194
Brunner, Emil, 36n53, 116n30
Buckareff, Andrei, 107n5, 119, 150n150, 251n13, 261
Buechner, Frederick, 234n10
Bullard, Roger, 33n44
Bultmann, Rudolph, 34
Burpo, Todd, 31n35
Bush, George W., 245

Cain, James, 135
Callahan, Sidney, 64, 101, 156, 178, 217n117, 231–32
Calvin, John, 30, 40, 53, 56–57, 84, 91
Casey, John, 28n26, 53n18, 54, 56, 71, 109n12, 255
Cassian, John, 123, 144n130, 146n135, 204n74
Catechism of Catholic Church, 25, 27, 54, 85n39, 113n21, 117n36, 134n88
Catherine of Genoa, 78–79
Catherine of Sienna, 273n89
Chambers, Arthur, 99
Charlesworth, James, 26n16
Chesterton, G. K., 138
Christensen, Michael, 55n23, 76n7
Christian Reformed Church, 42–43, 155, 253
Chrysostom, John, 116, 117n33, 218–219, 260, 262
Church of England, 22, 46

Ciurria, Michelle, 139n112
Clement of Alexandria, 76n7, 125, 130, 138, 258–60
Clephane, Elizabeth, 105n2
Cockburn, Bruce, 46, 176
Colquhoun, Frank, 241n25
Connelly, Douglas, 63n68
Cooper, John, 82n25
Cosden, Darrell, 54n19, 197n50
Council of Florence, 78, 83
Council of Trent, 78
Cox, Samuel, 254
Craddock, Fred, 176n67, 176n68, 185
Craig, William Lane, 115n29, 135n95, 263–69
Crossan, John Dominic, 33n42, 194n37
Crump, David, 207
Cullmann, Oscar, 34–35
Currie, David, 35n52, 82n25, 88–89, 94n65
Cyril of Alexandria, 116n33
Cyril of Jerusalem, 116n33, 219n121, 230

Dalai Lama, 167n32,
Daley, Brian, 55n23, 56n24, 77n12, 119, 262
Dante Alighieri, 56, 79, 106n4, 126n66, 155
Date, Christopher, 116n30
Davis, Stephen, 129, 135n94, 143, 147
Diodore of Tarsus, 114n25
Dixon, Larry, 222n133
Dodd, C. H., 34
Donne, John, 177
Dorr, Donal, 197
Duclow, Donald, 172n55, 176n67
Dunham, Maxie, 201, 203

Eastern Orthodox Church, 79, 85, 107, 116–17, 155
Edwards, David, 116n30
Edwards, Jonathan, 30, 57–58, 70, 92n60, 219–20
Elliot, Jim, 189
Eno, Robert, 76n8
Ephrem the Syrian, 114n25, 117n33

NAMES INDEX

Episcopal Church, 2, 22, 27–28, 43n80, 46, 48, 50–51, 81, 154n169, 169–70, 174, 177n71, 178n75, 179–80, 190, 208n90, 208n91, 231n3, 233, 234n9, 235n11, 238n19, 240n21, 241n24, 243n34, 251
Erasmus of Rotterdam, 237n15
Eriugena, John, 114n25
Eusebius of Caesarea, 114n25
Evagrius of Pontus, 114n25
Evans, Rachel Held, 168n35, 211n98, 216
Evans, Rod, 221

Fackre, Dorothy and Gabriel, 17–18, 24, 73n1
Fairbairn, Donald, 197, 199, 204
Fairlie, Henry, 200
Farrar, Frederick, 254
Fensham, Frank, 130n77, 130n78
Ferguson, Everett, 61
Fifth Ecumenical Council, 114
Fischer, John Martin, 61
Flint, Thomas, 159, 263n60
Florovsky, George, 117n37
Ford, David, 88n48
Forest, Jim, 180n87
Formula of Concord, 91n55
Fourth Lateran Council, 112n21
Fra Angelica, 30
France, R. T., 110
Francis of Assisi, 98
Frankfurt, Harry, 251
Friesen, Todd, 227
Fudge, Edward, 116n30
Fulghum, Robert, 73

Gandhi, Mahatma, 255, 267
Geach, Peter, 136n97
Giles of Rome, 30
Gilligan, Carol, 105n1
Goldsmith, Dale, 176n67, 176n68, 185
Goldsmith, Joy, 176n67, 176n68, 185
Graham, Billy, 218n118
Green, Melody, 159n3
Gregory of Nazianzus, 114n25, 258

Gregory of Nyssa, 52, 57–62, 69, 93–94, 97, 114, 140n115, 144n130, 152n160, 260
Gregory the Great, 59, 77–78, 97
Grenz, Stanley, 193
Griffiths, Paul, 25n15, 74
Groleman, Daniel, 167n32
Gulley, Philip, 123n57, 147, 151, 211, 213, 215, 216n116, 222
Guroian, Vigen, 169n40
Gushee, David, 86n43

Habermas, Gary, 13n8, 36n55, 132n84, 140, 142, 152n161, 173, 185n5, 261, 265n63, 266, 268n71
Hadot, Pierre, 166
Hall, Douglas John, 182, 196n46
Handel, George Frideric, 33
Hardy, Edward, 82
Hasker, William, 186n8, 187
Hauerwas, Stanley, 169n40, 179
Havener, Timothy, 221n128
Hawkins, Peter, 28n26, 61, 79n17, 97, 102
Hayes, Zachary, 80, 81n20
Heatherton, Todd, 93n62, 208
Hebblethwaite, Brian, 28n26
Heidegger, Martin, 172
Heidelberg Catechism, 27, 91n56, 159
Herion, Gary, 257
Hershenov, David, 68n85, 98n80
Hick, John, 70, 76n6, 85n40, 99n82, 116n30, 134n90, 141n117, 144n130, 148n144, 152, 187, 215, 270
Hiers, Richard, 31n38
Hildegard of Bingen, 56
Hitler, Adolf, 98, 256
Hodge, Alexander, 62–63
Hodge, Charles, 91
Hoekema, Anthony, 35n51, 38n59, 40n68, 42, 70
Homer, 28
Homily on Prayer, 91n56, 112n21
Hooker, Richard, 157n184
Hotz, Kendra, 37, 203n71
Hugo, Victor, 175

Ignatius of Loyola, 203
International Theological Commission, 54, 76–77, 107, 140, 190
Irenaeus of Lyons, 29, 55, 113–14
Isaac the Syrian, 131n79, 260

Jennens, Charles, 33
Jersild, Paul, 176n70
Johnson, Andy, 249
Johnson, Thomas, 149n146
Jordan, Clarence, 126
Judisch, Neal, 82n26, 86n42
Julian of Norwich, 45–46, 151, 229
Justinian I, 114, 140n115

Kagan, Shelly, 98n80
Kant, Immanuel, 86n42, 188n15, 268
Kantzer, Kenneth, 155n173, 222n133
Kastenbaum, Robert, 176n70
Kelsey, Morton, 66n78
Kempis, Thomas, 172–73
Kershnar, Stephen, 265
Kierkegaard, Soren, 182
Kimel, Aidan, 115n26
Knight, Gordon, 255, 267–69
Konstan, David, 111n16
Kornfeld, W., 248n4
Kreeft, Peter, 89n50, 115n29, 118n39, 129, 151n156, 225
Kronen, John, 2n2, 60, 93n61, 115n29, 133n86, 138n103, 138n106, 146n136, 150n150, 210, 212, 216, 225, 227n149, 256, 266, 270, 272
Kuhn, Karl, 249n6
Kukota, Irina, 117n34, 211n95
Kuyper, Abraham, 45n84
Kuzmic, Peter, 192–93
Kvanvig, Jonathan, 106, 153n164

LaDue, William, 91n59, 117n37, 134n90
Labberton, Mark, 189n17, 197n49, 201, 209–210
Lamont, John, 124n58, 135, 146, 262–63
Lamott, Anne, 101

Lane, Dermot, 27n19, 32n41, 34, 53n17, 62, 85n39, 145n132, 193n35, 207
Lang, Bernhard, 27n19, 28–29, 54n20, 56, 255n26
Larchet, Jean-Claude , 117n37
Lausanne Committee, 192–93
Lee, Frederick, 39, 177, 230–31
Lewis, C. S., 21–22, 38n58, 57, 62, 81–82, 85n40, 86–87, 96–97, 101, 102n89, 106n4, 126n66, 128n70, 133, 136n98, 137n100, 138n104, 141n117, 144n131, 145n132, 147n139, 150n150, 164n19, 167n33, 174, 175n65, 177, 178n76, 185, 197, 202n68, 206, 256–57, 271
Louth, Andrew, 40, 85n41, 117n37, 157n185,
Lucian of Samosata, 172
Luebering, Carol, 178
Lustig, Andrew, 176n70
Luther, Martin, 30, 83–84, 90–91, 124

MacDonald, Gregory, 116n30, 118, 126n64, 132n81, 138, 149n146, 149n147, 186n8, 215–16, 225, 248n2, 261, 266–69, 272
Macchia, Frank, 184, 194
Macquarrie, John, 124n58, 188n13
Macrina the Younger, 114n25
Malarkey, Kevin and Alex, 31n35
Manning, Brennan, 88, 153n161, 210n94, 212
Mark of Ephesus, 83
Marshall, Christopher, 128n68, 259
Marshall, Peter, 23
Marty, Martin, 227–28
Marx, Karl, 191, 197
Matthews, Matthew, 37, 203n71
Matthewes-Green, Frederica, 175, 223
Maurice, Frederick, 124, 254
Mavrodes, George, 188n15
Maximus the Confessor, 3, 114n25
McDannell, Colleen, 27n19, 28–29, 54n20, 56, 255n26
McGrath, Alister, 28n26
McLaren, Brian, 89n51, 199, 201–2, 204, 220–21, 222n131

NAMES INDEX

McMahan, Jeff, 69n86
Mealy, J. Webb, 116n30
Merricks, Trenton, 247
Merton, Thomas, 201
Methodius, 114n25
Meyendorff, John, 52, 83n31
Milgrom, Jacob, 248–49
Miller, Lisa, 51
Miller, Mary, 180
Molina, Luis, 263–65
Moll, Rob, 172, 176n67, 181n89
Moltmann, Jürgen, 25, 31, 34n47, 42, 62n60, 69–70, 85n40, 116n30, 131, 139, 169, 173, 187–88, 192, 195–96, 198, 206, 210–11, 213, 225, 259
Moreland, J. P., 13n8, 36n55, 132n84, 140, 142, 152n161, 173, 185n5, 261, 265n63, 266, 268n71
Mouw, Richard, 64n71, 164–165
Mulholland, James, 123n57, 147, 151, 211, 213, 215, 216n116, 222
Mulholland, M. Robert, 88n48
Murray, Michael, 135n92, 137n99, 143, 146n136

Neuhaus, Richard, 109n11, 149n148
Newman, John Henry, 254
Nicene Creed, 26, 159n3
Nichols, Terence, 51n8, 80n19, 80n20, 84, 101n88
Nicole, Pierre, 30
Niebuhr, H. Richard, 73n1
Nietzsche, Friedrich, 191n23
Nussbaum, Martha, 130n76

O'Callaghan, Paul, 45, 46n94, 63n65, 65, 71, 76n7, 102, 134n88, 134n90, 141, 156
O'Keefe, Mark, 169n40
Ochs, Peter, 170n47
Oden, Thomas, 39
Oepke, Albrecht, 35n50
Olson, Roger, 85n40
Ombres, Robert, 85n39, 87–88, 103n94
Origen of Alexandria, 29, 56, 76, 111n18, 114, 116n33, 132n84, 140n115, 144n130, 148n143, 152n160, 153n162, 257–58, 260

Pamphilus of Caesarea, 114n25
Pannenberg, Wolfhart, 207n84
Parker, James, 226n147
Pascal, Blaise, 171, 174
Passion of Perpetua, 113n23
Pawl, Timothy, 96n70
Paxton, Frederick, 176n67
Payne, David, 46n94
Peace, Richard, 199n58
Pelagius of Rome, 77n9
Perry, John, 10
Peterson, Eugene, 3–4
Peterson, Michael, 186n8
Phan, Peter, 40n69
Phelps, Elizabeth, 30
Philo of Alexandria, 28, 55
Pieper, Josef, 45, 71, 102, 156
Piguet, Leo, 233n8, 236n13, 244n35
Pinnock, Clark, 85n40, 106, 116n30, 149–50, 227n150, 258
Piper, Don, 31n35
Plantinga, Alvin, 265n63
Plato, 28, 36, 37n57, 54–55, 60, 113, 137, 152n160, 153n162, 188n15, 250
Plotinus of Rome, 29n28, 55
Plug, Allen, 107n5, 119, 150n150, 251n13, 261
Plumptre, Edward, 254
Polkinghorne, John, 1, 39n63, 50, 60, 64, 85n40, 188, 194n39, 224
Pope Benedict XII, 26–27, 53n17
Pope Benedict XVI, 7, 56n26, 58n33, 59n40, 77n10, 89, 100n85, 119n45, 160, 165, 170n43, 174, 198n54, 229
Pope Francis, 89n49, 121–22, 126n66, 129, 139n112, 151, 153n163, 213, 215, 223–24, 272–77
Pope Innocent IV, 78
Pope John XXII, 27n18
Pope John XXIII, 223, 275
Pope John Paul II, 101, 275
Potts, Michael, 262n58
Powys, David, 113, 253, 255
Prior, Kenneth, 200, 205

Procksch, Otto, 249n6
Pseudo-Dionysius, 114n25, 131n79
Pseudo-Justin, 66
Punt, Neal, 136n96
Purtill, Richard, 177
Pusey, Edward, 81, 143n126, 154, 219, 254

Ragland, C. P., 143, 145, 151, 272
Rahner, Karl, 59, 84–85, 91n59, 116n30, 123, 140, 141n119, 144n130, 145n132, 156n175
Ramelli, Ilaria, 110–11, 113n23, 114n24, 114n25, 114n26, 116n32, 128n69, 131n79, 137n101, 140n114, 140n115, 144n130, 150n151, 152n160, 153n162, 258n40
Raphael, 36
Ratzinger, Joseph, 40, 65, 85n39, 88n48, 91n59, 95n68, 141, 145n133
Reddish, Mitchell, 26n16
Reisman, Kimberley, 201, 203
Reitan, Eric, 2n2, 60, 93n61, 115n29, 133n86, 138n103, 138n106, 146n136, 150n150, 210, 212, 216, 225, 227n149, 256, 266, 270, 272
Richardson, Samuel, 221n129
Ringgren, Helmut, 248n4
Roberts, Arthur, 36n55, 64
Roberts, Robert, 251–52
Robinson, John A. T., 35n49, 116n30, 147n142, 155
Root, Michael, 102
Rowell, Geoffrey, 84n37, 85n40, 125n64, 157, 254–55
Rowland, Christopher, 33n43, 35n50, 37
Russell, Bertrand, 220–21
Russell, Jeffrey Burton, 28n26, 31n35, 54n20, 56n26, 56n27, 58, 60, 144

Sachs, John, 145, 194, 212
Saliers, Don, 166, 169n40
Sanders, John, 134n90, 140n114, 227n150
Sankey, Ira, 105

Sartre, Jean-Paul, 155
Sasse, Hermann, 110n14
Saward, John, 237n14
Scazzero, Peter, 199n58, 200–201
Schliermacher, Frederick, 115
Schneider, Johannes, 130n78
Schulz, Charles, 186
Schweitzer, Albert, 34
Second Council of Lyons, 78
Second Helvetic Confession, 27, 91n56, 112n21
Second Vatican Council, 79, 198
Sells, Michael, 168, 171n48
Seneca the Younger, 171–72
Seymour, Charles, 111n17, 138, 267, 269
Sheppy, Paul, 233n8
Sickler, Bradley, 135
Sider, Ronald, 164, 196, 205n77, 226n147
Sider, Theodore, 106n4
Siegrist, Anthony, 165–66
Silouan of Athos, 157
Singer, Peter, 189n16
Smith, James, 133n86, 161n9, 162–64, 166, 167n33, 169n40, 170, 196n46, 227
Smith, Harmon, 182
Snow, Nancy, 208n89
Spafford, Horatio, 45n86
Stainton, Tim, 69
Stassen, Glen, 86n43
Stauffer, Ethelbert, 120n47
Stevens, R. Paul, 167, 199, 202
Storms, Sam, 70–71
Stott, John, 116n30
Studd, C. T., 173n58
Stump, Eleonore, 261
Swedenborg, Emmanuel, 30
Swinburne, Richard, 75, 95n70, 96, 138, 141n120, 142, 143n127, 144n128, 161–62, 251n13

Tacelli, Ronald, 89n50, 115n29, 118n39, 129, 151n156, 225
Talbott, Thomas, 61n55, 112n19, 114–15, 123–24, 129, 130n78, 146, 148n143, 149n146, 149n147,

NAMES INDEX

150, 152, 153n162, 216n116, 257, 260–61, 270–71
Taliaferro, Charles, 13n8, 182
Tasker, Randolph, 110, 128n68
Taylor, Alfred, 70
Taylor, Barbara Brown, 46
Taylor, Isaac, 99n80
Taylor, Jeremy, 176n67
Temple, William, 254
Tertullian of Carthage, 24n9, 170n43
Theodore of Mopsuestia, 111n18, 114n25
Thielecke, Helmut, 154, 243n32
Thiselton, Anthony, 58–59, 60–61, 92–93, 110n14, 112n20, 117–18, 130, 139, 140n114, 257
Thomas, Owen, 33, 34n48, 36, 37n57, 62, 88, 150n150
Thompson, Francis, 105n2
Timpe, Kevin, 96n70
Tolkien, J. R. R., 229
Tolstoy, Leo, 172
Traub, Helmut, 26n16
Travis, Stephen, 130n76, 257
Trumbower, Jeffrey, 113
Tutu, Desmond, 238n18, 243n32, 243n33

United Methodist Church, 154, 242n28
Ussher, James, 22

VanArragon, Raymond, 138, 260–61
van Tholen, James, 156
Vander Laan, David, 81
Vander Zee, 242n29
Vassiliadis, Nikolaos, 83n31, 85n41, 117n37
Vaux, Kenneth, 176–77
Verhey, Allen, 22, 35n51, 38, 42, 132, 176n67, 178–79, 181n89, 196, 228
Vincent, Lynn, 31n35

Walker, Daniel, 115n28
Wallis, Gerhard, 120n46
Walls, Jerry, 24n9, 28, 40n68, 52n13, 61n54, 80, 81n23, 82–83, 85n40, 88n4889, 93–95, 96n72, 97n77, 98n80, 100, 102n89, 118, 124n59126n66, 135–36, 137n99, 141–44, 145n131, 146, 150n150, 153, 157, 160n8, 186, 187n10, 188, 215n111, 228, 247, 251n13, 255–56, 261, 262n56, 267–69, 271
Walters, G., 226n147
Ware, Timothy, 84, 85n41, 173, 243n31
Washburn, Phil, 133n87
Watts, Isaac, 57n30, 181
Webb, Stephen, 3, 11, 13–14, 25n15, 89, 189, 197n47
Weiss, Johannes, 34
Welker, Michael, 50
Wenham, John, 116n30
Wesley, Charles, 45n86
Wesley, John, 40, 50–51, 66, 91
Westminster Catechism, 231
Westminster Confession, 27, 91n56, 113n21
White, Edward, 253–54
Whittemore, Thomas, 221n129
Willard, Dallas, 9n4, 88n49, 100n85, 137n102, 139, 162, 164n18, 166–167, 170, 194, 200n60, 202, 207n86
Williams, Bernard, 61
Williams, Rowan, 57, 175n65
Willimon, William, 120, 169n40
Wills, Gary, 192n29
Wilson-Kastner, Patricia, 194n40
Winner, Lauren, 171
Wink, Walter, 160
Winter, David, 179
Wittung, Jeffrey, 55n23
Wolters, Al, 38n59
Wolterstorff, Nick, 180
Wright, J. Edward, 26n16
Wright, N. T., 18, 23, 26, 32–33, 35, 37–42, 44–45, 62, 71, 74, 81, 84, 91–92, 109n10, 112, 116n30, 128, 143n126, 144n131, 149, 154, 159, 166n30, 169, 179–80, 186n8, 191, 197–99, 206–8, 225–26, 227n150, 261
Wright, Richard, 253

Yancey, Philip, 168

Yang, Seung, 228
Yong, Amos, 11–12, 67, 69

Zagzebski, Linda, 53n18
Zimmerman, Dean, 98n80
Zobel, Hans-Jurgen, 120n46

Scripture Index

HEBREW SCRIPTURE

Genesis
1:20–30	11
3:24	76n8

Exodus
12:14	167
13:3–10	167
15:26	66
33:11	55
34:6–7	131

Leviticus
19:2	86n44
19:18	65, 248

Numbers
20:11–12	83n29

Deuteronomy
4:9	167
4:19	26
6:5–8	65, 167, 248, 250
8:2, 11, 18	167
11:2	248
11:11	26
26:19	86n44, 248

Joshua
4:1–24	167

2 Samuel
7	31
12:13–15	83n29

2 Kings
2:1	26

2 Chronicles
36:14–23	129

Job
29:14–16	173

Psalms
1	226
1:1–2	167, 185
2	33
6:4	228
7:1–10	128n69
13:1–2	22
15:1–2	86n44
16:8	168
23:6	105n2
24	31, 86n44
25:6	277

Psalms (cont.)

30:5	131
35:17	128n70
35:23–24	228
41:3	66
42:1–2	203
51	103, 237n16
51:5	158n1
51:10	209
53:2	26
77:11–12	167
90: 5, 12	172
90:13–17	194
93	31
98:3	149
98:9–10	128
102:9	181
103:3	66
103:8–9	131
103:15–16	172
103:17	120
104	45
115:3	112n19
119	167
119:9–11	168
119:33–37	162–63
136	120, 224, 273
139:7–12	151
147:3	66
147:8	26

Proverbs

4:5, 23	181

Ecclesiastes

7:2	172

Isaiah

1:10–17	249
2:1–5	32
4:4	76n8, 80
5:8–23	248
5:16	86n44
9:6–7	21, 31
11:1–9	32
19:16–25	130, 132, 148
25:6	25n15, 63, 149
25:7–8	187
27:2–3	257
29:18	66
33:14–15	248
34:1–4	132
35:1–10	32, 66, 87n44
43:4–7	121, 149
45:20–25	132, 149
46:10–11	112n19
49:5–16	151, 243n32
51:3	26
51:6	38n59
54:7–8	131
54:10	120
57:15	86n44
58:3–7	249
58:11	26
60:1–16	64
61	256
62:4	131
62:5	75
64:8–9	240n20
65:17	37
66:18	149
66:22	37

Jeremiah

22:13–19	249
31:3	120
31:8	67
31:10	132
31:33	168
33:14	21

Lamentations

3:22	120
3:31–33	131, 257

Ezekiel

16:53–55	132
31:8–9	26
36:25–27	168

Daniel

2	43

6:10	168	**Micah**	
7	43	3:9—4:5	132
7:14	32	4:6-7	67
12:2	50	6:8	105n1, 249
		7:18	131

Hosea

1:14-2:23	120, 151	**Habakkuk**	
11:1-9	120, 129n74, 131-32, 151, 257, 274	1:2	128n70
		1:13	86n44

Joel

		Zephaniah	
2:13	131	3:9	149
		3:19	67

Amos

5:18-20	127	**Zechariah**	
5:21-24	249	2:11	149
8:4-7	128n69	14:9	31

Jonah

		Malachi	
3	143	3:2-4	38n59, 76n8, 80
4:2	131		

APOCRYPHA

2 Maccabees

12:39-45	79

CHRISTIAN SCRIPTURE

Matthew

		8:11	25n15
3:7	127	8:12	127
4:29	38n59	9:20-22	68
5:4	196	9:27-30	68
5:8, 20	86n44	10:28	224
5:12	190	11:4-5	66
5:13-16	253	11:20-24	135n95, 267
5:25-26	80	11:28	217
5:43-48	86n44, 101n88, 212, 214, 249	12:22-29	32n40, 66
		12:32	80
6:10	32	13:3-9	200
6:21	163, 173	13:23	162
6:33	173	16:24-26	188
7:13-14	226	18:10-14	105, 120
7:21-23	139n110	18:33	275
		19:28	46, 229

Matthew *(cont.)*

19:29	190
21:31	32n40
22:1–14	63
23:34–40	249
23:37–39	65, 151
24–25	32n41
24:3	35
24:42–44	206
25:1–13	25n15, 206
25:21	173
25:14–30	193
25:31–46	50–51, 110, 112n19, 130, 139n110, 148, 173, 190, 221
26:64	44
26:69–75	161n9
28:18	32

Mark

1:14–15	32, 206
2:1–12	69
2:14	253
3:29	80
5:1–20	69
9:43–48	127
10:46–52	68
14:25	32n41

Luke

1:50–53	128n70
1:75	248
4:16–20	256
6:22–23, 35–38	190, 275
6:36	213n106, 275
6:40	200
7:18–23	32n40
9:23	186
10:8–9	66
10:25–28	249–50
11:37–42	249
12:10	80
13:24	226
14:1–23	67
14:12–14	190
14:15–24	25n15
15	151
15:3–7	212
15:11–32	120, 153, 273
16:19–31	50
16:26	109
17:20–24	32n40
18:1–8	128n70
18:28–30	190
21:27	44
23:34	139, 214
23:39–43	26, 41, 50, 81, 143

John

1:14	38
3:3	88n48, 158n1
3:16	120
3:17	212
3:36	32n40, 127
5:2–9	69
5:24, 40	32n40
5:28–29	109–110
6:40, 47, 54, 68	32n40
7:37	217
8:34	137n102
9	68
10:10	32n40, 188, 226
10:27	168
11:24	28
11:25–26	92n60, 177
11:33–35	179
12:32	149
13:1–17, 34	249
13:10	92n60
14:2	41
15:1–11	200
15:9–17	249
15:3	92n60

Acts

1:11	26
3:21	229
4:21	130n78
5:1–11	127
10:10	188
10:36	33, 44
22:5	130n78
23:6	29
24:15	29
26:6–7	29
26:11	130n78

Scripture Index

Romans

1:18	127
4:5	87
4:17	177
5:2	92n60
5:6–8	120n47
5:18	149
6:6–7	92
6:10–13	87, 92
6:16–17	137n102, 138
7:17	137n102
7:14–25	163, 250
8:1	83
8:5–7	162
8:10–13	92n60, 171, 200
8:13	88n48
8:18	187
8:19–25	38n59, 42, 228
8:31	120
8:38–39	119, 181
9–11	132
10:9	33, 44
11:32	149, 213
12:1–2	158, 165
13:8–10	249
13:11	173
13:12	206

1 Corinthians

2:9	25
2:16	168
3:1–7	200
3:10–15	79–81
3:16–17	87n44
6:9	87n44
9:24—10:13	87n44
12:3	33, 44
13:1–3, 13	249
13:8	121
13:12	3, 53
15:22–23	35, 149
15:26	175
15:28	149
15:51–52	68
15:54	174–75
15:58	198
16:22	22

2 Corinthians

3:3	168
3:18	50, 71, 87, 200, 250
4:4	138
4:17	187
5:1	26
5:6–8	23, 40, 50, 81
5:10	109, 224
5:15	75
5:17	88n48, 215
6:2	173
7:1	249
10:4–5	165
12:4	26

Galatians

3:6	87
4:19	75, 87
5:6	249
5:16–23	163
5:22–26	200, 249

Ephesians

1:4	249
1:10	38n61, 148, 229
1:20–22	33
2:4–7	120
2:10	95
3:18–19	215
4:8–10	26
4:13	75, 250
4:14–15	200, 250
4:22–24	87, 249–50
5:2	189
5:6	127
5:18	200
6:12	33

Philippians

1:6–10	29, 33, 38n61
1:14	83
1:21–23	23, 40, 50, 81
2:3–8	189, 249
2:5	168
2:9–13	33, 95, 149, 167, 200, 207
3:12–14	200
3:13	58
3:19–20	26, 173

Colossians

1:14	83
1:15–20	33, 149
1:28	200
2:9	38
2:11–13	92
2:15	33
3:2	165, 173
3:5–12	87
3:12–17	168, 170, 200, 249

1 Thessalonians

4:13–18	50, 63, 179
4:17	35n51
5:23	35, 103, 237n16

2 Thessalonians

1:9	110, 112n19, 127
2:1	35
3:6–14	193

1 Timothy

1:13	139
2:4	112n19, 120
4:17	35n51
6:14	35
6:15	33
6:17–19	190

2 Timothy

3:16	182
4:1, 8	35
4:3–4	224

Titus

2:11–14	35, 193, 206
3:7	29

Hebrews

2:14–15	175
5:12–14	168, 200
9:27	109
10:16	168
10:29	130n78
10:31	224
11:16	173
11:40	42
12:2	190
12:14	87n44

James

1:2	190
1:21–24	168
2:8	249
2:14–16	94n65

1 Peter

1:3–9	187, 190
1:13	228
1:15–16	86n44, 87
2:1–2, 24	87
2:5	200
2:11	160
3:18–21	116
4:6	116

2 Peter

1:5–10	200
1:6	35
2:9	130
2:11	160
3:1–14	193
3:9	112n19, 120
3:10–13	37, 38n59, 46n94, 206
3:13	75

1 John

1:5	86n44
1:7	83, 92n60
2:28	35
3:2–3	25, 29, 206
3:11–18	249
3:21	53
4:8	120
4:18	130
4:20–21	249

Revelation

1:7–8	43–44

2:7	26	14:10–11	127
2:10	190	19:6, 16	33
3:16	200	19:7–9	25n15, 63
3:20	217	20:10–15	33, 127, 132
4–5	25n15	21–22	25n15, 29, 248
4:1—5:14	29	21:1–5	23, 37, 38, 75, 187
4:10–11	62	21:2, 9	63
5:12–13	62	21:24–27	64, 87n44, 132
6:9–11	41, 50, 128n70	22:4	53
7:9–10	64, 213n103	22:20	22
11:15	33		

www.ingramcontent.com/pod-product-compliance
Lightning Source LLC
Chambersburg PA
CBHW021650230426
43668CB00008B/575